The
Sociological
Vision

Revised Printing

Kendall Hunt
publishing company

Christopher Pieper

Cover image © Shutterstock, Inc.

www.kendallhunt.com
Send all inquiries to:
4050 Westmark Drive
Dubuque, IA   52004-1840

Published in the United States of America

Contents

About the Author

Christopher Pieper, Ph.D. is Senior Lecturer and Undergraduate Program Director in Sociology at Baylor University. He earned his B.A. in Communication with Honors in 1996 from Southwestern University and his graduate degrees from the University of Texas at Austin in 1998 (M.A., Journalism) and 2011 (Ph.D., Sociology).

Prior to returning to academia in 2004, Pieper was for six years Communications Director at the Center for Public Policy Priorities, a research and advocacy organization working on behalf of low-income Texans. He has also taught at UT-Austin, Southwestern University, and the College of William and Mary. He teaches introductory sociology, Senior Colloquium, social psychology, social movements, and graduate courses in political sociology and contemporary theory.

Pieper is the author of numerous publications on religion and social movements, political sociology, media culture, and conflict. His first book, *Sociology as a Spiritual Practice: How Studying People Can Make You a Better Person,* was published in 2015. Using illustrations from current events, comparative religion, and new social research, the book demonstrates that practicing social science cultivates empathy, mindfulness, and the virtues that bring lasting happiness. Far from being enemies, spirituality and social science are seen as complementary paths toward personal and collective flourishing.

Chapter 1

Why Sociology Is Awesome and Why You Haven't Known This Before

In the pages to follow, you will begin an exciting adventure through what some have called the *sociological imagination*. By embarking on this journey, you will discover and learn many fascinating things about various aspects of the human condition.

As we humans move through life, we engage in many activities and play out several roles. During childhood, we progress from self-centeredness and inexperience in social relations to learning how to show empathy for others and live according to a set of social rules. Adolescence is a time for learning how to make the transition from the dependency of childhood to the world of adult responsibility. It is also a time of sexual awakening and sexual exploration. The social rules we learn and the adaptations we make in attitudes and behavior during this period set the stage for adulthood.

During our adult years, the process of social adjustment continues and becomes more complex as we are called on to play several parts and to adapt to a variety of changing social roles. We learn to adjust to the many demands placed on us by the various social conditions in which we find ourselves. Most of us take on an occupation or profession as well as family responsibilities in the role of spouse and/or parent. Some of us continue schooling as you are doing now. Often we are required by our various social responsibilities to do what may seem the impossible—to keep family, employer, and teachers all happy at once. But we seem to manage it most of the time. This is because we have acquired behaviors and skills that, in most cases, allow us to cope successfully with the demands of the social world around us. These behaviors and skills, which we often carry out unconsciously, are acquired largely from the society in which we live. The systematic study of how all this takes place as well as insights into how to address these challenges more successfully are included in the domain of a science called *sociology*.

WHAT IS SOCIOLOGY?

Questions commonly asked by students taking the introductory course include "What is sociology?," " What is it about?," "Why should I take this course?," "How does sociology work?," and "What do sociologists do?" These and other basic questions will be addressed in the pages to follow.

In essence, sociology is the science of human social behavior at all levels. Because humans by their very nature and development are social beings, most everything they do involves group interaction and interpersonal relationships. This fact makes sociology a particularly fascinating area of investigation. When we humans act, we tend to act socially, and this social behavior along with its causes and consequences represents what sociologists study. Such an area of investigation is as broad as it is interesting and includes such far-ranging topics as mate selection practices, the causes of crime, propaganda techniques used by politicians and advertisers, bureaucratic organization, and the head-hunting practices still used on occasion by some people in a handful of tribal societies (Service, 1971).

Beyond "Common Sense:" The Nature of Sociology

As the science of human social behavior, sociology focuses on the examination of everyday life and familiar forms of social organization in an objective and systematic way. The human condition has long been the focus of study by the world's major religions, philosophic systems, and the other humanities, including history, literature, poetry, and music. These and other related disciplines and art forms have provided many valuable insights and observations and countless anecdotal pronouncements about human behavior that have been espoused by many people as "common sense." Such "obvious" sources of conventional wisdom and "truth" resulting from "common sense" are often accepted at face value by many people, but not by the sociologist.

Sociology and the Nature of "Truth": An Illustration   The truth about human behavior—as discovered through the science of sociology—is always tentative and depends on the historical, social, and cultural contexts of the behavior under study. For example, in the nonindustrial, agricultural societies of the past with low technology and high mortality rates, having large families made very good sense and, therefore, was seen as "common sense" because large numbers of offspring helped to ensure the survival and prosperity of the group. Large numbers of children also represented an economic asset in these societies because children worked in the fields alongside their parents and other adults, and contributed to the economic well-being of their family and community. And finally, somewhat larger families were inevitable because of a lack of knowledge and technology concerning birth control.

In modern industrial and postindustrial societies, however, the reverse is true. Children in modern economies are consumers, not producers, and represent a drain on family income. This is because they must be sustained by the cash wages of the adult members while they complete the many years of schooling required in order to gain a meaningful place in society as adults. By first obtaining a high school diploma and then technical training and certification, and/or academic degrees, they as adults are then able to be competitive in modern economies that demand technical expertise. This helps to explain why fertility rates are much lower in modern societies as compared with nonindustrial economies. For most people in such societies—given their sociocultural context—it has become "common sense" to limit family size.

In addition, within modern societies such as the United States, Western European countries, and Japan, the better educated and most affluent classes have the fewest children per family, while the less educated and poorest classes as a whole have significantly more offspring. For most families with the fewest educational resources and the largest numbers of children, the sociological consequences resulting from this often include poverty, powerlessness, economic exploitation, and often despair. Such despair resulting from socioeconomic strain can then contribute to other negative consequences including alcohol and drug abuse, crime and delinquency, and various forms of family disorganization.

"Isn't It Just Common Sense?" From the preceding discussion, many people might ask this question: "Isn't it just 'common sense' to have fewer children in a modern society with a cash-based economy?" To this, many sociologists would answer: "That depends on how you perceive common sense." The more educated people in modern societies—to a significant degree—are able to insulate themselves from socioeconomically derived strain, poverty, and despair because they understand the overall impact of large numbers of offspring on their life chances. Therefore, "common sense" tells them to limit their family size.

The poor and less educated, lacking such insight, fail to see the larger picture and, for whatever reason or reasons, often do not take the proactive steps needed to improve their life chances and those of their children by planning and limiting their numbers of offspring. Trapped in a fatalistic mindset that often renders them incapable of self-determination, they use what they see as "common sense" to have large families. In their life situation, their relatives, friends, and neighbors mostly have large families and traditionally have always had many children. So it then becomes "common sense" to many of them to have a large family also. In addition, their religious belief system may define children as a blessing and a gift from God, and effective "artificial" means of birth control as a sin. Consequently, "common sense" means to many of them that (1) the more children they have, the more blessed they will become in the eyes of God because "the Lord will provide for our needs" and (2) going against God by practicing "forbidden" forms of birth control may damn them to everlasting hell when they die.

"Common Sense" and the Sociocultural Context In the pages and chapters to follow, you will learn how and why people operating in different cultural contexts define "common sense" differently as a result of their own distinct social interaction experiences. These experiences, which sociologists call socialization, are shaped by a variety of factors that often include culture of origin, gender, racial or ethnic background, age, class, and religious orientation. The systematic process used in acquiring information and insight about the factors that shape how people see the social world and their place in it is the *sociological imagination,* the focus of this first chapter.

Levels of Sociological Analysis

As sociologists examine the nature of human social behavior, they focus on two levels of analysis, macrosociology and microsociology. Macrosociology refers to the study of major institutions and entire societies or civilizations (Schaefer, 2012, p. 13). The prefix "macro" means large. In this regard, sociologists study the structure, functions, and consequences of the basic structural building blocks or major institutions that make up societies and the nature of societies themselves as a whole. For example, how are the family, government, and economic institutions in the United States organized today versus fifty or one hundred years ago? How does the United States today differ from China, India, Nigeria, and other countries regarding these and other aspects such as religion, dietary preferences, clothing and architectural styles, and a host of other aspects?

Let us also consider these and other questions relating to macrosociology. Why, for example, do Americans see dogs as pets while in Vietnam they are eaten as a delicacy and, in some parts of the world, eating dog meat is alleged to enhance sexual performance? Why do Americans drive on the right side of the road while in the British Commonwealth and some other areas of the world, people drive on the left-hand side. And why is it that almost all married Americans, despite the fact that over eighty-five percent are right-handed, wear their wedding rings on the third finger of the left hand? These and a myriad of other behaviors that we routinely carry out today have their origins in major social institutions and their norms, which may have originated in different times or cultures hundreds or thousands of years ago. Through culture contact, these customs and habits found their way into our society and were then accepted. Today, we continue to hand them down to future generations of our children through a process called socialization.

Microsociology, by contrast, is the study of social behavior primarily at the interpersonal, local, and community levels of society. How is your family organized, for example, as compared to that of your neighbors, coworkers, and associates? While most families in the United States in the 1950s were traditional nuclear families consisting of a full-time working father, homemaking mother, and two or more school-aged children, families today vary tremendously in composition (e.g., dual-earner families, single parent families, stepfamilies, etc.). How and why has all this diversity emerged in family structures at the microlevel during the past half century? In addition, why are some families loving and supportive of their members, while others are abusive and violent? These are sociological questions that are microlevel in focus.

In attempting to answer these and dozens of other inquiries, sociologists conduct comparative studies of all varieties of human social behavior occurring at the interpersonal level in local communities. They compare and contrast not only different families using the case study and other approaches, but many other areas of social behavior as partially reflected in the different topics contained in this text. In their investigations, they may look for patterns of behavior in such diverse social groups and organizations as fifth grade classrooms, shopping malls, local businesses, places of worship, and even prisons and houses of prostitution. In addition, sociologists examine folkways, traditions, and practices and their origins that occur mainly in a particular region of a country or sometimes in only one city or town. For example, in Louisiana, crawfish étouffée is a regional delicacy while in Flatonia, Texas (settled by Czech immigrants during the nineteenth century), locals host the "Chilispiel"—a combined Czech folk festival and Texas chili competition—during October of each year.

WHAT IS SCIENCE?

The word "science" comes from the Latin *sciens,* which means "to know" (Nachmias and Nachmias, 1987). As a means of explanation, **science** represents a systematic method of observing and explaining reality in a verifiable manner. Scientists, therefore, make no prejudgments about their subject matter, but seek the truth in whatever form it is revealed through a systematic process of investigation.

Basic Assumptions of Science

The scientific method is influenced by several basic assumptions about the nature of reality. Stated as propositions, they include the following: (1) *all in nature can be known,* (2) *nature can be understood through sensory investigation,* and (3) *phenomena in nature are linked through cause-and-effect relationships* (Goode and Hatt, 1952). Together, these propositions are key issues of discussion and study in epistemology, an area in the philosophy of science devoted to the study of knowledge and how it is validated. Although the ultimate truth of these assumptions about nature that underpin science cannot as yet be demonstrated, science remains a superior method of investigation because of its objectivity and openness, its self-correcting nature, and the strict rules of evidence that govern its method and those who use it.

Science As a Means of Explanation: Its Two Key Aspects

In almost any definition of sociology, terms such as "science," "scientific," or "study of" appear in places of prominence. Therefore, to truly understand and appreciate the nature and goals of sociology, one must first possess a basic understanding of the two key aspects of science and how the scientific approach differs from others.

Science Is a Method of Investigation   First and foremost, science is a *method of investigation,* a specific way of examining reality.

Because many individuals do not possess a basic understanding of how the scientific method works, the term "science" often means different things to different people. Some confuse it with technology and use phrases like "science moves onward" as captions for pictures that illustrate space voyages to other planets. Others see science as little more than a specific body of knowledge and use phrases like "science informs us" or "according to science." In truth, science represents far more than the products of investigation, such as spaceships and computers or everything known about cancer or crime. Instead, science is mainly a means of explanation or method of investigation. It represents one way of discovering and explaining various aspects of reality (Hoover, 1988).

Science Is a Body of Knowledge The second aspect of science is that it also represents a *body of knowledge*—a systematic and tested archive of accumulated data. Such a body of knowledge exists in every scientific discipline ranging from physics to sociology. One of the fascinating aspects of the scientific enterprise is that this body of knowledge is constantly expanding. Therefore, in the case of sociology, we know more about human social behavior today than we knew last last year and we will continue to know more in the future as our understanding of social behavior continues to grow.

Characteristics of Science

Science Is Theoretical As illustrated in Figure 1–1, science, first of all, is theoretical. Scientific theory consists of clearly stated propositions about reality that have been verified to some degree. Have you ever heard someone say, "Well, it's only a theory"? This inaccurate perception is held by many in the American public. It is almost as if "theory" (propositions) is placed in one box and labeled unreliable, undemonstrated, and unproven, while "fact" (verification) is placed in another and labeled as reliable, demonstrated, and proven.

Contrary to such erroneous notions, about science held by many in the general public, the truth is that in science, theory and fact are not separate, but instead, are intimately intertwined, two parts of the same whole. In science, the state of theory is the state of knowledge about some area of investigation, whether it is crime, cancer, or the

Figure 1-1

Many people have the mistaken notion that theory (propositions) and fact (verification) in science are separate concepts with little or no relation to each other. In actuality, nothing could be further from the truth. It is much more accurate to say that in science, "theory" represents one or more propositions about some aspect of reality that have been verified to some degree. Consequently, the state of theory about some topic in science is the state of knowledge about that topic. As more evidence is gathered (which is a continuing enterprise in science), that state of knowledge (scientific theory) is continually expanded and refined.

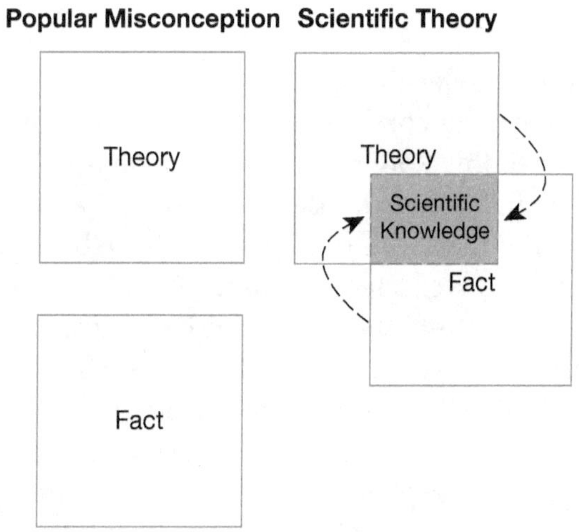

Box 1-1
Only a Theory
John H. Lienhard

Today, let's theorize. The University of Houston's College of Engineering presents this series about the machines that make our civilization run, and the people whose ingenuity created them.

A listener left a phone message. I'd mentioned Darwin's theory of evolution, and he said, "Wait a minute; Darwin's theory wasn't about evolution. His theory was that evolution occurs by means of natural selection." Warning flags went up. There was more here than met the eye. When I turned to dictionaries I saw the problem more clearly. The word "theory" has shifted under our feet.

The classical dictionary definition says that a theory is a mental plan or a systematic set of principles. A theory, unlike a hypothesis, has been *verified*. It has been shown to fit the facts, and it has stood up against attempts to prove it false. The atomic theory of matter and Einstein's Theory of Relativity are good examples. All the older dictionaries tell us that we're talking slang when we use the word *theory* for a hunch or a guess.

But that definition changes in dictionaries of current usage. They tell us that a theory is a *belief* or a *proposal* or a *hypothesis*. Theoretical knowledge now means a tentative idea and one that's been divorced from practice. The old meaning––an established body of knowledge—withered while I wasn't looking.

What Darwin proposed was not that evolution occurs—it obviously did. He set out to explain why it occurs. He explained how natural selection works. I expect that caller wanted me to be more cautious in a world where you hear people saying "Evolution is only a theory!" Evolution, of course, has long been a theory in the old sense of the word. But to call it a theory today is to scoff at it.

Few people still use the word theory in its old sense, and we have no new word to replace it. Meanwhile, in fields like math, physics, and engineering absolutely depend on intellectual constructs. To work in them, you have to traffic in theory. Yet, according to current usage, to be a theoretician is to be vague and ineffective.

All this has a chilling effect in our schools. Arithmetic, math, and science now have to be results oriented. Subjects that are inherently theoretical (in the old sense of the word) are being stripped of their theoretical subtlety. Students can smell that subtlety a mile away. They sense that they can shrug it off when the teacher tries to introduce it. Textbooks try to teach science by presenting solved examples rather than asking students to deduce their own results.

We need to do something about all this. We need to make analytical deduction respectable again. So here's what I ask of you: The next time a friend voices suspicions about something and you find yourself starting to say, "That's only a theory," stop and bite your tongue. Save that fine word "theory" for established knowledge. Save it for things like the photon theory of light, evolution by natural selection, or the laws of thermodynamics. Reserve the word theory for established structures of knowledge. And give our students a chance to see the kind of subtlety that turns isolated facts into whole bodies of understanding.

I'm John Lienhard, at the University of Houston, where we're interested in the way inventive minds work.

Source: Lienhard, J. H. 2008. "Only a Theory." Engines of Our Ingenuity. Episode No. 1531: A radio series broadcast each weekday on KUHF FM Radio, Houston Texas. For additional information consult: http://www.uh.edu/engines.htm

wing design for the next generation of jet aircraft. In this regard, scientific theory is often confused with theory in religion and philosophy. Both religion and philosophy also contain propositions, or theory. However, they lack the means of objective verification that is the hallmark of science. Therefore, "theory" becomes scientific theory only when there is some degree of objective evidence to support it (Lienhard, 2008) (Box 1–1).

Science Is Empirical Empiricism represents the manner in which evidence in science is gathered through the organized use of the senses. (Nation, 1997, p. 7). We all use our senses to "verify" reality for ourselves. Yet, when sensory measurement is used without the scientific method, our senses may easily fool us. Most all of us have been betrayed by our senses from time to time. Parents often think they hear their newborn baby crying in the middle of the night, but when they check, the child is sound asleep. In many other ways, our senses may play tricks on us. However, when the scientist is engaged in research, the senses are used for verification according to a strict system of safeguards called the rules of evidence.

Science Is Objective Objectivity refers to an unbiased and unprejudiced approach aimed at determining truth. Scientists seek only the truth wherever it leads them. They carry no preconceived notions into the research process. Instead, they let the facts point the way to the formulation and reformulation of theory (propositions). As practitioners of the scientific method, they are duty bound to report truth as revealed by the bulk of research findings and then acknowledge that evidence concerning a particular phenomenon, regardless of personal feelings. Therefore, truth in science is always tentative, as the investigator continues to look for increasingly more precise explanations. This self-correcting aspect of science is one of its most distinguishing features. Consequently, the scientific method is open-ended, requires no leap of faith, and can be replicated with the same results by anyone who uses it correctly.

Science Is Cumulative Through objectivity, science becomes based on cumulative knowledge, a characteristic of science in which what is known (the state of knowledge) is constantly being added to, modified, and refined. As more precise evidence is discovered, theory (the state of knowledge) is continually refined and sometimes even reformulated. Research being conducted today thus adds to what we already know in all fields of endeavor. Take, for instance, scientific research as applied to powered flight. At the dawn of the twentieth century, the Wright brothers flew only for a few brief seconds at Kitty Hawk, North Carolina. Today, given the cumulative effect of thousands of scientific studies in several related disciplines, manned flights to the moon have been made several times, and similar flights by men and women to the other planets and beyond seem almost a certainty in the future.

How Science Differs from Other Means of Explanation

The *hallmark* that distinguishes science from other means of explanation lies in the concept of verified propositions. Science, therefore, concerns itself with propositions about reality that have been verified to some degree (Lienhard, 2008). Unlike most other forms of explanation, the state of theory in science represents the state of knowledge about the area under study, whether it be the analysis of rock formations in geology or the study of human social behavior in sociology. Other methods of explanation also have their forms of theory (propositions about reality). However, their propositions or assumptions often (1) do not make use of objective evidence or (2) are not amenable to empirical and objective verification. These approaches to explanation, which predate science, include appeal to authority, mysticism, tradition, religion, and philosophy.

Appeal to authority involves trusting others—politicians, physicians, teachers, religious leaders, news commentators, for example—to discover, understand, and disseminate knowledge and truth for us. While it is tempting to blindly trust these "authorities," such an uncritical perspective can result in exploitation and victimization by those who would abuse their power and position.

Mysticism is similar to an appeal to authority, except that authority figures may or may not be consulted. For those who believe in mysticism, the authority figures that are consulted are those with "supernatural powers" such as faith healers, prophets, and "channels" (mediums), who make use of ritual and ceremony to create the conditions necessary for the mystical experience. In other instances, mystical states may be drug-induced, as with Indians in Mexico and the American Southwest who use peyote cactus and sacred mushrooms to produce hallucinations and visions (Lingeman, 1984). Those most likely to accept mystically derived "knowledge" tend to do so "under conditions of depression, helplessness, and intoxication" (Nachmias and Nachmias, 1987, p. 5).

Tradition involves accepting what worked in the past. Advantages include feelings of connection with previous generations and one's culture, as well as security and peace of mind in using "what's tried and true." Disadvantages include undue bias and narrowness of viewpoint, particularly given changing social conditions. Some "traditional" people, for example, continue to espouse racist views, male domination over women, and families having unlimited numbers of offspring.

However, two of the most important and widely used of these various alternatives to science as a method of explanation in examining the world are religion and philosophy.

Religion The term religion refers to a method of explaining human life and the universe usually through the concepts of the sacred and divine as acknowledged through ritual and worship. As such, this method of explanation contains and combines elements of authority, mysticism, and tradition in explaining the human condition. In essence, this approach depends on "subjective knowing" based on faith, because much of the foundation for religious belief deals with aspects of reality—such as god, heaven, hell, the soul, etc.—that cannot be objectively verified. Some religions are monotheistic (one god), others are polytheistic (multiple gods and/or goddesses), and some, such as pagan nature religions, contain no deities at all. Therefore, religion is easier to describe than to define, because it means different things to different people. In fact, the variety of religious beliefs and practices is almost limitless. According to sociologist Elizabeth Nottingham (1971), religion

> has given rise to the most spacious products of . . . imagination, and it has been used to justify the extremist cruelty . . . . It can conjure up moods of sublime exaltation, and also images of dread and terror. Although preoccupied with the reality of a world that cannot be seen, religion has been involved in the most mundane details of daily life. It has been used to blaze new trails into the heart of the unknown, and utopias have been founded in its name; yet it has also served to shackle . . . [people] to outworn customs or beliefs (p. 8).

Philosophy Philosophy is a systematic and rational method for organizing the thought processes that are used to address critical questions. The philosophical method originated about 600

BCE with Pythagoras, who saw it as the pursuit of wisdom. Today, philosophy includes such fields of study as aesthetics (art and beauty), metaphysics (reality), epistemology (knowledge), ethics (moral values), and logic (reasoning). The development of philosophy represented a tremendous step forward in the history of humankind, because it furnished a systematic way to organize thought in order to address intellectual questions and problems. It remains a valuable tool of analysis today. However, philosophy—unlike science—does not contain a reliable empirical means of verifying propositions in the world of human experience. This is where philosophy and science differ in approach, although science, in large measure, was built on a philosophic foundation, particularly in its use of logic.

The sociologist looks at different means of explanation, which include religion and philosophy, through the eyes of science. Combinations of these perspectives, along with science, help us to perceive and interpret the world around us and our place in it. When such combinations of perspectives are commonly held by groups of human beings, they form the basis for an agreed-upon "worldview." These agreed upon assumptions about reality, in turn, form much of the "common ground" or social cement that binds people together in social groups, organizations, institutions, and societies. The ongoing process through which these cultural worldviews emerge and evolve, along with their social consequences, furnishes much of the subject matter for sociology and the other social sciences.

Physical Sciences and Social Sciences

The sciences are divided into two general categories, the physical or natural sciences and the social sciences. The physical sciences focus on the study of physical and biological reality. They include such disciplines as biology, botany, chemistry, mathematics, and physics. The social sciences, by contrast, study various aspects of human behavior. These disciplines, in addition to sociology, include such fields of study as

Table 1-1

Physical Sciences and Social Sciences: Comparative Characteristics

The Physical Sciences	The Social Sciences
1. Are more concrete with a focus on physical matter	1. Are more abstract with a focus on human behavior
2. Contain universal laws	2. Do not contain universal laws
3. Examine the unpurposeful actions of matter	3. Examine the purposeful behavior of human beings

Source: Green, A. W. 1968. Sociology: An Analysis of Life in Modern Society. New York: McGraw Hill.

anthropology, economics, political science, and psychology.

As portrayed in Table 1–1, there are three basic distinctions between the physical and social sciences. First, the physical sciences focus on the concrete physical world, which include such readily observable and predicable things as molecules, chemical compounds, and the positioning and motion of objects. The social disciplines, by comparison, deal with the abstractions of human behavior in which no two people appear to think or act in precisely the same way. Second, the physical sciences have the luxury of universal or natural laws with which to predict with precision such things as the effects of gravity on a falling object or the boiling point of water at sea level. The social sciences, to date, have no universal laws because human behavior varies from society to society and from one social condition or situation to another. Finally, the subject matter of the physical sciences is without will or purpose, although some nonscientists do talk to their tomatoes and others play Mozart concertos to their geranium plants. The social sciences deal with the purposeful behavior of human beings, who possess keen intellects with both rational and emotional dimensions (Green, 1968; Landis, 1995).

THE SOCIOLOGICAL IMAGINATION

Sociology and Common Sense

The sociological perspective is a scientific one that goes far beyond obvious "common sense" explanations. The sociologist studies the underlying causes that shape human behavior. This analysis is carried forth using the scientific rules of evidence. Consequently, the sociologist, because of the method of investigation used, is not likely to be influenced by the personal and cultural biases and emotionalism that often shape and characterize the interpretations of the nonscientist.

When one peels back the onion called human behavior, the investigator, particularly if he or she is a sociologist, discovers that social reality is multilayered. As such, it has an impact on the lives of individuals that goes much beyond the overly simplistic notions we often refer to as "common sense." Does "absence make the heart grow fonder" or does "out of sight, out of mind" provide a more accurate assessment of what happens when lovers are separated for significant periods of time? Sociologists seriously examine these and a myriad of other fascinating questions that run the entire spectrum of human experience.

In addition, the sociologist examines all aspects of human behavior, not just those seen as acceptable or comfortable but also the popular biases expressed by certain individuals, communities, or societies. Conflict is studied as well as social harmony, deviance as well as conformity, and homosexual and bisexual behavior as well as heterosexual behavior. As a scientist, the sociologist enters the research arena with no preconceived ideas about anything, only the desire to discover "What is?" and "Why it is so?"

To embrace the sociological perspective is to be caught up in a special type of passion: the desire to know what lies behind the obvious and apparent human behaviors, social structures, and social policies of society at all levels. As Peter Berger has stated (1963):

> The fascination of sociology lies in the fact that its perspective makes us see in a new light the very world in which we have lived all our lives. This also involves a transformation of consciousness . . . . The sociologist will occupy himself with matters that others regard as too sacred or as too distasteful for dispassionate investigation. He will find equally rewarding the company of priests and prostitutes, depending not on his personal preferences, but on the questions he happens to be asking at the moment. He will also concern himself with matters that others may find much too boring. He will be interested in the human interaction that goes with warfare or with great intellectual discoveries, but also in the relations between people employed in a restaurant or between a group of little girls playing with their dolls. His main focus is not . . . ultimate significance . . . but the action itself, as another example of the richness of human conduct (pp. 19, 21).

The Sociological Imagination

Sociologists use objectivity and the tools of science to look beneath the surface of the society that many of us take for granted because of our beliefs, customs, and traditions. This perspective is often referred to as the sociological imagination.

The expression sociological imagination was coined by C. Wright Mills (1959) to refer to the ability of individuals to see how interrelated their private lives are with the nature of their society. By going beyond the obvious "common sense" explanations that are readily available and convenient to use, the sociologist comes to understand that the lives of individuals and groups are profoundly affected by the structural characteristics of their society. Most of us have a view of the world that is limited by our own spheres of social relations. Social factors such as ethnicity, class, education, religion, income, occupation, and place of residence shape to a significant degree the way we look at the world and how we act and interact with others in the larger community and society.

Try posing a few questions to your friends to see what types of response you receive. One question that many people are sure to have definite opinions about is: "Why does the United States make use of capital punishment for certain violent crimes?" Although responses may vary, some people will invariably say that it is because it deters crime. Sociological research to date, however, has shown that capital punishment in general—as it is currently structured in the United States—has little if any deterrent effect. In summarizing the extensive literature on this subject, criminologists Hugh D. Barlow and David Kauzlarich have stated (2002, p. 202) that "more than fifty years of research has yet to uncover a deterrent effect for capital punishment" (Archer and Gardner, 1984; Baile, 1998; Cochran, Chambers, and Seth, 1994; Peterson and Bailey, 1991). State execution in America has more to do with the desire for revenge, resulting from fear and other emotions, than its actual deterrent value. To seek out, understand, and perhaps even conduct such research represents the sociological imagination put into practice. It represents the desire to look beyond the obvious "accepted" answers to uncover the real "whys" of social behavior in a scientific and systematic way.

What Sociologists Do: Careers in the Field

One important issue of concern to many first- and second-year college students is how to choose a major and decide on a career. It is fairly common for students to change majors several times as they take the various required survey courses during their first two years. So if you feel confused or conflicted at this stage in your experience at college, take heart. You are typical of thousands of students who, at this stage, have not decided on a firm career path. Be patient with yourself. Most likely it will begin to "gel" and then become clear to you in the next year or two which path to follow.

The pursuit of a degree in sociology may or may not be the right thing for you. However, one thing is clear. Whatever career you pursue, whichever occupation you decide on, will require that you work and deal effectively with other people. Consequently, your job most likely will have one or more sociological dimensions. Getting along with people, understanding their interests, motives, and needs, sizing up all kinds of

Sociologists engage in a variety of activities aimed at observing, analyzing, and understanding the diverse aspects of human behavior.

© Robert Anthony, 2009. Used under license from Shutterstock, Inc.

different social situations, and knowing and understanding how bureaucratic organizations work (and sometimes do not work) are among the many sociological skills possessed by most people who succeed in their chosen fields of endeavor. So, regardless of which major you choose, a few sociology courses chosen as electives could provide you with many invaluable insights that can benefit you in the years to come.

The Baccalaureate Degree   A common misconception among some college students is that they will obtain a job after college in their major field. Often, this is not the case. A person with an undergraduate major in sociology is unlikely to obtain a position in sociology per se. Instead, a bachelor's degree in sociology may prepare a student to enter a variety of occupations and professions that require an in-depth understanding of people and social behavior (Billson and Huber, 1993; American Sociological Association, 1999; University of Notre Dame, 2013). A few of these are listed (also see Figure 1–2):

Prelaw	Corporate training
High school teaching	Diplomacy
Professional sales	Drug counseling
Probation and parole	Government administration

Law enforcement	Labor relations
Rehabilitation counseling	Health services
Public relations	Communications
Fund raising	Recreation services
Personnel	Community organization and development
Social work	Children's day care administration

Advanced Study and/or Graduate Degrees   Full professional standing as a sociologist normally requires at least a master's degree; a doctorate is preferred and often necessary for the highest positions. The master's degree involves at least one or two years of advanced study, depending on thesis requirements. Master's level sociologists often teach at community colleges and hold professional and administrative positions in business and industry, as well as in government. The doctoral degree (normally the Ph.D. in Sociology) requires at least four years of advanced study beyond the baccalaureate and includes the completion of a dissertation, a scholarly study resulting in an original contribution to knowledge. Some sociologists with doctorates may choose to teach at community colleges.

Figure 1-2

Employment Classifications for Bachelor Degree Holders with Majors in Sociology

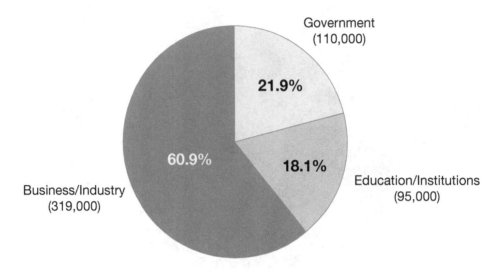

Source: American Sociological Association. 1999. Employed Social Scientists with Bachelor's Degrees by Sector, 1999. Updated October 23, 2008.

However, doctoral level sociologists, because of their extensive research training, typically teach at four-year colleges and universities. Sociologists with doctorates who choose careers in the private sector and government often occupy professional, research, and administrative positions at the highest levels.

The occupations of professional-level (master's to doctorate) sociologists are varied. A few thousand sociologists with doctorates hold full-time teaching positions in colleges and universities. Sociologists in business and industry hold positions ranging from advertising and marketing analysts to human resource development executives and consultants. Governmental agencies employ a large number of sociologists. The federal government uses such professionals in the departments of Agriculture, Defense, Health and Human Services, Homeland Security, Justice, Treasury, and Interior. Sociologists are also employed by federal agencies such as the Bureau of the Census and the Central Intelligence Agency (CIA), as well as by international organizations such as the World Bank, the World Health Organization, and the United Nations. In addition, some sociologists are in private practice as counselors, researchers, and consultants (Crossman, 2013).

Career Prospects for the Twenty-First Century

As we move more into the mainstream of the century before us, career prospects in sociology and related fields most likely will expand. For example, social gerontology, the study of the aged and aging, will require many more masters and doctoral level sociologists with specialties in this field. As more and more "baby boomers" (those born during the years 1946–1964) reach retirement age and beyond, they will require many more services than those currently available. Social gerontologists will conduct much of the research to assess such needs and help design the organizational structures (e.g., multi-level care centers and retirement communities) and services geared to the interests and accessed needs of this growing segment of the population. Other areas of sociological research and practice likely to experience a growing demand include but are not limited to college teaching, human services and social work, criminology, the sociology of deviance, the sociology of health care and medicine, and applied research and practice in both government service and business and industry.

Chapter 2

Society and Culture: Similar but Not the Same

In some parts of the world, people worship cows. The homage paid to these animals in some countries even extends to politics and law. For example, a group of holy men in India staged a demonstration involving 120,000 people in 1966 before the Indian parliament to lend support to the All Party Cow Protection Campaign Committee. In addition, a U.S. government official working in Nepal once killed a cow in a motor vehicle accident. In that country—a neighbor to India—murder of a cow is as serious as murder of a person. To avoid the diplomatic problems that surely would have resulted from the arrest of this unfortunate American, the Nepalese government ruled that "the cow had committed suicide" (Harris, 1987, p. 208).

Yet today in India, the rising middle class is embracing many Western cultural elements including American fast food—particularly "hamburgers." How do Indians reconcile the apparent contradiction between their religious beliefs and eating at McDonald's restaurants? They accomplish this by Indianizing the menu. At McDonald's in India, they sell the politically correct Maharaja Mac, a burger made of 100 percent ground lamb, and the Veg Surprise Mac, which uses a meat-like patty consisting of vegetable meat substitutes (Kannan, 2005).

During the 1970s, the Peace Corps began experiencing problems with their volunteers in the South African country of Botswana. Among other things, these Americans were experiencing burnout and hostility toward the Botswana people. A social scientist sent to investigate the situation found that much of the problem resulted from different cultural perceptions of "appropriate" behavior between the Americans and the Botswana. For instance, each time an American would attempt to go sit alone or otherwise obtain some privacy, he or she would be quickly joined by one or more Botswana. This annoyed the Americans because of the high premium placed on privacy in American culture. The Botswana, however, believe that only witches and the insane wish to be alone because of the social nature of human life. So every time they saw an American alone, they would rush to make social contact, to avoid breaching the rules of hospitality in their country (Schultz and Lavenda, 1987).

Each of these accounts serves to illustrate the arbitrary and ambiguous nature of human social behavior. The Americans and the British speak the same language but drive on opposite sides of the road. Americans eat with their mouths closed in order to be polite; in India, people eat with their mouths open for the same reason. In cities throughout Mexico and in some other Latin American countries, it is common for adolescent girls to demonstrate friendship by holding hands as they walk together and to kiss each other on the cheek when saying hello and goodbye. In American society, similar behavior might be interpreted by some as homosexual in nature. In these and hundreds of other ways, behavior—or the interpretation of similar behaviors—may vary from one society to another.

Such variability in our actions and perceptions is due in large part to the culture in which we live and the meaning and structure culture provides to our lives. Culture, in the sociological sense, refers to the socially established patterns of perceiving and acting that one acquires as a member of society. A person's culture thus represents a way of life as taught by the society in which that person lives. This way of life is passed from parent to child and consists of many elements, including a learned system of symbolic communication called language, a particular set of beliefs about the world and one's place in it, a history or ethnic heritage, and a set of socially standardized rules and values to live by. Indeed, it is largely this blueprint for living that gives our lives meaning and substance.

After having established a foundation concerning what sociology is, where it came from, how it developed, and how the sociological enterprise is conducted, we can now begin our journey through this fascinating science called sociology. In doing so, we will embark on a topical survey of the key areas of knowledge generated from the science of society. Central to the systematic study of social behavior is the concept of culture.

CULTURE: THE BASIS FOR HUMANITY

It is largely culture that separates human beings from the lower animals. As such, "human nature" is extremely variable because of the wide diversity of cultures in different parts of the world. Humans speak different languages, eat different foods, wear different clothes, and pray to different gods. The lower animals, by contrast, have a much more specific nature that is shaped to a large degree by inborn, biological factors.

The Nature of Humans

Compared to lower animals, human behavior is largely free of instinctual control. In fact, according to available research, humans have no definite instincts. The human being is virtually helpless at birth, is equipped with only a few basic reflexes, and would surely perish if not cared for by parents or other adults. By contrast, lower animal species often are able to achieve independence from their parents and become completely self-reliant within minutes or hours after birth. The salmon, for instance, never meets its parents; it carries out its life cycle guided largely by instincts alone, and then, guided by an instinctive imperative, ultimately goes up river at the end of its life cycle to spawn and die. Humans, lacking such inborn mechanisms, must rely on culture to equip them with the life strategies needed for survival.

"Instincts" in Humans: A Commonly Held Myth   The term *instinct* has become one of the most misused and overused terms in the English language. It is used in the popular culture as a catch-all term to describe any behavior that cannot readily be explained otherwise. Therefore, some people claim to have an instinct for cooking or gardening, and others say that they can instinctively dance, play chess, or make love.

Early in the twentieth century, anthropologist Franz Boaz (1911) asserted that since *Homo sapiens* represented a single species, any genuine instincts would have to be universally present in all humans. In his research, as well as that of scientists since, no universals that could be called human instincts have been found or agreed upon by the scientific community. Thus, the so-called "maternal instinct" is contradicted by child abuse and child-killing parents, the "aggressive" or "killer instinct" by pacifists, and the "survival instinct" by the many thousands who commit suicide each year. Yet the instinct myth continues to hang on tenaciously in popular culture, sparked in large part by simplistic labels perpetuated in the mass media to maximize profits. By way of illustration, Anthony Hopkins in 1999 starred in a movie titled *Instinct* about a primatologist who goes to Rwanda to study the mountain gorilla but instead lives with them, reverts to becoming gorilla-like himself, and allegedly kills two park rangers because of his primal instincts. In addition, the fragrance "Instinct" by David Beckham is now marketed to men with the implied message that women will be drawn "instinctively" to any man who wears it.

Behaviors Often Confused with Instincts: Reflexes and Drives   Two behaviors often confused with instinct are reflexes and drives. Both meet the first two preconditions that define an instinct—they both are (1) unlearned and (2) are universally present in all humans. However, both reflexes and drives fail to meet the criterion of complexity necessary to be regarded as an instinct.

A reflex is an automatic physical response to an external stimulus by the nervous system. The child whose hand is jerked back automatically after touching a hot stove is engaged in a reflex action, as is the person whose knee jerks back when tapped by a physician's mallet during a medical exam. However, they both represent simply a reactive response. There is no proactive message as in an instinct. The complexity criterion, therefore, is not met.

A drive is a physiological state in the form of internal tension that signals an individual that a particular need demands satisfaction. The drives for hunger and sex serve as notable examples. Both may manifest themselves in the form of tension, excitement, and sometimes discomfort. However, neither the hunger drive nor the sex drive tells the human being what steps to do next and in what order to complete the cycle. In lower animals, instincts for food acquisition or mating would take over. We humans, by contrast, must look to our culture to provide the answers as to how such drives can and should be satisfied.

Other Ways Humans Differ from the Lower Animals   In addition to the lack of definite instincts, human beings differ from the lower animals in several other important ways. Humans have a *superior intellectual capacity* because of a brain that is more complex—with about ten billion nerve cells—than that of other species. This makes it possible to think both rationally and abstractly and to develop, among other things, the technology to overcome the limitations of the natural environment. The *upright posture* of humans frees the hands for grasping and manipulating physical objects. In addition, humans' *sophisticated hands with opposable thumbs* allow the grasping of tools and the manipulation of a wide variety of objects with fine dexterity. With this capability, our ancestors were able not only to construct weapons and kill animals for food, but to develop a wide variety of sophisticated tools and machines with which to overcome the limitations of their physical environment. Finally, humans have *vocal chords of a refined nature*. This permits them to produce the thousands of nuanced sounds consisting of words and inflections needed for articulate speech. The use of symbolic language is essential to the social sharing of thoughts, feelings, and goals and the building of culture.

These four characteristics—superior intellect, upright posture, sophisticated hands, and refined vocal chords—along with the lack of rigid instincts, allow humans a flexibility unique among Earth's many species. With such capabilities, humans have devised various cultures and social systems throughout the world that have functioned to provide social order and stability as well as social change and progress. With this as a necessary background discussion, we will now examine human culture, beginning with its essential characteristics.

Characteristics of Culture

Culture Is Learned   First of all, *culture is learned* rather than instinctive or innate. Thus, a person is born *into* a culture rather than being born *with* one. Culture, as such, is a social invention created by people to lend order and predictability to their lives. It is acquired by the individual as a result of membership in a society. Largely because of the lack of biological imperatives for human behavior, societies throughout the world have very diverse cultures that differ from one another in fundamental ways. Family structures, economic systems, methods for governing, religious beliefs, educational systems, and other uniquely human dimensions of life are arranged differently depending on one's cultural context.

Culture Is Socially Shared   Second, *culture is socially shared*. Such cultural elements as beliefs, norms, values, symbols, and means of communication are passed from parents to children and are shared in general with people in the larger community and society (Kottak and Kozaitis, 2008, pp. 12–14). The process by which culture is passed from person to person is called *socialization*.

Culture Is Cumulative   Because it is passed from generation to generation, culture also is subject to change. Therefore, *culture is cumulative*. This third characteristic of culture is particularly apparent in modern societies like the United States that are affected by new technologies and other developments that continue to alter the way we live. Recent innovations like electronic synthesizers, MP3 players, and DVDs have changed our music and the ways we listen to it; microcomputers and the internet have affected the way we carry out our jobs, shop, and attend school; automated teller machines and electronic transactions have affected the way we bank, get paid by our employers, and pay our bills; and email, cell phones, and text messaging have changed the ways we communicate with family, friends, and associates. Many other developments in recent years and emerging today likewise have changed and are continuing to change if not transform much of our lives. The disease HIV/AIDS and other sexually transmitted diseases have had an impact on our sexual behavior. The consequences that rising economic powers such as China and India are having on the U.S., European, and global economies are changing

the ways we live as well. As a result of these and other influences, our culture is constantly changing as we adapt to new conditions that arise in our society and in the larger world that surrounds us. Think, for example, of the many changes that have occurred in American culture during the past one hundred years. We now drive cars rather than ride horses, our children attend modern schools with computer terminals rather than one-room, country schoolhouses, and we now can shop at home online or by watching one of several "home shopping" channels.

Culture Consists of Expected Forms of Behavior   In addition, *culture consists of expected patterns of behavior*. For the most part, these patterns for living are socially agreed upon and accepted by members of a society. They represent mainly the rules we live by. These rules are kept relatively uniform and stable by social pressures to conform and are made visible by group habits. Sociologists study these habitual forms of behavior that make up much of the subject matter for the scientific study of culture.

Culture Satisfies Basic Human Needs   Finally, because of the learned, socially shared forms of behavior that comprise culture, *culture satisfies basic human needs*. Culture is gratifying to us because it gives our lives structure and predictability. People typically feel relatively secure and comfortable in most situations because their lives are patterned after the cultural habits of family, friends, community, and society. Take your day-to-day activities as an example. Your life probably revolves around a continuous cycle of socially acquired habits focused on family, school, work, and friendship relationships. Your daily routine likely begins in the morning when you rise from a particular side of a bed and ends when you crawl into the same side of the same bed at night. Much of what you do in between involves a group of regular behavioral patterns, such as the likelihood that you sit in the same seat (by choice or assignment) each time your sociology class meets.

By contrast, most people feel quite anxious when everyday habits and routines are unexpectedly disrupted and they have their "cultural rugs" yanked out from under them. For example, most Americans remember with vivid clarity where they were and what they were doing on September 11, 2001 when the United States was attacked at the twin towers of New York's World Trade Center and the Pentagon in Washington, D.C. It was a day of much confusion, horror, anger, and sadness for many Americans that they perhaps will never forget. To avoid various forms of confusion, anxiety, panic, and mistakes, culture provides security and stability for society members in hundreds of different ways by showing them just what to do in most social situations. Public schools throughout the country, for instance, conduct fire drills periodically so students will have a pattern to follow in case of a real emergency.

Cultural Identification

Ethnocentrism: Three Key Characteristics From our exposure to society while growing up (socialization), we develop our own special view of the world and how we should relate to it. For most people, this cultural identification takes the form of ethnocentrism, the tendency to regard one's own culture as superior and other cultures as inferior. This form of cultural bias is

Ethnocentrism takes a variety of forms and occurs at all levels of society.

© Zdorov Kirill Vladimirovich, 2009. Used under license from Shutterstock, Inc.

common to all cultures. So whether one is an American, Italian, Nigerian, or any nationality, there is a marked tendency to perceive one's own culture as the best one. In fact, most people regard their own culture as the only really important one and are largely oblivious to the different life styles and perspectives of those who live in other parts of the world.

In terms of characteristics, first, *ethnocentrism exists at different levels of society.* For instance, many high school students exhibit school pride at pep rallies and ball games by cheering on the "best" team which, of course, is their own. Many people likewise claim that their hometown, state, or region is the best in the country. Some Texans are among the most ethnocentric of all Americans, and place bumper stickers on their cars that say "Native Texan," "Don't Mess with Texas," or "Love New York? Take I–10 East." In a similar fashion, some Southerners take deep pride in being from "Dixie" and refer to those from the North as "Yankees." In the hilly regions of rural Vermont, people who have not lived there for at least twenty years are sometimes called "flatlanders" and may not be seen as quite as acceptable as "long timers" or those who are native born.

Second, *ethnocentrism may foster social cohesion and stability at various levels of society.* At the micro level, a local disaster such as an earthquake or tornado may result in ethnocentrism in the form of community spirit, which would influence people to aid the victims. It also fosters social cohesion and stability at the societal level by encouraging people to take pride in their cultural heritage and way of life. In wartime, ethnocentrism may take the form of patriotism, so essential in sustaining the effort needed to vanquish a foe.

There is a third characteristic of ethnocentrism, however, that can result in negative or disruptive consequences. *Taken to an extreme, ethnocentrism may foster conflict and discord among different groups.* For example, if people become so ethnocentric about their own gender, race, ethnic background, religion, class, or sexual orientation that they are unwilling to be sensitive to the needs and concerns of others, their prideful intolerance can drive a wedge between groups with different backgrounds. On a macro to super-macro level, if diplomats from two countries with different ideologies cannot find common ground and reach a workable compromise, war may be the result.

Xenophobia   Some individuals become so culture bound and intolerant because of their ethnocentrism that they develop xenophobia, an irrational fear of foreigners or of cultures significantly different from one's own (Portes and Rumbaut, 1990). Many of those who are xenophobic simply avoid people from different cultures or situations that would bring them into contact with such people.

Another fairly typical manifestation of xenophobia is an aversion to foreign travel. The idea of traveling thousands of miles at significant expense to experience "strange" people with different languages, lifestyles, foods, and religious beliefs, living in a place with different laws and customs, makes them feel very uncomfortable. So they stay within their comfort zone at home in their own country. In addition, some who have traveled to a foreign country vow never do it again because it was so "different"—in their ethnocentrism, they cast this in a negative light.

Taken to the extreme, xenophobia sometimes can lead to negative and, on occasion, tragic consequences. On September 16, 2001—a few days after the 9/11 attack on America—a fifty-two-year-old man in Mesa, Arizona was murdered for wearing a turban. The perpetrators—a gang of unidentified, armed vigilantes "patrolling" the streets looking for members of Al Qaeda—shot and killed Balbir Singh as he was waiting on a customer at the gas station he owned. In reality, Singh was an East Indian immigrant to America, not an Arab Muslim extremist, and was wearing a turban as part of his religion, Sikhism—a monotheistic, Indian religion that frowns on the cutting of one's hair ("Sikh, Pakistani Shot in USA," *The Tribune,* September 17, 2001).

Subcultures and Countercultures   Cultural identification is also influenced by ancestral background and geographical mobility. In several European and Asian countries, for instance, most people have a similar ethnic heritage because their parents and ancestors have lived in the same city or village for many generations. Consequently, a country like Japan or Switzerland would be seen as a *homogeneous society.* By comparison, the United States is a *heterogeneous society* because it consists of people with diverse ethnic backgrounds who tend to be geographically mobile.

Heterogeneous societies like the United States often contain what sociologists call subcultures.

Some young people referred to as "Goths" represented a counterculture of the late 1990s and early 2000s.

© magicinfoto, 2009. Used under license from Shutterstock, Inc.

A subculture represents the heritage and lifestyle of a particular group that, although in basic harmony with the dominant culture, has some distinctive cultural features of its own (Schaefer, 2013). Some subcultures are regional, including those in California, the Midwest, or the deep South, while others are occupational, as illustrated by physicians and college professors with their jargon and professional standards, or rodeo cowboys and rock musicians with their special modes of dress, language, mannerism, and lifestyle. Some sociologists would also designate special subcultures by age or marital status, as illustrated by the adolescent subculture or the singles subculture. Others might identify specific subcultures by social class or by hobbies like coin collecting, fishing, or quilting.

However, the most visible, multifaceted, and influential subcultures are those based on the ethnic heritage of their members. In the United States, these groups include Americans with African, Italian, Mexican, Greek, Chinese, and Native American backgrounds, to mention only a few. They tend to be distinguished by characteristics that include family structure, language patterns, religious beliefs, holiday observances, types of food and ways to prepare it, and other life patterns. Other subcultures, such as the Amish, exhibit a distinct way of life based largely on their religious beliefs.

Although subcultures typically are in basic agreement with mainstream society in general, countercultures usually are in disagreement or opposition. A counterculture is a type of subculture that is in basic disagreement or conflict with the ways of the dominant culture of a society (Robertson, 1974; Yinger, 1982). During the 1960s, many college youths essentially dropped out of mainstream society and subscribed to a "hang loose" ethic. These young people, generally called "hippies," practiced an alternative lifestyle that included mind-altering drug use and permissive sexual practices. They were alienated from many of the underlying tenets of middle-class society, including the work ethic, deferred gratification, materialism, and individual responsibility (Suchman, 1968). In the 1970s and 1980s, countercultures typified the lifestyles of such diverse groups as the Hare Krishna, the "Moonies," and other religious sects; some factions of the "Skin Heads," the "Weathermen," and other extremist groups; and "punk" groups in Great Britain and the United States (Brake, 1985). During the 1990s and 2000s, the "Goth" lifestyle became a popular countercultural alternative for some young people who wore black clothing, boots, and cosmetics (e.g., lipstick and nail polish), and often made use of body piercings and tattoos as fashion statements. Some countercultures, therefore, are "different" but relatively harmless. More extreme countercultural groups today, however, are those whose activities revolve around criminal activity, such as delinquent gangs, drug rings, hate groups, and terrorist organizations such as Al Qaeda.

Culture Shock

When some of us are exposed to an unfamiliar cultural environment, it is not unusual to experience culture shock, a disorientation that occurs when one is placed in a cultural setting significantly different from one's own. Most Americans, for instance, are taught that certain body noises are inappropriate in a public place. Yet in some Middle Eastern countries, custom encourages dinner guests to give forth with boisterous belches to show the host that the meal was fully enjoyed. When Americans travel in certain parts of Europe, they are often surprised, if not dismayed, by such things as body odor brought on by infrequent bathing, women who do not shave their legs and underarms, and topless or nude sunbathing at many parks and beaches. Visitors to the United States are likewise shocked at many American practices including—in the European view—the "crass commercialism" involved in "littering" the landscape with billboards and neon signs, and—for the Japanese—the "cruel" and "inhuman" practice of placing the elderly in nursing homes.

In a pluralistic society like the United States, a citizen can experience culture shock even within the borders of his or her own country. Those from Northeastern cities such as New York and Washington, D.C., who relocate to cities like

Atlanta and San Antonio, often must adjust to a much slower pace of life and people who are "laid back" and much less harried. Similarly, those accustomed to the friendly, slow-paced environment of a quiet village in a rural area can find the anonymity of urban life, coupled with the hustle and bustle of rush hour traffic, very unsettling.

Even a trained social scientist can experience culture shock when exposed to a culture drastically different from his or her own. Anthropologist Napoleon Chagnon (1983), after receiving his research training, decided to conduct a participant observation study on a South American tribal group called the Yanomamo. These Indians live in the rain forests of Brazil and are extremely fierce and warlike. They regularly raid other tribes to steal women and often have the same done to them. The men proudly wear their often hideous battle scars as badges of masculinity. Because they rarely bathe, they sometimes can be detected before they are seen in the thick jungle. In addition, they make a fermented soup from bananas that they crush with their bare feet in large vats and then offer to visitors as a sign of friendship.

When the anthropologist first met the Yanomamo, a dozen men greeted him with drawn arrows. They had green tobacco stuck behind their lower lips and large amounts of green mucus hanging from their noses, the product of a green hallucinogenic powder that they regularly ingested by sniffing. Chagnon (1983) found all this quite repugnant and reports that he:

> . . . pondered the wisdom of having decided to spend a year and a half with this tribe before I had even seen what they were like. I am not ashamed to admit that had there been a diplomatic way out, I would have ended my fieldwork then and there. I did not look forward to the next day when I would be left alone with the Indians. I did not speak a word of their language, and they were decidedly different from what I had imagined them to be. The whole situation was depressing and I wondered why I had ever decided to switch from civil engineering to anthropology in the first place (p. 10).

Cultural Relativity

Early explorers and missionaries from the 1500s through the 1800s gave us the first written descriptions of simple, non-literate societies. Limited by the cultural blinders of their own ethnocentrism, they portrayed the cultures of these people as barbaric, uncivilized, and heathen. Indeed, even the highly trained social scientists of today, as evidenced by the Chagnon's description of culture shock, are hard pressed to remain objective when faced with a culture drastically different from their own.

Nonetheless, today's sociologists and anthropologists make every effort to put into practice cultural relativity, the principle that each culture should be seen and understood in its own context apart from a biased comparison with others (Lindsey and Beach, 2000). Taken out of its cultural context, any behavior can seem strange or unacceptable to the outsider, as evidenced by Chagnon's reaction to chest-pounding duels and other practices exhibited by the Yanomamo. Likewise, a visitor to the United States or Canada might find the body-punishing contests in football and ice hockey to be equally strange and unsettling.

Social scientists have established that there are no universally agreed upon standards for morality, religion, justice, beauty, art, or almost anything else. Instead, each society develops its own cultural adaptations necessary for survival and prosperity, regardless of how distasteful they may appear to outsiders. Sexual expression provides one example of cultural variability. Tibetan monks remain celibate for life, while the machismo orientation in some Latin American countries encourages the compulsive seduction of women. Among the Nayar of India, adolescent girls are encouraged to take lovers and later, as adults, "visiting husbands." By comparison, Sudanese girls in West Africa undergo surgical amputation of the clitoris to prevent sexual relations before marriage (Saxton, 1972). Some of these practices might seem strange or even barbaric to most Americans, but sociologists and anthropologists attempt to understand them within their respective cultural contexts.

Cultural Universals

Despite tremendous variations in cultures, there are some general elements found in all societies. These are called cultural universals, patterns and practices common to all cultures. Every culture, for instance, has one or more specific forms of religion, although religion varies greatly in different parts of the world. Likewise, all societies prohibit murder, although what constitutes unjustified killing differs greatly from culture to culture. In fact, the list of cultural universals is quite long. It includes the following practices: athletics, body decoration, cooking, courtship, dancing, division of labor, family, folklore, funerals, games, incest taboos, medicine, music, sexual restrictions, and tool making (Murdock, 1945).

KEY COMPONENTS OF CULTURE

American sociologist William F. Ogburn (1922) divided culture into two subdivisions, material culture and nonmaterial culture. In his formulation, *material culture* consists of physical objects or technologies that provide meaning to a group of people or society. Means of transportation provides one example. In the United States, most people drive cars. On the streets of small towns in the provinces of the Philippines, families of four or five travel in small, three-wheeled, motorized tricycles, which are also used in Thailand and there are called Tuk Tuks. In rural China and India, a wagon pulled by a buffalo is a fairly common means of transportation, while in parts of North Africa and the Middle East, some people still travel by camel. In similar fashion, architecture, clothes, foods, eating utensils, tools, weapons, art, and any other physical things that people own, use, or value are a part of material culture. By contrast, Ogburn asserted, *nonmaterial culture,* consists of ways of using material objects along with such aspects as beliefs, customs, and means of communication.

A more useful and sophisticated paradigm in use today takes Ogburn's typology and expands it into four key components—material culture, cognitive culture, normative culture, and language (Semones, 1990). Together they represent the four essential building blocks that constitute the patterns for living—our culture—that we use to survive and prosper in society (Figure 2-1).

Figure 2-1

Culture is comprised of four overlapping elements. Together they form the basic social support system that give our lives order, security, and some predictability.

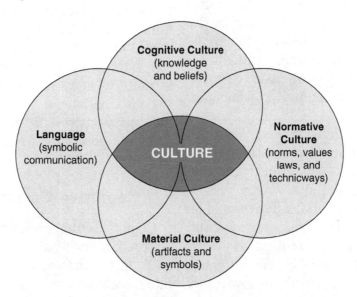

Source: Semones, J. K. 1990. Sociology: A core text, 77. Fort Worth, TX: Holt, Rinehart & Winston.

Material Culture

In dividing culture into its four key components, we will begin with material culture, which consists of cultural aspects, including technologies, that for the most part are physical and tangible in form. Material culture consists of two key elements or subtypes, artifacts and symbols.

Artifacts   Physical objects that represent a specific culture are artifacts. Archeologists study the remnants of artifacts in trying to piece together the characteristics of an ancient culture. If you were to go to a museum to see an exhibit of artifacts from colonial America during the 1600s and 1700s, you would probably notice things like floor-length dresses, plows, axes, butter churns, candle molds, and spinning wheels, which would tell you a great deal about the way people lived during that time.

Suppose ten thousand years from now archaeologists sift through the remains of American culture left from the first two decades of the twenty-first century. What do you think they would find, and how would they interpret these artifacts? They might discover, for example, huge circular structures with seating capacity for tens of thousands of people with a small rectangle of earth in the center. At first they might think that these were huge cathedrals, houses of worship where people paid homage to their god or gods. Then they would realize that they had found a huge sports stadium or the remnants of one. They might also find thousands of huge golden arches and eventually arrive at an understanding of the late twentieth and early twenty-first century phenomenon called "fast food."

Obviously, material things have no objective meaning based solely on their physical characteristics, but must be understood chiefly in terms of their cultural settings and how they were or are used. To Americans, a railroad car would be an artifact that was used to transport people and freight from one place to another. However, among impoverished Indians in North Central Mexico today, abandoned rail cars are sometimes used as homes.

Symbols   Symbols are objects or acts that have a special meaning within a specific culture. Many symbols are also artifacts, in that they have tangible properties and have meaning within a specific cultural context. However, what separates a symbol from an artifact is its ability to stir emotions and/or communicate a special, sometimes abstract meaning. Take a country's flag as an example. Its presence has the ability to stir strong emotions of love, pride, and patriotism—even hatred if it is the flag of an acknowledged enemy. The flag is used in various rituals, and certain norms specify when it is to be raised or lowered, how it is to be handled physically, and how it is to be accorded respect. This expresses the special meaning attached to a cultural symbol that, physically, is no more than a rectangle of bright-colored cloth (Turner, 1967).

Many symbols have special emotional meaning in American culture. They include the bald eagle as the national bird, the Statue of Liberty, the Liberty Bell, and numerous other patriotic symbols. The wedding ring and the cross also evoke strong emotions. Symbols may also have commercial meaning, such as logos for television networks, automobiles, fast-food chains, and designer clothes. Clothing itself is often a symbol of an occupation, as evidenced by the uniforms worn by police officers, military personnel, nurses, and postal workers. Clothing may also symbolize social class, particularly when one looks at extremes like the society matron in her mink coat compared to the "bag lady" in her ragged attire who lives on the street. Additionally, symbols often take nonmaterial form such as gestures and facial expressions that project various emotions or "body language" that may indicate a variety of things, including saying hello and good-bye, flirting, or even signifying insults.

Cognitive Culture

Cognitive culture refers to the ways in which a culture defines what is real or what exists. As such, this component of culture is subdivided into three basic subtypes or elements: knowledge, beliefs, and ideologies.

Knowledge   One form of cognitive culture is knowledge, defined as propositions about reality that have been scientifically verified. We know, for example, that the United States has landed men on the moon, that there really is such a thing as global warming, and that Barack Obama began his second term in January, 2013 after having been re-elected as President of the United States. *Knowledge* (the state of scientific theory) is based on demonstrated facts that have been objectively gathered and empirically demonstrated. As such, it takes several forms. These range from *pure knowledge* (information for its own sake) generated out of scientific research, to *practical knowledge* (technology) aimed at improving the quality of life in such diverse areas as horticulture, education, medicine, and industry.

Beliefs   Beliefs represent the other basic form of cognitive culture. Beliefs are propositions about reality that either are not based on scientific evidence or cannot be demonstrated through scientific means. Within the United States, beliefs that are not based on scientific evidence are often held by people who tend to be poorly educated or who appear to have an anti-intellectual bias. Through their beliefs, they sometimes seem to be saying, "Don't confuse me with the facts. I believe this way." Examples include the Flat Earth Society whose members believe that our planet is flat and thousands of Americans who insist that manned flights to the moon never occurred. The other type of belief—namely, propositions about reality that cannot be demonstrated or have not been verified (so far) through scientific means—are also diverse. Beliefs of this type include the other-worldly aspects of religion, such as the concepts of heaven, hell, god (or gods and goddesses), and reincarnation, and a multitude of other beliefs such as those relating to UFOs, visits from alien life-forms, ghosts or poltergeists, and mythical creatures such as unicorns, the Loch Ness monster, and a creature called "Big Foot."

Ideologies   When a group of beliefs becomes strongly held, an ideology may form. An ideology is a set of ideas aimed at promoting the interests of a particular segment of society. In *German Ideology* (1846), Karl Marx and Friedrich Engels argued that the ideology of the ruling class—its basic set of social, political, religious, and economic ideas—was used to underpin existing social policy and maintain the status quo. In their view, it operated mainly to reinforce and perpetuate the existing class structure. Therefore, they argued, the ideology of the ruling class mandated for all German people what behavior was seen as lawful or unlawful, moral or immoral, and otherwise acceptable or unacceptable.

Modern sociologists, particularly conflict theorists, view this concept from a much broader perspective. The various classes and segments of society are seen to have their own ideologies aimed at promoting their own interests. This is particularly evident in a pluralistic society like the United States that is comprised of many interest groups. Today, for example, there are conservative versus liberal ideologies in politics, Catholic versus Protestant ideologies regarding religion, and various other forms of ideology related to class, race and ethnicity, sex roles, and other social characteristics and issues.

Normative Culture

Another important cultural component is *normative culture,* which many sociologists consider to be the most important in maintaining social order and stability. Normative culture consists of socially agreed-upon standards for thinking, feeling, and acting in society. These cultural standards include norms, values, laws, and technicways.

Norms: Rules of Conduct   Much of the foundation for normative culture lies in the concept of **norms**, cultural rules that specify appropriate and inappropriate behavior. There are literally thousands of norms that comprise the standards that we are expected to live by. Some are explicit—you must pay your income taxes—while others, like washing your hands after using a toilet, are implied. Some norms called *mores* are seen as very important and are strongly reinforced by a formal system of rewards and punishments, while others termed *folkways* seem almost trivial by comparison and usually are followed but generally are not required. Some apply to everyone, while others guide the behavior of only a few. Taken together, they constitute much of the blueprint for survival that is the fabric of culture. Therefore, norms as rules of conduct furnish each of us with a fairly detailed map for negotiating our journey through life.

Mores   Among the most important norms are mores, which have a compelling moral connotation whose violation is met with general condemnation and sometimes severe punishment. As children, we are taught mores as moral imperatives that specify both what must be done in many circumstances and, likewise, what is forbidden. These notions of right and wrong later become internalized in us as the basis for our most cherished, if not sacredly held, values. Consequently, because most societies place a high value on life, killing another person may be defined as murder and punished by lengthy imprisonment and, in some cases, death. Most people in the United States would find it repugnant to kill and eat the family dog, not simply because of its impracticality in a society full of food or the threat of legal punishment, but because mores in American culture have elevated the dog to the position of family member. Therefore, many if not most of us would be emotionally incapable of doing such a thing. In addition, one can be arrested, fined, and imprisoned for engaging in cruelty to animals. By contrast, in portions of China and other parts of Asia where different norms are practiced, dogs are considered a delicacy, are raised and sold for food, and animal cruelty is largely an unknown concept. Indeed, mores are often structured in an opposite manner in different cultures. For instance, American women often bare their legs but must cover their breasts under threat of arrest for public indecency. By contrast, Balinese women must hide their legs but are free to expose their breasts (Stevens, 1970).

Folkways   In contrast to mores, folkways are broad-based norms such as general customs and social conventions that, when violated, result in only mild punishment, if any. As such, they involve little or no moral connotation. Instead,

folkways represent the habitual or customary ways in which things typically are done. For instance, if you traded your car for a bicycle, gave up meat to become a vegetarian, and quit watching television, you would be violating several American customs. Although your friends and neighbors might see you as a little strange or eccentric, you would not be the subject of severe condemnation or punishment. Some folkways, however, do carry a slight "ought to" connotation, with some pressure to conform along with the likelihood of mild but emotionally significant punishment. If, for example, you forgot the birthday of a parent, spouse, or child, or suddenly decided the day before Christmas or Thanksgiving not to celebrate it, the consequences might be emotionally hurtful for others and for you as well if there were not an acceptable explanation. Folkways are the most pervasive form of norms and cover practically everything we do, from standards of social etiquette and personal hygiene to compliance with community standards and observance of cultural traditions and holidays.

Some of the most interesting types of folkways—*fads, crazes,* and *fashions*—are those limited to particular time frames and certain groups of people within a culture. These folkways are particularly important in urban, highly technological societies like the United States because they provide both guidelines and insights into how people form and adapt to customs in light of rapid cultural change.

Values: Our Standards of Evaluation   The norms of any culture are often a reflection of the values held by its members. In this sense, values are the standards used by people to evaluate the relative desirability and worth of practically everything in their lives and in the social world around them. This includes people, objects, ideas, acts, and feelings. Values occur at all levels of culture and thus are held by individuals, groups, and even whole societies. They define for us what is good and bad, moral and immoral, artful and in poor taste, beautiful and ugly, and worthwhile and worthless.

Values, however, differ from norms in three fundamental ways. First, values *are attitudes that*

Table 2–1

Values Versus Norms: Comparative Characteristics

Values	Norms
Personal attitudes/feelings (can be held by one person)	Social rules for conduct (are established and enforced by groups)
Are general and abstract (love, beauty, justice)	Are specific and concrete (address specific forms of behavior)
Cannot be rewarded or punished	Include a system of sanctions

can be held by one person while norms are social rules established and enforced by groups. In addition, values *are general and abstract,* while norms are specific and concrete. For example, we may value the general concepts of marriage and freedom, but norms specify the concrete conditions and limitations under which both take place. Finally, values *cannot be rewarded or punished,* whereas norms include a system of sanctions. As such, the way one thinks or feels (one's values) is internal and cannot be sanctioned one way or another. However, when values become transferred into behavior, this action like any other behavior is subject to rewards and punishments that are attached to the group, community, and societal norms one is expected to follow and live by.

Because the United States is a heterogeneous society with a large number of subcultures, it is somewhat difficult to identify in specific terms an American value system. The fact is, some subcultures hold certain values while others have different priorities. For instance, both Mexican Americans and Vietnamese Americans place a high premium on family cohesion and the work ethic. As another example, Jewish Americans as a subcultural group place a different emphasis on the use of both time and money than do many Americans. This condition of cultural pluralism is further complicated by rapid cultural change brought about, in significant part, by changes in social and economic conditions and technology. Consequently, value orientations regarding the roles of women and minorities, consumer behavior, sexual practices, the size of families, recreation, and many other things have experienced significant change in recent decades.

Nonetheless, sociologist Robin Williams (1970) identified several traditional value orientations in American culture that remain dominant well into the twenty-first century. They include orientations toward achievement and success, activity and work, humanitarianism, practicality, material comfort, equality, freedom, democracy, and individuality.

Laws Officially recorded norms formulated and enforced by government are laws. While other norms may vary in terms of the proportion of people in a society to which they apply, everyone is obligated to obey laws. Most laws are codified mores that act to reinforce and protect the maintenance of social order. Those who choose not to conform are subject to a penalty that, for minor offenses, may be only a traffic fine or a court judgment in a civil suit. In some extreme cases, however, punishment may take the form of imprisonment or even execution. Most people conform to laws simply by knowing what they are. Others who might be tempted to deviate are at times deterred by the threat of legal punishment.

Sometimes laws correspond closely to norms regarded as important in the larger culture. In other cases, they reflect the political power of certain segments of society to have their agendas officially formulated as the public policy for all to follow. Although the 55-mile-per-hour federal speed limit passed during the 1970s contributed to the reduction of the number of highway deaths, it was highly unpopular and largely ignored by many Americans during the first few years it was in effect. Due to its unpopularity, the federal law was changed and most states have returned to higher speed limits. The felony statutes mandating harsh prison terms for possession of small amounts of marijuana were equally unpopular during the same period when at least twenty-five to thirty million Americans were using this drug recreationally. This resulted in the laws being changed so that possession of small amounts of marijuana today constitutes a misdemeanor rather than a felony in most jurisdictions.

In addition to laws operating as mechanisms of social control, they also act as vehicles for social reform. When laws become outmoded and no longer reflect the mores of society, people in the United States have the right to sue, and the courts rule on whether or not a law is constitutional. In this manner, laws that are no longer in accord with the dominant mores are changed or abolished. During the 1960s, for instance, the U.S. Supreme Court—in the wake of the civil rights movement—struck down miscegenation laws, which forbade interracial marriage as unconstitutional. In similar fashion, the rulings by the high court established the legal right to abortion during the 1970s. Legislative bodies can also write new laws that correspond to changing conditions, as illustrated by the Civil Rights Act of 1964 passed by Congress. As a recent example, the U.S. Supreme Court, in a groundbreaking case handed down in June, 2008, struck down a Washington, D.C. law which prohibited a law enforcement officer—who was required to carry a gun on duty—from keeping a firearm in the home to defend his or her family. This case established a legal precedent by the high court in ruling that U.S. citizens have an individual right to keep and bear arms as set forth in the Second Amendment to the Constitution (Greenhouse, 2008).

Language

In addition to cognitive culture and normative culture, language represents the third key component of nonmaterial culture and the fourth component (in addition to material culture) overall. Those who travel to foreign countries know how difficult it can be at times to function in a culture where a different tongue is spoken. Indeed, language is "the storehouse of culture" (Harroff, 1962) and represents for each of us the primary means through which we receive, understand, and pass on our way of life to others.

In this sense, language refers to a learned system of symbolic communication that furnishes the framework for the sharing of meaning and culture with others. Without understanding the language of a culture, it is not possible to participate in it in a meaningful way (Fishman, 1985).

Humans are unique in the animal kingdom because, unlike all other species, they use language, which furnishes them with a history and a means of passing on their thoughts and experiences to others after they die. In pre-literate societies, culture is passed on through oral tradition. Societies with greater material technology make use of the written word and electronic media that allow thoughts and feelings to be permanently recorded for posterity.

Key Functions of Language First of all, language *serves as the primary means of cultural transmission*. Second, *it acts as the main vehicle of thought*. We think in symbolic terms using the words furnished us by our culture. If reared in a Spanish-speaking culture, we think in Spanish. If taught English as a child, this linguistic system furnishes the primary structure for our thoughts. In addition, language *allows us to transcend the world of concrete experiences*. By talking to a person about their trip to foreign country or by reading a book about an event from one hundred years ago, we can transcend space and time and experience these things vicariously. Finally, language *allows us to assign meaning to abstract or nebulous ideas or concepts*. Consequently, we are able to conceptualize our feelings about love, hate, beauty, God, and other intangibles.

Limitations of Language Although language is liberating in many respects, it can also be limiting because it restricts the manner in which we view reality. In addressing this issue, the linguist Edward Sapir (1929) said that "the worlds in which different societies live are distinct worlds, not merely the same world with different labels attached." Some languages stress the masculine or feminine genders showing a bias in the culture, as illustrated by the masculine bias in traditional English up until the 1970s. Other languages and how they are used reflect additional concerns and themes prevalent in given cultures. For example, anthropologist Margaret Mead (1971), in her research on the Arapesh of New Guinea in the 1930s, found that they counted in terms of dogs probably because dogs have four legs. Thus the number five was expressed as "dog and one," eight was "two dog," and twenty-four was "two dog, two dog, two dog."

The Sapir–Whorf Hypothesis The perspective that language structures and limits the way people in different cultures think about and perceive reality was developed by Edward Sapir and Benjamin Whorf and is often referred to as the Sapir–Whorf hypothesis. Cross-cultural examples are abundant. While English-speaking people are very time conscious; see time in a linear fashion of past, present, and future; and have numerous time concepts in their language, the Hopi Indians of the American Southwest have no words in their language for time or concepts related to time such as days, months, and years. Everything in their view has "become" or is "becoming." Americans generally have only a handful of words for "snow." Eskimos, by contrast,

have between twenty and thirty different terms for snow because weather conditions are important in their world. Whether language strictly determines how we see reality, as Sapir and Whorf contended, or basically reflects existing realities of the larger culture as others argue (Eastman, 1975) is a matter of debate. However, one thing is clear. Language as taught to the members of any society determines in large part how they conceptualize reality and then act on such conceptions.

CONFORMITY AND SOCIAL CONTROL

So far, you have learned basically what culture is, why humans alone have a definite way of life that varies from society to society, and what the basic components of culture are and how they are structured. Now we turn to an examination of how certain mechanisms of social control act to maintain cultural conformity and social order and how cultures change.

The Need for Social Control

In examining how societies maintain social order and control, we will trace the need for social stability by first looking at some notable

---

"Dressing up" is one of the symbolic ways in which people perceive their location in society and project themselves to others.

examples that emerged as historical benchmarks first in Babylonia and then later at various times in Western Civilization.

The Code of Hammurabi: Origins of a Rationalistic Tradition In ancient Babylonia over four thousand years ago, its ruler, Hammurabi developed a system of law called the Code of Hammurabi. This code consisted of 282 laws that the king required be written on huge tablets and placed in the center of the city for all to see. The purpose of these laws, as stated in the Code's prologue, was "to cause justice to prevail in the land . . . and to further the welfare of the people" (Browne, 1946). These laws were comprehensive and covered the spectrum of social issues from political and military affairs to social relations with one's family and neighbors. In addition, each law contained prescribed punishment for its violation.

Ever since the time of Hammurabi, a rationalistic tradition has emerged in many cultures which recognized the need for social control to be exerted over human behavior rather than dependence on divine intervention to control people's actions. The promise of otherworldly pleasure or pain in the afterlife was found to have little or no impact on the behavior of many people whose lives were guided by the "here and now" rather than the distant future. What was needed was a culturally designed and enforced system of social control aimed at maintaining conformity to the dominant norms of society.

The Social Contract School of the Enlightenment Period (1650–1770) Among the first scholars to inquire systematically into the origins of systems for social control and the complex issue of conformity were the social contract theorists of the seventeenth and eighteenth centuries. The English philosopher Thomas Hobbes (1588–1679) was an early proponent of the *social contract* idea. In *Leviathan*, Hobbes (1651; 1881) attempted to explain the origins of both society and government. He asserted that early humans lived in a state of nature and pursued their selfish desires as best they could. This ultimately led

to a war of "all against all." In order to ensure survival, peaceful coexistence, and social order, people entered into a social contract with each other in which they mutually agreed to give up some freedom in order to live under a system of enforced social rules.

The social contract school continued to be popular during the eighteenth century and had several European exponents, such as John Locke (1632–1704) and Jean-Jacques Rousseau (1712–1778). Both argued that the people of any society, when faced by authoritarian rule that usurped their "inalienable rights" and ceased to address their needs, had a right to overthrow this type of government and form a new contract that was more equitable (Locke, 1690; Rousseau, 1762). Locke maintained that governments had a sacred trust to guarantee and protect the freedoms of their people. Whenever a government violated this trust, the people had a right to set it aside. Thomas Jefferson, the primary author of the Declaration of Independence, was deeply influenced by enlightenment thinkers and particularly by Locke. Therefore, the writings of John Locke formed much of the ideological foundation for the American Revolution, whose influence is reflected in this brief excerpt from the Declaration:

> We hold these truths to be self evident, that all men are created equal, that they are endowed by their Creator with certain inalienable rights, that among these are life, liberty, and the pursuit of happiness. That to secure these rights, governments are instituted among men, deriving their just powers from the governed . . . That whenever any form of government becomes destructive of these ends, it is the right of the people to alter or abolish it and to institute a new government, laying its foundation on such principles and organizing its power in such form as to them shall seem most likely to effect their safety and happiness.

The social contract idea represented an important benchmark in the development of social thought pertaining to the nature of social order and how it should be maintained. As such, it represented a rational explanation for the origin of society and government that provided several useful insights. However, its basic propositions about people "wandering around alone in nature" and "deciding suddenly to form a comprehensive social contract" are largely unsupported by modern science and are dismissed as myth. Humans have always been social creatures, and mechanisms for social control have evolved gradually, in step with general cultural evolution. Nonetheless, the social contract theorists were correct regarding one fundamental issue. Effective mechanisms of social control must be put into place by every culture to ensure social order and stability.

Mechanisms of Social Control

Sanctions Social control in any culture is maintained primarily through the use of a system of sanctions. These are socially recognized and enforced rewards and punishments that are applied to conforming and nonconforming behavior. Sanctions may be positive or negative, formal or informal. In addition, they are usually flexible, in that the norms to which they relate prescribe a certain *range of tolerance* before sanctions are invoked. For instance, if a child strays momentarily from expected behavior but then returns to conforming behavior after acknowledging a look of disapproval on the face of a parent, no application of a sanction will be necessary in most cases. In like manner, motorists usually are given a leeway of about five miles an hour or so before being ticketed for speeding. The range of tolerance varies from situation to situation and from one group or culture to another. College students, for example, are treated with much more tolerance by their professors than are high school students by their teachers in terms of personal freedom of action (they are adults), but generally with less tolerance regarding work assignment deadlines and other academic responsibilities.

Types of Sanctions *Positive sanctions* are rewards given for compliance with norms. Because the most effective form of social control involves voluntary conformity, most people will conform if provided a set of positive rewards that are meaningful for them. In small rural societies and in our relations with family, friends, and

coworkers, *informal positive sanctions* usually are sufficient to reinforce conformity. Informal sanctions may range from a smile, a nod, or a "thumbs up," to a declaration of support and appreciation ("I like your work"), or even physical affection. Informal positive sanctions are particularly important when given to or received from a close family member because of the emotional bond present and the wish to be appreciated by a loved one. In school and career settings, *formal positive sanctions* are also very necessary in motivating people to conform and achieve. These too take several forms and occur in various degrees. For example, a person may receive a raise or promotion at their place of employment, earn an "A" or make the Dean's list in college, or receive a formal award or honor from his or her profession, community, or nation.

Negative sanctions are punishments given for the violation of norms. They usually indicate incomplete or inadequate socialization and, like positive sanctions, take both informal and formal forms. *Informal negative sanctions* are often applied to children who are attempting to learn how to become successful social beings. However, some parents over-use them and, in doing so, fail to understand that a balance of rewards and punishments would be much more effective. As adults, most of us have a large variety of informal negative sanctions we can apply to others, just as we do with informal rewards. We can frown, scowl, be sarcastic or critical, voice displeasure or anger, ridicule and belittle, give the "silent treatment," and even slam doors or make someone sleep on the couch. These types of sanctions are often quite effective because of the emotional bond between the parties, and because it is emotionally painful when we displease or upset our friends and loved ones. Sometimes, however, negative sanctions must be applied formally. This usually occurs in organizations and in the relationships of people with their larger community and society. *Formal negative sanctions* may range from official reprimands, demotion, dismissal from a job or failing grades at school, to arrest and imprisonment in extreme cases for violation of criminal law.

Chapter 3

Socialization: Learning How to Be Human

Earlier, we began our survey of key topics in sociology by examining culture, the way of life we acquire as members of society. Through exposure to a culture, we are provided with a set of socially accepted patterns for thinking and acting that gives our lives order and predictability. In this chapter, we will focus on socialization, the process through which culture is transmitted to the individual and the personality and self concept are developed. To begin, we will first examine the nature—nurture debate.

THE NATURE VERSUS NURTURE DEBATE

The crux of this debate is the question of how personality is determined and self-concept is formed. Personality refers to the sum total of a person's unique yet consistent patterns of thoughts, feelings, and actions. Are humans equipped at birth with a set of traits that largely direct and shape their personality development? Or are they instead shaped and influenced primarily by their experiences with the social environment that surrounds them? Proponents on both sides of this issue have argued vigorously for their respective viewpoints for well over a century. While each of us most likely possesses a

genetic predisposition for being introverted or extraverted as demonstrated through neuroscience (Canli, 2004; Canli et al., 2002, 2004), much of what determines who we are and who we become depends on our cumulative experiences with others and society as we move through our life experience.

Socialization also provides the individual with a sense of identity in terms of "Who am I?," "What am I worth?," and "Where am I going?" This identity or self-image we each possess sociologists call the self-concept, the personal assessment people have of their own identity and self-worth and how they fit into the larger community and society. Our self-image forms much of the foundation for our personality. It is a complex area of study for the sociologist because (1) it has several dimensions and (2) it is constantly evolving due to a continuous, dynamic interplay that occurs between individuals and their social environment.

The Nature Argument

Those who subscribe to the nature position maintain that human beings possess a definite set of qualities determined largely by inborn traits. One's environment, therefore, represents only the background against which these inherited characteristics are played out (Adams, 1974).

The notion of an "innate human nature" was proposed by social contract theorists of the seventeenth and eighteenth centuries. Some, like Jean-Jacques Rousseau, argued that humans are basically good but tend to become corrupted by modern civilized society. Others, such as Thomas Hobbes, argued that humans by nature are untrustworthy and selfish, characteristics that necessitated the formation of society with rules to keep people under control.

Social Darwinism   In 1859, Charles Darwin published his *On the Origin of Species,* which gave the nature argument a great deal of scientific legitimacy. He argued that human beings, like lower animals, are products not of divine creation but of evolution through natural selection. Those with the ability to adapt to changes in their environment survive, while those without such adaptability perish. Consequently, environment affects the genetic makeup present in all species and biological traits that are most adaptable emerge through natural selection.

The social Darwinists, led by Herbert Spencer, expanded this argument to include the nature of human societies. Social Darwinism was the argument that governments should not interfere in the lives of individuals or the operation of organizations so that the fittest can survive. Spencer and his followers asserted that European societies and the United States were more dominant in the world than other societies because they were more highly evolved. Other, less-advanced social systems were biologically and socially inferior because they occupied an earlier, and thus more primitive, stage of evolution (Spencer, 1860, 1874). The social Darwinists also used the natural selection argument to explain why certain individuals within modern societies were affluent, successful, and more "fit," while others, struggling in the throes of poverty were, therefore, "unfit." The glaring flaw in this argument soon became clear as the behavioral sciences developed substantively during the early part of the twentieth century: In the biological world, each member of a species—lions, for example—are born with essentially the same attributes and are exposed to the same environmental circumstances. However, humans are distributed throughout each society with diverse characteristics that are treated quite differently according to how each society is structured.

Instinct Theory   Another popular approach used by nature proponents during the late nineteenth and early twentieth centuries was that human behavior is determined mainly by "instincts." Instinct theory argued that human behavior was shaped largely by genetically inherited predispositions called instincts. Some proponents of this perspective held that such "instincts" caused specific types of behavior. Thus, people got married because of a "mating" instinct, fought wars due to a "killing" instinct, lived in homes and societies as a result of "nesting" and "herding" instincts, and birthed and raised children guided by "maternal" and "parenting" instincts. One researcher documented the increasing popularity of instinct theory during this period and, in reviewing academic and popular literature, found that over ten thousand alleged instincts had been claimed to exist (Bernard, 1924). However, by the 1930s researchers like anthropologist Margaret Mead and others were finding that, while some individuals and cultures had traits some called "instinctive," others did not. Therefore, *instinct* by this time had become a useless concept in science with which to explain human behavior in a meaningful way.

Sociobiology   Although most of the thinking of the twentieth century was dominated by "nurture" or environmental explanations of human behavior, a new discipline called sociobiology emerged during the late 1970s and 1980s that gave nature proponents renewed vigor. Sociobiology is the study of the biological aspects of social behavior in all species including humans (Wilson, 1978). The founder of this perspective is Edward O. Wilson, an entomologist (one who studies insects) who originated the term *sociobiology.* Wilson and his followers attempted to integrate or synthesize the research results of both the biological and social sciences. They argue that although culture rather than genetics is the prime cause of specific human behavior (Wilson, 1975), some forms of social behavior in general have a genetic foundation. They claim, for instance, that there are tendencies toward the exhibition of male dominance, territoriality, the incest taboo, the eating of meat, and religion that are genetically encoded in humans at birth.

This biological explanation has come under a barrage of criticism. In a debate with Wilson over three decades ago, Marvin Harris, an anthropologist, categorically rejected the idea that traits such as aggressiveness, territoriality, and male dominance were inherited by humans. He argued that there is tremendous variability in all these traits from culture to culture, and that even if there are certain biological tendencies for behavior, they are so weak and general as to be meaningless because they are so easily overridden by culture (Harris, 1980). Others argue that even some human behaviors long thought to be primarily biological—such as sexuality—are now being shown to be greatly influenced by cultural factors (Lauer and Handel, 1983). In short, there is little, if any, hard evidence to support the contention that most behaviors specific to humans as individuals are determined wholly or even significantly by genetic factors.

The Nurture Argument

While biology does play a role in affecting who we are as humans and our actions, available research indicates that we are impacted at least as much by environmental or "nurture" factors. We will begin a brief overview of this research with examples of findings on complex lower animals that are also capable of learning and that also need satisfying social contact with others of their kind.

Animal Studies: Examples by Pavlov and Harlow   A little over a century ago, researchers began to discover the impact of learning on behavior that previously was thought to be purely instinctive or otherwise inherited. At that time, the Russian physiologist Ivan Pavlov (1849–1935) demonstrated that, even among dogs, much behavior is subject to environmental conditions. Pavlov observed that dogs salivated any time

food was present, a condition that appeared instinctive or reflexive. Through a process later referred to as *classical conditioning*, he conducted experiments with dogs in which, each time they were presented with food, a bell was rung. Gradually, he taught the dogs to salivate at the sound of the bell alone even when food was not present.

During the second half of the twentieth century, psychologist Harry Harlow and associates conducted experimental research to study the effects of social deprivation on rhesus monkeys (Harlow and Zimmerman, 1959; Harlow and Harlow, 1966; Novak, 1979). The researchers reared baby monkeys in total isolation from other monkeys, including their mothers. Instead, each monkey was given two artificial surrogate mothers made of wire. One "mother" was constructed of plain wire and was equipped with a bottle for feeding. The other "mother" was covered in terry cloth but contained no bottle. The monkeys became attached to the terry cloth mother and would cling to it most of the time, and went to the plain wire mother with the bottle only for food.

In his experiments with classical conditioning, Russian physiologist Ivan Pavlov demonstrated that, even among lower animals such as dogs, much of their behavior is learned.

Invariably, these animals grew up extremely maladjusted. When approached, they would bite themselves repeatedly and cower in corners. They exhibited fear and hostility when exposed to others of their kind. The females, after reaching maturity, would not mate and, when artificially inseminated, refused to care for or nurse their offspring. In a few cases, they even killed their babies before their caretakers could save them. Although one must be careful in generalizing from the behavior of lower primates to that of humans, it is clear that even with these animals, both sexual and maternal behavior are learned to a remarkable degree. Perhaps more important is the fact that monkeys, like humans, need love and nurturance in order to grow into functioning adults. Also, like humans, they may grow into neglectful and abusive parents if they themselves are neglected and abused while growing up (Kempe and Kempe, 1978; Polansky et al., 1981).

Even before the modern findings of Harlow and others, experimental animal studies cast such a serious shadow on biological explanations of human behavior that, by the 1920s and 1930s, the idea of human instincts ceased to be a meaningful concept in mainstream social science. The dominance of the nurture argument became fully established in the scientific community during the 1930s where it has remained to the present day.

Social Isolates In 1924, psychologist James B. Watson (1878–1958) made his famous statement about the primacy of "nurture" over "nature" in human behavior:

> Give me a dozen healthy infants, well-formed, and my own specific world to bring them up in and I'll guarantee to take any one of them at random and train him to become any type of specialist I might select—a doctor, lawyer, artist, merchant, chief, yes even a beggarman and thief, regardless of his talents, penchants, tendencies, abilities, vocations, and the race of his ancestors (p. 104).

While Watson perhaps overstated the case, instances of children suffering extreme isolation from social contact with others provide a good illustration of the importance of socialization.

Consider, for example, an experiment in which children were systematically isolated from certain socialization experiences and then observed to see how they developed. Such research, of course, would be condemned by present-day social scientists because of humane and ethical considerations. Nonetheless, this type of experiment was ordered by Emperor Frederick II during the thirteenth century. The emperor wanted to find out what types of speech patterns children would exhibit as adults if they had no interaction with others growing up.

> So he bade foster mothers and nurses to suckle the children, to bathe and wash them, but in no way to prattle with them or to speak to them, for he wanted to learn whether they would speak the the Hebrew language, the oldest, or Greek, or Latin, or Arabic, or perhaps the language of their parents, of whom they had been born. But he labored in vain because the children all died. For they could not live without the petting and joyful faces and loving words of their foster mothers (Ross and McLaughlin, 1949).

The twentieth-century cases of Anna, Isabelle, and Genie in the United States during the twentieth century all serve to illustrate clearly that children deprived of adequate social contact and stimulation in their early years do not develop into functional adults as a result. Sociologists refer to such deprived children as social isolates.

First, the cases of Anna and Isabelle reported by Kingsley Davis (1940, 1947, 1948) provide prominent early twentieth-century examples. Both were illegitimate children discovered and rescued by the authorities during the 1930s when they were about six years old. They both had been hidden from view in small attic rooms by their mothers because they were unwanted. Although the cases of these two little girls were unrelated and they were found nine months apart, their lack of socialization and states of physical condition were similar. Neither showed any human characteristics; they could only grunt and groan and were extremely ill from poor diet and lack of exercise. Anna could not walk, and Isabelle could only shuffle around because her legs were so bowed. Anna was placed in a county home and later in a school for the retarded where, by the time she was seven, she had advanced to the level of an average two year old. When she died at age ten from an extreme case of jaundice, she was toilet trained, could dress herself, and was able to show affection for a doll. The girl known as Isabelle was more fortunate. She had experienced greater social contact with her mother and, in contrast to Anna's limpness and total lack of expression when found, was often fearful and hostile around strangers. Her care and treatment were supervised by specialists who provided her with a much more intensive learning environment than Anna. Consequently, she made extremely fast progress so that by age eight and one-half years old, she was functioning almost at a normal level and eventually was able to enter school.

In a more recent case study involving a social isolate named Genie, the results were not so successful. Genie, a thirteen-year-old California girl, had been locked naked in a room and tied to an infant's toilet seat by her father since before her second birthday. When rescued in 1970 by the authorities, she could not utter a sound because her father had severely beaten her every time she tried to vocalize. In addition, she could not stand or straighten her arms and legs and could not chew because she had never been given solid food. When tested, she had the social development of a one year old. Placed in a special developmental program at UCLA, she made limited progress with speech over the course of four years, yet never learned to behave according to social norms. She learned to speak in short phrases but never learned to read. Her social behavior, however, was manifested by such acts as grabbing strangers she liked and refusing to let go, peering into people's faces from a distance of only a few inches, and near compulsive public masturbation (Curtiss, 1977).

Institutionalized Children Research conducted on groups of *institutionalized children*—socially deprived children in institutional settings such as state-sponsored orphanages—have yielded similar results. One groundbreaking study was conducted in Europe during and after World War II. Rene Spitz (1945), in a two-year study, compared

populations of infants in two different types of institutions, an orphanage and women's prison. Both groups of children had their physical needs attended to adequately, including food, clothing, cleanliness, and room temperature. In addition, each child in the orphanage saw a physician daily. In the prison, the children's mothers were with them regularly and were allowed to play with their babies for hours at a time. The children at the orphanage never saw their mothers and were rarely given any affection or emotional support from anyone, largely because the staff was small and overworked. They were also kept socially isolated from one another, whereas the children in the prison were in a collective nursery. Consequently, all the children in the orphanage were deficient both emotionally and socially by age two, and some were retarded. Most startling of all was that by the age of four, slightly over one-third of the children in the orphanage had died. When examined over the same period, the children in the prison had developed normally and none had died.

More contemporary examples of abandoned and isolated children continue to shock those who live in postmodern societies. India today has many orphanages where children, warehoused with no one to interact with them, lie in bed all day in darkened rooms. Behavioral scientists recently have conducted experimental research on these children. Their findings show that regular, structured 90-minute play sessions with groups of these children resulted in significant increases in motor skills and improved IQ scores (Taneja et al., 2002). Recently, China has furnished some of the most glaring and pervasive examples of socially neglected children in the world. As a result of its one child per family policy, implemented during the 1980s to address dire overpopulation issues coupled with a largely village-focused agricultural economy, boys have been highly desired and prized. Girls, by contrast, were seen as worthless and have met an entirely different fate. Millions had been killed by their parents at birth, put out on the streets of large cities to beg from tourists, or abandoned outright and hidden in human warehouses away from the prying eyes of the world. Orphans who do survive to adulthood are often so developmentally deficient that they cannot live functional lives (Meese, 2005).

Feral Children   A final perspective that underscores the importance of nurture is the notion of *feral children,* alleged children of nature isolated from social contact with others and supposedly raised by wild animals. Largely devoid of evidence of actual cases, such "stories" have retained their romantic fascination to many people. In Roman mythology, Romulus and Remus, the founders of Rome, were suckled and raised by a wolf. During the twentieth and now the twenty-first century, several generations of Americans have been entertained by the fictional exploits of Tarzan the Ape Man, a boy from British nobility who, after his parents died in Africa when he was an infant, was reared by Kala, an ape. While these and other fictional accounts make interesting stories, it is unrealistic that a human being could actually survive with animals in early childhood, much less develop into a fully functional adult.

Malson (1972), in reviewing the literature of fifty-three alleged cases of feral children between 1940s and early 1960s, found that almost all such persons who had spent significant periods in mid to late childhood living "in nature" had significant to severe problems of functioning and in adapting in a social environment. Most, for example, could not adequately work or communicate verbally with others. Therefore, real cases of so-called feral children are, in actuality, unfortunate children who are lost, abandoned, or cast out by their parents with very negative consequences to their emotional and social development (Ogburn, 1959).

Nature versus Nurture in Perspective   Each of us represents a unique combination of biological heritage and environmental experiences. From our biological backgrounds, we each are born with a genetic blueprint that includes a wide range of inborn traits and predispositions. Genes contained in this blueprint determine our complexion, our eye and hair colors, our body build and general size, our sex and blood type, and a variety of other characteristics. They also contain certain biological triggers that govern the aging

The fictional exploits of Tarzan the Ape Man have been enjoyed by generations of Americans. In reality, however, there is no evidence that a human child, virtually helpless as an infant, could be raised to maturity by animals.

Courtesy of the Library of Congress.

process by signaling the onset of puberty, young adulthood, middle age, and old age. Biological factors also influence our level of intelligence, our personality, and our native talents.

However, unlike the lower animals, we humans are provided by nature with only the platform or the foundation necessary to reach our potential as the most advanced and sophisticated creatures on this planet. To actually reach this potential, to become a person and develop into a fully functioning human being with a fully developed personality and self-concept, each of us must rely on the environmental influences provided by socialization.

FUNCTIONS (NEEDS) SERVED BY SOCIALIZATION

The human infant is virtually helpless at birth and is born *tabula rasa,* a social blank without any encoded experiences. Many lower animal species develop mainly in the womb and are fully capable of taking care of themselves within hours, weeks, or months after birth. The human infant, by contrast, cannot stand alone for the first year, is incapable of sexually reproducing for well over a decade beyond this, and may not be totally self-sufficient for still another ten or twelve years in many societies. Acquiring the skills and information necessary to get along with others and survive in society begins at birth and continues throughout the life cycle. How this process of acquiring culture and developing a personality takes place is one of the most fascinating topics within social science. To explore it, we begin with a brief examination of the basic needs served by socialization.

Bonding and Emotional Support

We humans are social creatures who require regular and satisfying contact with others. As we have already seen, the debilitating effects of social deprivation in small children can lead to dramatic maladjustment and, in some cases, even death. Although comprehensive studies to measure the effects of deprivation cannot be carried out on human subjects for obvious ethical reasons, research of this type has been conducted on some of the more sociable lower animals, most notably by Harry Harlow and others as previously discussed.

In humans, emotional needs are met primarily through bonding, the process of forming close personal relationships with other people, such as the relationship between a parent and child. There are three major types of bonded relationships: (1) parent–child, (2) cross gender, such as a married couple, and (3) same gender, as typified by two close friends (Beach, 1973). Of these, the parent–child relationship is most crucial for the development of a well-adjusted child.

A growing body of research shows that the bonding that is important to the child's later social development may take place immediately after birth (Klaus et al., 1972; Kennell, Voos, and Klaus, 1979; Klaus and Kennell, 1982). Marshall Klaus and his associates, for instance, compared the bonding effects of two groups of women with their newborns. Those women in the control group had the typical level of contact with their newborns during the first few days after birth. Women in the experimental group had much more intensive contact with their newborns and, in addition to regular feeding times, spent at least one hour with their babies immediately after birth and an additional five hours each day with them during the first ten days. In longitudinal research conducted on these women over five years, it was found that children in the "extended contact" group developed more readily than the other children

---

Bonding begins early in life and sets the stage for later emotional and social development.

© Kurhan, 2009. Used under license from Shutterstock, Inc.

in several ways. As a result of more intensive bonding, these children were healthier physically; received more physical, emotional, and verbal contact from their mothers; and, at the age of five years, performed better on IQ and language exams than did the other children.

The Establishment of Behavioral Boundaries

In addition to meeting emotional needs, socialization also teaches the individual how to behave in a disciplined manner by placing behavior within certain boundaries. Undisciplined behavior is self-centered behavior that operates for the most part on impulse. Small children are self-centered or egocentric in orientation and, because they lack significant socialization, see the world as revolving around them. However, living in a society requires that each person learn to control impulses and act according to social rules. To do so, the child must learn to take the needs and wishes of others into consideration. Socialization, therefore, is a cultural process through which the developing child becomes equipped with guidelines for acceptable behavior. This in turn later will allow a mature person to survive and prosper as a member of society.

Goal Setting

Disciplined behavior simply for its own sake can be very unrewarding. Therefore, it is important for the individual to learn how to set and achieve meaningful goals so that disciplined behavior will have meaningful and beneficial results. Goals, therefore, act as rewards that reinforce disciplined behavior. To succeed as a society member, life essentially involves setting meaningful goals, achieving them, and then setting new ones. Some goals are short term, like getting out of bed in the morning, mowing the yard, or going out to dinner and a movie on Friday night. Others may be long-term goals, such as completing a college degree, reaching a certain career level, or raising a family. In any case, the nature of the socialization experiences one has significantly affects one's ability to set and achieve meaningful goals.

The Development of a Self-Concept

As discussed earlier, *self-concept* refers to the personal assessment people have of their own identity and self worth, and how they fit into their community and society. One way to describe self-concept is to say that it includes at least three key elements: *self-identity* ("Who am I?"), *self-worth* ("What am I worth?"), and *self-direction* ("Where am I going?") (Semones and Romero, 2007). Consequently, self-concept is much more multidimensional and complex than the overly simplistic "self-esteem," a term often used in the popular culture.

Social Survival Skills

To succeed in society, each individual needs to acquire a variety of coping skills. Some are general and needed by everyone, such as the skill to communicate effectively through mastery of both spoken and written language and the ability to get along well with others. Other skills are more specialized, such as occupational skills acquired primarily through formal education, training, and experience. Some socialization skills are gradually acquired as we learn the role demands placed on us by the social positions we occupy. For instance, during the course of a day, a person may carry out obligations that are the result of being a family member, an employee, a college student, a neighbor, and a consumer. Given the limitations of time and energy, it can be quite challenging to develop and implement the skills needed to balance all of these demands.

CLASSICAL SOCIALIZATION THEORISTS

How the personality and self-concept are formed and how we acquire culture have been investigated by socialization theorists throughout the twentieth century and continues today. In the next section of this chapter, we will examine the pioneering work of several theorists who have greatly enlarged our understanding of the socialization process. We will begin by discussing the work of two pioneering interactionists in sociology, Charles Horton Cooley and George Herbert Mead. Then we will briefly examine some of the work of psychoanalytic theorist Sigmund Freud, one of the founding fathers of modern psychology.

Cooley: Interactionism and the Looking Glass Self

One early American theorist who did much to popularize the interactionist perspective in sociology was Charles H. Cooley (1864–1929). This quiet, unassuming scholar, who spent his academic life teaching sociology at the University of Michigan and the University of Chicago, was greatly influenced by the work of William James, the nineteenth-century psychologist. James (1890) developed a concept of social self, rooted in the idea that the way people see themselves is greatly influenced by how others interact with and see them. Cooley built on this foundation to argue that, just as we see a physical reflection when we look at ourselves in a mirror, we also see a social reflection of how we look to others as we interact with them. This image we see of ourselves as a result of interacting with others is the **looking glass self**.

The Three Components of the Looking Glass Self   Cooley (1902, 1909) asserted that our self-image is shaped largely by three constantly interacting elements within the personality: (1) *presentation:* how we think we are seen by others, which affects how we present ourselves in each interaction situation; (2) *identification:* how we think others judge or evaluate us each time we interact with them; and (3) *subjective interpretation:* how we feel about and deal with their evaluations. This process, which is largely unconscious, occurs as a result of our varied and constantly evolving relationships with individuals and groups. Therefore, our self-concept is continually being influenced by these interactions as we "take readings" (*identification*) on how we appear to others by

examining the image we see reflected in our social mirror.

Two Applications: The Thomas Theorem and the Self-Fulfilling Prophesy   Think back to when the interactionist perspective was first discussed. The basic premise of interactionism is that *perception drives behavior;* i.e., we act on our perceptions of reality. Let's now break this down by examining two applications of Cooley's looking glass self.

The Thomas Theorem   Early in the twentieth century, American sociologist W. I. Thomas issued a simple yet profound statement known today as the Thomas theorem. When individuals "define situations as real, they are real in their consequences" (Thomas and Thomas, 1928, p. 572). In other words, we socially construct (invent) how we see ourselves, the world around us, and our place in it based on our socialization experiences. If a child is loved, encouraged, and consistently shown approval and affection while growing up, this will set the stage for how positively the child sees him- or herself and expects to be seen by others when he or she gazes into the social mirror. Abuse, neglect, and discouragement will tend to have an opposite impact. Therefore, if we then expect to be accepted or rejected, we often are. This theorem also has applications for specific areas of life and the roles we play including work, school, and relations with family and friends. What we invest in time and energy (behavior) in all these areas depends on how we see them (perception). In each instance, what we then receive (consequences) will depend on our priorities and what and how much, in terms of time and energy, we choose to invest or not invest in them.

The Self-Fulfilling Prophecy   Second, adults can chose the types of social looking-glass they peer into, although children, because of the accidents of birth, are limited in their early years by the influences of family socialization. Those with positive self-concepts are conditioned to seek out positive people, and those with negative self-images often become caught up in the "misery loves company" syndrome. This often results in what sociologist Robert Merton has called the self-fulfilling prophecy, a prediction by a person that something will occur—their perception—which is then caused by that person to become true because of his or her actions (Merton, 1957). Therefore, if we believe in ourselves, we often make success happen, while if we expect to fail, we often do so and then blame our shortcomings on the situation or on others. Our inner realities—perceptions of reality based on what we think is true—become our outer realities—behaviors and actions—which then cause our perceptions to become true with very real positive or negative consequences.

Mead: Interactionism and Role Taking Theory

A contemporary of Cooley's who also viewed social behavior from an interactionist perspective was George Herbert Mead (1863–1931). Mead, a philosopher and early social psychologist, served on the faculty at the University of Chicago. Regarded as the Father of Social Psychology and a founder of symbolic interactionism, he disagreed strongly with the atomistic view of humans popularized by the social contract theorists and other "scientific" philosophers of the seventeenth and eighteenth centuries. These views assumed that humans could have a self-concept and reason in nature apart from the influences of society.

Mead noted that while we have many potentialities at birth, it is only through contact with society that we develop our humanity as manifested in the personality and self-concept. He felt that the important thing to be studied and understood is how society gets into the individual, shapes the personality or "self-hood," and determines to a great degree a person's social behavior. This takes place essentially during childhood as we acquire the norms of society and learn to engage in role taking, the ability to imagine ourselves in the social roles of others and act them out in order to learn the social standards that will be applied to our behavior.

The Three Stages of Role Taking In Mead's view, we learn to take on the roles of others and become social beings in three general stages—the imitative (preparatory) stage, the play stage, and the game stage (Mead, 1934).

In the imitative stage (the first three years), children learn to imitate the behavior of others in their immediate environment such as parents and other close family members. Small children will indiscriminately imitate the behavior of parents, for instance, some attempting to read the paper, dress up, shave, or talk like Mom or Dad.

As children become older, they move into the play stage in which they begin seriously to act out the roles of adults. Children from three through seven or eight years of age typically go through periods of wanting to be a parent or a nurse, a doctor or astronaut, or any one of the myriad of fantasy figures like cowboys, Indians, Tarzan, Wonder Woman, Spiderman, and so forth. Although children at this stage do not understand the obligations that go with certain roles, the role taking itself facilitates social development.

Finally, in middle to late childhood and early adolescence, children enter the game stage in which they learn to play the game of society according to the rules or role obligations. As part of this process, children typically become significantly aware of the impersonal sanctions that increasingly will be applied to their behavior by the larger society as they grow to maturity.

The Emergence of Self: The "I" and "Me" As children progress through these three stages of role taking, two components of the self emerge, which Mead called the "I" and the "Me." The "*I*" is the acting self as represented by one's natural drives and impulses, talents, and creative energies. The "*me*," by contrast, represents the socialized self that acts in response to the demands of society. The small child, undersocialized and dominated by the "I," acts on selfish whim and impulse. Older children and adolescents, because of the role-taking influences of socialization, become increasingly dominated by the "me."

For most of us as adults, Mead argued, the "me" normally keeps the "I" in check except in certain circumstances where it is acceptable, if not desirable, to allow the "I" to express itself. Although the "me" as the social component of the self is necessary for the purposes of conformity and social order, we must guard against the other extreme in which we become oversocialized automatons who have lost the spark and spontaneity of the "I" that we need in order to reach our creative potential as unique human beings.

Significant Others and the Generalized Other   As the self develops, it is most influenced by significant others, people with whom the individual has close personal ties. Parents and siblings are our first sources of intimate, personal relationships, followed by the friendship circles formed within our peer groups and important role models outside the family (e.g., a favorite teacher, a coach, or a public figure). Later, as adults, most of us typically form additional bonds with significant others such as best friends, lovers, and/or spouses. In addition to the specific demands placed on us by our loved ones, our social behavior is also subject to universally and applied norms in the form of community and societal standards for behavior. Thus, each of us is expected to conform to the requirements of the generalized other, standards of community behavior expected of anyone placed in a given social position. If a child is socialized by parents and other significant others to develop pro-social values and skills, the child will tend to "fit in" with the demands and expectations of the larger community and society (generalized other).

Freud: Elements of the Self in Conflict

Unlike interactionist theorists in sociology such as Cooley and Mead who saw socialization as largely a smooth, relatively uneventful process (in most cases) of merging the individual with society, Sigmund Freud (1856–1939) saw childhood socialization quite differently. Freud, an Austrian physician and the founder of the psychoanalytic school in psychology, viewed socialization as a process of coercion in which the child's freely expressed feelings and urges came under the force and control of parents and the norms of society.

Freud's Components of the Personality   According to Freud (1930), the personality (psyche) consists of three components—the id, the ego, and the superego—that develop in the child in stages and interact together in a dynamic mental process, which he termed the *psyche*. The first to develop is the id, a person's natural urges and "instincts" such as sex and aggression. Children under two years of age are thereby dominated by the "pleasure principle," are completely self-centered and obsessed with doing whatever feels good.

During the ages of two, three, or four years, the rational part of the self called the ego—the governor or manager of the personality—begins to emerge. The child's ego, governed by the "reality principle," consciously thinks through the consequences of acting before doing so. In a small child, the ego is aware of the power of parents to sanction behavior and, thus, learns to do what is rewarding and avoid what is punishing.

Sigmund Freud. The psychoanalytic approach.

Courtesy of the Library of Congress Prints and Photographs Division

The superego, an inner voice or conscience that makes us feel proud when we act properly and guilty when we do wrong, develops in middle childhood. Ruled by the "principle of ideals," it represents the ideal standards of behavior we live by in the form of internalized ethics or morality.

The Relationship between Components of the Psyche (Personality) According to Freud, the ego comprises the most important component of our self-concept. It represents the governor or the main control mechanism in the psyche or personality. As mediator between the conflicting demands of the id and superego, it channels selfish id impulses into socially desired forms of behavior while, at the same time, reduces ideal expectations of the superego into realistic and manageable modes of behavior that conform to societal standards. If, however, the ego becomes weakened or destroyed, and either the id or superego becomes dominant in the personality, then maladjustment may set in, the result being deviant or antisocial behavior. Id-dominated individuals, in extreme cases, might commit a violent crime such as murder, assault, or rape. Likewise, people whose superegos have taken over could, in the extreme, become religious fanatics or political terrorists who become so obsessed with ideals that they lose their perspective. Freud might have interpreted the events of September 11, 2001, as having resulted from superego-dominated, personality maladjustment in the nineteen young Saudi men who—as functionaries for Osama Bin Laden—sacrificed themselves to kill over twenty-eight hundred innocent Americans. In this view, superego driven fanaticism drove this "mission from god."

LATER SOCIALIZATION THEORISTS

While Cooley, Mead, and Freud were among the most prominent pioneers, others have greatly refined and extended our modern understanding of the socialization process. Among those who stand out in this respect are Erving Goffman, Jean Piaget, and Lev Vygotsky.

Goffman: Interactionism and Dramaturgical Analysis

One sociologist who sought to extend the work of interactionists such as Cooley and Mead was Erving Goffman (1922–1982), who used a somewhat novel and provocative approach. As discussed previously, Cooley sought to explain how the interacting self is created in a constant intermeshing of personality elements—*presentation*, *identification*, and *subjective interpretation*. His colleague and mentor, Mead, stressed how the self develops during three stages of role taking as we interact with others. Goffman's approach, however, perhaps could best be introduced with a brief quote from the great bard of English literature:

> **" *All the world's a stage, and all the men and women merely players: They have their exits and entrances; And one man in his time plays many parts . . . " ***

—William Shakespeare,
As You Like It, Act 2, Scene 7

Freud's Elements of the Psyche

Id	Ego	Superego
(Pleasure)	(Reality)	(Ideals)

Interaction as Dramaturgy: The Calculated Presentation of Self In Goffman's view, our day-to-day, face-to-face interactions with others are the central ingredients or "stuff" that society is built from. This micro to macro perspective he called dramaturgical analysis, the study of how and why people intentionally interact with each other like actors in a play titled "society." Society, in this sense represents a continuous theatrical performance that, like the daily episodes of television daytime soap operas, go on for decades or a lifetime without end. In Goffman's view, each of us socially constructs how we will play each role that we take on according to socially agreed to scripts that we then often embellish with our own style and carry out according to our own purposes (Goffman, 1959, 1967).

Life as Theater: The Role of Impression Management and Face Work As we carry out our roles or play our parts in this theatrical production called society, Goffman argues that it is not just what we do that matters but how we do it, and not just what we say but how we say it as well. And there is also the possibility, Goffman implies, that what we mean to do or what we mean to say may be misinterpreted by others or used against us in some way. Politicians, for example, must be very careful in what they say and do because those competing with them for political office may use their utterances and actions, often taken out of context, to discredit them.

Impression management refers to the conscious efforts we make to present ourselvesto others in a way they will see as favorable. In doing so, we devote energy to studying for and practicing the role we will play so that we will give a good performance. Our role preparation includes the proper costuming or dress we should wear like the uniforms worn by nurses, police officers, and airline pilots or the "proper" attire for business professionals or exotic dancers. We also use what Goffman calls "expressions given," that is, our intentional use of language as a script we verbalize, and our "expressions given off," which are the nonverbal messages we convey with our facial expressions and eye movements, our mannerisms, and our body language usually aimed at creating a certain impression in our audience. In this regard, the verbal and nonverbal cues intentionally given off by politicians, professors, professional boxers, prostitutes, and bus drivers are all very distinct and different because they involve different scripted roles. In addition, each player needs the proper setting or *set* and the correct *props* in order to give a convincing performance. Examples would include soldiers in a battle formation with tanks, automatic weapons, and air support; professors with classrooms, lecterns, and media equipment for PowerPoint presentations; and physicians with examining rooms, white coats, thermometers, and stethoscopes (Goffman, 1959).

Face work is Goffman's term for efforts made by people to present themselves to others in a favorable light in order to avoid public embarrassment or "losing face" (Ibid.). In some places like Tokyo, Japan, for example, it is not uncommon for unemployed business executives to dress up in suits and ties, go downtown as if going to work, pass the day by frequenting movie theaters, museums, or libraries, and then go home. They do this because they want to "save face" in the eyes of their families and friends who are unaware they are unemployed (French, 2000). Other people use a variety of face work techniques as verbal rationalizations or "spin" when they feel ignored, embarrassed, marginalized, or rejected in social situations. For example, a student failing a particular course might say to his or her friends "That professor was such a lousy teacher that I dropped his course."

AGENTS OF SOCIALIZATION

Children are influenced in their individual and social development by a variety of factors. The family, peers, school, church, media, and the larger community and society all play an integral part in shaping our personalities and equipping us with skills for social survival and prosperity. In this portion of the chapter, we will focus on three of the most important agents of socialization—the family, the peer group, and the mass media—which, in the case of family and close friends, represent our primary sources of significant others and continue throughout our lives to play a significant role in shaping our attitudes and behaviors.

The Family

Of all sources of childhood socialization, the family is the most important. As mentioned earlier, the human infant is virtually helpless at birth and must rely on parents and other family members for physical care and protection during the many years required for maturation. More important for humans, however, is that our experiences with our families shape the way we see ourselves, the larger world, and our place in it. An American child grows up with a very different culture, language, and worldview than a child reared in Peru, India, or Japan. Likewise, family socialization patterns within pluralistic societies like the United States are quite diverse. For example, children reared in a rural farming community in the Midwest come to look at the world through a different filter than those brought up in a large industrial city in the Northeast. Likewise, children whose parents practice religious fundamentalism tend to grow up with different values and life priorities than those reared as Presbyterians, Catholics, or Jews.

Class as a Socialization Factor   One important factor involved in the transmission of culture to a child is social class. A family's socioeconomic level is important because different class levels represent distinct subcultures. Children's class backgrounds shape to a significant degree the values and beliefs they hold, their self-concepts, and how they come to relate to the rest of the world. These class subcultures are further reinforced by other factors, which include region, rural or urban residence, race and ethnicity, and religion. Children reared in lower socioeconomic circumstances, for instance, may tend to be fatalistic and see success as determined largely by luck. Those reared in more affluent circumstances, by contrast, tend to have an achievement orientation and see success in terms of individual effort and hard work.

Sociologist Melvin Kohn (1963, 1977) conducted studies that show distinct differences in how children are raised in working-class versus middle-class families. Working-class parents tend to stress strict conformity to traditional standards, punish the consequences of unacceptable behavior (what children do), and are more likely to use physical punishment. They stress to their children the importance of obeying the rules and keeping out of trouble. This parenting style, according to Kohn, is at least partially influenced by the fact that working-class parents typically have blue-collar jobs. In such occupations, they are given little, if any, discretion in how they do their own work and are expected to follow instructions precisely.

Middle-class parents, by contrast, tend to have white-collar jobs that, due to their complexity, require more independent thought and discretion. This is then reflected in how they socialize their children. Middle-class parents tend to stress and reward their children's initiative and creativity. When punishment is given, it is for the motives behind behavior instead of what the children did. Children in middle-class families are taught the importance of self-control rather than strict obedience and are less likely to be physically disciplined.

The impact of the family on the formation of self-concept is also important. As we saw with the cases of Anna, Isabelle, and Genie, and in Harry Harlow's deprivation research on monkeys, the lack of adequate emotional support during the formative developmental years can be devastating. Small children need consistent love, affection, support, and encouragement in order to develop positive self-images and the confidence required to deal effectively with life's adversities and challenges (Mortimer and Simmons, 1978). The family is the first social group to which they become members, and parents represent their first teachers, guides, and role models.

Birth Order   Even so, parents tend to treat their first-born and later-born children differently. Some research indicates that the first-born children tend to receive more attention, affection, and discipline than later-borns. These first-borns then tend to become higher achievers than their younger siblings, who tend to be more relaxed and sociable (Forer, 1976; Dunn and Kendrick, 1983). For instance, first-born children tend to earn better grades in school, score higher on IQ tests, and appear more likely to go to college. In addition, they are overrepresented among Rhodes scholars, those in *Who's Who in America,* and even presidents (52 percent) of the United States (Vander Zanden, 1985).

Methods of Family Socialization

There are three key methods of family socialization: reward and punishment, imitation and modeling, and didactic teaching. A combination of each of these methods occurs to some degree in almost all families as children progress through infancy into childhood, and then move into and through the years of adolescence. We will consider each briefly here.

The Continuum of Parenting (Use of Reward and Punishment)

Authoritarian (Mainly punishments)	Authoritative (Balance: Rewards and Punishment)	Permissive (Mainly rewards)

Reward and Punishment: Three Parental Approaches   The dominant method of family socialization is reward and punishment, the primary tool used by parents to establish and enforce behavioral boundaries and standards for their children. There are three broad yet distinct parenting styles: the authoritarian approach, the permissive approach, and the authoritative approach (Baumrind, 1968, 1989). Each is practiced to a larger degree in some cultures or socioeconomic levels than others. In examining mothers cross-culturally, for example, German mothers are the most authoritarian, American mothers the most permissive, and Japanese mothers the most authoritative. In the discussion to follow, we will examine the viability of each approach as a parenting approach in America. In this brief narrative, each parenting strategy will be explained in terms of a definition, the primary parental tool used by such a parent, and their chief parental role. As you read the brief explanation to follow, keep in mind that each parent or set of parents tends to fall somewhere on the continuum that appears below in terms of parenting style.

Authoritarian Parenting   The authoritarian approach is one in which the parent uses mainly punishments and few if any rewards, and makes most if not all decisions concerning the child's behavior. With this strategy, *the parent's chief role is that of traffic cop or drill sergeant,* while the primary parental tool used is coercion or intimidation. While this strategy may be effective in village-focused, agricultural societies where children work shoulder to shoulder with their parents in the fields, participate directly in the economy as producers, and learn responsibility hands-on at a very young age, the authoritarian approach is very ineffective in modern and post-modern societies. Even with the best of intentions by such parents who love their children, this approach often spells disaster because it infantilizes children and shelter's them from the reality-testing experiences they will need to become full-functioning and responsible adults. While it is not difficult to intimidate small children, they do eventually mature into teenagers, physically as large or larger than their parents. Teenagers then often rebel against their parents and do wild and often destructive things to themselves and others because they have not been allowed to grow up.

Permissive Parenting   The second strategy, the permissive approach, is one in which the parent uses mainly rewards and few if any punishments and makes few if any decisions concerning the child's behavior. The *parent's chief role* with this approach *tends to be the parent as pal when children are young and the parent as martyr as they mature.* Like the authoritarian approach previously discussed, the permissive strategy represents an expedient, a parental shortcut, used by unprepared, ill-informed, and often overwhelmed adults. Usually they have not given parenting much thought or preparation beforehand and often are distracted by other demands placed on their time. As such, this parent's primary parental tool is bribery, which is every ineffective. Such parents often do not understand that small children are children, not miniature adults. As such, they are egocentric, extremely astute observers, and are and will continue to be very selfish and manipulative unless parents exert consistent and competent control and guidance very early on. In order for children to grow into competent adults, they must learn and appreciate that they are not the centers of the universe and that the world is not going to cater to them. Permissively raised children grow into immature, selfish, and incompetent adults who, even into their thirties and forties, sometimes are dependent on their parents to rescue them or "bail them out" when they prove incapable of being autonomous, self-reliant adults.

Authoritative Parenting   Finally, the authoritative approach is a parenting strategy in which the parent uses a balance of rewards and punishments, sets clear and consistent boundaries for the child's behavior, and gradually allows the child to participate in personal decision making. Behavioral research has clearly established that authoritative parenting is the most effective approach (Dorius et Al., 2004; Eisenburg et al., 2005). The *chief parental role* employed by such parents *tends to consist of five dimensions: teacher, counselor, coach, facilitator, and guide.*

Authoritative parents tailor which parental role dimension or combination is appropriate in a given circumstance with each child and parenting situation. How do they know which one or combination to use? They know their child. How do parents come to know their children? This can only be accomplished by investing large amounts of time and energy in them. By doing this and implementing the *primary parental tool of patience,* these parents tend to gradually guide their children, over an eighteen- to twenty-year period, into becoming competent, autonomous, and well-adjusted adults with the tools and strategies needed to survive and prosper in an increasingly complex and ever-changing world.

Imitation and Modeling   A second method of family socialization is imitation and modeling, a process in which, by imitating the behaviors and methods employed by parents, children use them as models for their own lives. Parents often may be unaware of the power they as role models have over their children. For small children, parents usually are the first and most important adults in their lives and they usually want to be just like them. It is important to note that children will imitate their parent's bad habits and behaviors, as well as those seen as positive and adaptive. From a child's perspective "If mom and dad do it, it must be great. I want to do it too and be just like them." Consequently, parents should take care to model pro-social behaviors that, should the child employ them later as a life habit, will facilitate adjustment to the social demands of the larger community and society.

The family is the primary agent of socialization.

© Iana k, 2009. Used under license from Shutterstock, Inc.

Didactic Teaching   The third and last method of family socialization to be discussed is didactic teaching, the actual hands-on instruction of a child by a parent in some skill or activity. Parents instruct their children in a variety of behavioral techniques they will need to acquire the skills to carry out a wide variety of behaviors and social habits necessary as adults. This instruction begins early in infancy as small children learn how to eat without being spoon fed, and dress themselves, tie their shoes, wash their hands, brush their teeth, and pick up their toys and clothes. Later they can be taught and required to make their beds, keep their rooms neat and tidy, and do a variety of household chores (e.g., washing, folding, and putting away their own clothes, mowing lawns, helping with cooking and washing dishes, etc.) as responsible members of a household. Recreational pursuits are also commonly taught by parents such as riding bicycles, playing ball, swimming, and playing a variety of games. Finally, beginning early in childhood, parents can teach their children how to talk properly, read, learn their numbers, and later, how to manage money, use their time wisely, etc.

The Peer Group

By the time children are five or six years old (and younger for the many children in daycare situations), their relationships with peers begin to play an important and integral role in their emotional and social development. Peer groups are groups of people of about the same age and social position whose members have significant influence on one another. Children are fascinated with one another because of the special standing of equality they share. This sets their relationships with each other apart from the inequality inherent in their dealings with adults. Because their states of physical, emotional, and intellectual development are about the same, they have experiences in common that are not applicable in their relationships with adults.

The Youth Subculture   In today's fast-changing modern society, children grow up in a very different world from the one their parents knew as children. This, among other things, has resulted in a gap between generations in several respects. Most notably, the twentieth century witnessed the emergence of a youth subculture consisting of life-style characteristics and preferences among children and adolescents very distinct from those of their parents. This is readily seen today in their use of "pop slang," distinct modes of dress, hairstyles, music, and other special consumer preferences.

The youth subculture acts to reinforce the impact of peer group socialization and can have both functional and dysfunctional consequences. On the positive side, it supports development of interpersonal communication skills and relationships outside the home, which become very important during adulthood in both career and recreational settings. Overidentification with the more superficial aspects of the youth subculture, however, can retard the development of an adult sense of responsibility. Involvement by children and adolescents with deviant elements such as the "drug scene" or delinquent groups can also have pronounced negative results.

Characteristics of Peer Groups   Peer groups function in several ways. First, *they introduce children to the impersonality of social rules.* In the home, rewards and punishments are administered by parents in a very personal manner, while in the peer group rules are impersonally set and sanctioned, and few if any people are given "special" consideration. Second, *they test the limits of adult tolerance.* Children will attempt things in peer settings that they would not dream of doing on their own in order to test adult authority and the strength of peer support and influence. In

addition, *children's peer groups may or may not reinforce adult values.* For instance, one group of twelve year olds may have a lawn-mowing service to make money in the summertime, while another forms a burglary ring to rob the community (Broom and Selznick, 1968). Finally, *they teach children some of the more informal aspects of the larger culture that they often are not taught at home.* These may be adaptive or maladaptive in preparing a child for life success as an adult: Getting along with others, acquiring the etiquette of male-female social relations, learning about sex, the use of profanity, and the use of drugs are often reinforced or acquired in peer groups.

Mass Media: Its Impact on Child Development

Mass media consist of the various methods used to transmit information to large numbers of people in an organized manner. Through its many sources—including books, magazines, newspapers, television, movies, the internet—both children and adults are exposed to a vast array of images and topics.

Peer groups influence our behavior throughout the life cycle.

© carme balcells, 2009. Used under license from Shutterstock, Inc.

© mandy godbehear, 2009. Used under license from Shutterstock, Inc.

Parents, in most cases, represent the most important source in guiding socialization for the developing child. There is an established and growing body of behavioral research on cognitive development—as related to the use and misuse of media—that parents can utilize to maximize the cognitive development of their children. Based on dozens of studies conducted over the past fifty years, cognitive research findings can perhaps best be summarized in the form of two key recommendations for parents who wish to foster intellectual development in their children.

Read to Your Child   A common characteristic of high school students who score in the top ten percent on college entrance exams is that they were consistently read to by their parents when they were small children. It is well established in the scientific literature that children who are read to each week from twelve months of age until they begin reading on their own typically are reading by age four and one-half years and, upon entering first grade, often read at the third to fourth grade level. Through such socialization, these children learn to love to reading and are intellectually curious and thirsty for knowledge. Parents who make an investment of their time and energy in fostering the development of their children's minds in this manner help to prepare their children for success rather than failure. The degree to which a child's mind is nourished by learning how to read as soon as possible provides a firm foundation for later development and self-actualization as an adult.

The following are key reasons why children benefit from being read to by their parents:

1. It activates listening skills.

2. It activates the imagination.

3. It provides interesting conversation topics.

4. It provides important language modeling.

5. It develops the ability to think critically.

6. It enhances the ability to think symbolically.

7. It stimulates writing abilities.

8. It's fun.

9. It's an affordable source of entertainment.

10. It increases a child's attention span.

11. It provides a peaceful family activity.

12. It develops a child's desire to read.

13. It models a rewarding lifelong habit.

14. It gives a child a sense of language rhythm.

15. It helps to pattern neural pathways.

16. It expands a child's vocabulary.

17. It increases a child ability to concentrate.

18. It gives a child needed practice in predicting information.

19. It expands a child's world view.

20. It's the single most important thing a parent can do to help a child succeed in school.

(Source: "Television, Computers, and Brain Development,"
Speechgoals.org 2004)

Set Quality Standards for a Child's Access to Television and Other Multi-media   Depending on which study is consulted, American school-age children spend an average of twenty-two to twenty-eight hours each week watching television. Do the math. There are twenty-four hours in a day. A minimum of eight hours are needed by children for nightly sleep. Two to four additional hours a day are required for getting dressed and undressed, bathing, eating meals, and taking care of physical hygiene and elimination needs. Subtract these hours from twenty-four and you get twelve to fourteen hours of functional living time each day. If a child watches twenty-two to twenty-eight hours of TV per week, this means that up to two-sevenths of a child's functional waking life may be spent sitting passively in front of a glowing screen. This is passive learning. By contrast, reading is active learning. Children being read to or reading on their own conjure up in their mind's eye what the characters in a story look like and how they relate to each other. In addition, they can determine the pace of their reading and stop to reflect on and think about what they just read. With television, everything is done for the viewer who is simply a passive receiver.

Too much television and other media with no quality controls can pose serious implications for cognitive development. If parents do not impose quality and quantity boundaries and limits on the television programming to which their children are exposed, the results, in extreme cases, can result in a variety of maladaptive consequences. These include impaired cognitive ability, deficiencies in reading skills, symptoms of attention deficit hyperactivity disorder (ADHD), poor social interaction and communication skills, social isolation, a negative self-concept, depression, a propensity toward aggressive and violent behavior, and poor performance in school. How much television should my child be exposed to? Of course, television is a wonderful medium for educational enrichment and entertainment. Used in moderation, it can enrich people's lives. Yet, like many things, including fat- and salt-laden fast foods, too much of it can have harmful effects particularly for young children. According to Jane M. Healy (1998) in "Understanding TV's Effects on the Developing Brain," too much television—particularly at ages critical for language development and manipulative play—can impact negatively on young minds in several different ways including the following:

Higher levels of television viewing correlate with lowered academic performance, especially reading scores. This may be because television substitutes for reading practice, partially because the compelling visual nature of the stimulus blocks development of left-hemisphere language circuitry. A young brain manipulated by jazzy visual effects cannot divide attention to listen carefully to language. Moreover, the "two-minute mind" easily becomes impatient with any material requiring depth of processing.

The nature of the stimulus may predispose some children to attention problems. Even aside from violent or overly stimulating sexual content, the fast-paced, attention grabbing "features" of children's programming (e.g., rapid zooms and pans, flashes of color, quick movement in the peripheral vision field, sudden loud noises) were modeled after advertising research, which determined that this technique is the best way to engage the brain involuntarily. Such experiences deprive the child of practice in using his or her own brain independently, as in games, hobbies, social interaction, or just "fussing around." I have talked to many parents of children diagnosed with attention-deficit disorder who found the difficulty markedly improved after they took away television viewing privileges.

The brain's executive control system, or prefrontal cortex, is responsible for planning, organizing and sequencing behavior for self-control, moral judgment and attention. These centers develop throughout childhood and adolescence, but some research has suggested that "mindless" television video games may idle this particular part of the brain and impoverish its development. Until we know more about the interaction of environmental stimulation and the stages of pre-frontal development, it seems a grave error to expose children to a stimulus that may short-change this critical system.

Excerpt from "8 Ways to Keep Television from Stunting Brain's Growth" by Jane M. Healy. Reproduced with permission from AAP News, May 1998, 14(5), p. 23. Copyright © 1998 by American Academy of Pediatrics.

A fair consensus among scientists who research learning would strongly suggest the following guidelines for parents: Infants and toddlers under two years should be discouraged from having little if any television exposure; for preschool children, one to five hours per week is recommended but no more than eight to ten; school-age children should have no more than ten to fifteen hours per week (American Academy of Pediatrics, 2001). Yet by age seventy, the average American will have spent seven to ten years of their waking life sitting passively in front of a television set (Strasburger, 1993). The foundation for such a lifestyle as a spectator rather than engaged participant is established early in childhood. One study found that one-third (32 percent) of children two to seven years old and nearly two-thirds of children and adolescents aged eight to eighteen years of age had a television set placed in their bedrooms

(Gerbner, et al., 1994). In a policy statement issued by the American Academy of Pediatrics in February, 2001, it was recommended that parents "remove television sets from children's bedrooms" (American Academic of Pediatrics, p. 424.)

However, there is a huge disconnect between what experts (behavioral scientists, neuroscientists, and pediatricians) recommend regarding TV and other media exposure by children and what children actually experience in their socialization. According to research reported by the Nielson company, American children age 2–11 were watching an average of 24 hours of TV per week in 2012, down from 28 weekly hours in 1997 (Derusha, 2013). Yet if one looks at TV exposure from all social media sources on line, the figure rises again to over 28 hours per week. If we add to that the total weekly exposure to media that children experience from all sources—TV, ever changing and proliferating social media (e.g., facebook, twitter, YouTube, Skype), and the thousands of applications (apps) now available on so-called "smart phones," total exposure to media, according to recent research by the Kaiser Family Foundation, is nearly 55 hours per week or 7 hours and 38 minutes a day (Shapely, 2010).

Effective childhood socialization requires that parents be engaged with their children by spending significant periods of time each week interacting with them one-on-one and in family activities. Too many uninformed and disengaged parents use television and other forms of information technology at potentially harmful levels as surrogate baby sitters to distract and entertain their children while they engage in things they consider more important. One price the child pays for too few restrictions on television and exposure to other media (e.g., movies, video games, internet) is impaired literacy development, which, according to recent research, is associated with poor performance in school (Sharif and Sargent, 2006; Moses, 2008). By contrast, children whose parents take the time and expend the energy to actively parent and guide them experience quite a different set of socialization experiences than "overstimulated children" whose minds are constantly bombarded and distracted by relatively unrestricted levels of

"useless" information a mile wide and an inch deep. Children who are the recipients of competent parenting grow up learning how to concentrate for extended periods on key cognitive tasks, engage in introspection and critical thinking, and are able to stay task-oriented and focused in order to complete complex tasks and achieve meaningful life goals.

ADULT SOCIALIZATION

As behavioral theorists and researchers have known for quite some time, socialization does not end with adulthood but continues throughout the life cycle. Upon leaving childhood, we experience the transition to the world of adult responsibility and make various adaptations as we grow older and mature. These adaptations take several forms. Some have to do with the role transitions we make as we leave or continue school, obtain a job, and perhaps get married and start a family. Others involve how we adjust to our own aging process as we adapt first to being a young adult, then a middle-aged person, and finally a senior citizen.

Rites of Passage

Adult socialization is often reinforced by rites of passage, formal events that signal the end of one position or stage in life and the beginning of another. These key life events often take the form of ceremonies or rituals such as school graduation, marriage, completion of military training, and promotions or awards. These events, often involving the taking of photographs and attendance by close family and friends, are very special occasions that are remembered for years. But most important, they serve as benchmarks that mark our journey from one stage or period of life to another as we progress through our life cycle.

Anticipatory Socialization

The informal preparation for future life stages and life responsibilities is what Robert Merton and Alice Rossi (1968) have called anticipatory socialization. As George Herbert Mead found in his observations, this process of social preparation for the future actually begins in early childhood as children first imitate and then play out social roles they see enacted by parents and other adults. Children, for example, often look forward with eager anticipation to becoming a "teenager." Teenagers then prepare for entering the adult world. These mental rehearsals for the future, however, have their greatest impact during adulthood when we experience the greatest number of life transitions.

Anticipatory socialization is also evident in our personal relationships. Going steady prepares a couple to see if they are sufficiently compatible to carry it further. If the relationship endures and intensifies, a couple may become engaged. This, in turn, is a special period that allows two people to prepare for a married life together. If they do get married, the first year or two of marriage may be needed to decide about children and prepare for the responsibilities of parenthood. Life involves a series of these transitions that, if planned carefully, soften and make easier the changes and adjustments we all make as we grow older.

Resocialization

Role transitions made in adulthood often involve resocialization, an abrupt and often basic change in life style and life priorities. It involves, in most cases, the abandonment of one way of life for another. Being married, for example, involves a significant shift in priorities and a very different life style as compared to being single. A much more dramatic example is that of a person who experiences a religious conversion or joins the priesthood. The convert will sometimes claim a feeling of being cleansed or "born again," and essentially begins a new life as a believer. Resocialization is also in evidence when one joins the military. Other examples of resocialization would include becoming a parent, going to prison, getting divorced, losing one's job, winning the lottery, inheriting a fortune, or entering retirement from one's profession.

Resocialization tends to take two forms—voluntary and involuntary. *Voluntary resocialization* involves an independent and conscious choice by a person to undergo a fundamental change in his or her social identity and lifestyle. Sometimes, however, resocialization is imposed on people by virtue of the type of society in which they live or particular life circumstances. In this regard, *involuntary resocialization* is a basic life change imposed on a person by others or society. In rural areas of countries such as Indonesia, India, and China, for example, children are essentially forced by circumstances and parental pressure to become farmers or herds people. In several cultures, marriage is involuntary because it is arranged by parents who often give their children little or no choice in the matter.

The Middle Years and Becoming Elderly

As we become older, both anticipatory socialization and resocialization experiences play an important role in shaping our life course. During the middle years of the forties, fifties, and sixties, people look back introspectively at their previous accomplishments and examine their current life situations. "Have I used my life productively?" "Am I successful?" "Have I made a difference in the lives of others and in society?" The way such questions are answered affects how people see middle age and the future.

The middle years can be fulfilling and productive, or fraught with stress and crisis. Many mid-lifers experience some of the positives and the negatives both. This is a time in which income is highest, free time is often the greatest, and parental responsibilities are being phased out as children become adults and ultimately leave home. Although middle-aged people do not have the physical appearance of their youth, health and vitality are usually good and, combined with greater maturity and affluence, often provide them with very fulfilling lives. In fact, for many, the middle years are among the best.

Others in middle age, however, may experience crises in a variety of forms. Some feel they are caught in a "sandwich generation" between responsibilities to their adolescent and young adult children, and to elderly parents in poor economic circumstances or failing health. Others may have a mid-life crisis in which they feel trapped in a boring and unfulfilled life with no excitement or challenge. In any case, the middle years are a period of consolidation and reflection. For most, the majority of life decisions and accomplishments have been made, time is getting short, and the challenge is to make the most of what time they have left and to use it most productively to build the best future possible. Becoming elderly usually begins at about retirement. Because thirteen percent of Americans are now over sixty-five years of age or older (U.S. Census Bureau, 2000a), the elderly population is now much more visible than it once was.

Senior citizens face many challenges and problems. First, they live in a society that, during most of the twentieth century, had a "youth orientation," which viewed and treated many of the elderly as second-class citizens. The trend now, however, is shifting toward a much more positive view regarding the elderly and their capabilities, as evidenced by an increased use of elderly role models in the media and the abolition or extension of the mandatory retirement age formerly set at sixty-five. Second, the elderly often live on fixed retirement incomes that average only about one-half the earnings they had while working. Combined with increasing health problems and the difficulty in obtaining and paying for health insurance, senior citizens often face significant financial problems. Finally, retirement often brings reduced self-esteem, and the elderly must face grief crises when friends and spouses die.

Despite these problems, those over sixty-five often live healthy and productive lives for an additional fifteen years or so, and for some, much longer. As the ranks of the elderly continue to swell, with the numbers of those eighty-five and older increasing the fastest, positive role models are also becoming more common. At the age of seventy-eight, Ronald Reagan completed his second term as president of the United States in 1988; Senator John McCain was nominated for the presidency in 2008 at age seventy-one. Comedian and actor George Burns, who lived to

Resocialization carries with it a fundamental change in both life style and the norms one is expected to obey.

© koh sze kiat, 2009. Used under license from Shutterstock, Inc.

be one hundred years old and made movies until he was 94, once said that people get old and feeble because of their attitudes. They "practice to get old. The minute they get to be sixty-five or seventy, they sit down slow, they get into a car with trouble. They start taking small steps." His approach was to attack life with "moxie" (Toufexis et al., 1988).

Evidently, an increasing number of senior citizens agree. Hulda Crooks, age ninety-one, climbed ninety-seven mountains between the ages of sixty and ninety, including Japan's Mt. Fuji. Other examples include seventy-four-year-old Dr. James Jay who, along with fifty-five others over the age of seventy, completed the New York City Marathon, and author Jane Stovall, one hundred three, who became a senior golf champion in her eighties and a student pilot at eighty-nine (Gibbs, et al., 1988). And more recently in 2013, sixty-four year old American Diana Nyad became the first person to swim from Cuba to the United States without a shark cage (Sloane, et. al, 2013) and Yuichiro Miuro from Japan became the oldest person ever to reach the summit of Mount Everest at age seventy-six. (Associated Press, May 23, 2013).

Chapter 4

Groups: The Basic Unit of Sociology

It was almost midnight in San Diego on a cold night in February and young Christopher Valva was arriving home from his second shift job at a printing company. The nineteen-year-old noticed three juveniles "hanging out" near his house, told them to go away, and then, after an angry exchange of words, was attacked and stabbed in the heart with a long hunting knife. As his assailants fled, Chris stumbled into his house, and his shocked mother, seeing her blood-soaked son, dialed 9-1-1. Within minutes, police and paramedics were on the scene and Chris was rushed by ambulance to the trauma center at Mercy Hospital and Emergency Center. En route, while the driver communicated with Mercy and a surgical team was hastily assembled, paramedics continued to apply CPR to Chris although he had almost no blood, collapsed veins, no pulse, and dilated pupils.

Upon his arrival at the hospital, Dr. Eugene Rumsey, Jr. and a team of other trauma surgeons, nurses, and technicians went to work on a patient that by most traditional indications was already dead. Knowing that the young man had only a one percent chance for survival, the team opened his chest and, while a breathing bag forced oxygen into his lungs and intravenous lines sent blood and solution coursing through his veins, Rumsey held Chris's heart in his hand and massaged it until it showed signs of life and finally began beating on its own. As it beat, the heart spurted blood through a one and one-half inch wound, which was carefully sewn shut and repaired by a thoracic surgeon. Over the next several hours after the surgery, the crises of restoring liver and kidney functions, treating heart arrhythmias, and combating the sudden drop in body temperature with blankets and blood transfusions were dealt with and successfully overcome. In March, thirty-five days after entering the Mercy Trauma Center, Chris Valva was released from the hospital. By Christmas, he was able to return to work and resume a normal routine after having been given a second chance at life (Michelmore, 1986).

This rather dramatic incident serves to illustrate how fundamentally important groups are and how critical they can be to each of us. In Chris Valva's case, one group of delinquents almost caused his death, while the intercession of his mother and two other groups—paramedics and the medical trauma team—saved his life. While nothing this extreme may happen to most of us, our group contacts and relations with others nonetheless have a profound impact on our behavior, emotional and social well-being, and happiness.

As we have already seen, both culture, and socialization are the products of group processes.

Likewise, the way we affiliate with and interact in groups play a crucial role in shaping the social organization of a society. In the discussion to follow, we will build upon this foundation and focus our attention specifically on groups and how they operate in society.

Social Groups The most important and fundamental of all group types is the social group, a group of people bound together by common interests and values in a definite pattern of social relations. A person's family, a circle of close friends, a sociology class, two couples on a picnic, and several neighborhood children at play with one another all serve as representative examples. They each possess common attributes, consciousness of kind, and patterned social relations.

Social groups and the relations members share with each other are at the core of the human experience. Culture, socialization, and social organization all take place within group settings. In addition, both a person's self-concept and social identity are shaped primarily through patterned social relations with others. For these reasons, this chapter is devoted primarily to an exploration of the different types of social groups, the factors that shape the way they are organized, and the forms of behavior that take place within them.

Formal Organizations The last of the five types of groups is the formal organization, a group deliberately formed to pursue one or more specific practical goals. Like social groups, formal organizations also are very important to human survival and prosperity, particularly in large technological societies with differentiated institutions and a specialized division of labor. They too are characterized by common attributes, consciousness of kind, and patterned social relations. However, unlike most social groups, formal organizations have the additional characteristic of calculated formation, which allows the most complex of human endeavors, from performing open heart surgery to landing men on the moon, to first be planned and then carried out in a highly organized and efficient manner. Through calculated formation (the intent, plan, or means), the formal organization is then able to achieve its primary goal, whatever it might be, such as earning a yearly profit, curing a disease, or winning a military battle (Table 4-1).

SOCIAL GROUPS

Because culture, socialization, and social organization take place largely within the framework of social relations, the bulk of this chapter is devoted to a discussion of how sociologists

Table 4-1

Types of Groups and Their Characteristics

	Typical Characteristics			
Type of Group	**Common Attributes**	**Consciousness of Kind**	**Patterned Social Relations**	**Calculated Formation**
Physical Aggregate	Yes	No	No	No
Statistical Category	Yes	No	No	No
Social Category	Yes	Yes	No	No
Social Group	Yes	Yes	Yes	No
Formal Organization	Yes	Yes	Yes	Yes

distinguish between two fundamental types of social groups, primary groups and secondary groups.

Primary Groups

Charles Horton Cooley (1909, 1956) originated the concept of primary group, a small group characterized by personalized, ongoing relationships. In his formulation of the "looking glass self" theory of personality, Cooley was particularly interested in examining group relationships that have the greatest impact on the developing child. He felt that the family and children's play groups are among the most important influences on a child's socialization because they are the first groups a person is exposed to and they represent the primary source of social and emotional support. In elaborating on primary groups, he had this to say:

> By primary groups I mean those characterized by intimate face-to-face associations and cooperation. They are primary in several senses, but chiefly in that they are fundamental in forming the social nature and ideals of the individualities in a common whole, so that one's very self, for many purposes at least, is the common life and purpose of the group . . . Primary groups are [also] primary in the sense that they do not change in the same degree as more elaborate relations, but form a comparatively permanent source out of which the latter are ever springing. Of course they are not independent of the larger society, but to some extent reflect its spirit . . . . These groups, then, are the springs of life, not only for the individual, but for social institutions (1956, pp. 23–29).

Characteristics of Primary Groups   Based on Cooley's initial formulation and subsequent observations and refinements by other sociologists (King and Koller, 1975), it is clear that primary groups have several distinct characteristics. The eight key characteristics are listed below.

1. *Relative Smallness.* Given the fast-paced and relatively specialized nature of social relations in technological societies today, it is relatively rare for primary

groups—such as one's family or circle of best friends—to exceed more than eight to ten individuals. Most contain only two to five people. Indeed, given the geographically mobile nature of life for many Americans, it is difficult to sustain long-term and personalized relationships with relatives and friends that one no longer lives near or sees more than a few times a year or less.

2. *Strong Affectional Ties.* The relationships among primary group members are personal and emotion laden. We tend to build an emotional investment with our significant others, and they with us. Given this degree of intimacy, our primary group relations serve as our basic source for emotional and social support.

3. *Strong Personal Identification.* As a result, in large part, of our very personal relations with our primary group members, we also identify strongly with them and desire their approval. Therefore, primary groups play an instrumental role in socialization, and influence to a remarkable degree the formation of a person's self-concept.

4. *Multidimensional Relationships.* Interaction among primary group members tends to be relatively open, free, and extensive. Because our fellow members care about us and accept us as we are, it is possible to interact with them as a whole person and to "be ourselves." In many social encounters, however, we share only a single facet of our personality with others because of the special role demands—such as those of an employee, student, or customer—placed on us as well as on those with whom we interact.

5. *Continuous Face-to-Face Contact.* Members of primary groups interact with one another on a one-to-one basis frequently and over a continuous period

Primary group relations are very personalized, with levels of emotional intimacy and social sharing that make them special for each of us.

© Anthony Harris, 2009. Used under license from Shutterstock, Inc.

of time. We usually see and interact directly with our immediate family and best friends daily or weekly on an ongoing basis over many months, years, and in some cases, several decades during our lives.

6. ***Durability.*** Primary group relations are very durable and often border on permanence. This is partially due to the fact that personal relationships, especially in modern technological societies, are difficult to form and maintain and, once established, are not easily transferable to other people. It is quite difficult, if not impossible, to replace the strong ties felt with a close relative or best friend.

7. ***Trust.*** As a result of the close personal nature of primary group relations and their durability, we tend to trust our fellow members; likewise, they feel they can trust us. Most of us, for instance, would not hesitate to take the word of a close family member or close friend but might be skeptical about many things told to us by acquaintances or strangers.

8. ***Informal Social Controls.*** Because of many of the preceding factors, formal or official social controls are usually unnecessary in primary groups. Informal sanctions such as praise (positive) or criticism (negative) are usually sufficient in maintaining conformity to group rules or standards.

The Scope of Primary Relations   Our interactions with others in our primary groups represent "the ties that bind." By connecting to others in a personal and ongoing manner, we not only obtain satisfaction of our basic needs for emotional intimacy and social sharing, but we also contribute to the cohesiveness of the larger community and society. Primary group relations thus furnish us with a sense of belonging, a feeling of being connected to the larger human experience. This need to belong is important to us and manifests itself throughout life not only in family and typical friendship groups, but in a number of other diverse primary group circumstances as well. Two interesting examples involve primary group bonding in the military and among social deviants.

Secondary Groups

In contrast to the primary group is the secondary group, a relatively large collection of people with whom one has superficial and somewhat impersonal relations. Our interactions with secondary groups tend to be more task oriented and specialized compared to our primary relations, which are focused on friendship and personal intimacy. Although our experiences with them may be pleasant (such as discussing career possibilities with a school counselor) or unpleasant (like complaining about poor service in a restaurant), we tend to feel neutral and somewhat aloof concerning most of our secondary group encounters and interactions.

Characteristics of Secondary Groups
Secondary groups have these characteristics:

1. ***Relatively Large Size.*** Secondary groups generally are larger than primary groups

and may include thirty, forty, or fifty people or more (e.g., students in a college sociology class, employees who work in a particular department or division of a company, etc.).

2. ***Weak Affectional Ties.*** Relationships among members of secondary groups tend to be relatively impersonal with little, if any, emotional investment. As a result, secondary relations are easily transferable to other people and social situations. Take the "face-to-face classes" in which most students enroll each semester for example. At the end of each college term, few, if any, people feel pangs of loss at the prospect of never seeing their classmates again. Most people enroll for the next semester or term, form new secondary relations with teachers and students, and have at most only fleeting thoughts concerning the "relationships" they left behind. Courses taught over the internet tend to be even more impersonal. Distance learning classes are becoming increasingly popular for some students and provide some advantages, particularly for highly disciplined and autonomous

learners for which they often provides a good fit. However, under the best of circumstances, such courses tend to be less personal than on-campus classes because of a lack of face-to-face contact and interaction with professors and fellow students.

3. ***Little or No Personal Identification.*** Because our secondary group relations are generally interchangeable, they tend to have much less influence on our self-concept than our relations with family and close friends.

4. ***One-Dimensional Relationships.*** Interaction in these groups tends to be specialized and somewhat inhibited. Secondary group relations are structured primarily in terms of specialized social statuses (positions) and the role demands that go with them. Therefore, especially in modern societies, people in most social situations tend to reveal to others only the single facet of themselves required by positions such as employer or employee, teacher or student, store clerk or customer, IRS representative or taxpayer. Some of us—particularly

---

Secondary group relations are the most common. They involve superficial and somewhat impersonal relations with others.

© Iofoto, 2009. Used under license from Shutterstock, Inc.

sociologists—realize that, because of the highly specialized and complex nature of modern society, we remain unaware of the multi-dimensional nature of most people with whom we come into contact. However, most of us probably are so preoccupied with our own lives and priorities that we do not even think about it.

5. *Limited Face-to-Face Contact.* Members of secondary groups tend to interact with each other rather infrequently on a one-to-one basis over a relatively short period of time. Take most college students, for example. Think for a moment about your status as a member of a sociology class and perhaps other classes that meet on campus two or three times per week. How many of your classmates have you verbally interacted with directly in a one-on-one, face-to-face manner during the course of the semester? How often? What does this say to us about the quality of our relationships at school or, for that matter, in most of the social encounters we have with others in modern society? What does it say about the way your society is organized in terms of social relations as compared with a much smaller, village-focused, nonindustrial society?

6. *Nonpermanence.* These group interactions tend to last for only a relatively short period of time, in part as a result of their specialized nature and easy transferability to other people and to other situations. A secondary group transaction between a customer and a counter person at a fast-food restaurant may last only a minute or two. A college class will meet for a school term or semester and then disband forever.

7. *Distrust.* Because of the somewhat reserved, impersonal, and temporary nature of secondary groups, distrust often tends to replace trust as an assumption on which relationships between members are based.

8. *Formal Social Controls.* Conformity to group standards, in most cases, is ensured through a system of formal rules that apply equally to all members. Company employees must conform to rules related to working hours, workloads, lunch hours, and vacations. Students must contend with rules concerning attendance, curriculum requirements, grading standards, and registration procedures.

The Scope of Secondary Group Relations In mass urban societies today, most social contacts with others involve secondary rather than primary relations. Most Americans, for example, spend the bulk of each weekday either at school or at work. Both schoolchildren and college students typically come in contact with several teachers and dozens, if not hundreds, of other students each day. Likewise, physicians, teachers, department store cashiers, and those in numerous other occupations come in contact with many people in a variety of different specialized circumstances. In a given day, a college professor, for instance, may teach several classes, have individual conferences with students, interact with colleagues, administrators, and textbook salespeople, and sit on one or more committees. In fact, many occupations involve working with people in a variety of capacities including project groups, task forces, and committees, which are all typical secondary groups. Members usually know little about one another so that liking or disliking one another personally tends to be irrelevant as long as they can interact together successfully in the context of their jobs or the task at hand (Olmsted and Hare, 1978).

Regarding the scope of secondary relations, Luis Wirth commented (1938) that

the city is characterized by secondary rather than primary contacts. The contacts of the city may indeed be face to face, but they are nevertheless impersonal, superficial, transitory, and segmental. The reserve, the indifference, and the blasé outlook that urbanites manifest in their relationships may thus be regarded as devices for <u>immunizing themselves</u> against the personal claims and expectations of others (pp. 1–2).

The Psychological and Interpersonal Impact of Secondary Relations The German sociologist Georg Simmel (1918, 1950 A), a contemporary of Wirth's, spoke of the psychological and interpersonal impact that resulted from the indifference and reserve characteristic of social relations in the modern metropolis:

> As a result of this reserve, we frequently do not even know by sight those who have been our neighbors for years. And it is this reserve which, in the eyes of small town people, makes us appear to be cold and heartless. Indeed, if I do not deceive myself, the inner aspect of this outer reserve is not only indifference but, more often than we are aware, it is

a mutual strangeness and revulsion, which will break into hatred and fight at the moment of a closer contact, however caused (1950 A, p. 415).

Social Group Relations in Perspective

Although the concepts of primary and secondary groups are useful for discussion purposes, few social groups are strictly one type or the other. Instead, most are composites that, though they may be predominantly primary or secondary in nature, still contain elements of the other type. Consequently, primary groups and secondary groups are perhaps best understood as ideal types at either end of a continuum as shown in Figure 4-1.

Figure 4-1

Primary and Secondary Group Relations: A Continuum

Primary Group Relations ——————— ± ——————— Secondary Group Relations

<u>Secondary</u> group elements may <u>develop</u> <u>within</u> <u>primary</u> group relationships and vice versa. In the family group, for example, a young person may move back home with parents for a while after graduation from college and pay rent just like any other boarder. Likewise, a person who works for a large corporation will interact socially with most fellow employees on a secondary group basis. However, within a given department or office, people may see each other socially outside work and sometimes form fairly strong friendships. Behavioral scientists find that one important factor leading to the formation of primary groups among relative strangers and acquaintances is <u>continued</u> <u>proximity</u>. The longer we are near people on a regular basis, the more likely it is that we will develop an ongoing pattern of interaction, get to know them, and form meaningful friendships (Gergen and Gergen, 1981).

SOCIAL STRUCTURE AND THE QUALITY OF GROUP RELATIONS

The manner in which a society is structured or organized affects to a significant degree the overall quality of social relations that occur within it. This is perhaps best illustrated in the work of two late nineteenth century and early twentieth century European sociologists, Ferdinand Tönnies and Emile Durkheim.

Tönnies: *Gemeinschaft and Gesellschaft*

Ferdinand Tönnies (1855–1936) was a German sociologist who spent his entire academic life at the University of Keil in northern Germany. His most important contribution to sociological theory, *Gemeinschaft und Gesellschaft* (community and society), was published in 1887. In this ground-breaking work, which was subsequently published in six other editions, Tönnies developed a typology in which he distinguished between the social organization of village-focused societies and that of mass societies characterized by large cities and an urban way of life. His pioneering use of the polar typology—the placing of two dissimilar concepts as ideal types at either end of a continuum—is a tool of analysis still used by sociologists today (Timasheff, 1967). There are illustrations of polar typologies throughout this book, including Figure 4-2.

Figure 4-2

Tönnies's Polar Typology of Societies. Based on the discussion in this chapter, where would you plot the United States along this continuum? What about Thailand or Bolivia?

Gemeinschaft Society ———— ± ———— Gesellschaft Society
(Primary Group Relations)   (Secondary Group Relations)

The *Gemeinschaft* Society: Basic Characteristics The *gemeinschaft* is a community-oriented society in which most social relations are personal, informal, and tend to be based on tradition. Both horticultural and agrarian societies, for example, tend to be largely *gemeinschaft* in terms of how social relations are organized. In speaking of this, Tönnies (1887, 1957, 2003) said:

> Family life is the general basis of life in the *Gemeinschaft*. It subsists in village and town life. The village community and the town themselves can be considered as large families, the various clans and houses representing the elementary organisms of its body . . . . Here, original kinship and inherited status remain an essential, or at least the most important condition of participating fully in property and other rights (1957, pp. 228–229).

In the *gemeinschaft* environment, primary group relations abound because of a variety of structural factors. These nonindustrial, village-focused societies typically have *low levels of material technology* and *slow rates of change*. These attributes, coupled with *common ancestry*, combine to produce a system of *commonly held norms and values*. In a farm-based economy, life tends to be organized around *tradition-based social positions* into which people are socialized from birth. Men, women, and children all have their own prescribed roles that govern not only how they interact within the family but also how they identify with and contribute to the community as a whole. Because most occupations and functions revolve around farming and animal husbandry, people have a great deal in common with one another and form *close-knit and long-term ties* with family and community members. In these societies, there is also *geographical stability* as many of their members grow up, get married, raise their families, and grow old and die within a few miles of their birthplace. These factors tend to create a societal climate conducive to primary group relations.

The *Gesellschaft* Society: Basic Characteristics By contrast, Tönnies argued, the *gesellschaft* is an urban, industrial society with impersonal and somewhat informal relations that tend to be based on contract. Tönnies was concerned about the decline of primary relations and offered at least a partial explanation by identifying several key characteristics of emerging urban societies. In his view, the intimacy and sense of community characteristic of *gemeinschaft* societies were being replaced by

> the rational will of the *gesellschaft*. In the course of history, folk culture has given rise to the civilization of the state. The main features of this process can be described in the following way: Economic control is achieved in many forms, the highest of which is planned capitalist production or large-scale industry. It is through the merchants that the technical conditions for the national union of independent individuals and for capitalist production are created. This merchant class is by nature, mostly

also by origin, international as well as national and urban, i.e., it belongs to *gesellschaft* not *gemeinschaft*. Later all social groups and dignitaries and, at least in tendency, the whole people acquire the characteristics of the *gesellschaft* . . . . Simultaneously, along with this revolution in the social order, there takes place a gradual change in the law, in meaning as well as in form. The contract as such becomes the basis of the entire system, and rational will of the *gesellschaft* formed by its interests combines with the authoritative will of the state to create, maintain, and change the legal system (1957, pp. 225–226).

Largely because of its size and complexity, the way a *gesellschaft* society is organized acts to create barriers to primary group relations. Given such factors as *high technology, rapid change,* and *diverse ancestry* among society members, *diverse and specialized norms and values* emerge. People develop very different perceptions of appropriate and inappropriate behavior, given their particular cultural heritage, varied occupations, and other quite diversified life situations.

An industrial economy results in *contract-based social positions* in which long-standing traditions may be of little relevance in light of changing social conditions. Personal relationships give way to business and professional relationships that are highly specialized in nature. Relationships based on friendship, trust, and good will are replaced by those that stress profit, productivity, and the achievement of other rational goals. Long-term close ties are replaced by *temporary and specialized friendships,* which are spread over several groups and tend to change in membership as time passes and conditions change. Finally, a *gesellschaft* society is characterized by *geographical and social mobility* among members. In a modern cash economy, people often must go where the jobs are, even if it means leaving extended relatives and friends behind and moving to another city or state.

Durkheim: Mechanical and Organic Solidarity

The French sociologist Emile Durkheim, a contemporary of Tönnies, also was interested in exploring the relationship between the way a society is structured and the overall manner in which social group relations take place. Like other analytical sociologists of his day, including such notables as Tönnies, Georg Simmel, and Gabriel Tarde, he favored the comparative approach, particularly that of comparing simple versus complex societies.

Durkheim's main research interest throughout his academic career was focused on the issue of social solidarity (social order) and its fundamental causes. In his first book, *The Division of Labor in Society* (1893, 1933), he sought to explain from a historical perspective the types of social solidarity characteristic of both simple rural societies and modern industrial social systems. Although he concentrated mainly on social solidarity, much of what he said had significant relevance toward explaining the quality of social relations in different types of societies.

Durkheim distinguished between simple nonindustrial societies characterized by *mechanical solidarity,* and complex industrial societies characterized by *organic solidarity.* He felt that social solidarity (order and cohesion) was the result of a collective conscience, a state of mental and moral agreement among members of a society concerning basic norms and values. Thus the collective conscience of a society, as expressed in a particular form of social solidarity, was the moral and social cement that held society together.

Mechanical Solidarity   Among the results of Durkheim's analysis was his finding that the primary group relations prevalent in simple nonindustrial societies was related to mechanical solidarity, the solidarity (cohesion) of resemblance characteristic of traditional nonindustrial societies. Most people in simple societies of the past, such as feudal societies of preindustrial Europe, were almost identical in their occupations, interests, and values. The low level of material technology in these societies resulted in a very simple division of labor. Therefore, the actions of most people tended to take the form of automatic or mechanical responses to rather predictable life situations. With everyone engaging in the same activities and thinking similar thoughts about most things, it then followed that social relations in these small societies tended to be personal and open for the most part. Because almost everyone knew almost everyone else in the hamlet or village, there were few obstacles to interfere with primary group relations. Durkheim found that in these societies the collective conscience was very strong and social solidarity was, therefore, relatively easy to maintain. This friendly, open sort of orientation toward others in the community can still be observed even today in rural pockets of largely industrial societies and postindustrial societies like the United States.

However, something developed in recent history to undermine mechanical solidarity, weaken the collective conscience, and alter the nature of social relations. That something was the Industrial Revolution, which began about 1750 but did not have a significant impact until after 1800. The factory system of production, Durkheim asserted, resulted in the emergence of a specialized division of labor and with it a different type of social cohesion, which he termed organic solidarity.

Organic Solidarity   Durkheim used the term organic solidarity to mean the solidarity of differences. In modern societies, individuals are differentiated by their occupations, values, and life styles. The result of this societal condition brought on largely by industrialization is a society composed of different types of people. These different individuals function much like the various organs of the body. They carry out different functions, but ones that complement or blend with each other for the smooth working of the society as a whole. Just as the heart, lungs, stomach, and other organs perform different yet complementary functions to maintain equilibrium in the physical organism, the same could be said for the way differentiated occupations interrelate smoothly to maintain order in the industrial society.

To carry the organic analogy further, a breakdown in one functional area can cause dislocation all across the system in either a physical organism or a human society. If, for example, a person experiences a heart attack or a serious back injury, his or her entire body is rendered incapable of functioning properly until the injured part recovers. Durkheim asserted that the same is true in a society. In the United States, for instance, coal miners produce coal and coal runs the steel mills; steelworkers produce steel and steel is used in the production of automobiles; car manufacturers distribute the cars to car dealers and the dealers then sell the cars to consumers. Hypothetically speaking, a long and unresolved coal miners' strike could create somewhat of a domino effect, which in turn could possibly impair a large part of the economy.

Durkheim was concerned because organic solidarity was more precarious than the earlier type and, given the differentiated nature of modern societies, the collective conscience was weakened. He felt that the sheer complexity of these societies often resulted in a condition of *anomie* the absence or breakdown of norms.

In terms of social relations, modern societies—composed of huge numbers of people who are different from one another in occupation, values, and life styles—are structured in a manner that discourages primary group relationships. One may come into contact with so many different types of people in so many different situations that it becomes difficult to maintain anything other than secondary group relationships with most of them.

Social Group Relations Today

Some sociologists such as Harold L. Wilensky and Charles N. Lebeaux have argued that "the breakdown of primary group life and informal controls has been greatly exaggerated" (1958, p. 125). They cite studies that show that the need to form primary relations is fairly universal and manifests itself in urban as well as rural settings. Even in a geographically mobile, industrial society, people who are isolated from one source of primary relations seek out and find others.

While it is true that people everywhere desire and need primary group relations, an impressive body of research shows that the nature of urban industrial society makes it difficult for people to form and sustain primary relations. Stanley S. Guterman (1969), for instance, concluded from his research that urban dwellers are less likely to have primary group bonds with close friends than those who live in small towns. In 1985, a national study asked those in the sample to identify the person with whom they could discuss important matters. Through the use of this measure, the study found that the average person had strong personal ties with only three other people as close confidants (Marsden, 1987).

Since that time, Americans have increasingly become a nation of observers rather than participants in meaningful social connections with others, their community, and society. In 2000, Robert Putnam's thoroughly researched book *Bowling Alone* chronicled the fact that Americans have become increasingly disconnected from one another in civic engagement; by the mid 1990s participation in church, community organizations, clubs, volunteerism, and philanthropy was only one-tenth of what it was during the 1970s. Civic and organizational participation had declined significantly in every measurable area "from the most common—petition signing—to the least common—running for office" (p. 41). In addition, based on national sampling data, the average number of close confidant relationships for typical Americans had been reduced from three people in 1985 to only two confidants in 2004. Nearly twenty-five percent reported that they had no one with whom to discuss personal matters important to them (*Science Daily*, 2006).

Relating to Groups as an Individual

In-Groups and Out-Groups Probably the most fundamental way each of us relates to groups as an individual is in terms of "us" versus "them." Early in the twentieth century, William Graham Sumner (1906) addressed this issue by distinguishing between in-groups and out-groups. An in-group is a group that a person belongs to or identifies with. It is a "we" group as compared to a "they" group. In-groups have a sense of "we-ness" or *consciousness of kind* that usually is based on commonly shared values or experiences among group members. Nongroup members are typically viewed as outsiders or

"they." Our in-groups may range in size from the smallest of social groups, such as a marriage or friendship circle, to the largest of social categories, such as "we" women, "we" Methodists, "we" New Yorkers, or "we" Americans. These types of group identifications reinforce both our need to belong and social cohesion as manifested in *ethnocentrism*.

An out-group, by contrast, is a group that a person does not belong to or identify with. It is a "they" group as compared to a "we" group. Groups distinguished according to in-groups and out-groups differ in membership and orientation, and are often characterized by rivalry and tension. If one is Catholic, an out-group would be Protestants. In similar fashion, the old would represent an out-group for the young, those who like mainly classical music would be an out-group for country-western fans, and Palestinians would be an out-group for Israelis. (Lindsey and Beach, 2000)

Social Distance The manner in which an individual relates to groups can also be examined by measuring social distance. This refers to the degree of acceptance an individual feels toward those who belong to various groups to which he or she does not belong. Sociologist Emory S. Bogardus (1959) devised a seven-point system to measure social distance. When it is administered to research subjects in the form of a scale, they are asked to answer yes or no to whether they would be willing to include a certain category of person—a member of a different ethnic group for instance—as (1) a family member by marriage, (2) a personal friend, (3) a close neighbor, (4) a co-worker, (5) a citizen in their country, (6) a visitor to their country, or (7) would ban the person from their country.

Through the use of the Bogardus Social Distance Scale and other measures, sociologists are able to ascertain how close or distant people feel toward certain groups according to certain characteristics, such as age, ethnicity, race, class, religion, sexual orientation, and nationality. This allows us to predict with some accuracy the extent to which some groups will either be cooperative or antagonistic towards one another. (Macionis, 2007)

Reference Groups In 1942, Herbert Hyman used the term *reference group* to describe another way people relate to the groups that surround them. A reference group is a group to which a person may or may not belong, which is used as a standard of comparison to evaluate his or her values, behavior, and goals. A person's primary groups, including family and close peer relations, may be reference groups in the sense that they usually are seen as models for value formation and behavior.

Many reference groups, however, are social categories that we use strictly as a basis for comparing our own attitudes and performance. Using them as benchmarks can be a valuable device for assessing or own social identities, performance, and decisions regarding what we wish to achieve in life. For example, it is important for a person serious about obtaining a college degree to identify strongly with college graduates, just as high school and college athletes often identify with professional ball players, aspiring writers with published authors, and beginning employees wishing to get ahead with those in the upper ranks of management.

Both success and failure tend to be defined in terms of the groups in which we choose to participate and those with which we identify. To identify with the success of a particular reference group only as a dream, with little or no commitment or effort devoted to it, will not be sufficient to attain a wished-for standard of performance or objective. However, without beginning with a vision, as measured by the behavior and accomplishments of others, the achievement of success, regardless of how it is socially defined and measured, will most likely not occur.

Social Networks and Networking

Each of us possesses one or more social networks, linkages maintained with specific types of people for the satisfaction of personal and practical needs. By way of elaboration, some people may have developed a variety of large, established social networks while others may have only a few that tend to be very small. Some reclusive and socially disconnected people may have no social

networks to speak of at all. Most of us, however, tend to have a family network, a friendship network, a network of work associates, a network of classmates if we attend college, a network of fellow church members if we are affiliated closely with a church organization, etc. (Schaefer, 2013)

A very important life skill is learning how to engage in networking, the conscious and planned cultivation of social networks to achieve personal or practical goals. Politicians and those successful in business and careers are masters of networking. Similarly, people with large circles of fairly close friends usually have expended significant time and energy to cultivate them.

MICROSOCIOLOGY: SMALL THINGS THAT MAKE A BIG DIFFERENCE

Concert tours for popular entertainers like Lady Gaga and Justin Beiber require a tremendous amount of planning and organization. Hundreds of details must be worked out starting with the necessary time set aside in the entertainer's schedule—decisions about the cities to be included; the concert locations to be used; negotiations concerning the "cut" of the proceeds to be received by promoters, ticket sellers, and concert halls. As the tour gets under way, "roadies" are hired to transport and set up the musical instruments and sound equipment, and advance people are sent ahead to ensure that arrangements for hotel accommodations, limousines, security, concession workers to sell programs, buttons, sweatshirts, and posters, and local publicity are all properly taken care of. Finally, a day or two before the concert series begins in each city, the performer and musicians, backup singers, choreographers, and technicians arrive to rehearse, to be interviewed by local media, and to ensure all details related to the performances are complete. In addition, some concerts today are technological spectaculars, often requiring computer-sequenced laser lights, smoke and fireworks explosions, wires and cranes to levitate the entertainer above the stage or over the audience, or other special effects. Only after all preparations are completed do the concert performances take place—often creating the illusion of spontaneous events that just unfold naturally.

In similar fashion, practically all aspects of social life involve social organization, the process by which society is structured as a system of social interaction to meet the needs of its members. Just as we may watch a live concert without thinking about the organization behind the scenes, we often carry out our day-to-day lives without consciously thinking about the organization or structure that surrounds us at all levels of our society (Schaefer, 2013).

Social organization actually is based on two concepts. First, there is social interaction, the process through which two or more individuals mutually influence each other's thoughts, feelings, and actions. We humans are social beings who need satisfying contact with others of our kind. We therefore engage them in conversation and make plans and decisions together that provide the rich texture and focus for social life. However, people do not interact with each other in random fashion. Instead, social interaction is shaped by social structure, a set of organized norms that govern how people are to interact with each other in various social situations. For example, there are norms that govern the structure of social interactions in the family, school, and the workplace. These two dimensions of *social interaction* and *social structure* then result in a comprehensive system of human interaction on various levels of society called social organization.

LEVELS OF SOCIAL ORGANIZATION

Almost every social act we perform—from the one-minute encounter with a department store clerk to the complex interworkings of large-scale organizations, basic institutions, and whole societies—involves structured forms of behavior. In this regard, sociologists generally distinguish between two basic levels of social organization: microlevel organization and macrolevel organization.

Microlevel Social Organization

Microlevel organization is concerned with the patterned ways people act at the local community level in social encounters, relationships, and groups. The emphasis here is on how we act, react, and interact in our everyday encounters with others and how the smallest elements of a society's social structure, such as social relationships, are structured. When we interact with others, even in the most brief and casual encounters with strangers, our behavior is usually somewhat patterned

As societies have become larger, more diverse, and more complex, external social controls have become increasingly necessary.

© Lisa F. Young, 2009. Used under license from Shutterstock, Inc.

© James Steidl, 2009. Used under license from Shutterstock, Inc.

and predictable. In fact, much of what we do at the microlevel of society approaches social ritual. Many of us get up on the same side of the bed each morning, begin on the same side of the grocery store each time we do our shopping, and sit in the same seat at the kitchen table when we eat meals with our families. While it is true that the human experience is rich with individual diversity and opportunities for spontaneity, most of us operate within the structured boundaries set by our society and the habits we have acquired from our experiences with it. These habits take several forms.

Social Encounters For instance, even the way we encounter people in our society is highly structured. Typically, many of us avoid making eye contact with a total stranger we pass on the sidewalk. A person we recognize as only a casual acquaintance is usually met with a "Hi," at which point he or she will respond back with a "Hi." This is a one-stroke greeting ritual. If we pass someone we know better, we will say "Hi," the other person will say, "Hi," we will then say, "How are you?" and he or she will usually respond with "Fine." This is a two-stroke greeting ritual. If the interaction goes beyond two strokes, the individuals normally will engage in a conversation that could last for several minutes or longer.

Using the family as an illustration, microlevel organization in the family begins with how we encounter our family members. Unlike an encounter with a stranger that may involve a nod or smile, or a business associate with whom we shake hands and begin by saying "How are you doing today?" followed by their response of "Fine, and you?," initial encounters with family members are different. Often, a family greeting includes a hug, a kiss, or both. Then when we part, the hug or kiss (or both) is often repeated. The way encounters (in the form of greetings) take place in family settings also vary by culture. In American families, males often shake hands. Among Filipino males, the younger male may take the hand of the older male relative and touch it to his forehead as a sign of respect.

Social Interaction In numerous other ways, our social behavior at the microlevel is highly

organized. Many of us say "Hello" when answering the phone, "Have a nice day" in a customer service role, and "Bless you" when someone sneezes. Likewise, many of us learn how to use certain cues to get people to respond to us in predictable ways. Depending on one's needs or purposes, a long and silent stare will cause most people to talk, standing up during a long meeting is a useful cue to end the meeting, and placing one's coat or sweater on a theater chair will usually reserve a seat in American society.

Social Relationships Our relationships with family, friends, and co-workers are also structured in particular ways. Take a person's own individual family, for example. Most Americans come from a family background organized around a father, a mother, and one or more siblings. Others experience a childhood in which elderly grandparents or other relatives live in the home with them and the rest of their family members. Some, because of divorce, abandonment, poverty, or other disruptions, are reared partially or totally by grandparents or a single parent.

When a family is considered as a total group, individual family organization may depend to some degree on other factors including class, ethnicity, religion, and size. Some parents, because of these and other factors, may be more likely to be authoritarian, permissive, or authoritative in terms of how they rear their children. Size alone can affect the dynamics of the family as a group. Older children in large families, for instance, have often found themselves in the role of surrogate parent, responsible for the behavior of their little brothers and sisters. The eldest child with only one or two siblings rarely is expected to take on this responsibility. Other examples of microlevel organization include the structured patterns of interaction evident in a local high school, church, rock music band, grocery store, or garden club.

Macrolevel Organization

By contrast, macrolevel organization represents the manner in which large-scale organizations, basic institutions, and societies are organized and interact with one another. In other words, while microlevel organization focuses on how the small pieces of a society's social system are structured, macrolevel organization is concerned with how the large building blocks of a society are organized and interrelate together.

Large-Scale Organizations What sociologists call *large scale organizations* include formal organizations like school systems or colleges, church denominations, and corporations, as well as whole industries devoted to the production and promotion of such things as cars, computers, rock music, education, defense, and health care. To illustrate, compare a community college with a major university as large-scale organizations. Both provide their students with a fine education but are organized very differently. The community college offers two-year academic degree programs along with vocational-technical certificate programs and continuing education courses. It stresses quality teaching with faculty members who teach in small classes and use a student-centered approach. A community college is often smaller than a university and is strictly a commuter institution that serves primarily a local population. A major university, by comparison, offers four-year academic degree programs and graduate programs leading to advanced degrees. Its faculty members are mainly research and publishing oriented, often teach large auditorium classes, and typically use a subject-centered approach. A major university also tends to be a large residential institution that attracts a regional and often a national or international student body.

Institutions As mentioned earlier, an institution is a major structural part of a society that addresses a special area of human needs. Some simple societies are organized around one institution, the family group of kinship clan, in which all necessary social functions are carried out. Other more complex societies have *differentiated institutions,* each with its own specialized area of focus and concern. In modern social systems, there are five of these fundamental, yet specialized, institutions—the family, the economy, education, government, and religion—which

together comprise the essential structural building blocks of society. Institutions in different societies vary in the ways they are organized. Government in the United States, for example, is structured as a representative democracy with a two-party political system and three relatively equal branches: the executive branch headed by a president, the legislative branch, and the judiciary. Cuba, by contrast, is governed by a military dictator as head of state; Western Samoa has a tribal chief; Oman, a sultan; Kuwait, an emir; and Jordan, a king (*The CIA World Factbook, 2013*). The religious institution in some societies is predominantly Christian, while others may practice Buddhism, Islam, Confucianism, Hinduism, or any one or a combination of religious belief systems. In addition, the family institution is organized very differently in various societies, some allowing only monogamous marriage (one spouse), while others allow polygamous marriage (multiple spouses).

Societies (and Their Characteristics) The largest and most complex system of social interaction is a society, the largest possible grouping of individuals with specific characteristics in a particular system of social interaction. Given this definition, there are two basic varieties of societies: animal societies and human societies. Many lower animal species including ants, bees, wolves, baboons, and whales have social interaction systems similar in many respects to those of humans (Table 4–2).

Animal Versus Human Societies *Animal societies* have the following key characteristics: They (1) occupy a definite territory, (2) perpetuate their membership through sexual reproduction, (3) are completely autonomous and self-contained (like a hive of bees or a pride of lions), and (4) possess a way of life shaped in large part by instincts. Human societies have the first two characteristics in common with their animal counterparts: (1) territoriality and (2) perpetuation through sexual reproduction (although asexual means are possible now such as in vitro fertilization and possibly cloning in the future). However, human societies are (3) relatively independent

Table 4-2

Macrolevel Organization of Animal Versus Human Societies

Animal Societies (Characteristics)	Human Societies (Characteristics)
1. Occupy a definite territory	1. Occupy a definite territory
2. Sexual reproduction	2. Sexual reproduction*
3. Completely independent	3. Relatively independent
4. Way of life shaped by instinct	4. Way of life shaped by culture

This today is beginning to undergo some change. Various reproductive technologies that do not require sexual intercourse are now available or are in development.

(ties to other societies), and (4) possess a way of life shaped by culture rather than instinct (Biesanz and Biesanz, 1973).

Territoriality   One of the most interesting characteristics of both animal and human societies is territoriality. Like the lower animals, we humans also are territorial creatures who use various devices at both macro and microlevels to claim space. However, unlike lower animals who use, among other things, urine and claw scratches on trees to establish territorial boundaries, humans accomplish this politically at the macro level through treaty arrangements with other societies. Societal or national boundaries are taken very seriously and, if threatened, are defended under force of arms if necessary. In fact, disputes and wars between both tribal societies and nations are often caused by disputes over territory.

At the microlevel, most of us carry an invisible bubble of personal space with us everywhere we go. The size of this territorial bubble is influenced by one's culture and the social situation. In America, except for situations such as standing in line or riding in an elevator, it is normally about three to four feet in diameter. In American culture, this is usually the minimum distance we prefer to keep from other people, especially strangers. Americans will usually skip at least a seat or two, if possible, between themselves and other people in a movie theater. Suppose that two Americans are seated in a restaurant at a table that could seat four. Two strangers enter and sit down with them rather than occupy one of the

available empty tables. The original occupants at the table would probably be very surprised and might feel threatened or offended. However, in Germany and other parts of Europe where other standards of territoriality apply, to sit at a separate table when two chairs are available at a table already partially occupied might be considered ill mannered. Physical objects are also used to "stake a claim" to personal space "as when sunglasses and lotion claim a beach chair, or a purse a seat in an airliner" (Goffman, 1972, p. 41). To further illustrate how territoriality differs from society to society, in some parts of both the Middle East and South America, it is not uncommon to get close to another person's face when interacting with them, close enough to feel the other's breath. Think of how most Americans and even Europeans might react to this.

Relative Independence   The third characteristic mentioned previously, relative independence, requires some further elaboration. Societies among the lower animals may require total group autonomy. In this sense, animal groupings—a hive of bees, a pride of lions, a band of hyenas—tend to be *independent*, wholly autonomous and self-contained.

They typically do not interact with other animal groupings of their kind outside of their own territorially occupied group. Human societies, by contrast, tend to be much more *interdependent* and interconnect with one another through various alliances, treaties, and agreements. The United States, for example, is a voting member of the United Nations, has the NAFTA trade agreement with Mexico, and is a member of the North Atlantic Treaty Organization (NATO), the World Bank, and numerous other international bodies. In addition, most European countries are now members of the European Union (EU), an effort designed to combine Europe's separate national economies into one consolidated block of worldwide influence to compete favorably with the American dollar. With this move, the eurodollar has replaced French francs, German dueschmarks, and Italian lira, to name a few, which now are seen largely as artifacts of the past.

KEY FORMS OF ORGANIZATION WITHIN SOCIETIES

Within the different types of societies [e.g., preindustrial (hunting-gathering, horticultural, agrarian), industrial, postindustrial] at both micro- and macrolevels are several forms of social organization. Among the most fundamental of these are those that are found in every society—kinship, fealty, groups, social statuses, and contract. Together, they comprise much of the foundation for the way human social interaction and social relationships take place.

Kinship

Kinship is a form of social organization involving the manner in which family relations are organized. In all societies, blood and marriage are universal bases for kinship organization, but it varies in which one or the other tends to be predominant. Most societies, particularly nonindustrial ones, have consanguineal kinship, a type of family organization based primarily on blood ties. These societies normally have an *extended family* of several generations of kin who depend on one another for mutual support and protection. Given the relatively simple division of labor in hunting-gathering and horticultural cultures, all societal functions are family-based and carried out mainly within this single institution. In these societies, male dominance is the usual pattern, women (wives and daughters) take a secondary role, and family name and property are passed from father to son. Some, however, such as the Navajo of the American Southwest, are female-focused or matrilineal, with property being passed between generations through the women's bloodlines (Witherspoon, 1975).

Industrial societies and emerging postindustrial societies are more likely to have affinal kinship, a type of family organization based primarily on marital ties. Here the *nuclear family,* consisting of only the married couple and

---

With the emergence of the information revolution, and service-oriented economies, the United States and other technological societies are making the transition to postindustrial societies.

their children, tends to be the dominant family form. This transition from consanguineal to affinal kinship began with the dawn of the Industrial Revolution as several functions that were once primarily family based—like education, religion, and economic production—gradually fell within the domain of separate, specialized institutions. With the shift away from an agrarian economy to one characterized by specialized occupations and cash wages, the consanguineal kinship system, with its emphasis on the extended family as a cooperative, self-supporting unit, became obsolete, at least from an economic standpoint.

Today in modern societies like the United States, extended family kin—including assorted grandparents, aunts, uncles, and cousins—tend to live in separate locations. In fact, given the demands for geographical mobility placed on many technical and professional workers in industrial and postindustrial societies, the nuclear family has become the only meaningful family unit in many instances, because extended kin often live several hundred miles away or farther. Consequently, affinal kinship became the primary family pattern in the United States and remains so today.

Groups

One of the most fundamental forms of social organization is the group. A group consists of two or more people with one or more characteristics in common. Most groups are easily recognizable and have clear-cut boundaries that allow us to distinguish members from nonmembers. Group boundaries are established by the characteristics of members, the norms that govern their behavior, the behavior patterns that stem from such norms, and group goals. *Social groups* (informal social interaction) and *formal organizations* (formal social patterns) are types of groups largely governed by these factors. Therefore, family is easily differentiated from friends, members of a rock music group from members of a country-western band, and employees of General Motors from members of the U.S. Marines.

Other types of groups may be more difficult to precisely identify or understand because of their temporary nature and constantly changing characteristics. *Physical aggregates* that include *crowds* and *publics* (widely dispersed categories of people who share an interest in an issue or group of issues) are notable examples. Nonetheless, the groups we belong to and interact with play an important role in determining who we are and in shaping our social behavior. More detailed information about groups is provided in Chapter 7, which deals exclusively with specific types of groups and group behavior.

Statuses

The term status, as used by sociologists, refers to a socially defined place or position a person occupies in society, along with a set of expected behavior patterns that act to regulate that person's behavior. Most of us are involved in several statuses (social positions) simultaneously. In the most general sense, we are, first of all, members of a society. This status carries with it the responsibility to act in ways acceptable to the norms of our culture—speaking a certain language, obeying the laws, working at a job, paying taxes, and following a multiplicity of folkways. We also occupy several specialized statuses that may include family member, spouse, parent, employee, supervisor, student, citizen, or consumer. Take the position of family member as an example. As a member of this group, we may occupy a status as spouse, parent, child, sibling, in-law, etc. Therefore, every group or organization in which we participate involves a specific place or status that we occupy as participants within it. Each of these statuses, in turn, requires some of our energy and time and results in portions of our behavior being organized in particular ways.

Take your status as a college student for instance. Each week, you devote time and energy to attending class, taking notes, reading this textbook, and, it is hoped, organizing your work by completing the accompanying study guide in preparation for successful performance on exams. Your other statuses related to family and job can be demanding also. Thus, the statuses or social positions you and others occupy act to organize social behavior to a remarkable degree.

Basic Types: Ascribed, Achieved, and Master Statuses The two most fundamental status types are ascribed and achieved statuses. An ascribed status is a social position assigned to a person at birth or otherwise imposed by society. The individual has little or no choice in determining an ascribed status he or she occupies. Examples include being born male or female, belonging to a particular racial or ethnic group, nationality, and being a child, teenager, or senior citizen. Although committing a felony and going to prison is a choice, how society labels and treats the felon upon release from prison is an ascribed status. By contrast, an achieved status is a social position earned through individual effort. Becoming a high school or college graduate, employee, spouse or parent, winner of the Nobel prize, and murderer are all examples of achieved statuses.

In addition, most adults typically choose to identify with or are defined in terms of one of their social positions above all others. This becomes the master status, the social position held by a person that becomes the primary source of his or her identity. In the United States, when two men meet for the first time at a social gathering, they usually will project a master status related to their employment or occupation. This is because men have been socialized traditionally to see themselves primarily in terms of being a family breadwinner. Women traditionally have identified primarily with the marital-homemaking position. Today, however, women typically choose from either their family status as wife-mother or their job or career. For college-educated, professional women in a dual-earner marriage, there is a pattern for some to see themselves primarily in terms of their jobs or careers, particularly after their marriages are established and their children are older with a firm foundation for their socialization having been firmly established.

Related Concepts: Status Set and Status Inconsistency Two other concepts related to the status (or position) in society one holds are status set and status inconsistency. A status set refers to the sum total of social statuses (social positions) a person occupies in his or her life situation. For example, one person may hold the statuses of family member, student, employee, church member, and club member (a hobby or personal interest organization) as his or her major social statuses. Another person may have a status set larger, smaller, or different in some regards. Because life in modern society is complex, it is relatively easy to take on more statuses (positions) than one can handle comfortably and overcommit time and energy resources that one might not have. For example, trying to work at a full-time job, take a full course load at college (another full-time commitment), and be an effective spouse and parent may be more than many people can handle comfortably. This, in turn, can lead to various problems such as *role strain* and *role conflict* that we will discuss shortly.

A second interesting concept related to statuses in modern society is status inconsistency. This refers to a contradiction or mismatch between statuses in which a person ranks high in one and low in another. For example, a person might rank low in their occupational position as an unskilled laborer but high in their social status as a deacon in their church. As another example, there is a wealthy "businessman and investor" who lives in a large mansion in a New Jersey village, has a chauffeur drive him into Manhattan each morning to work, and donates large amounts of money to his church and various charities. Then, he is arrested by the FBI, charged with racketeering, is convicted, and goes to prison. No one in his little village knew of his other status as head of a large criminal "family" that coerced millions in "protection money" over the years from dozens of businesses in New York.

Roles and Their Complications In Chapter 3: Socialization, we saw how, according to George Herbert Mead and other interactionists, children mentally rehearse for the statuses they will carry out as adults by engaging in role taking, the imitation and playing out of adult roles. By adulthood, when statuses are actually occupied, each is characterized by a role, the expected forms of behavior, obligation, and privilege that go with a social status. Roles form the building blocks that make up the structure of the social positions we hold. They also determine in large part how we behave as participants. Largely through the influence of roles and how they are sanctioned by the larger society, the statuses we occupy not only shape our behavior but determine to a significant degree who we are. As Peter Berger (1963) says:

> One feels more ardent by kissing, more humble by kneeling and more angry by shaking one's fist. That is, the kiss not only expresses ardor but manufactures it. Roles carry with them both certain actions and emotions and attitudes that belong to these actions. The professor putting on an act that pretends to wisdom comes to feel wise. The preacher finds himself believing what he preaches. The soldier discovers martial stirrings in his breast as he puts on

the uniform. In each case, while the emotion or attitude may have been present before the role was taken on, the latter inevitably strengthens what was there before. In many instances there is every reason to suppose that nothing at all anteceded the playing of the role in the actor's consciousness. In other words, one becomes wise by being appointed a professor, believing by engaging in activities that presuppose belief, and ready for battle by marching in formation (p. 96).

Statuses in modern societies often involve a role set, two or more distinct roles that relate to a single status or social position (Merton, 1968). The physician for example, carries out one role in regard to patients, another in relation to nurses, and others attached to interactions with colleagues, medical students, and pharmaceutical salespeople. In similar fashion, a college baseball coach has different role obligations to players, the

Figure 4-3

Each of us has a status set through which our life is organized according to the statuses we hold and the role that goes with each. Some of these statuses or social positions—such as family member or occupation—may also contain a role set.

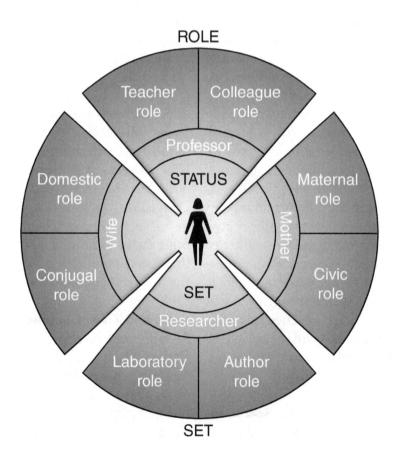

college as his or her employer, other college coaches, high school coaches while recruiting new players, and professional scouts.

Sometimes the obligations associated with our various social positions cause complications or problems for us in the form of role ambiguity, role strain, and role conflict. Role ambiguity occurs when the obligations attached to a social status are unclear. This often takes place in a new status or relationship. Most of us have felt a little unsure of ourselves on a first date, in the first few days at a new job, or in the first few weeks as a college student. Likewise, adolescence is often a confusing time for many young people with few, if any, clear-cut role demands. Role ambiguity can also occur when we are placed in an awkward situation in a social position that is normally well defined. A person might, for instance, feel very uncertain of how to proceed if a best friend asked for advice in how to handle his or her failing marriage.

Role Related Problems: Role Strain and Role Conflict One problem commonly experienced in modern society is role strain. This is stress that occurs when conflicting role demands are built into a single status, a person cannot fulfill the role demands of a given position, or both (Goode, 1960; Merton, 1976). Take the middle-management supervisor in a production plant, for example. Upper management wants lower labor costs and tries to freeze wages, while lower-level workers want wage increases and promotions. The clashing role demands placed on the middle manager by these two groups—whose needs, priorities, and demands are sometimes in opposition—can sometimes make it difficult to succeed in such a position.

The teenage marriage represents a good illustration of role strain that can occur when the role demands of a given social position simply cannot be met and the individual is overwhelmed by obligations. Young couples who marry while one or both are still in high school face role strain brought on by emotional and social immaturity, inadequate financial resources, the lack of credentials and experience needed to obtain adequate employment, family pressure, and a

number of other problems. Taken as a whole, these elements of role stain contribute to a high teenage divorce rate. Regardless of type, unresolved role strain can lead to a negative self-concept, and, in some cases, even illness, heart attack, and premature death (Krantz, Grunberg, and Baum, 1985).

Role conflict is stress caused when conflicting role demands are built into separate statuses or positions, each of which an individual is expected to carry out successfully. Most of us experience role conflict from time to time when the obligations of the different positions we occupy interfere with each other. The role demands of one's job may conflict with those of one's marriage. If the requirement to spend extra hours at work becomes a long-term condition, a spouse may feel neglected and the marriage could suffer. You may have experienced role conflict as a college student, particularly if you have an outside job, are married, or both. If you do not put in sufficient study time, you may fail. But if you are not available to work when your employer needs you, you could lose your job. Obligations to a spouse or other family members may also require your attention. Consequently, many of us often feel like a juggler who must keep several balls in the air at the same time. It can be a difficult task and often requires careful planning and prioritizing. Even so, sometimes we must be wise enough to realize when we are overextending ourselves, and must establish firm priorities and reduce our obligations in certain areas when necessary (Schaefer, 2013).

Contract

Ever since the Middle Ages, *contract* has been an important basis for social organization, particularly in Western societies. A contract is a social bond between two or more parties that involves the exchange of one promise for another. As such, it has represented an important way to structure social relations for several hundred years. In feudal times, free peasants would often contract with a territorial lord to exchange their services for his protection. Unlike the general and implied nature of promises made and benefits received through kinship and fealty, contractual relations, as they evolved in Western societies, were very specific and explicit. As societies became larger and more complex, the need for specific and clearly defined contracts became more important. The rise of modern business economies after the Middle Ages, followed first by the Industrial Revolution and later by the high technology of the twentieth and twenty-first centuries, have made them even more necessary.

Today, the formal and specific nature of contracts has made them an indispensable form of organizing a wide variety of relationships in modern society. At the microlevel, we enter into contracts on a continuing basis each time we participate in the consumer economy by purchasing goods and services. All the activities of modern life, from charging a meal to a credit card, paying college tuition, to purchasing the clothes we wear, the cars we drive, or the houses we live in, usually involve contracts with one or more parties. Contracts at the macrolevel of society are more likely to have political and social, as well as economic, dimensions. They may include areas as diverse as labor contracts, corporate mergers, and nuclear test ban treaties.

Bureaucracy

With the development of early civilizations such as Mesopotamia and Egypt, decision making eventually came under the control of centralized authority. This was accompanied by the rise of *bureaucracy,* a form of social organization in which the work of participants (in large-scale organizations) is rationally coordinated by professionally trained managers. Without such leadership, the building of the pyramids in Ancient Egypt, the construction of the roads and aqueducts by the Roman Empire, and similar historical developments could not have occurred.

In modern times, the emergence of industrialization in the 1800s and the development of the factory system brought revolutionary changes to the production process. Of these changes, the most important involved the problems of managing extremely large numbers of factory workers engaged in a variety of specialized occupations.

Many traditional forms of leadership were ineffective in an industrial setting. Historically, those who rose to positions of authority did so as a result of personal power or charisma or were appointed on the basis of political favoritism by a king, lord, or other authority figure. The factory, however, represented a new phenomenon that had as its central purpose the mass production of economic consumer goods. In order to succeed, this type of enterprise required a rational, efficient form of management. In response to this need, professional managers were educated and trained especially for that purpose. This process of the professionalization of work roles has continued to evolve up to the present day. In speaking of this, Max Weber said that, in "place of the old-type ruler who is moved by sympathy, favor, grace, and gratitude, modern culture requires for its sustaining external apparatus, the emotionally detached and hence rigorously 'professional' expert" (Bendix, 1960, p. 422).

Today, most large-scale formal organizations involve the coordination of large numbers of people engaged in diverse and specialized functions. This applies not only to industrial and business organizations in modern societies, but also to institutions such as government. In France, for instance, government consists of a huge civil service apparatus. To qualify for a high-level civil service position, one must complete a special two-year school for government training after college graduation and score high on a battery of competitive examinations (Ridley, 1979). In the United States, many occupations are becoming increasingly professionalized, including law enforcement administration, nursing administration, and hotel and restaurant management. Given these trends, bureaucracy as a form of social organization appears destined to remain with us in the foreseeable future.

PATTERNS OF SOCIAL INTERACTION

Although many aspects of social organization vary from society to society—as in kinship structure and means of subsistence—social relations everywhere involve similar patterns of social interaction. *Social interaction*—previously defined as a process through which two or more individuals mutually influence each other's thoughts, feelings and actions—take five basic forms: cooperation, exchange, conflict, competition, and accommodation.

Cooperation

The most common form of social interaction is cooperation, the sharing of responsibility by people who work together to reach a shared goal. This joint effort and teamwork represents much of the foundation for maintaining social order and stability at all levels of society. By cooperating with each other through compliance with group and societal norms, our actions contribute to social survival, harmony, and, it is hoped, progress. More specifically, social cooperation makes it feasible to achieve goals that would be difficult if not impossible for a single individual to attain. Among the Eskimos of northern Canada, for instance, hunting and fishing are conducted in groups in order to acquire enough food for subsistence. The legislative bodies of modern governments operate under systems of parliamentary procedure in order to make laws and conduct related business. Throughout history, cooperation has made it possible to accomplish feats ranging from the construction of temples in ancient Athens to the development of space flight technology, computers, and particle accelerators today.

Forms of Cooperation According to sociologist Robert Nisbet (1970), there are four basic forms of cooperation. By far, the most common in both past and modern societies is *spontaneous cooperation,* which takes place face-to-face at the microlevel in the form of mutual aid. Conditions that result in this type of cooperation tend to emerge from a set of situational circumstances. If a person's house catches fire, neighbors often work together to put out the fire and provide temporary support to the affected family. Likewise, college students sometimes form study groups to prepare for an upcoming exam. *Traditional cooperation,* by comparison, takes the form of social habit that is passed down from generation to generation as established custom. Americans, for example, cooperate with each other traditionally in hundreds of ways, ranging from standing in a line to get a check cashed at the bank to attending the weddings and funerals of close relatives and friends.

However, modern societies—characterized by ongoing change and increasing complexity—tend to depend less on spontaneous and traditional cooperation than on two other types. One of these, *directed cooperation,* involves cooperation that is enforced by an authority figure such as an employer, teacher, or police officer.

As members of a community and society, people learn the value of many forms of cooperation.

The other, *contractual cooperation,* takes place when two or more parties mutually agree to specific conditions for cooperation. This can vary in form, from the teenager who agrees to baby sit a child for a married couple (microlevel), to several countries that form a formal trade agreement with each other (macrolevel).

Exchange

Cooperation is often reinforced by exchange, a form of social interaction in which all parties expect to benefit by receiving a reward. Sociologist George Homans (1961, 1974) has argued that we seek rewards in all our relations with others, and avoid negative consequences or punishments. We tend to continue relationships that offer more benefits than drawbacks and try to avoid those in which the negatives outweigh the positives.

Another exchange theorist, Peter Blau, has said that what is rewarding or punishing is not always clear cut or visible to the casual observer, but may be quite symbolic and subjective. In other words, what is meaningful as a reward may depend on the person, the situation, and the priorities or goals the individual seeks to have addressed or satisfied. For the student of behavior possessed by "the sociological imagination," Blau (1964) says that

> [s]ocial exchange can be observed everywhere once we are sensitized . . . to it, not only in market relations but also in friendship and even in love . . . as well as in many social relations between these extremes in intimacy. Neighbors exchange favors; children, toys; colleagues, assistance; acquaintances, courtesies; politicians, concessions; discussants, ideas; housewives, recipes (p. 88).

Exchange is based on the principle of *reciprocity,* the idea that people provide assistance to those who have helped them in order to maintain equality in social obligations (Gouldner, 1960). If someone comes along with jumper cables and helps you start your stalled car, you may reciprocate by offering to pay the person for his or her trouble. When you invite someone to your home for dinner or a party, that person may fulfill a felt obligation to you by returning the favor. If someone remembers your anniversary or birthday or sends you a Christmas card, you may respond in kind. In these and countless other ways, we exchange courtesies and resources with one another at all levels of society. This promotes alliances between individuals and groups and helps ensure cohesion and order throughout society.

Competition

Competition occurs when two or more parties attempt to reach a mutually prized goal that is limited in quantity. Unlike cooperation (shared goals) and exchange (mutual rewards), competition occurs when there can be only one winner of a ballgame, election, job promotion, or award for salesperson of the year. In these and numerous other situations, one must compete with others for scarce rewards. However, like the two previously mentioned forms of interaction, competition is governed by a particular type of norms (Friedsam, 1965). These norms act as rules of engagement to prevent competition from deteriorating into conflict which can be very destructive. The primary purpose of competition, therefore, is to achieve the goal, not to injure the other party or subvert the competitive process. If this process is threatened, it is sometimes necessary to impose punitive sanctions. These might include expulsion from the game for the abusive athlete, or job demotion or dismissal for the unethical sales representative.

Competition, like other forms of interaction, is found in all societies to some degree, whether it involves territorial hunting rights, soil resources for farming, cattle for breeding, or markets for industrial commodities. In the United States, the competitive spirit is an underlying element in dominant traditional norms that stress individualism, capitalism, and the upwardly mobile pursuit of the American dream. In this context, the primary advantage of competition is its usefulness as a mechanism to allocate scarce resources as rewards for hard work and high achievement. However, it can also result in discouragement and a sense of failure for those who, by virtue of poverty or emotional and social deprivation brought on by the accidents of birth and socialization, are not equipped with the necessary "cultural currency" to compete on an equal basis.

Conflict

When cooperation, exchange, and competition break down, there is often conflict, a pattern of interaction in which two or more parties seek to reach a goal by neutralizing, dominating, or destroying all adversaries against their will (Williams, 1970). Conflict occurs in all types of groups, from the most intimate to the most impersonal, and at all levels of interaction, from the two people who bash their cars together on the freeway and pursue the matter in court to two or more countries that go to war. As the opposite of cooperation, conflict is characterized chiefly by hostility on the part of the concerned parties and often a lack of norms almost to the point that "practically anything goes." Although physical confrontation and violence sometimes occur, conflict more typically involves less dramatic approaches including verbal disagreements, written position papers, or exercises in social (e.g., petitions or demonstrations) and economic sanctions.

Conflict is a pattern of interaction that may occur at any level of society and take a variety of forms.

© unitypix, 2014. Used under license from Shutterstock, Inc.

Forms of Conflict The German sociologist Georg Simmel (1858–1918) argued that there were four basic types of conflict: wars, feuds, litigations, and ideological conflicts (Simmel, 1955). *Wars* represent the most extreme and destructive type of conflict from the standpoint of violence. During World War II (1939–1945), over 50 million people lost their lives. During the Vietnam conflict nearly a third of a century later, more than 58,000 Americans were killed and the civilian death toll for the Vietnamese exceeded 1,500,000. *Feuds* are disputes between or within groups, whereas *litigations* represent legal conflicts between parties that are fought in the courts. *Ideological conflicts,* the last of Simmel's categories, are conflicts over ideals or principles as illustrated by capitalism versus communism, conservatism versus liberalism, and Christianity versus agnosticism.

Accommodation

When conflict becomes disruptive, a process is needed to foster its reduction or resolution so that opposing parties can function together successfully. This process is called accommodation.

Forms of Accommodation Although accommodation takes several forms, two of the most common are compromise and toleration. *Compromise* involves give-and-take negotiations between two parties in an attempt to find common ground sufficient to build a successful relationship. Examples might include the married couple with marital conflict (microlevel) that reaches an accommodation with or without the mediation of a professional counselor, or a labor-management dispute that is settled with or without third-party arbitration. Formal compromise often takes the form of written agreements, like labor contracts or treaties. In 1987, for example, twenty-four countries signed a treaty in Montreal, Canada, designed to help protect the ozone layer in the atmosphere. The ozone layer protects us from the harmful effects of the sun's ultraviolet rays. They agreed, among other things, to freeze world production of certain chlorofluorocarbons and fluorocarbons used in refrigerators and aerosol cans, which contribute to the destruction of the ozone layer.

Toleration is an agreement between two opposing parties to coexist since neither can easily defeat the other. In contrast to compromise, which involves active negotiations and sometimes formal agreements, toleration usually involves an implied arrangement between two relatively equal parties. In essence, they agree that although they do not like each other, it is in their best interests not to engage each other in direct conflict. The former Soviet Union (which dissolved in 1987) and the United States were bitter ideological enemies for over forty years. Yet, because each had sufficient nuclear armament to destroy the world several times over, they found it advantageous—through a condition called *détente*—to avoid direct confrontation and overt war. Although they did engage in compromise with each other in some areas and signed treaties together, the primary relationship between these two super powers was toleration.

Chapter 5

How We Actually Do Sociology: The Research Process

Two social scientists—one a sociologist and the other an anthropologist—embark on a study of American funeral rituals. They use as their key contacts some employees of "funeral parlors," who inform them about types of funerals that are scheduled and where and when they will take place. Using an approach called *participant observation,* the two researchers attend these funerals, blend in with the mourners, and make their observations. Not only do they discover how varied funeral rituals are in America, but they also observe that a small number of "professional mourners" exist who, for a variety of reasons, often attend the funerals of people that they did not even know.

Late one night, a sociologist and a research assistant participate in a stakeout with officers of a local police department in a large metropolitan city. The suspects being watched engage in a major "drug buy," and the stakeout team closes in and make several arrests. The sociologist and the assistant observe and record many things, including police procedure, interaction patterns of the police officers before and after a successful

vice squad operation, and the "street smarts" exhibited by experienced felons caught in the act. As a bonus, the rapport established between the sociologist and the officers yields an unexpected result. Because several of the officers are the sociologist's students in a Sociology of Deviance course, the officers are quite willing to discuss the issue of police corruption within the department—the way honest cops feel about "dopers" who sell confiscated drugs they "skim off" from "the take"—and the bureaucratic problems within the department in dealing effectively with crooked cops.

Using the survey approach, a sociologist completes a study on sociologists in the state of Texas who teach in public, two-year colleges. The results of this research reveal a variety of characteristics and practices that are descriptive of this research population, which included the following: the background and education of the sociologists, the theoretical perspectives in sociology with which they identify and use, their teaching methods and techniques, work load [number of courses (preparations) and sections taught], hours worked per week, committee obligations, record keeping duties, report writing, time spent on research and writing, and other pieces of information.

A sociology professor, after obtaining proper clearance, takes a group of undergraduate students on a day-long visit to a maximum security prison in Texas. Before the day of the visit, the students are given an orientation seminar on the prison as a separate society with its own set of norms, routines, and practices. They discuss how to act in such a cultural environment and how to formulate research questions to ask of the warden, the prison guards, and even the inmates themselves. In this manner, students using the interview approach are able to gather information on the various perceptions of "prison" held by people placed in different prison roles and to acquire, in an objective and systematic way, insights about crime and its consequences both as a form of behavior and, for some, as a way of life.

These illustrate the variety of research methods used by sociologists, as well as the wide diversity of sociological subject matter that is available to investigate. With this in mind, in this chapter we will build on previous information to explore how sociologists as scientists conduct research.

TYPES OF SOCIOLOGICAL RESEARCH

The research enterprise in sociology takes two basic forms: *pure research* and *applied research*. As scientists, many sociologists seek to extend the frontiers of knowledge and add to what is known about the nature of their own society and other societies around the world. Others seek to link research to the world of social action surrounding us and to related issues of social need, public policy, international policy, and social reform.

Pure Research

The first and foremost task of sociology is to develop a constantly expanding base of reliable knowledge about the social behavior of human beings at all levels of society. This is pure research, scientific investigation aimed at expanding the base of knowledge. In his 1930 presidential address to the American sociological society, William F. Ogburn emphatically stated the rationale for pure research and his position concerning sociology's proper role:

> Sociology as a science is not interested in making the world a better place in which to live, in encouraging beliefs, in spreading information, in dispersing news, in setting forth impressions of life, in leading the multitudes, or in guiding the ship of state. Science is interested directly in one thing only, to wit, discovering new knowledge (1930, p. 301).

The desire to seek knowledge for the sake of knowledge, in the view of many traditional sociologists, represents the true spirit of the scientific method. During the early twentieth century, some in the sociological community were afraid that this young discipline might not be accepted as a legitimate science if allowed to become associated with addressing practical issues and solving social problems. In those early days, when sociological knowledge was sparse and the complexity of social issues was great, it was also politically expedient for sociologists to sidestep what some have called "social responsibility" by wrapping themselves in the robes of academic respectability and claiming the need to keep science "pure."

However, as sociology matured and gained legitimacy in the academy of sciences, the distinctions between pure and applied research became less of an issue in the minds of many practitioners. Today, pure and applied research are seen by most sociologists as complementary, rather than at odds with one another. Whether or not sociological knowledge is to be used is no longer an issue. The question now is, "For what purposes?"

Applied Research

In 1906, Lester F. Ward, the first president of the American Sociological Society, stated his position on the applied approach in sociology in the following manner:

Just as pure sociology aims to answer the question, What, Why, and How, so applied sociology aims to answer the question, what for? . . . Applied sociology is essentially practical. It appeals directly to interest. It has to do with social ideals, with ethical considerations, with what ought to be . . . . The most that it claims to do is to lay down certain general principles as guides to social and political action (as quoted in Wilkinson, 1980, p. 3).

Today, over a century later, applied sociology is seen as a legitimate area of investigation and practice within the mainstream of the sociology profession. Applied research is the study of how sociological principles and knowledge might be applied to social issues, programs, and problems. Many involved in "sociological practice" are employed by or act as consultants to organizations and institutions in business and industry, government, health and human services, and education. Others are in private practice as counselors and clinical sociologists.

Areas of applied research in sociology are becoming increasingly diverse and include corporate marketing, consumer and advertising research, human resources research in the corporate sector, studies of and practice in the legal and criminal justice systems (e.g., applied sociologists often work as consultants in helping attorneys choose juries), and research on aging (Freeman, Dynes Rossi, and Whyte, 1983; Larson, 1995). Over one-quarter of all doctoral level sociologists today pursue careers in applied sociology outside of academia (Lyson and Squires, 1993).

Three areas of applied sociology in particular are receiving much attention today: policy research, evaluation research, and clinical sociology.

Policy research refers to studies related to social issues and problems, the results of which may be used as a basis for the formation of public policy. During the past several decades, social scientists have participated in government research and served on presidential commissions and committees devoted to various social issues including civil disorders, the Vietnam and Iraq conflicts, pornography, drug abuse, law enforcement, and, more recently, international terrorism and national disaster planning.

Evaluation research examines the consequences of various public policies by evaluating their degree of effectiveness or ineffectiveness. In recent years, for example, sociologists and other social scientists have investigated the effects of the Federal Communications Commission (FCC) standards regarding violence on television, the impact of capital punishment on rates of violent crimes, the preventable human costs incurred by the inhabitants of the Gulf Coast in the aftermath of Hurricane Katrina in 2005, and the impact of gun control on rates of crime.

A third area of sociological practice, clinical sociology, is an applied profession within sociology dedicated to helping people better cope with their social identities and social relations through the use of sociological principles. Clinicians in sociology have their own international organization (Sociological Practice Association) and certification credentials (Certified Clinical Sociologist, or C.C.S.). They engage in professional practice in several areas ranging from counseling and therapy to public health care and human resource development in both the public and private sectors.

Sociological Research in Perspective

Today, pure research and applied research represent two halves of the same whole—the sociological enterprise. Both pure and applied sociologists use the process of discovery and analysis called the scientific method. As introduced in Chapter 1, science is a means of explanation that is theoretical, empirical, objective, and cumulative. Science produces verifiable knowledge and, in this way, differs from explanations based on authority, tradition, belief, and simple logic. As such, the scientific approach is a formal one involving a series of steps that must be carried out according to a specified set of rules. Yet science, like most forms of discovery, offers an exciting and intriguing adventure for the practitioner who yearns to see what others have not seen and know what others have not known. Just how the scientific method works in sociological research, the steps involved in conducting the sociological enterprise, and the ways in which the sociologist makes observations and arrives at conclusions are the main topics in this chapter.

DOING SOCIOLOGICAL RESEARCH: AN OVERVIEW

Three Levels of Analysis

The goal of scientific research is the expansion of knowledge. To accomplish this, sociologists as scientists examine their subject matter on three levels. First, there is *description.* Researchers must begin by describing what it is that they wish to investigate, whether it is geological rock formations in the physical sciences, criminal activity, or family interaction patterns in sociology.

Second, researchers wish to find an *explanation* for the occurrence of their subject matter. If, for example, crime rates are rising or fertility rates are declining in a given society, what factors account for these phenomena?

Third, scientists ultimately aim at *prediction.* They try to predict how, when, and why various aspects of their subject matter will occur in the future. Sociologists operating on this level of analysis engage in forecasting in which they attempt to predict a variety of social trends based on description and explanation.

Consider college enrollments as an example. At the *description* level, women have, over the past several decades, surpassed men in terms of undergraduate college enrollments and may soon do the same regarding graduate school enrollments as well. In 1984, women accounted for 44 percent of undergraduate enrollments in the United States; in 2006, they accounted for nearly 56 percent. As of 2006, women were earning more bachelor's degrees than men and forecasts were that, by the year 2020, women would constitute 60 percent of undergraduate students. In terms of the *explanation* level, factors impacting this trend include the impact of such factors as the woman's movement (modern feminism) that emerged and evolved from the early 1960s to the present, better birth control technology that empowers women to control when and if they have children, enabling legislation and Supreme Court decisions that protect the rights of women and other minorities, and several other variables.

What then, might such changes mean? What *predictions* might we make based on such trends? If such trends continue for several more decades, women could and most likely will

Clinical sociologists use the knowledge generated from sociological research in applied settings.

© Lisa F. Young, 2009. Used under license from Shutterstock, Inc.

come to occupy many to most of the desirable and powerful positions in many sectors of society. Because the United States is a rational-legal system, driven by expertise and credentialing, in the future those with the credentials will essentially dominate our major institutions—from business and industry to politics, academia, and perhaps even the military establishment (commanding generals). Sociologists are beginning to predict that women, if they collectively choose to, could form a truly matriarchal society within the next century in which women would dominate. While they may or may not elect to do so, one thing seems very clear. If current trends continue, women most likely will constitute the brain trust in American society within 50–75 years and, by the end of the century, could have the power to set the standard for cultural norms, make the rules, and dominate social policy. Whether or not they decide to exercise such an option and what reactions, if any, would come from men is, of course, an open question.

The Scientific Research Cycle: Seven Key Steps

Learning How Science Works: Scientific detection involves seven essential steps normally followed in chronological order to complete an investigation or study. These are the seven steps, which will be explained in detail as we proceed through this chapter:

Step 1. Statement of the Research Problem

Step 2. Review of the Literature

Step 3. Statement of Hypotheses

Step 4. Research Design / Methodology

Step 5. Data Collection

Step 6. Analysis of the Findings

Step 7. Reporting the Results

Every educated person should know and understand the seven basic steps—in their proper order—listed above that are used in the scientific method each time a study is conducted and completed.

Because of the diversity of human behavior, every form of social experience is of interest to the sociologist—professional wrestling for example. What are the similarities and differences among those who attend wrestling events and those who go to basketball games or modern art exhibits? What are the backgrounds of those who become wrestlers? These are but two of many questions the sociologist might explore.

© Danny Lehman/Corbis

Box 5-1

The Scientific Method

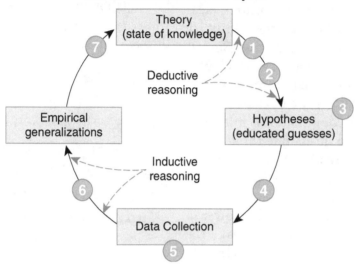

The Scientific Research Cycle

Most scientific studies involve the completion of a series of steps or stages. The researcher typically begins with the state of knowledge (theory) about the phenomenon to be investigated. The project ends with the discovery of additional information that, when integrated with what is already known, acts to reinforce, modify, and extend the state of knowledge. Each study thus represents the completion of a scientific research cycle. The scientific enterprise itself, whether in sociology, psychology, physics, chemistry, or any other discipline, represents a never-ending series of such cycles.

The Seven Basic Steps in Conducting a Scientific Study

Step 1: Statement of the Research Problem

The researcher begins by taking what is generally known (the state of knowledge or theory) about a phenomenon and, using deduction, narrows the focus down to a specific research instance called the -problem.

Step 2: Review of the Literature

The scientist next takes into full account previous research (the state of existing knowledge) concerning the phenomenon under study. This aids in prediction, maximizes efficiency, and maintains objectivity. Scientists must stay current in their areas of specialization (the literature) as knowledge is expanded.

Step 3: Statement of Hypotheses

Based on the review of the literature, hypotheses are formulated. They represent specific predictions (derived deductively from previous studies) about what the researcher expects to find when observations are made.

Step 4: Research Design / Methodology

The research design represents the method or methods to be used in making observations (survey, experiment, participant observation, content analysis, etc.)

Step 5: Data Collection

Once the re-search design is decided upon, it is closely followed and all observations are made.

Step 6: Analysis of the Findings

Findings are then analyzed to see whether or not the hypotheses are supported by the observations (data) gathered. Once the findings have been fully interpreted, the researcher can make empirical generalizations from them through inductive reasoning. In other words, specific observations can then be generalized to a larger population.

Step 7: Reporting the Results

To conclude the study, research results are reported in scientific and professional journals, books, papers presented at academic conferences, and popular publications. Through this process, the results of research then become added to the state of existing knowledge or theory. Future researchers will then take these results and conclusions into account when they review the literature in the future and conduct subsequent research.

Source: The diagram "The Scientific Research Cycle" is from: Wallace, W. 1972. The Logic of Science in Sociology, *p. 18. Chicago: Aldine-Atherton.*

GETTING STARTED: STEPS 1–3

Sociological researchers also use the scientific method in similar fashion to the study briefly described above by completing the same seven steps. The first of these is the development of a research problem or question.

Step 1: The Research Problem

To begin, many questions about reality are not amenable to scientific investigation and verification, at least not at the present time; for instance "Does God exist?" "Are there UFOs from outer space?" "Does 'Bigfoot' or 'The Loch Ness' creature exist?" "Are there really such things as poltergeists or 'ghosts'?" These and other similar topics have to do with subjective beliefs, value judgments, and unpredictable variables. Other questions and variables, however, can be investigated and determined scientifically with measurable results such as "Does the amount of education members of a group possess affect their relative degrees of racial prejudice, and if so, how, and how much?" These are the types of questions addressed by scientists called sociologists.

A scientific study normally begins with a research problem, or the statement of a specific research problem (topic) related to a general scientific theory. In this sense, a research problem is aimed at testing, verifying, extending, or refining the existing level of explanation (knowledge) about the subject under investigation. To illustrate this, suppose a sociologist wants to test the theory that "the amount of formal education influences the degree of racial prejudice that people may exhibit." This is general scientific theory, because previous research has demonstrated a relationship between these two factors. In deriving a testable research problem from such a theory, however, the sociologist has to narrow his or her focus to identify needed specifics, such as the target population to be studied (the who), the type of racial prejudice to be examined (the what), and the geographical area (the where) such as town,

state, or even the country or society in which the study will be carried out. These specifics are necessary in order for a research problem to be testable.

Step 2: Review of the Literature

The second step in conducting scientific research is the review of the literature, a thorough examination of previous research concerning the scientific theory that is to be tested. By examining previous research, the sociologist is able to weigh the evidence and then make predictions concerning what might be found in the study about to be carried out. In sociology, as well as in other sciences, investigators must keep abreast of the latest developments in their research fields. The responsibility to stay current with the scientific literature, in light of rapidly expanding knowledge, largely accounts for the necessity for sociologists and other scientists to specialize.

Three Reasons Why Review of the Literature Is Needed   The review of the literature is needed for several reasons. First, a properly conducted literature review *aids in prediction*. It gives the researcher a firm foundation on which to base predictions or hypotheses. Thus, it aids in making the scientific method coherent and systematic. Second, it *promotes efficiency*. A review of the literature may show that the behavior or event the sociologist wants to observe or explain has already been thoroughly researched. As a result, needless and unproductive repetition of previous research can be prevented. The review of the literature, therefore, aids in making science cumulative. The state of reliable knowledge is continuously added to and refined, and scientists can avoid "reinventing of the wheel." Finally, a thorough and properly conducted review of the literature *ensures objectivity*. The researcher cannot legitimately be accused of being biased or unscientific if the hypotheses concerning expected findings are based on or grounded in the body of previous research findings.

By contrast, the scientific community looks with great disdain on those who use the language and imagery of science to make facts fit into their own preconceived "theories." This is pseudoscience, which takes many forms in its attempt to befuddle and sometimes defraud the public. Practitioners today abound in many places and take several forms, from the psychic surgeons of the Philippines with their sleight-of-hand trickery, to some authors of popular books who masquerade as social scientists by publishing biased reports on various forms of social behavior. Such devices prey on the innocent, the ignorant, and those desperate for assistance of some kind. The best defense against such "flimflam" is maturity and a sound understanding of the scientific method.

Step 3: The Statement of Hypotheses

After completing the review of the literature, the sociologist next makes educated guesses or predictions about what he or she expects to find when the study is carried forth. These predictions are called hypotheses. In scientific research, a hypothesis is a formal statement of an expected relationship between two variables that can be tested.

In science, the term *variable* generally is defined as anything subject to change or variation, such as rain in meteorology, soil erosion in geography, or rates of cancer in medicine. In sociology, a variable is defined specifically as any social characteristic or form of social behavior that may differ in some regard or change. A family sociologist, for example, might examine variables such as marital satisfaction, family violence, and sex roles, while the demographer (one who studies population characteristics) might focus attention on such variables as fertility, mortality, and rates of immigration.

A hypothesis contains both an independent and a dependent variable. Together they represent the two basic types of variables included in scientific research. The independent variable is the causal or influencing variable. It causes or influences to some extent the occurrence of another variable called the dependent variable. Sociological research has shown, for instance, that violence in the home while a person grows up is one independent variable which may influence him or her to engage in family violence—a dependent variable—as an adult.

The *dependent variable* is the effect variable that is the subject of research. In science, all investigation focuses on the dependent variable, the effect that the research attempts to account for or explain. Let us take, for example, a sociologist who specializes in criminology. This researcher wishes to investigate recidivism (the rate at which released felons engage in new crimes and return to prison). Consequently, recidivism would be the dependent variable for the purposes of this research. It is the effect being examined and, as such, is dependent on certain causes or explanations. These causes or explanations represent the independent variables that the sociologist must search for, make predictions or hypotheses about, and then test to see if expected relationships between such independent variables and the dependent variable are indeed the case (Lindsey and Beach, 2000).

Durkheim: A Pioneer in Hypothesis Formation and Testing The modern sociological method of hypothesis formation and testing was pioneered by Emile Durkheim in his research on suicide conducted late in the nineteenth century and later reported in his seminal book *Suicide*. Durkheim's basic theory was that the industrialization and rapid urbanization people experienced as the Industrial Revolution took hold had weakened their loyalty and attachment to their communities and group affiliations (social integration). As a result of these changes, he contended, some of these people became somewhat dehumanized, detached from the community and the group support mechanisms they had previously enjoyed. They became confused and alienated and were more likely to engage in various forms of behavior harmful to themselves including, in extreme cases, suicide.

Durkheim's general hypothesis was that the degree of *social integration* in a society or group (independent variable) was inversely related to suicide rates (dependent variable). In other words, the higher the degree of social integration in a society or social group, the lower would be the expected suicide rates. As specific indicators of social integration, he used measurable independent variables such as religious affiliation, marital status, degree of economic stability, and parental status. Some of his hypotheses are summarized below:

> Catholics (who have a stronger church affiliation) should have lower suicide rates than Protestants.
> Married persons should have lower suicide rates than single people.
> Married persons with children should have lower suicide rates than married persons without children.
> Times of economic prosperity should be accompanied by lower suicide rates than times of economic instability (Durkheim, 1966).

When the data Durkheim gathered were statistically analyzed, the results confirmed many of his hypotheses, including the examples given. He concluded that the social bonds people have or do not have in their social affiliations affect the way they act in times of personal crisis. In most cases, those with the strongest social affiliations (social integration) are least likely to take their own lives, because they have more social supports than those with weak affiliations. In addition, the social norms under which they operate are more clearly defined. Not only were Durkheim's findings significant in furthering our understanding of such factors as social integration and suicide, but the way in which he stated his hypotheses, gathered his data, and analyzed the findings have furnished us with a model for conducting much of what makes up sociological research today (Durkheim, 1966).

STEP 4: PLANNING THE STUDY

So far we have examined the first three steps involved in moving through the scientific research cycle—Step 1: Statement of the research problem, Step 2: Review of the literature, and Step 3: Statement of hypotheses. Step 4 has to do with planning the study or the *research design,* one of the most fascinating and critical components of scientific research.

The Concept of Research Design

In the process of conducting a sociological study, the research design represents the decision by the researcher to use a particular method in making scientific observations. The scientist, like the average citizen and consumer, wants simply to "find out" and will use a variety of strategies in order to do so. Earl Babbie (1983) in addressing this topic has this to say:

> Suppose, for example, that you want to find out whether a particular automobile—say the new Burpo-Blasto—would be a good car for you. You could, of course, buy one and find out that way. You could talk to a lot [of] B-B owners, or talk to people who considered buying one and didn't. You might check the classified ads to see if there were a lot [of] B-Bs being sold cheap. You could read a consumer magazine's evaluation of Burpo-Blastos, or other ways. The same situation occurs in scientific inquiry (p. 27).

The particular method used in sociological study depends on a variety of factors. What is the nature of the research problem? How much time and money are available as resources to be used in the study? Where does the research need to be conducted—locally, two thousand miles away, or perhaps in another country? How accessible and cooperative are the people being studied likely to be? These and several other questions must be considered when developing a plan for how observations are to be made. Although there are several types of research designs that may be used, three of the most prevalent ones used by sociologists are the survey, the experiment, and field research.

The Survey

The survey approach uses questionnaires to gather information about people's attitudes and their social behavior. Sociological surveys take a variety of forms, including face-to-face and telephone interviews (in which typically a questionnaire is read to a respondent), and questionnaires either administered in person or mailed to large numbers of people with stamped return envelopes. Advantages include (1) efficiency and

The survey approach sometimes involves face-to-face or telephone interviews. At other times, a questionnaire may be administered in person to a group of research subjects or sent to them through the mail.

© Rob Marmion, 2009. Used under license from Shutterstock, Inc.

low cost; (2) the gaining of information that can be easily be generalized to a larger population; and (3) flexibility, in that several different kinds of questions can be asked. Disadvantages include (1) a format that does not allow in-depth answers and (2) a "snap-shot" view of reality, in which answers to questionnaires often portray largely what the subjects were feeling at the time of the study (Black and Champion, 1976). Sociological surveys are used in a variety of applications, including certain forms of demographic research such as census taking; public opinion polls on social, economic, and political issues; and studies conducted on employee morale and job satisfaction in industry.

When sociologists use the survey approach, they are very careful to examine the research instrument (questionnaire) for validity and reliability. A questionnaire or survey has *validity* if it measures what the researcher hopes to measure. *Reliability* has to do with the consistency or repeatability of the information gathered. Thus, a questionnaire would be reliable if each time it was administered to the same or similar group of research subjects, the results were about the same.

Populations and Samples In survey research, the total group of people, events, or things being

examined or observed is called the universe or *population*. A population could be represented by all registered voters in a county, all civil disturbances in the United States each year between 2005 and 2015, or all marriage records contained in a municipal courthouse. In most cases of sociological research, however, the population is the total group of people with specific characteristics being studied. The characteristics that define the boundaries of a research population usually include such factors as geographical location and time frame. For instance, a population that a criminologist uses for research purposes might consist of all males between eighteen and twenty-five years of age convicted of felony property offenses in the state of Ohio between the years 2005 and 2015.

In some studies, it is feasible to use an entire research population as a source of observation, particularly when the numbers of people involved are less than four or five hundred. In these cases, many researchers prefer to use the entire population. However, in instances where numbers are large and an entire population is not readily accessible, it is permissible to use a sample, a smaller number of people taken from the larger population being studied.

In scientific research, it is essential to use a random sample, a sample chosen in such a way

The major television networks use the results of stratified random sampling to predict which presidential candidate will carry certain states on election night.

© Stephen Coburn, 2009. Used under license from Shutterstock, Inc.

that every member of the larger population being studied has an equal chance of being included. If, for example, a sociologist conducted research on all public school teachers in the state of Texas during the 2014–2015 school year, the large size of the research population (over 100,000 teachers) would necessitate the use of some sort of random sample. Through the use of random sampling, findings could be generalized to the total population from which the sample was drawn. By contrast, a similar study of teachers in Livingston, Texas (less than 100) would make use of the entire population of teachers who live and work there.

When carried out correctly, survey research can offer a sophisticated method of analysis. In this regard, there are several different types of random sampling approaches. One is the stratified random sample, a random sample chosen in such a way that certain characteristics of the population being studied are represented in accurate proportions. In network coverage of the presidential election returns on election night, news commentators will project winners in certain states with only a few percentages of the votes counted. This is done through stratified random samples taken of certain chosen precincts cumulatively in each state in the weeks and days leading up to the election that accurately reflect the different constituencies within the voting population. These data are then assessed in conjunction with exit polls of voters conducted in the same sampled precincts the day of the election.

Sampling Problems: Bias and Error When sampling is not carried out with precision, there are usually significant amounts of bias and error. An unscientific or biased sample is one that involves a lack of random selection and, in some cases, self-selection by the participants. Examples would include straw polls, on-the-street interviews, phone-in responses, and letters to the editor that, while sometimes interesting, have little or no scientific value because their findings cannot be generalized to a larger population. They are representative only of the people who participated by furnishing information.

In Alfred Kinsey's research on sexual behavior, conducted in the 1940s, there was significant sample bias because he solicited volunteers who responded to newspaper ads and who were paid for furnishing their sexual histories. About one-half of the men used in his survey were from only one state, Indiana, and were predominantly well-educated and middle to upper middle class. Consequently, his subjects were not representative of

Americans in general (Kinsey, Pomeroy, and Martin, 1948).

The chief result of using a biased sample in survey research is sampling error, the degree to which characteristics of a sample do not represent those of the population from which it was drawn (Borg and Gall, 1979). In the 1948 presidential election, Harry Truman, the Democratic incumbent, ran against Thomas Dewey, a formidable Republican. The major polls listed Dewey as ahead, and on election night, with the final results undecided, some newspapers (including the *Chicago Tribune*) printed headlines announcing Dewey's victory. The next morning, many people were surprised to learn that Truman had been reelected president. The pollsters had stopped sampling voters far too soon before the election to account for shifts in attitudes in the closing weeks of the campaign. They had also used telephone surveys. In 1948, because a significant proportion of the American population still did not have phones, the predictions were skewed and the margin of sampling error was significant. Today, however, sampling techniques are greatly improved with a margin of error, in most cases, of only about 3 percent (Davis and Smith, 2005).

The Use of Interviews Sometimes, sociologists and other social researchers make use of an interview in conjunction with or instead of a group-administered or mailed questionnaire. An *interview* involves the direct questioning of research subjects by an investigator. One form is the *structured interview* in which the interviewer reads a set of predetermined questions to a respondent in which the answers are limited to yes or no, a set of predetermined answer choices, or a fill-in-the-blank response (e.g., "Would you call yourself a Democrat, Independent, or Republican?"). The advantage to this approach is that interviewers often do not need to be degreed professionals and the little training required can be completed in a brief period. The *unstructured interview* approach allows the respondent to answer freely in his or her own words. This requires a much more highly trained and experienced interviewer, often with professional credentials. In such cases, the interviewer knows what general areas need to be covered but also can "bore in" and use the responses of the research subject to ask more in-depth, follow-up questions. The less the researcher knows about details of the topic being explored, the more unstructured the interview might be, particularly in the beginning. In this sense, the interview might begin with this question: "Tell me about . . . ?," which places the respondent in the role of teacher. However, the researcher controls the pace, flow, and direction of the interview and knows how to establish the needed rapport with the respondent by respecting and protecting their key rights while obtaining needed and valuable information to better understand a given aspect of human behavior (Weiss, 2004).

The Experiment

The Greek philosopher Aristotle, once argued that a heavy object, when dropped from a great height, would fall at a much greater speed than would a much lighter object. Yet, for almost two thousand years, no one, including Aristotle himself, ever bothered to empirically test this idea. During this long period, mathematicians developed a formula that basically said that the speed at which an object fell was largely a function of weight. Consequently, a two-pound object would fall at twice the rate of a one-pound object, and a five-pound object would fall five times as fast. Finally, as legend has it, a young Italian professor named Galileo (1564–1642), one day in 1591, dropped a one-hundred-pound cannon ball and a one-pound cannon ball from the top of the leaning tower of Pisa at the same time. This experiment and others that followed demonstrated that objects fall through space at about the same rate of speed, regardless of weight. Such studies by scientists during the late sixteenth and early seventeenth century marked the beginning of the experimental method (Butterfield, 1957).

Sociologists today sometimes use the experiment as a research design. However, instead of comparing the actions of two cannonballs or other objects, they compare the behavior of two groups of people. Specifically, an experiment consists of a study in which two matched groups of people are compared in terms of how they act in a specially designed social situation. Both groups are examined to see how they act or perform in relation to an identified dependent variable that is the focus of the study. One group, called the experimental group, consists of subjects exposed to a particular independent variable. The other group, called the control group, is not exposed to the independent variable. The two groups are then compared with each other to determine whether the variable that was supposed to change (i.e., the dependent variable) did so because of the impact of the independent variable on the behavior of the experimental group.

Study Skills and Student Grade Performance: A Sociological Experiment Suppose a sociologist decides to study the grade performance of over two thousand randomly chosen students enrolled in their first semester at college. In this case, grade performance would represent the dependent variable. One-half of these students (the experimental group) are then randomly chosen to be exposed to a study skills seminar called "Effective Study Skills: A Step-By-Step System for Student Success" or ESS. Exposure to ESS would then represent the independent variable. This is done after midterm grades are computed, which are then used as the basis of comparison. The other first semester students (the control group) are not exposed to this independent variable. At the end of the semester, the grade performance of the two groups are compared to see if exposure to and implementation of the ESS study system (independent variable) made a difference in the end-of-semester grade performance (dependent variable) of those in the experimental group as compared with the control group (Semones, 1991).

Research similar to this actually was conducted by the author in 1979 and 1980 and again ten years later on a larger scale in 1989–1990. Students randomly chosen to attend the seminar in ESS (the experimental group) were further divided into two subgroups after the seminar and tracked to measure their end of semester performance. Experimental Group 1 (EXG-1) consisted of those who merely attended the ESS seminar and who showed no evidence afterward of having implemented the entire system. Experimental Group 2 (EXG-2)

consisted of students who demonstrated implementation of the entire study system through a special tracking mechanism built into the system called Diagnostic Follow-up. The results showed that those in EXG-1 had only marginal improvement at best. However, students in EXG-2 generally reported significant and, in some cases, dramatic improvement in their grades (Semones, 1991).

Structured Environments and Social Behavior: Zimbardo's Experiment Experiments are often used by sociologists and other social scientists to test how the structure of social environments impacts human behavior. In a much-publicized experiment, social psychologist Phillip Zimbardo (1972) and colleagues at Stanford University attempted to see how the social environment of a prison affected the behavior of guards and prisoners. They placed an advertisement in a local newspaper for students willing to work as paid research subjects for two weeks. Twenty-four "mature, emotionally stable" students were chosen for the experiment and, at the flip of a coin, were divided into two groups, "prison guards" and "prisoners." The basement of a campus building was converted into a "prison," and those chosen to be prisoners were unexpectedly "arrested" at their homes by "police officers," handcuffed, then transported to the "prison" on campus by "patrol car."

The experiment had to be abandoned after only six days, however, because the students were so affected by the "prison" environment that they lost the capacity to differentiate between the role-play and reality. They actually turned into guards and prisoners. Zimbardo, in commenting on this, said,

> There were dramatic changes in virtually every aspect of their behavior, thinking, and feeling. In less than a week, the experience of imprisonment undid (temporarily) a lifetime of learning; human values were suspended; self-concepts were challenged, and the ugliest, most . . . pathological side of human nature surfaced. We were horrified because we saw some boys (guards) treat others as if they were despicable animals, taking pleasure in cruelty, while other boys (prisoners) became servile, dehumanized robots who thought only of escape, of their own individual survival, and of their mounting hatred for the guards (1972, p. 243).

The Hawthorne Effect One potential problem in experimental research with human subjects is the Hawthorne effect, a temporary change in the behavior of people in a group because of the presence and influence of outsiders. During the 1920s and 1930s, Elton Mayo and his associates (Roethlisberger and Dickson, 1939) conducted research at the Western Electric Company to study the effect of working conditions on employee productivity and morale. At the company's Hawthorne plant in Chicago, they first set out to ascertain the workers' normal rate of output in what was called the bank wiring room. A "bank" was a set of switchboards; it was determined that the work standard for each worker was to complete wiring of two banks per day.

Once this standard of expected output had been established by the scientists for a control group, an experimental group consisting of several women was separated from the larger group of bank wirers. While working conditions for the larger control group remained the same, several changes—one at a time—were introduced into the work environment of the experimental group. However, it did not matter in what area the change was made—work breaks, lighting conditions, the length of working hours, the length of work week, production goals—production increased with each change.

This puzzled the researchers at first and they thought the study had failed. It had failed in its original intent, because the research design was flawed. The presence of the researchers "tainted the data" in that it emphasized to members of the experimental group that they were being studied and were, therefore, "special." By being segregated from the other workers and made to feel special, members of the experimental group developed greater degrees of cohesion and friendship, which in turn led to mutual reinforcement and greater productivity.

In addition, the special way they were treated influenced them to try and please the researchers by being "good" research subjects. While managers in large-scale organizations can use insights derived from this and other related research to maintain and improve morale and productivity among participants, the results of the Hawthorne studies also have implications for social research. Consequently, sociologists and other social scientists must take care that their presence does not influence research results. By being as unobtrusive as possible in conducting social research—especially with experiments and field research—they can minimize the Hawthorne effect.

Experiments: Advantages and Disadvantages The experimental approach has certain advantages as well as some potential drawbacks. Unlike the survey, which gathers information about the social world as it exists naturally, the experiment involves intentional manipulation of one or more independent variables. This makes the experimental approach superior in some situations because of its ability to measure more precisely the cause-and-effect relationship between specified independent and dependent variables (Simon and Burstein, 1985). In addition to its ability to be controlled, the experiment has the added advantage of being easy to replicate should a researcher find it useful to do so. Disadvantages include the probable overuse of college students, who are readily available as research subjects, and the problem of artificiality in some experimental situations.

Field Research: Participant Observation

The method known as field research involves the study of certain forms of social behavior within their natural settings. Field research techniques take a variety of forms and are referred to by such names as the case study, the in-depth interview, the community study, and participant observation. Field studies are largely descriptive or qualitative in nature, whereas surveys and experiments typically are more explanatory and stress quantitative measurement. The field approach is particularly useful when little is known about certain social phenomena or when certain forms of behavior do not lend themselves easily to quantification through surveys or experiments. Areas examined through field research include deviant behavior, nonliterate foreign cultures, and "campus demonstrations, courtroom proceedings, labor negotiations, public hearings, or similar events taking place within a limited area and time" (Babbie, 1983, p. 245). These forms of social behavior are perhaps best studied, at least initially, within their natural settings (McGuire, 2002).

Participant Observation   One of the most fascinating forms of field research is participant observation, an approach in which the researcher actually joins the group being studied in order to obtain an inside view of social behavior (Crossman, 2013). By gaining admittance to and actually participating in the group under investigation, the sociologist is able to obtain both a depth and breadth of understanding not possible with many surveys and experiments. This technique allows the sociologist the intimacy of an inside view, gaining knowledge of how people perceive their social world, and how they think, feel, and act in it (Dewait and Dewalt, 2002).

Playing the role of imposter and sometimes even disguising one's true identity is neither new nor limited to the field of sociology. During ancient Muslim times, it was rumored that Harun al-Rashid, the caliph (king) of Baghdad, often wore the disguise of an average citizen, and sometimes a beggar, in order to observe firsthand the mood and behavior of his subjects. A story in modern literature familiar to many is *The Prince and the Pauper,* in which the little prince swaps identities with a street urchin. Novelist John Steinbeck (1939) lived for a time in a migrant worker camp in order to understand more fully the people he wrote about in *The Grapes of Wrath.* In the world of modern espionage, the United States and several other countries have agents posing in the guise of diplomats and embassy workers, who live and work in the country of the "enemy" to gather information about the other side.

Other scientific disciplines also make use of participant observation. The late anthropologist Margaret Mead was a pioneer in the use of this research approach. During the 1920s and 1930s, she lived among and studied several non-Western tribal cultures in portions of the North and South Pacific. Her comparative studies of family structures and sex roles in simple societies in the

Admiralty Islands, New Guinea, and Samoa are regarded as classics in anthropological literature. More recently, the research of primate anthropologist Jane Goodall has given us much of what is now known about the social behavior of lower primates, particularly chimpanzees. Since the 1960s, she has devoted her professional life to living among and gathering data on chimpanzees at great sacrifice and, at times, risk to her personal safety. A colleague of Goodall's Dian Fosse, was murdered while pursuing similar research on gorillas in Africa.

Weber's Influence: *Verstehen*   In sociology, participant observation has its roots in Max Weber's concept of verstehen, or empathetic understanding. By "walking in the shoes" of different types of people in various social situations, the sociologist is able to understand what Weber called social action at the individual, group, and community levels. This approach was also used in the pioneering research of "Chicago School" sociologists during the 1920s, which included Nel Anderson's (1923) study of hobos and Frederic Thrasher's (1927) analysis of gang behavior.

Goffman's Undercover Work in a Mental Institution   More recently, there have been other classic studies, such as sociologist Erving Goffman's (1961) study of the "underlife" that patients in a mental institution experienced apart from the conventional roles played out in doctor–patient relationships. Goffman essentially went underground and worked for a year as an assistant athletic director in a mental hospital where he could "snoop" around the wards, get to know the patients, and study the hospital as a "total institution" without interference. He found that patients in such a totally controlled environment developed their own subculture, through which they were able to manipulate and deceive the staff and gain some personal control over their own lives.

Griffin and Halsell: Racial Group Impersonation   Obviously, participant observation research can be both intriguing and potentially dangerous. Two studies in modern sociological literature that illustrate this involved two Caucasian journalists, a man and a woman, who each conducted separate observations in different parts of the country and at different times. Both of them underwent medical treatment to temporarily darken their skin in order to pose as black people.

John Howard Griffin (1961), on assignment for *Sepia* magazine, was assimilated into the black subculture of the deep South during the fall of 1959 and lived and traveled through the region as a black man for several weeks. In a daily journal he kept, he was able to document his experiences at the hands of white society and furnished a penetrating portrait of the pervasiveness of white racism at this time in a published book titled *Black Like Me*. When his research became known, his life was threatened, racists hung his effigy from a streetlight in his home town, and a cross was burned in his yard.

Almost a decade later, Grace Halsell (*Soul Sister*, 1969) replicated Griffin's study and spent time living as a black woman in both Harlem and the deep South. Like Griffin, she underwent treatments to darken her skin. She too kept a journal and made numerous observations about what it was like to be black and live in a white-dominated society during the late 1960s. During much of this experience, she worked as a maid in white households and was once sexually assaulted by "the man of the house."

Participant Observation: Advantages and Potential Problems   Like surveys and experiments, participant observation studies have their pluses and minuses. This approach is very useful in studying social behavior among people who either lack the sophistication to draw sociological insights about their own behavior or are unwilling to share such information because of their own vested self-interests or deviant status. In addition, because of the large amount of time and energy spent by the researcher in making contact with the subjects of such a study, a picture of group processes can be obtained in greater depth than through other types of studies that tend to take place over a relatively short period of time.

However, these very advantages pose certain problems, such as maintaining scientific

John Howard Griffin, a white journalist, used the participant observation approach to pose as a black man in the deep South during the civil rights era and wrote a book about his experiences.

© Bettmann/Contributor

objectivity in light of such intense contact, and the ethical problems that sometimes occur. For instance, should subjects be told that their new member is a sociologist conducting research? In some cases, this should be done, while in others, to do so would result in altered or uncooperative behavior by those being investigated. In all instances, however, the sociologist must guard against any individual or group being injured or damaged by such research (Babbie, 2013).

Research Design in Perspective

For the sake of clarity, two points should be made. First, the research designs just discussed—the survey, the experiment, and field research (participant observation)—are only representative, not exhaustive, in describing the richness and diversity of sociological research. Other approaches are also used, which include content analysis, the case study method, etc.

Some sociologists, for instance, make use of content analysis, a research design in which the content of communication is studied to assess its impact on social attitudes and behavior. Like the historian, the sociologist may examine a variety of existing sources including government records (census data, laws, court decisions, and reports), popular written communication (newspapers, magazines, and advertisements), and literary, artistic and entertainment media (novels, plays, paintings, and sculpture, motion pictures and television, and so on). Data derived from content analysis may tell us much about the nature of a given society as well as how it changes over time. Take television programming for example. How is its content today similar to or different from that of television in the 1950s? What does this tell us about American society? Which values, priorities, issues, and social patterns have remained essentially the same? Which have changed, and why? As the structure of American families changed during the last half of the twentieth century, so did its portrayal in situation comedies. Throughout the 1950s and early 1960s, *I Love Lucy, Leave it to Beaver, Father Knows Best* and a myriad of other shows painted a fairly idealistic picture of the traditional nuclear family with a

breadwinner father, homemaker wife, and one or more school-aged children. But by the mid 1960s through the 1970s, family life became portrayed differently as in *The Andy Griffith Show* (single dad Andy, son Opie, and great aunt Bea), *The Brady Bunch* (blended family), and *All in the Family* and *Maud*, which portrayed young adult offspring—married or single—returning home to live with their parents. By the 1980s and 1990s, we were observing the Huxtables on *The Bill Cosby Show* (a two-career, upper-middle black class family) and the Bundys on *Married with Children* (a lower-middle class, dysfunctional, traditional nuclear white family) and by 2014, the comedic antics of a real family in Louisiana were portrayed weekly in a reality TV series called *Duck Dynasty.*

The content in motion pictures has also changed in concert with changes occurring in the larger American culture. In 2003, the movie *Kill Bill* was the number one box office hit in the United States for several weeks in a row. Using it an example of a very violent film with an R rating, the author chose to conduct an analysis of this motion picture using the content analysis approach. During approximately 110 minutes, the heroine, played by actress Uma Thurman, proceeded to slice-and-dice 93 people in an orgy of bloodletting, killing 76, most of them up-close-and-personal with a Hattori Hanzo samurai sword. What does this motion picture and others with women as violent protagonists—such as *Charlies' Angels: Full Throttle* (2003) and *Monster* (2003) (which won Charlize Theron the Oscar for best actress for portraying serial killer Aileen Wuornos) tell us, if anything, about changing gender roles in American society, how women see themselves compared with previous times, and how they are perceived and treated by society?

As a second point, the various research designs used in scientific research, as illustrated by the approaches just discussed, are not mutually exclusive. Instead, they sometimes overlap with two or more approaches being used in the same study or different phases of the same study. The basic principle here is that sometimes two or more research methods, when used together, may yield more precise results than one method used alone. As an example, it is not uncommon for sociologists to use a broad-based survey involving hundreds of people in combination with a few in-depth interviews or case studies (Simon and Burstein, 1985).

STEPS 5–7: OBSERVING, ANALYZING, AND REPORTING

The scientific enterprise is much like building a house. The first three steps—Statement of the Research Problem, Review of the Literature, and Statement of Hypotheses—are analogous to planning and preparing the site of the project in terms of what is to be built (or studied), where it will be constructed, and who will be involved. Step 4, the Research Design, answers the "how" question by providing the blueprint for the completion of the project. Once that blueprint or research design has been established, then what remains is simply a matter of carrying out and completing the study, analyzing the results, and reporting the findings.

Step 5: Making Observations (Collecting Data)

After the research design has been fully decided on, the planning phase is over and it is time to carry out the study by making observations. This data collection phase represents Step 5 in the scientific research cycle and, in most cases, must be carried out as set forth in the research design in order for the results to be valid.

One important consideration in implementing any study is its time frame. How much time is required to complete the study and make all necessary observations? If a study is broad-based and takes place over a brief period of time, it is a cross-sectional study. Many surveys and experiments are cross-sectional studies. Observations in such studies are usually gathered within a period ranging from a day or two, to a few weeks. In the middle 1970s, for example, a team of sociologists conducted a national survey of life satisfaction in a sample of 2,702 American

households. It found that among other things, married people were happier than single individuals (Campbell, Converse, and Rogers, 1976). A longitudinal study, by contrast, is focused on a single group of people over an extended period of time. Many such studies take several years to complete. In a study completed in the late 1970s, sociologists spent nine years tracking 2,000 randomly chosen high school freshmen to study the factors that accounted for their career choices five years after graduation from high school (Bachman, O'Malley, and Johnson, 1978).

Step 6: Analysis of the Findings

Once the observations have been made and all data collected according to the specifications of the research design, it is time to carry out the analysis of the findings, a determination of whether or not the hypotheses set forth in the study were supported by the information that was gathered. This is Step 6 in the scientific research cycle. In sociological research, such analysis usually involves the use of statistics, mathematical procedures that describe the characteristics of variables and explain or measure the relationships among them. Statistical analysis in survey research typically involves establishing the degree to which an independent variable is associated or correlated with the dependent variable.

Correlation   One statistical test used by sociologists in survey research is a measure of association or correlation. A correlation refers to the simultaneous occurrence of two variables together in a particular type of relationship. In other words, where you find one, you find the other in a particular type or direction or association. A particular change in one is accompanied by a specific type of change in the other. Correlations may be either positive or negative and may range from 11.00 (100 percent positive) to 21.00 (100 percent negative) between two factors or variables (Babbie, 2013).

Suppose, for example, researchers in a particular study found a 2.80 (negative) correlation between amount of education (independent variable) among Italian Americans and their degree of racial prejudice focused on Chinese Americans (the dependent variable). This would mean that, among Italian Americans, one could predict the dependent variable or effect (their degree of prejudice against Chinese Americans) 80 percent of the time by knowing their amount of education (the independent variable). In other words, there would be an 80 percent probability that those high in formal education (independent variable) would be low in racial prejudice focused on this group (dependent variable). By knowing the independent variable (the causal or influencing variable), one could predict the occurrence of the dependent variable (the effect) most of the time.

Spurious Correlation The appearance or correlation of one variable with another does not mean, in and of itself, that the two are causally related. Therefore, it is also important to determine the probability that a correlation between two variables is due to chance.

In this regard, sociologists and other social scientists must be careful not to accept a spurious correlation, the simultaneous occurrence of two variables caused by a third or intervening variable. For example, in some parts of the United States, when the consumption of ice cream in the population goes up, so does the sexual assault rate. There is over a 90 percent positive correlation. However, just because these two factors are highly correlated does not mean that one causes the other. What we have here is a spurious correlation. The intervening third variable in this case is the climate. Sexual assault rates are highest in the summer months. The fact that people also eat the most ice cream during the summer months—as far as sexual assault rates are concerned—is a coincidence, or a serendipitous finding.

A Test for Statistical Significance To guard against the acceptance of spurious correlations, sociologists conduct a statistical test called a test for statistical significance. This is a measure designed to determine the likelihood that the correlation found between two variables was due to chance. In this regard, the standards for acceptance of any correlation found in sociological research are very high. In social research, if there are more than five chances out of one hundred (5 percent) that the relationship (correlation) found between an independent and dependent variable is due to chance or sampling error, the results typically are seen as inconclusive and are thrown out. This high standard of acceptability in statistics is referred to as the *.05 level of statistical significance.*

Presentation of the Data In addition to determining whether or not the hypotheses in a study are supported through the use of statistical tests, the analysis of the findings also involves *summary and presentation of the data.* The findings of sociological research, particularly with surveys and experiments, are often summarized and presented in the form of tables, graphs, and charts. The use of these devices furnishes the reader with a logical and visually clear means of fully understanding what was found. The results of statistical analysis are also summarized at the bottom of such graphic displays.

Empirical Generalizations *Empirical generalizations* refer to the process by which inductive reasoning is used to move from the specific observations made in the study to general conclusions or generalizations concerning a larger social process or group of people and their behavior. By using a random sample, for example, the findings of a study can be generalized to apply to the entire population from which the sample was drawn. For example, in political polling, a stratified random sample of people (perhaps 1,200 voters) is drawn from all U.S. registered voters likely to vote. Each respondent is asked: "Who would you vote for if the election were held today?" Based on the scientific way in which such polls are conducted, an empirical generalization is made and the public can see how an election would have been determined had the election been held on the day the sample was taken.

Step 7: Reporting the Results

Do you remember the analogy we used in which the scientific research cycle was compared to the face of a watch? Just as the minute hand of a watch approaches the twelve at the top of the circle to begin the hour-long journey again, *reporting the results* of research (Step 7) signals the completion of the scientific research cycle. This, in turn, adds to the state of theory (knowledge) and sets the stage for future research.

Sharing the Findings of Research The process of *reporting the results* of sociological research usually involves publishing a study or a summary of it through one or more academic sources. Results of research, therefore, are shared in a variety of ways. A summary of the results of doctoral research in sociology are reported in *Dissertation Abstracts,* an index resource available in every major university library in the United States as well as other research libraries, such as the Library of Congress. In addition, much of the most important sociological research is summarized in article form and published by a variety of professional journals in sociology. Some of the more prominent publications include the *American Journal of Sociology,* the *American Sociological Review, Social Problems,* and the *Journal of Marriage and the Family.* In addition, the American Sociological Association and other regional sociological societies hold annual conventions where the results of research are presented as professional papers, and are discussed and critiqued by sociologists at roundtable discussions and group forums.

The Impact on the State of Knowledge With the completion of each scientific research cycle, a new page is added to the library of sociological knowledge. The results of some studies represent "blind alleys" that add nothing per se to what is known about a certain aspect of social behavior. Yet, such findings tell us where not to look next time and aid sociologists in narrowing down the possibilities in terms of getting at cause-and-effect relationships. Other studies are groundbreaking in significance, such as Durkheim's work on suicide and Goffman's research on "total institutions" previously mentioned. They act as powerful beacons that point the way for others to follow. Most research efforts, however, add tiny increments of information in creating a grand

mosaic of understanding about the human condition. In this sense, sociological research is truly cumulative, with those engaged in science today building on the legacy created by those who came before and then setting the stage for those who will follow tomorrow.

RESEARCH ISSUES AND TRENDS

As exciting and rewarding as sociological research is and can be, it carries with it some serious and sober responsibilities. Unlike the geologist who studies rocks, the chemist who works with chemical compounds, and others in the physical sciences, the sociologist (1) is a part of the subject matter he or she studies and (2) deals with human beings instead of physical matter. This means that special care must be taken to ensure objectivity in the research process and to ensure that certain safeguards are used to protect the rights and sensibilities of human research subjects.

Ethical Issues

Much has been written about the medical experiments conducted on Jewish prisoners in Nazi concentration camps during World War II. Yet, on a much smaller scale, similar research has occurred in the United States. Between 1932 and 1972, the U.S. Public Health Service conducted biomedical research on 400 black males infected with syphilis who were living in poverty in Alabama. The purpose of the study was to examine the long-term effects of the disease. During this forty-year period, the government provided these men (and 200 non-syphilitic black males used as controls) with "free" medical treatment.

However, they were never told they had syphilis nor were they ever treated for it, even though penicillin had been available as an effective treatment since the early 1950s. Approximately one-third of these men died from the disease while the study was in progress. This research was finally brought to light by the Alabama advisory committee to the U.S. Commission on Civil

"Tumbleweeds" cartoon by Tom K. Ryan.

Rights, which characterized it as involving "violations of basic human rights" (*Los Angeles Times,* May 13, 1973; Part 1A, p. 6).

During the early 1960s, the U.S. Army budgeted over six million dollars to study conditions relating to social and political unrest in Latin American countries. Several sociologists, economists, and political scientists were employed to do much of this research, which became known as Project Camelot. The strong implication given by the name "Camelot" was that the United States was trying to find ways to encourage progress in certain South American countries without violence and possible human rights violations.

When it became obvious that the results of this research would be shared with South American dictators such as military dictator General Pinochet of Chile and used to quell dissension and unrest, a public outcry arose in Chile and other South American countries and among social scientists in the United States. The results of this furor led to a cancellation of the project by the U.S. government in 1965 (Horowitz, 1967; Sjoberg, 1967).

In the wake of "Camelot," a debate developed among many in the social science community about the propriety of conducting certain types of social research without specific safeguards. In 1968, a committee of the American Sociological Association developed a code of ethics to govern social research. The code was formally adopted in 1971 and revised in 1980 and, most recently, in 1997. Its fundamental principles include the following:

1. Value research subjects rights to privacy and dignity.

2. Shield research subjects from personal harm.

3. Ensure confidentiality.

4. Make use of informed consent regarding information gathered on research subjects or when their observed behavior takes place in a private setting.

5. Give proper credit to research collaborators and assistants (American Sociological Association, 1997).

Even given the ethical guidelines enumerated above, sociological research can involve some delicate choices between the rights of individuals, the rights of society, and the need to know by the social scientist. The rights of individual privacy and anonymity must be acknowledged and protected. However, some forms of sociological research, such as experiments or participation, usually require some degree of deception or the lack of full disclosure on the part of the researcher. To do otherwise would invalidate the findings, because people would not act or interact naturally. In this regard, sociological researchers generally agree that any behavior carried out in public may be studied (even if those being observed do not like it), as long as the researcher maintains confidentiality by not revealing the identities of those being studied.

> Some of the richest material in the social sciences has been gathered by sociologists who were true participants in the group under study but who did not announce to other members that they were using the opportunity to collect research data. "... It would be absurd ... to insist as a point of ethics that sociologists should always introduce themselves as investigators everywhere they go and should inform every person who figures in their thinking exactly what their research is about" (Erikson, 1967, p. 368).

The Challenge of Scientific Sociology

To study human social behavior systematically and do it well is not an easy task. Sociologists as scientists must stay abreast of the latest developments in their fields of specialization and in sociology as a whole. They must also maintain their objectivity in working with human subjects, yet at the same time hold fast to a *code of ethics* through which the fundamental rights of those same research subjects are protected.

Social scientists working for agencies and organizations as employees or consultants must also guard against the pressure to endorse blindly the self-serving positions or policies of such employers in how they plan their research, carry it out, and report the findings. The danger here is co-optation. Sociologists, more than anyone else, understand the power of organizations to shape behavior and, therefore, must strive to maintain the integrity of objective science.

Sociologists as researchers are often placed in the position of being "damned if they do and damned if they don't." Indeed, Robert K. Merton (1959, pp. xv–xvi) maintained that sociologists are often placed in a four-way bind. When their research shows that what many people think is the "obvious truth" is indeed supported by the

evidence, they are seen by some as terrible bores who do little more than place fancy names on simple things that people already know about and understand. When the results of their investigations support an unpopular view, they are sometimes lambasted as heretics or troublemakers. When their studies demonstrate that what was unlikely to be the case is indeed not true, they may be perceived as fools for questioning "common sense." And when their findings result in facts that appear to be unbelievable, they are denounced by some as charlatans whose aim it is to deceive.

In spite of all this, sociologists as scientists have no foreknowledge of what is true or untrue, and what is popular or unpopular is of little or no concern. Their task is to find out "what is" in an objective and systematic way, and to disseminate this knowledge to others. This is their primary imperative or mission, which is accomplished basically through the process outlined in the preceding discussion.

As a science, sociology consists of a never-ending series of research cycles in a variety of specialty fields. Through the scientific research process, each sociological study is completed. What we now know about human social behavior has come about through the completion of thousands of such cycles. Consequently, sociologists engaged in research today are standing on the shoulders of those who, through their research efforts, laid the foundation for what is now known. And those engaged in sociological investigation today will be the pathfinders who will take us through the twenty-first century. This sociologi-cal pilgrimage is bound to involve traveling some rocky roads at times for those who sign on for the trip. However, the scenery and experiences along the way promise to be very exciting. And the destination—an increased understanding of the human condition—is the magnificent obsession of all who call themselves sociologists.

Chapter 6

Explaining Society: Sociological Theory

By the 1700s, two thousand years after the death of Plato, several of the physical sciences had emerged and reached maturity. Galileo had invented a telescope and, most likely, had conducted the first true scientific experiment. Sir Issac Newton had made key contributions by discovering some key laws of physics. Human biology was beginning to develop as scientists began to acquire a modern understanding of the body and, with this knowledge, began to trace the causes and treat the symptoms of disease. Students in schools called academies were being trained not only in the Socratic method and Aristotelian logic but in the methods of the physical sciences as well. Some of these students and those who came after them would later, during the nineteenth century, become the founders of a new science called sociology.

Quiz 2:
103-124

Emile Durkheim.
"Social facts."

© Bettmann/Contributor

Emile Durkheim

Emile Durkheim (1858–1917) was a French sociologist whose thinking, along with that of Karl Marx and Max Weber, represented one of the three great "watersheds" of sociological thought during the nineteenth century. His ideas formed much of the basis for the development of functionalism, a dominant theoretical perspective in sociology today.

Durkheim's Perspective: Social Determinism Durkheim's view was that society, rather than the individual, should be the unit of analysis in the study of social behavior. Through this perspective, he became the first behavioral scientist, in effect, to take a principle in the physical sciences, the *principle of synergy* (i.e., the whole is greater than the sum of its parts), and apply it, by extension, to human behavior. Durkheim's restatement of the principle of synergy as applied to human behavior was in essence: Society as a whole is greater than the sum of its parts—the individuals that interact within it. Society and the social conditions it generates shape individuals and determine to a significant degree the way they think, feel, and act. In Durkheim's view, social groupings of people at various levels of society produce their own environments apart from and in addition to the individuals that make them up. These environments, in turn, shape our behavior, as in (to use modern examples) peer group pressure among some teens to take certain drugs, influence derived from a crowd's actions to stand up and cheer at a ball game, or the presence of a police patrol car influencing us to apply less pressure to the accelerator or to buckle our seatbelt.

Sociology as the Study of Social Facts Durkheim argued that sociology should be seen essentially as the scientific study of social facts. Social facts represent things or events external to the individual, such as customs, that have the power to shape behavior. These phenomena are generated by groups and are, therefore, independent of individuals who may find themselves under their coercive power. Take, for example, your behavior this morning as you left your home, got in a car, and headed for school or work. Did you lock the door to your home? Do you do so regularly? Do you regularly lock your car doors as well? If you do, why do you engage in such behavior? Could it be that something called "crime" is in the air and custom dictates that you "lock up" your home and car? If Durkheim were alive today, he might say that the social fact of crime causes people to lock their homes and cars in some communities and societies, just as a social fact called the lack of crime results in people not "locking up" in other communities or societies.

Durkheim's Organic Analogy Durkheim devoted most of his professional life to exploring and researching the nature of social facts and their impact on social behavior. He studied the nature of social order, the manner in which the division of labor in society is organized, and other diverse fields, including the nature of religion in simple societies. In *The Division of Labor Society* (1893), he used an organic analogy to study social cohesion or solidarity in nonindustrial versus industrial societies. By doing so, he established much of the foundation for what would emerge as the functionalist perspective in twentieth century sociology.

Durkheim's organic analogy deserves mention here. Influenced by Auguste Comte's ideas, Durkheim was very concerned about social order and stability. Like Spencer, Durkheim developed an organic analogy although he developed it to a much more sophisticated level than his colleague. His organic analogy is summarized as follows: A society is similar to a biological organism in that both biological and social organisms consist of major components (organs in the body; institutions in a society) that work together to produce a stable and healthy system.

First to Use Statistical Analysis In his book *Suicide,* published in 1897, Durkheim was the first sociologist to make use of statistical analysis. In doing so, he chose to examine suicide as a social problem. Due to this seminal research, he was awarded the first sociology professorship to be established by a university in France. In both his methodology and theoretical contributions, Durkheim appears to "embody what has proved to be conceptually most distinctive in the field and most fertile in its contribution to other disciplines. Durkheim, it might be said, is the complete sociologist" (Nisbet, 1965, p. 1).

The Concepts of Social Integration and Anomie In Durkheim's view, an orderly and stable society is one characterized by social integration. This is a social condition in which most people in a community or society basically agree on social rules (norms) and values, which cause them to feel socially connected and secure as a result. This, in turn, causes them to feel a sense of belonging and connectedness with family, friends, and community. Such a sense of belonging and social consensus is not only psychologically satisfying but also forms much of the glue that makes social stability and harmony possible.

In his book *Suicide,* Durkheim pondered this question: "Why are suicide rates much higher in modern, urban, industrial societies as compared to small, rural, village-focused societies?" He found part of the answer in the concept of anomie, which he coined and defined. Anomie, Durkheim asserted, is a state of confused norms or normlessness, brought about by rapid change

or social complexity. When a person is placed in a social situation in which norms are absent or confused, he or she feels disconnected from family, friends, and/or the community of society that surrounds them. This, in turn, can result in a sense of confusion and alienation, and depression can then set in. This, in turn, can lead to various forms of maladaptive behavior including suicide when people feel their "cultural rug" has been yanked out from under them and do not know what to do or where to turn.

The Stock Market Crash of 1929: A Classic Example The numerous suicides by several middle- and upper middle-class men in the wake of the stock market crash of October, 1929, provide an example. Having lost everything in the economic collapse that followed, the social integration of these men became compromised, they became socially disconnected, and the resulting anomie overwhelmed them psychologically. Their role of family breadwinner stripped from them and their masculine identity compromised, these men saw suicide as the only way out. Using Durkheim's analysis, it is clear that anomic suicides still occur today in the even more complex world of the twenty-first century.

The Katrina Effect: A Modern Application A recent example of the results of anomie occurred in the aftermath of hurricane *Katrina,* which breached the levees and flooded most of New Orleans when it made landfall August 29, 2005. Despite warnings by the National Weather Service 72 hours before the storm hit, local, state, and federal government officials essentially took a "wait and see" approach instead of mobilizing and implementing a coordinated, proactive plan.

The consequences in the aftermath of the storm can now be called the Katrina effect, an unnecessary expansion of social breakdown (anomie) caused when authorities charged with maintaining social stability fail to act decisively when a known, sudden change is imminent and/ or after a disaster occurs. The immediate reaction by President George W. Bush when Katrina hit was to say, in effect, that no one could have predicted it. Yet, experts cited in the *Houston*

Chronicle predicted such a breach of the aging levees in 2001, "the New Orleans Times-Picayune predicted it in 2002, . . . the National Geographic magazine . . . predicted it in 2004" and even experts in the Bush administration in published documents saw it as one of three potential major disasters (Wallerstein, 2005, p. 1).

In the case of *Katrina*, the collective indecisiveness, lack of a timely proactive response, and, in several instances, gross incompetence by government officials at all levels had dis-astrous human consequences. While most citizens who were middle to upper class were able to evacuate themselves, thousands of poor, handicapped, and elderly people were trapped inside the city by the floodwaters and could not get out. Because the National Guard, U.S. military personnel, and other relief agencies did not arrive in force for several days after Katrina hit, a state of pervasive and growing anomie enveloped New Orleans and social order broke down.

Desperate for food, water, and other essentials, hundreds of citizens—in a state of fear and confusion—panicked and engaged in the wholesale looting of grocery and department stores to feed and supply themselves and their families. Without the presence of adequate law enforcement and emergency military personnel to maintain order, the criminal element in significant numbers rampaged over the city stealing large-ticket items such as electronics from stores, breaking into houses, stealing cars, assaulting citizens with impunity, and generally creating an environment of mayhem. Despite the fact that Mayor Ray Nagin ordered a mandatory evacuation of the city two days before the storm, officials at the state and federal levels mounted only a tepid response until several days later when CNN and other major news agencies—broadcasting continually from New Orleans before, during, and after the storm hit—recorded and publicized to the world many aspects of this disaster (Wallerstein, 2005). America's allies responded by offering $854 million in cash and other resources for disaster relief. But nearly two years later, only $40 million had been collected and used by the U.S. government, the rest "delayed by

Karl Marx. "Class conflict."

Courtesy of the Library of Congress Prints and Photographs Division

red tape and bureaucratic limits on how it can be spent" (Solomon and Hsu, 2008, p. 1).

Karl Marx

Another major figure in nineteenth-century sociology was Karl Marx (1818–1883), the German philosopher and political economist. Marx was a controversial figure in his time and remains so today. Though German by birth, Marx lived in several countries before settling in England. Since he wrote in many subject areas—history, economics, philosophy, political science, and sociology—he did not accept the title "sociologist" or any other academic label. Instead, Marx saw himself primarily as a social activist dedicated to using the tools of science not only to understand the social world but also, in the Platonic sense, to change it for the better. He was particularly critical of what he felt was the "evil" and "exploitative" nature of modern capitalist institutions and societies. His most fervent wish was to see capitalist societies undermined and replaced with socialistic, social systems which he felt were more equitable.

Marx's Perspective: Class Conflict Marx essentially was an economic determinist who viewed all human history as a series of class struggles related to the economic means of production. In two works primarily, *The Communist Manifesto* (1848), co-written with Friedrich Engels, and *Das Kapital* (1867, 1894, 1907), completed by Engels after Marx's death, he set forth his main ideas. Throughout human history, he asserted, perpetual conflict had existed between the "haves" (those with economic and political power) and the "have nots" (those lacking in economic resources and power).

During the Middle Ages in Europe, this conflict was between the feudal lords and landed gentry and the peasant serfs who sharecropped the land. Because the aristocrats owned all the land, the peasants were left with little choice than to farm the land in exchange for enough of the crop yield to barely feed themselves. In the Industrial Age of the nineteenth century, the haves and the have nots were represented by the bourgeoisie and the proletariat, respectively. The bourgeoisie consisted of the capitalist owners of industry who made profits from exploiting the labor of the workers. The proletariat consisted of the workers, the exploited class, who subsisted on wages that were no higher than necessary for survival.

Marx's Flawed Prediction Marx predicted revolution. In his view, the proletariat in emerging industrial societies would develop *class consciousness* by fully realizing how and to what extent they were being exploited. They would then become alienated against the capitalist system of production and overthrow the bourgeoisie in a revolution that might be violent in some societies while relatively bloodless in others. This, in turn, would usher in a new era in human history in which, because of the sheer efficiency of industrial production, class conflict would no longer be necessary. Consequently, a classless form of society would ultimately emerge—communism—that would be devoid of class conflict. In such a society, Marx envisioned a social system in which people would work according to their abilities and receive according to their needs.

Marx's romantic vision of a classless society in a world of plenty brought on by industrialization was seriously flawed on two counts. First, to date communistic countries with Marxist governments have not met most criteria for success as judged by the historical record. His views did form the ideological basis for the emergence of the Soviet Union, which, with its totalitarian system of government, failed miserably. Born out of the proletarian revolution in Czarist Russia during 1917, the Soviet confederation finally collapsed and broke apart under the weight of its own bureaucratic inefficiency in 1987 followed by the fall of the Berlin wall shortly thereafter. In a world where everyone was paid about the same wages, there was no incentive to excel; those with energy, creativity, and an entrepreneurial spirit had their efforts quashed. In other parts of the world, communism at best has experienced limited success. The price paid for this oppressive form of government by the people who have lived under its rule have been threefold: (1) the loss of personal freedoms such as speech, press, and assembly, (2) a relatively low standard of living with a scarcity of housing, goods, and services, and (3) little or no opportunity for upward social mobility.

Second, Marx was incorrect in his predictions for several industrial countries, particularly for the United States. Indeed, there was mass exploitation of industrial workers in America at the hands of the capitalist owners of industry during the last half of the nineteenth and first part of the twentieth centuries. Marx failed to anticipate, however, the rise of the labor movement in America and the eventual success of labor unions in gaining economic and social power, which resulted in greatly improved working conditions and increased pay and benefits for workers.

Marx's Contributions to Sociology Nonetheless, his preoccupation with the questions of power and conflict furnished a firm foundation for the emergence of the conflict perspective in modern-day sociology. Various groups, organizations, and institutions do indeed compete with one another for rewards, particularly those in short supply. How they acquire power, the forms that power takes, and the consequences of how it is used affect the lives of rank-and-file citizens in a multiplicity of ways—politically, economically, and socially. How this takes place forms the basis for modern conflict theory in sociology today.

Max Weber

The last of the great theorists of classical sociology was Max Weber (1864–1920), a German legal scholar and economist. Unlike Durkheim (social facts) and Marx (class conflict), Weber concentrated on the interaction between individuals and their social situations.

Weber's Perspective: Behavior as Active Interpretation According to his assessment, people in general are not automatons who blindly follow social conventions as dictated by their society. This former view was at least partially set forth by Durkheim, who asserted that, for most of us, our thoughts, perceptions, and behaviors are largely the product of the society in which we live. Weber offered a different perspective. Instead of just being passive recipients of one world view, Weber argued, most people actively interpret the social world around them based on their own particular experiences with it.

Sociology as the Study of Social Action In Weber's view, sociology is the study of social action, the meaning people assign to their own behavior and their relations with others and society, and how this personal assessment of reality affects their own behavior and that of others. According to Weber, individuals and groups interpret reality based on their previous social experiences and the cultural context within which they live. To use a modern example, suppose a small dog walks by. If it is observed by an American, this animal probably will be perceived as a pet. If it is observed by a Vietnamese, the dog may be perceived as a meal. For the sociologist, a dog is neither a pet nor a meal, nor is it, as many male Koreans believe, a special delicacy that, when eaten, enhances sexual potency. Sociologically, the dog as a "cultural object" must

be interpreted in terms of its cultural context. The same principle applies to people. Each of us is influenced by our own cultural context and our particular experiences with it. For example, most Americans see monogamous marriage as "normal" while, in some cultures, polygamy is the preferred form of matrimony for both men and women. Yet, even within our own cultural framework, how each of us experiences "family" is based on our interactions with our social environment.

Sociology's Challenge: Verstehen Weber asserted that, for anyone who aspires to be a sociologist or to think and observe the world sociologically, the challenge is to develop verstehen, an empathetic understanding of how individuals and groups perceive the social world and their place in it. If, for example, you are a white male sociologist and you want to understand women, African Americans, Hispanic Americans, Asian Americans, the elderly over 80 or any other culture or subculture, you must be able to get inside their frames of reference, understand their social experiences and/or ethnic backgrounds, and see the world from their cultural experience of it. By being able to, in effect, "walk in their shoes" or look at the world through their eyes, the information and insights gathered from such an approach equip the observer, whether a sociologist or a student of the sociological approach, with one form of the *sociological imagination*.

The Importance of Value Neutrality Weber was among the most prolific of the early sociologists in his ideas and research efforts. Like Durkheim, he felt the necessity to use statistical analysis in the study of social behavior where possible. However, he differed sharply from Comte and Marx who espoused a social activist orientation in their sociology. Weber asserted that sociological analysis should include the study of human values as part of its subject matter (value relevance), but that the sociologist as a scientist must remain value-free or ethically neutral in matters of research methods, social policy, and reform. Thus, value neutrality was an essential part of his perspective. Sociologists, like all other human beings, have their own prejudices, opinions, and preferences. However, when they put on the hat of scientist, they must leave such biases at the door and be driven by where the evidence takes them. In addition, Weber asserted, to be a social scientist you must be able to change your views when evidence, objectively gathered, does not support it.

Other Contributions by Weber: An Overview In one of Weber's prominent works, *The Protestant Ethic and the Spirit of Capitalism* (1905, 1977), he correlated the development of capitalism as an economic system with the tenets of Protestant religion, particularly the work ethic contained in Calvinism. In his last book, *Economy and Society* (1922), published two years after his death, he traced the historical development of authority or leadership forms and the development of modern bureaucracies. Weber's ideas acted as forerunners of those developed by Charles H. Cooley (interactionism) and Talcott Parsons (functionalism) during the twentieth century (Timasheff, 1967).

One of Weber's most valuable contributions was his development of the ideal type concept. An ideal type is a conceptual model of something used as a basis for comparing phenomena as they actually exist. Take "urban" as an ideal type, for example. In this sense, urban is used in its ideal form as a mental or pure type to which to compare real societies and communities. If one were to use this device to analyze communities in the United States, Chicago, Illinois would be plotted much closer to the ideal type of "urban" than would Bristol, Tennessee or Liberty, Texas.

TWENTIETH-CENTURY SOCIOLOGY

While sociology as a formal discipline had its theoretical beginnings in Europe, it developed into a full-fledged science in the United States during the twentieth century.

The Emergence of American Sociology

Two Founding Mothers: Martineau and Addams During the nineteenth and early twentieth centuries, American sociology had its beginnings in the work of several social commentators, scholars, and activists. Of these luminaries, two in particular should be included under the description of "Founding Mothers," Harriet Martineau (1802–1876) and Jane Addams (1860–1935). The first of these founders, Harriet Martineau, was not an American but an Englishwoman who visited the United States and made detailed observations of its people. She is best known as the author of *How to Observe Manners and Morals* (1838), the first book ever published on social science research methods. Jane Addams, both a scholar and social activist, published articles in the *American Journal of Sociology* and also was awarded the Nobel Peace Prize in 1931 for her humanitarian work in helping to establish several programs to aid disadvantaged and depressed women and children (see Box 6–1).

Emphasis on Social Reform: Sumner, Ward, and Du Bois As American sociology took root and moved into the twentieth century, its founders

W. E. B. Du Bois
Reform-oriented sociologist.

Photo by Cornelius M. Battey, 1918.
Courtesy of the Library of Congress Prints and Photographs Division.

Box 6-1

The Development of Sociology: Two Founding Mothers

From its beginnings, sociology has benefited from the contributions of women, both as scholars (pure sociology) and as activists (applied sociology). Two notable early contributors to the emerging science of society were Harriet Martineau and Jane Addams.

Harriet Martineau.
"Comte's translator."

© Bettmann/Contributor

A contemporary of Auguste Comte, Harriet Martineau (1802–1876) was an English sociologist best known for her translation of Comte's work into English. However, she was a capable scholar in her own right. Martineau made extensive observations of social life both in her native England and in the United States. Her travels and studies in America served as the basis for her highly detailed *Society in America,* a book about American social customs. Another of her works, *How to Observe Morals and Manners* (1838), is considered the first book ever written on sociological research methods. In honor of Martineau and her contributions, a professorship in sociology has been established in her honor at the University of Massachusetts.

American sociologist Jane Addams (1860–1935), although a capable scholar, preferred the role of social activist, for which she was awarded the Nobel Peace Prize in 1931. An early and active member of the American Sociological Society, she published in the *American Journal of Sociology* and was offered a position at the University of Chicago. Instead, she cofounded Hull House in 1889, a Chicago commune consisting of women intellectuals and activists who provided housing for the disadvantaged and depressed, and worked for various social reforms, using sociological data in an applied fashion. Largely because of her efforts, social legislation was passed that improved the juvenile justice system, created safer work environments, provided social services for the poor, and improved public sanitation.

Yet Addams faced an uphill battle on two counts. First, she was a woman in a male-dominated culture that considered it "unladylike" and perhaps abnormal for a woman to be a social activist. Second, during a time when sociology was trying to gain legitimacy in the scientific community as a "respectable" science, applied research and social activism were not seen as appropriate activities by most in the academic establishment.

Jane Addams.
"Social Activist."

Photograph by Lewis Wickes Hine from the records of the Child Labor Committee, courtesy of the Library of Congress Prints and Photographs Division

Lienhard, J. H. 2008. "Only a Theory." *Engines of Our Ingenuity.* Episode No. 1531: A radio series broadcast each weekday on KUHF FM Radio, Houston Texas. For additional information consult: http://www.uh.edu/engines.htm

and early proponents—as represented by William Graham Sumner (1840–1910), Lester Frank Ward (1841–1913), and W. E. B. Du Bois (1868–1963)—largely embraced an activist approach in examining social life. William Graham Sumner taught the first sociology course offered at an American University (1875) and authored *Folkways* (1906), an influential treatise on early cultures. Lester Frank Ward, the first president of the American Sociological Society (1906), did much to popularize sociology through his writings, including *Dynamic Sociology* (1883), and through his lectures. In addition, he sought to break sociology into two major subdivisions, *pure sociology* (research aimed at increasing knowledge for knowledge's sake) and *applied sociology* (the use of sociological findings to reform and improve society). In their work, these early American sociologists showed themselves to be spiritual descendents of Comte in that they stressed a social reform orientation focused on solving social problems at societal, community, and organizational levels.

Another of the early reform-oriented sociologists during the early twentieth century was W. E. B. Du Bois (1868–1973). He became the first African American to complete a doctorate at Harvard University in 1895. After completing postdoctoral work in sociology and economics at the University of Berlin under the tutelage of Max Weber, he returned to the United States in 1897 and received an appointment to the faculty at Atlanta University. There he remained for most of his academic career. Du Bois devoted most of his efforts toward the study of race relations in the United States during the decades following the Civil War. His most important books on this subject were *The Philadelphia Negro: A Social Study* (1899) and *The Souls of Black Folks* (1903). Along with Jane Addams and other reformers, he founded the National Association for the Advancement of Colored People (NAACP), which grew to represent a key social action arm of the civil rights movement a half-century later and remains influential today (Stark, 1989; Schaefer, 2008). Du Bois is widely regarded today as the Father of African American Sociology.

1920–1940: Dominance of the "Chicago School" The reform perspective characteristic of American sociology reached its zenith during the 1920s and 1930s, led mainly by sociologists at the University of Chicago, where the first graduate programs were established. There, a unified school of thought in the spirit of Addams, Ward, Sumner, and Du Bois developed—the "Chicago School"—which focused on the study of everyday life and community and urban problems.

At the University of Chicago, the emphasis in sociological research and practice came to be centered on the effects of rapid urbanization and the various forms of social disorganization—termed social deviance—that occurred as a result. Such a reform orientation achieved its most sophisticated and widespread acceptance in the two decades leading up to World War II.

Prior to this time, the prevalent view regarding maladaptive or antisocial behavior was that such behavior originated from internal sources, such as biological makeup. According to the biological model, the person who violated the norms of their community or society did so because of an immoral or defective physiological makeup, personality, or character. This came to be the central argument of psychiatry, which arose during the first few decades of the twentieth century as a specialty field within medicine. This view remains a cornerstone of mainstream psychiatry with its focus on "mental illness," "treatment," and "cures" for maladaptive forms of behavior. While psychiatry does retain a legitimate place in the professions in terms of being able to effectively treat some people with organically based behavioral maladies, mainstream behavioral sciences today—most notably psychology and sociology—see most behavioral problems as mental disorders and not "disease," problems in living, and/or forms of deviant behavior.

By contrast, the central thesis of the "Chicago School" was that the major causes of social problems—including poverty, crime, delinquency, mental disorders, and drug abuse—stemmed from external causes that originated in the structural makeup of society that had changed dramatically as a result of the industrial revolution. Various forms of social disorganization seen mainly in large cities were the product of rapid urbanization and the stressful, impersonal, and fast-changing environment that it imposed on people's lives (Renzetti and Curran, 1998).

1940–1965: The Rise of "Systemic Theoretical Sociology" From about 1940 until the mid-1960s, the emphasis shifted away from the social problems and reform orientations of the Chicago School toward the development of comprehensive theoretical perspectives. This conservative shift from social activism was focused primarily on the development of comprehensive scientific models of how societies operate at all levels that could be tested empirically. As this occurred, modern orientations such as structural functionalism (macrosociology), conflict theory (macrosociology), and symbolic interactionism (microsociology) reached full expression through the contributions of sociologists at more than a dozen major universities, mainly on the east coast (Semones, 1990). Although some sociologists (e.g., C. Wright Mills and

Howard Becker) retained an activist orientation and bitter divisions arose between the scientific theoreticians and the social activists, sociological theory began maturing during this period and set the stage for the decades to come (Becker, 1967; Lipset, 1994).

1965–Present: Diversity and Globalization Over the past half century, changes in sociology, both as a science and as a practice, mirrored those occurring in both American society and other parts of the world. During the 1960s and 1970s, social reform and activism were in the air, as reflected in the civil rights movement, the war on poverty, protests against America's military involvement in Vietnam, and the rise of American feminism. Against this backdrop, "the number of American sociologists rose from 3,000 to 25,000 and sociology became the largest single academic major in many colleges and universities" (Lindsey and Beach, 2000).

With the shift toward conservatism from 1980 until well into the 2000s, people in the United States experienced eight years (1981–1989) under Ronald Reagan and twelve years (1989–1993; 2001–2009) with both George H. W. Bush and his son George W. Bush. Quite predictably, the fortunes of sociology as a college major—a questioning and debunking discipline by its very nature—waned. As people became cynical about the integrity of their leaders and the likelihood of meaningful social reform in the wake of both Watergate (the Republicans under Nixon) and the impeachment and disbarring from the legal profession of a President (the Democrats under Clinton), Americans as a people turned inward. Quite predictably, the alienation this spawned in the form of the "me" generation lead to a declining visibility and interest in sociology and a significant increase in the numbers of students majoring in business and psychology. However, with the election of Barack Obama as President in 2008 and his reelection in 2012, there were signs that a shift in public opinion toward social reform might be occurring.

Because social, economic, and political trends periodically reverse directions and occur in cycles, likewise the direction in which sociology is moving and its relevance are continuing to evolve and improve (Crossman, 2013). In the wake of changes occurring in American society in terms of gender roles, the interest in feminist theory within sociology is growing. As the population continues to age—as reflected in the large numbers of "baby boomers" (those born during 1946–1964) reaching retirement age—an increased interest also is being shown in social gerontology, the study of aging. And, as witnessed by such trends as (1) international terrorism, (2) the globalizing of the world's economy, and (3) the growing evidence of global warming and its threat to human populations in the near future, a global approach to the use of sociological methods and findings is becoming increasingly relevant and necessary.

Consequently, the sociological perspective is poised for a resurgence in popularity as more and more leaders around the world realize its indispensable value as an approach in both understanding the world and in better addressing and solving its growing problems. With that in mind, we will now examine the three major paradigms or perspectives dominant in contemporary sociology—functionalism, conflict theory, and interactionism—in order to better understand the social world around us, as well as how it might be changing in the future (Table 6–2).

Functionalism

Primarily a Macrosociology Perspective Structural functionalism, or functionalism as it is often called, refers to the analysis of the various parts of society (family, government, education, and so forth) in terms of how they function to promote social order and harmony. In other words, functionalism studies the various structures in society—its major institutions—in terms of how they operate to maintain a state of social order or equilibrium. Rooted in the work of Auguste Comte, with his identification of major institutions in modern, emerging, industrial societies, and Emile Durkheim, with his organic analogy, functionalism focuses primarily on a macrosociology approach (Lindsey and Beach, 2000).

Table 6-2

Three Major Sociological Perspectives

Sociological Perspective	Key Founders	Central Premise	Level of Analysis
Functionalism	Talcott Parsons Emile Durkheim	Order and stability	Macrolevel
Conflict Theory	Karl Marx	Conflict and change	Macrolevel
Interactionism	Max Weber	Perception drives behavior	Microlevel

Basic Premise: Order and Stability   According to functional analysis, the natural state of affairs in society is order and stability. A healthy society, therefore, is seen by functionalists as a stable and harmonious one. This preoccupation with social order and harmony is easy to understand when we consider the cultural milieu experienced by the intellectual fathers of functionalism—Spencer and Durkheim. Each grew up in France during the aftermath of the French Revolution and were deeply concerned about the disruptive effects of social disorganization.

Founders and Later Contributors   This theoretical approach, which originated in the work of Auguste Comte, Herbert Spencer and, to a greater degree, Emile Durkheim, became a dominant perspective in sociology throughout the twentieth century. Comte's preoccupation with order and stability—impacted, no doubt, by his exposure to the instability that characterized France in the aftermath of the French Revolution—was an influence on both Spencer and Durkheim, who each used the organic analogy as they compared a human society to a living organism. A society as a structure has specialized parts—institutions—that function and interrelate for the smooth operation of the whole, just as specialized organs in the body function to create equilibrium in the physical organism.

This approach was developed and expanded in large part by Talcott Parsons in *The Structure of Social Action* (1937), *The Social System* (1951), and *Toward a General Theory of Action* (1951).

Functional analysis was later refined by one of Parson's students, Robert Merton, in several works, most notably *Social Theory and Social Structure* (1968).

Two Types of Functions: Manifest and Latent   According to this approach, each of the various parts or institutions in society contains functions, benefits that result from a particular social structure or activity that help to promote social order and harmony. In this regard, there are two basic types of functions: manifest and latent. Manifest functions are intended and recognized consequences or benefits that characterize certain parts of society, such as the family (reproduction, socialization, the satisfaction of affectional needs, etc.) and education (career preparation and personal growth). Others are latent functions, which are unintended and unrecognized consequences (benefits) that result from the various parts of society. Latent functions usually are not obvious and occur as an extra benefit from participation in certain aspects of society. For instance, mate selection may occur at college although higher education was never designed for this purpose. In similar fashion, the family as an economic unit of consumption supports the toy industry and much of the construction industry.

The Role of Dysfunctions   Sometimes there are dysfunctions, negative and disruptive consequences that stem from a structural component of society. Examples would include deficit spending within the government or violence and divorce in the family. When such disruptions occur, modifications (social reforms) in the way such social structures are organized may be used to reestablish order and equilibrium. For example, sociological research strongly indicates that, if most engaged couples would complete premarital counseling from a qualified, certified, and licensed marriage and family counselor/therapist, the American divorce rate could most likely be reduced by half.

Criticisms Aimed at Functionalism As the historically dominant approach in modern sociology, functionalism has come under a great deal of criticism in recent decades. Some argue that it is far too conservative in orientation and thus convenient to those wishing to maintain the status quo. This argument centers on the assertion that what is seen as positive and harmonious for one segment of society may be seen as negative and dysfunctional for another. Functionalists counter with the assertion that in any society, there is basic consensus concerning what is seen as important, such as "family" in Mexican culture and "equal opportunity" in American society.

Another related criticism accuses functionalism, with its emphasis on consensus, of being inadequate in accounting for social change, particularly in highly technological societies such as the United States. Functionalists attempt to defend their perspective by saying that order and harmony in society take the form of a dynamic equilibrium. Consequently, there is order in society that evolves and adjusts constantly as society changes.

Conflict Theory

Primarily a Macrosociology Perspective Although the emphasis in functionalism is social order and how it is maintained, the conflict perspective focuses on change. Specifically, modern conflict theory represents the analysis of conflict and power as they relate to social policy and change within society. Although many social observers over the centuries have written on conflict and power, conflict theory as a sociological perspective originated in large part from the work of Karl Marx and his emphasis on class conflict between the "haves" and "have nots" in modern society.

The conflict approach originally was conceived as a macroperspective. Since that time, however, Marx's economic determinism has been broadened to include the analysis of conflict in all its basic dimensions—economic, political, and social—at all levels of society. Sociologists use this perspective today to examine a variety of issues, from types of social conflict and the forms they take, to the ways in which power is acquired and concentrated in society.

Basic Premise: Conflict and Change The basic premise of conflict theory is this: The natural state of affairs in society is conflict and a struggle for power among competing groups. Conflicts, for example, may exist between basic institutions such as church and state, between and within organizations such as political parties or major corporations, or between different subcultural groups including those distinguished by age, gender, race or ethnicity, sexual orientation, or position on social issues. In addition, some societies contain many interest groups, each of which competes with others for power and influence in shaping the social policies that affect the lives of all society members.

While the conflict approach has long dominated sociology in certain portions of Europe, it has gained prominence in the United States only since the 1950s and 1960s. Stimulated in part by the tumultuous events taking place in American society during that time, C. Wright Mills is credited with establishing the conflict perspective in the mainstream of American sociological thought through his controversial book, *The Power Elite* (1956), and other works. Mills, among his other contentions, argued that power in America was concentrated in the hands of a few leaders in the military, business, and government. Because of the work of Mills and other conflict theorists, including Lewis Coser (1956) and Ralf Dahrendorf (1959), conflict theory is now regarded as an increasingly viable approach in examining social behavior at all levels of society.

Interactionism

Primarily a Microsociology Perspective While functionalism and conflict theory are more amenable to analyzing the large structural building blocks (institutions) that make up society as a whole, interactionism is largely a microperspective. Its primary value lies in its ability to furnish insight about social behavior at the interpersonal, local, and community levels of society.

Symbolic interactionism, or interactionism as it is more commonly called, focuses on the personal meaning people assign to the social world around them and how they communicate these perceptions to others through language. This orientation was foreshadowed to some extent by the contributions made by Max Weber and his emphasis on the subjective nature of social life. Consequently, men often have a different perception of the roles of husbands and wives than do many women; rank-and-file workers typically see the world of work with a different set of priorities than do members of management; and Republicans perceive political reality in a way very distinct from Democrats.

Basic Premise: Perception Drives Behavior Stated very succinctly, the underlying proposition of interactionism is this: Perception drives behavior. People tend to act, for the most part, on their perceptions of reality. The emergence of this orientation in modern sociology was based to a significant degree on the contributions made by Weber and his emphasis on the subjective nature of social life. Weber asserted that each person looks at social life through his or her own perceptual screen shaped by unique personal experiences with the outside world. Because people from different cultural and family backgrounds have had different and often unique interactions with their social situations, they tend to look at the world and their place in it through their own experiential lens or spectacles.

Early Popularizers: Cooley and Mead The two most prominent founders and popularizers of the interactionist approach were both Americans, Charles Horton Cooley (1909, 1964) and George Herbert Mead (1934). Cooley (1864–1929), a sociologist at the University of Michigan—and later the University of Chicago—developed a concept that has been called the "looking-glass self." In his view, human beings, through their social encounters, develop their own distinct personal identities. We constantly assess and reassess how we imagine others see us. Our "identification" of how we think others see us then impacts our own self-image and how we then project ourselves to others in our social relations.

Mead (1863–1931), a member of the Chicago School, stressed how our acquisition and use of language affects our development of a self-image, as well as our ability to interact successfully with others. He argued that our thoughts and perceptions can be shared with others only through the use of language. This capacity to think and communicate symbolically is what separates us from the lower animals. Through symbolic communication with others, we develop a self-concept and learn to accept the way others view the world and how we must act in order to succeed in it. By interacting with and observing the roles of others and how they carry them out, the developing child then models this behavior by learning to play out social roles that Mead called role taking.

Later Contributors As the twentieth century progressed, other interactionists added to the perspectives furnished by Cooley and Mead. Herbert Blumer (1957), for instance, studied crowd behavior and people's tendency to redefine a social situation and act in certain ways when exposed to various types of crowds. Through a process called social contagion, crowds often spread their perceptions of reality to others, who then become caught up in the spirit of the moment and sometimes get caught up in mobs and even riots.

Another interactionist, Erving Goffman (1961, 1967), studied how the social roles people play, along with the scripted behaviors that go with them, affect the way people perceive reality and then act as a result of those perceptions. Consistent in the work of contemporary interactionists is the view that life in a society represents a "constructed reality" in which people share essentially the same worldview, interpretation of symbols, and definition of reality.

TWENTY-FIRST CENTURY SOCIOLOGY: A GLOBAL PERSPECTIVE

With the twenty-first century now fully upon us, the future of sociology promises to be one of increased growth and change. Given the shrinking size of the world in an era of instant internet communication and the increasing interdependence of the world's socie-ties in numerous ways, the information revolution is fundamentally changing the way we live and how social scientists are analyzing, assessing, and evaluating such changes.

Sociologists from around the world will need to approach social structures, social policy, and cultural systems not from the limitations of a classical nineteenth century European perspective or the twentieth century American view, but from a twenty-first century global perspective. To do so effectively, they will need to open dialogues with each other from across the boundaries of their own countries and cultures. As this occurs, they will learn from each other and develop some consensus regarding the nature of the postmodern world and how to better understand the place of humankind in it.

Sociological theory will continue to grow and diversify as we come to know more about the social world around us. Different methods of sociological investigation and measurement will emerge and become increasingly more sophisticated and diverse. The role of the sociologist will also continue to evolve. One indicator is that the new generation of sociologists appears to be increasingly eclectic in the use of the three major paradigms within the discipline—functionalism, conflict theory, and interactionism. Rather than choose one over the others, these new scholars possess the flexibility to see the value of each paradigm or a combination of paradigms as the research or applied situation dictates. In addition, they often are able to consider and use additional theoretical perspectives to better understand the many intricate and nuanced aspects of human social behavior at all levels of society.

As sociologists become more secure in their status as scientists, the issue raised by Weber of remaining value free and ethically neutral probably will become less of a debate. The sociologist as researcher must, of necessity, remain value free in his or her role as research scientist. However, the use of applied, clinical, or "public sociology" approaches at various levels will also become more prevalent and necessary as more sociologists become involved in matters of public policy and social reform.

Ultimately, the future of the science of society will depend on the development of great theorists in the tradition of Durkheim, Marx, and Weber, and, more recently, Mead, Parsons, and Mills. It is probable that some of these future theorists are already in school. Who knows? One of them might be you or one of your classmates taking this course. It all begins with something called the sociological imagination.

Chapter 7

Dividing the Ranking: The Functions and Effects of Stratification

The Conflict Perspective

While functionalists argue that stratification is beneficial to society because it matches individuals with the greatest skills to positions requiring the greatest expertise, conflict theorists take an opposite view. The conflict perspective sees stratification as harmful to society because it allows those with the most power, prestige, and wealth to dominate and exploit the less advantaged and maintain a condition of inequity.

Marx: Origins of the Conflict Approach The conflict perspective on stratification originated with the work of Karl Marx during the nineteenth century. As you will recall from our discussion in Chapter 6, Marx argued that human history is largely a chronicle of class struggles that have existed in every age between two basic groups, the "*haves*" and the "*have nots*." The "haves," whether they are represented by the feudal lords of the Middle Ages or capitalists of modern times, comprise the ruling class, whose members possess most of the power and wealth. The "have nots," as represented by feudal serfs and modern factory workers, are the economically dispossessed with

little or no hope for the future. In Marx's view, human history has consisted of a continuous cyclical process in which the tyranny and exploitation practiced by each ruling class ultimately led to its overthrow by the "have nots," who then became the new ruling class.

Marx viewed social class strictly in economic terms as related to the means of production. Those who owned the means of production were the ruling class, and those who worked for the owners were the "have nots." In the modern industrial era, he predicted the "have nots," whom he named the *proletariat*, would realize that they were being exploited, develop *class consciousness*, and overthrow the ruling class or *bourgeoisie* in a revolution that might be peaceful in some societies and violent in others. Then, he asserted, the sheer efficiency of industrial production would create such an abundance, that further class conflict over scarce resources would be unnecessary, the public would own the means of production and a truly classless society would emerge. Although Marx's notion of a proletarian revolt did not materialize in most societies and his ideas were far too simplistic by modern standards, his perspective was a powerful one and his ideas regarding the importance of power established an important foundation for further sociological exploration.

Modern Conflict Theory Since the 1950s, American sociologists have greatly expanded Marx's narrow economic perspective on conflict. One characteristic that distinguishes conflict theory from functionalism is its emphasis on the impact of social structure on stratification rather than on individual factors such as training and talent. Some conflict theorists, for instance, might argue that no woman or black person, regardless of ability, could have been nominated for—much less elected to—the presidency of the United States before 2008 because of the social and political inequities built into the structure of American society. Others, like Ralf Dahrendorf (1959), have examined how various groups such as unions, companies, and a multitude of interest groups compete with one another for political as well as economic power. Organizations like Mothers Against Drunk Driving (MADD) and the National Education Association (NEA), for instance, have no ownership in the means of production (as in Marx's view), but nonetheless wield a significant amount of political power.

LIFE CHANCES AND STRATIFICATION

Social rank profoundly influences both our general attitudes and our behavior. This process begins with early childhood socialization in which, because of the accident of birth, the social stratum that our family occupies significantly affects how we come to view the world and our place in it. In American society, children from different social classes develop distinctive value orientations. Working class adolescents, for example, must decide whether or not to go to college after high school graduation. Among upper middle-class teenagers in general and certain ethnic groups including several Asian American subcultures, not going to college is rarely considered an option because of the way they are socialized by their parents. Instead, their key decision

has to do with which college to attend. Upper middle-class and upper-class teens, for example, often are focused on choosing a college during their junior year of high school and often apply to several colleges during the fall and early spring of their senior year through a process called early admission. For adolescents occupying the lower social classes, such patterns of behavior are much less prevalent.

Differential Life Chances and Their Indicators

The Concept of Life Chances Stratification also affects what Max Weber termed life chances, the opportunities for survival and prosperity in society. These life chances which, together, determine in large part the way a person will live and what social mobility, if any, he or she will experience are identified and studied carefully by sociologists.

Life Chance Indicators In the United States and elsewhere, life chances significantly impact on both the length and quality of life. Take *life expectancy* as one example. The higher one's social class, the longer one's life expectancy tends to be, according to numerous studies. Infant mortality, for instance, is much higher among the poor (Gortmaker, 1979; Mare, 1982), and overall mortality rates as well as rates of specific diseases like cancer are also higher among the poor (Shai, 1986). Americans in the middle and upper classes are better fed, housed, and educated, and this contributes to longer life expectancy. They also have much better access to adequate *health care* than their less affluent counterparts. Although public assistance programs, such as Medicaid, have helped narrow the health care gap significantly, these programs tend to serve only those living in the most dire circumstances, such as the elderly, the disabled, and those living in single-parent households. The underemployed "working poor," who constitute the majority of people living in poverty, tend to have little or no health insurance and, consequently, receive only sporadic medical attention at best.

Another indicator of differential life chances is nutrition. Families with middle-class incomes spend about 15 percent of their income on food as compared with 35 percent spent by families with incomes below the poverty line (Gallo, Zellner, and Smallwood, 1980). The more affluent also pay less than the poor for food items because they can shop around for bargains in suburban chain grocery stores that buy foodstuffs in bulk. By contrast, the urban poor often have no personal transportation and, especially the disabled and elderly, are limited to small neighborhood markets where prices are higher and perishable goods like bread, produce, and diary products are often stale, overripe, or semi-spoiled. Consequently, the diets of those in the lower strata of society are substandard, and this contributes to high infant mortality, low birth weight in babies, and millions of malnourished children.

In terms of social policy, the 1980s under the Reagan administration was a period of declining support for several forms of public assistance, including maternal and child health care programs. These cutbacks were made in order to reduce federal bureaucracy and governmental costs (Aldous, 1986). Yet a growing body of research shows that public programs designed as preventive measures to enhance life chances actually save money in the long run, not to mention the social costs involved. In a study conducted at Harvard University, for example, it was found that the incidence of low birth weight in babies of mothers who did not receive supplemental nutrition benefits during their pregnancies was three times higher than babies of mothers who did receive such assistance. As a result, it was estimated that each dollar spent on such preventive prenatal care for poor mothers would net a savings of three dollars in long-term costs of health care for the children of these women (Amidei, 1981). Although some marginal improvements occurred during the Clinton administration (1993–2001), life chances among the poor did not improve on President George W. Bush's watch (2001–2009) except for reductions in poverty among the elderly. And the number of Americans living in poverty continued to grow during President Barack Obama's time in office

and by late 2012 had reached nearly 50 million (CBS News, November 15, 2012).

Poverty

Poverty is a condition experienced by those who possess the lowest levels of life chances in a given society. These not only include life expectancy, health care, and nutrition, but are also reflected in other indicators such as inadequate housing, low levels of education, high fertility rates, and low income. Sometimes referred to as the *underclass* (Myrdal, 1962), those experiencing poverty in America and elsewhere typically are people who lack the basic resources necessary for long-term survival and prosperity.

Absolute Versus Relative Poverty Sociologists define poverty in several different ways (Light and Keller, 1982). First, there is a distinction made between absolute poverty and relative poverty. Absolute poverty exists when people lack essential resources for survival, such as food and shelter. Compared to some societies, relatively few people in the United States starve to death each year. When these things do happen, they occur mainly among abandoned infants, the elderly poor, and "street people." In the world's poorest countries, however, absolute poverty is a reality for a large proportion of their populations. During the 1984–1985 drought in Africa, for example, two million people died of malnutrition and disease.

Relative poverty, by contrast, refers to a standard of living that is substandard in relation to that of the majority of society members. Using this definition, millions of Americans, including the underemployed and those in steady, but unskilled occupations, may have the essentials such as food, shelter, and basic health care but lack the purchasing power to acquire many of the nonessential "luxury" items many to most people in the middle class often take for granted.

Objective Versus Felt Poverty There is also a distinction made between objective and felt poverty. Objective poverty is a state of official deprivation as determined by an agreed-upon

These photographs were taken by Louly Contreras, an honors student in sociology at San Jacinto College. She analyzed them using the SIVSI™, a visual sociology assessment tool developed by the author. They portray life style elements of those who live on the streets of Houston and were part of a visual sociology project on stratification. How many SIVSI™ indicators can you find in each of these images? See *Achieving Sociological Fluency: An Interactive Guide and Workbook* that accompanies your text. Would you be able to write a brief essay on the sociological content contained in these photos and the messages they convey? If so, what do these photos tell you?

Courtesy of Louly Contreras

standard of measurement. Since 1964, the U.S. government has used a poverty index developed by Mollie Orshansky (1965) of the Social Security Administration. This index, now known as the "poverty line," is set yearly, based on the amount of money needed each year per person to maintain minimum but adequate nutrition under temporary circumstances. Researchers use an elaborate formula to establish this cutoff point; it is based on the type of family, the number of adults and children under eighteen years of age living in the household, the type of residence (farm or nonfarm), and other factors. They then calculate these factors in terms of the consumer price index. In 2013, the poverty line for a nonfarm family of four was $23,550 (U.S. Department of Health and Human Services, 2013). Consequently, close to sixteen percent of all Americans were officially poor in that year.

Felt poverty refers to hardships experienced by those who fall slightly above the poverty line and/or those who experience psychological and emotional deprivation. Many such families may be worse off in standard of living because they cannot qualify for federal assistance programs that are open to those who are "officially" poor. Others may be distinguished from the "officially" poor primarily because of felt emotional deprivation because their standard of living has been reduced. Felt poverty, therefore, should not be confused with relative poverty because it often has more to do with the psychological and emotional dimensions of poverty than with actual standard of living. Say, for example, a very affluent upper-class family lost their family business due to bankruptcy and were forced to live a middle-class lifestyle with only one home instead of several and with fewer amenities. While many people would feel little if any sympathy for them, members of this family, nonetheless, might perceive themselves as poor and experience a great deal of psychological and emotional distress.

The Poor in America

Those at the bottom of America's socioeconomic ladder vary widely in circumstances. Some are dislocated workers temporarily out of work who are "down on their luck." Although they and their families often suffer significantly and lose homes, cars, and other possessions, many if not most are able to return to work and/or retrain for other jobs. Others are marginal workers engaged in seasonal or unskilled jobs that offer low pay and often little job security such as farm workers, and manual laborers, domestics, dishwashers, car washers, and shoe shiners.

There are about fifty million people living in poverty within the United States which include more than ten million families (CBS News, 2012; U.S. Department of Health and Human Services, 2013). As many as sixteen million (approximately one-third), however, form the "hard-core" poor who appear destined for permanent poverty. Of these, an estimated one to three million are the homeless of various types, including those with mental disorders, who help make up the ranks of the "street people." An additional several million are undocumented aliens who live on the fringes of society and continually face deportation. A few million more are single women with dependent children caught up in a long-term cycle of poverty (Harrington, 1984; U.S. department of Health and Human Services, 2008; *The World Almanac Book of Facts*, 2013).

Regardless whether the experience of deprivation is temporary or long term, poverty appears to be a growing problem for the most vulnerable people in society. Most of America's poor occupy one or more of the following overlapping categories: women, children, minorities, the elderly, and the disabled (U.S. Census Bureau, 2012b).

Of these groups, the large majority of the poor are women, children, and minorities. A trend toward the feminization of poverty is obvious since most adults living in poverty today are women. In 2005, the poverty rate for all women eighteen years of age or older was nearly thirteen percent (14.6 million women) as compared with nearly nine percent of all American men. In addition, of the twelve and one-half million adults who participated in the Federal Food Stamp Program, about eight and one-half million (68 percent) were women, with forty-five percent of

these being young women in the eighteen to thirty-five year age group (U.S. Department of Health and Human Services, 2007). As a result of such factors as teenage pregnancy, divorce, desertion, and widowhood, more than forty-eight percent of households headed by single women suffer from poverty. In large part due to this factor, more than half of all poor children in the United States live in these households. Consequently, about thirteen million children—almost one out of every five Americans under eighteen years of age (eighteen percent)—live in households with incomes below the poverty line. When racial and ethnic backgrounds are factored in, ten percent of white children, twenty-eight percent of Hispanic children, and thirty-five percent of black children live in poverty (Fass and Cauthen, 2006) (U.S. Department of Health and Human Services, 2013).

The rates of poverty among the elderly are not as dismal. A couple of generations ago during the 1960s, about thirty percent of those over sixty-five were living in poverty. However, due to better retirement programs offered by both private and public employers and the fact that many Americans today who are sixty-five or older continue to participate in the labor force, the poverty rate for the elderly had fallen to only ten percent by 2005. Consequently, only about ten percent (more than three and one-half million) of all poor in the United States today are elderly.

The Culture of Poverty Hypothesis

A Culture of Poverty as a Cause? Perhaps the most popular explanation of poverty among social scientists historically has been the culture of poverty hypothesis developed by anthropologist Oscar Lewis (1961, 1966, 1968). Using data gathered from field observations made primarily among the impoverished in Mexico and the United States, he argued that poverty involves a subculture that socializes its children with attitudes of despair and acceptance of being poor as natural and normal for them. The poor, Lewis asserts, tend to have little sense of what is going on in the larger society and remain socially isolated

Poverty takes several forms. Although the urban poor are highly visible in the media today, there are many like this rural family who also suffer impaired life chances.

© Michael Zysman, 2009. Use under license from Shutterstock, Inc.

from it in their own neighborhoods and communities. They appear relatively unaware of opportunities for improving their life chances and fail to see how collective organization on their part could help to diminish their problems as well as influence public policy in the larger community and society. Poverty, then, can become a self-perpetuating cycle. On an individual level, the child reared in this environment tends to develop a set of values and personality characteristics very different from those of the middle-class child in the suburbs. As Lewis explains,

> The individual who grows up in this culture has a strong feeling of fatalism, helplessness, dependence, and inferiority; a strong present-time orientation with relatively little disposition to defer gratification and plan for the future, and a high tolerance for psychological pathology of all kinds (1966, p. 23).

A Critique: Poverty for Most Is Temporary

While Lewis's hypothesis may help to explain poverty at least in part among segments of the chronically poor (Kerbo, 1981), it has come under criticism by some social scientists. Perhaps most important is the fact that for most who experience poverty in the United States, being poor is a temporary situation from which they recover in a

few months or years (Duncan, 1984; U.S. Census Bureau. 2011). Consequently, many to most sociologists do not accept Lewis' hypothesis as having much validity today.

The majority of today's poor are represented by an ever-changing pool of unfortunates caught up in the throes of temporary deprivation. Some are single mothers with young children who, because of teenage pregnancy, separation, or divorce and other factors, experience poverty and must seek public assistance for a time until they can obtain jobs. Others are displaced workers victimized by structural unemployment, the loss of employment as a result of changes in the economy that render certain occupations obsolete. In recent years, for example, changes in demand and technology have affected the gas, oil, steel, auto, and farm industries, which in turn have resulted in millions of "new poor."

A Culture of Poverty as a Consequence?

Some sociologists, such as Garth Massey (1982) and others, have argued that the culture of poverty—when it does exist—is not so much the cause of poverty as it is the consequence or adaptation to the condition of being poor. Ian Robertson (1980), in summarizing much of the literature on this point, reports that from the perspective of some writers,

> any distinctive culture of the poor is the result, not the cause, of their continuing poverty, and their characteristics and attitudes are a realistic and understandable response to their situation. The poor have to abandon the attitudes, values, and expectations of the predominantly middle-class society around them because middle-class culture is irrelevant to their circumstances. For example, middle-class culture emphasizes "deferred gratification"—saving income and postponing pleasures today in order to reap greater benefits tomorrow. The culture of the poor, however, tends to emphasize "instant gratification"—spending one's money and enjoying what one has while it lasts. Clearly, the value of deferred gratification makes no sense to someone who does not have money to save and is pessimistic about the future. Instant gratification is a rational response to this situation, but it is the result not the cause of poverty. Indeed, empirical studies of impoverished ghetto residences show that if they do manage to get jobs that offer stable income, they become "mainstreamers," concerned with such middle-class values as deferred gratification and respectability (p. 189).

The Poor and Welfare: Myth and Reality

There are several commonly held myths about the poor and the amount of public assistance they receive in the United States. Perhaps two of the most prevalent and interconnected misconceptions are as follows: *The myth of able-bodied recipients* and *the myth that most of America's poor are on welfare*. In fact, so-called welfare chiselers, while they do exist, are the exception rather than the rule. Most public assistance dollars go to help children, the ill, the elderly, and the disabled. Of these, single mothers and their offspring represent the one category that comprises the large majority of welfare recipients. Factors that contribute to this include emotional immaturity and ignorance about birth control, rape, divorce, and abandonment or desertion by live-in partners or husbands. In addition, contrary to popular belief, only about one-third of America's poor today receive welfare assistance. Contributing factors include the increased stigma attached to receiving welfare, increased requirements including paperwork to receive benefits, and federal requirements imposed since 1996 that limit benefits to five years of lifetime eligibility (Shirk, Bennett, and Abner, 1999; Deparle, 2004; Etter, 2006).

A third misconception is *the myth that women on welfare keep having babies to increase their benefits*. In fact, adults in a "welfare family" (1) have a life-time limit of four years in which to receive federal Temporary Assistance for Needy Families (TANF) benefits, (2) must participate in a work plan designed to reach economic self-sufficiency to receive any benefits, and (3) ultimately receive benefits for an average of only eighteen months. Of those adults who are single parents receiving benefits, eighty-two percent have only one or two children and fewer than seven percent have more than four offspring (U.S. Department of Human Services, 2006).

As a final illustration, there is *the myth that benefits discourage working*. In fact, welfare payments alone in all fifty states are not sufficient to raise a recipient family's above the poverty line. And people have to eat to survive. Just for the sake of illustration, suppose a family of four living at the allotted poverty line of $23,550 (2013) spend one-third of its income on food and choose to purchase it at McDonalds. According to sociologist Leonard Beeghley, that would give each family member just one Big Mac sandwich and a one medium soft drink per day on which to live (Beeghley, 2008).

Chapter 8

Economic Inequality in the US

Every Christmas, the Parent-Teacher Association (PTA) at the school Elizabeth and Grace attend collects donations of presents for students from low-income families. Both girls wonder who among their classmates must rely on presents from strangers, and secretly hope that they will never have to do so. Grace started to worry about this possibility even more after recognizing class divisions among her classmates. Grace knows that Elizabeth receives more expensive presents than she does, and unlike Grace Elizabeth almost always gets what she wants for Christmas. Grace takes some comfort in the knowledge that her presents come from her parents and not the PTA, but she realizes that that could change.

Keenly aware of the long hours her parents work, Grace can't help thinking that if money were granted based on effort, her parents *should* have as much money as Elizabeth's parents. Elizabeth's parents, though, seem to be home much more often and can go on great vacations every year. It has become clear to Grace that the distribution of money in U.S. society benefits some people more than others—and that life is not fair. Who knows whom the PTA might be helping next year?

What is *your* economic situation? Are you financially stable? Do you believe you have your fair share of income and wealth? Do you think income and wealth are distributed equitably, or do you think economic inequality in the United States is a social problem? Chapter 8 examines the extent of economic inequality in the United States and compares it to that found in other nations. It also looks at the repercussions of this inequality, sociological explanations for inequality, and the efforts of some sociologists to address related social problems.

IS ECONOMIC INEQUALITY A SOCIAL PROBLEM?

Economic inequality refers to the unequal distribution of income and economic assets. Whether economic inequality in the United States is a social problem can be determined by using the criteria for defining a social problem:

- Is economic inequality in the United States part of a social pattern?

- Does economic inequality violate a core value of society?

- Does economic inequality negatively impact those in power?

- Can society do something about economic inequality if enough people choose to confront it?

The answers to these questions rely upon conducting research, using the sociological lens view. Without using the sociological lens, it's possible to overlook social patterns of inequality and draw incorrect conclusions. Most Americans tend to consider social issues in terms of only the people with whom they tend to interact, rather than considering social patterns across the United States or the globe. Sociologists focus on trends rather than individual examples of social phenomena. For example, when looking at economic inequality in a society, sociologists would measure the distribution of wealth and income throughout the population they are studying and across whatever subgroups they are interested in, such as racial, ethnic, and gender subgroups.

Inequality and Social Patterns

A recent study (Norton & Ariely, 2011) reveals that most Americans are unaware of the degree of economic inequality in the United States. A nationally representative online sample of Americans, randomly drawn from a panel of more than 1 million Americans, was given the following definition of wealth:

> Wealth, also known as net worth, is defined as the total value of everything someone owns minus any debt that he or she owes. A person's net worth includes his or her bank account savings plus the value of other things such as property, stocks, bonds, art, collections, etc., minus the value of things like loans and mortgages. (Norton & Ariely, 2011, p. 9)

The respondents were then shown three charts that illustrated different distributions of wealth, ranging from somewhat equitable to very unequal—the distribution of wealth is how wealth is divided among a population. When asked which of the three charts displayed how wealth is distributed in the *United States*, most respondents selected the chart that actually described the distribution of wealth in *Sweden*, which, of all nations, provides the most economic equality.

Figure 8-1 illustrates the *actual* United States distribution of wealth plotted against what respondents chose as the *estimated* and *ideal* distributions across all respondents. The bar labeled

Figure 8-1

Distribution of wealth in the United States

As this graph shows, the distribution of wealth in the United States is different from what many people think it is.

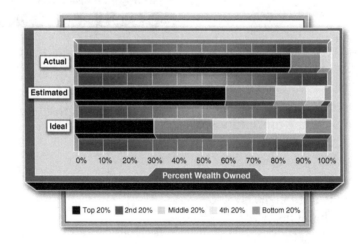

Maury Aaseng

Source: Based on data taken from Norton M. & Ariely D. (2011) Building a better America—One wealth quintile at a time. Perspectives on psychological science, 6(9).

"actual" represents the actual distribution of wealth in the United States at the time of the study. The bar labeled "estimated," the one chosen by the majority of respondents, represents the actual distribution of wealth in Sweden. And the bar labeled "ideal," the chart most often picked by respondents as an ideal distribution of wealth, represents an even *more equitable* distribution of wealth than that found in Sweden. Overall, the figure reveals the lopsided distribution of wealth in the United States and the inaccuracy of how most Americans perceive that distribution.

Why do Americans see themselves as better off than they are? Most Americans tend to live in proximity to those with comparable levels of wealth and income—it is relatively rare to find millionaires living next door to working-class people. This may be one of the reasons why most Americans describe themselves as middle class, when many academic models shows that only about 45% of Americans can be categorized as lower or upper middle class. By contrast, between 1% and 5% of Americans are considered upper class, rich, or "super-rich," and the remaining population, over 50%, is considered working class and poor (Gilbert, 2002; Thompson & Hickey, 2005; Beeghley, 2004). However, examining issues of economic inequality requires looking at the world from a sociological rather than an individual perspective. The high level of economic inequality in the United States can be examined only by looking beyond one's immediate circumstances and the individual experiences of the people one knows.

Using the sociological lens for a broader look beyond one's own neighborhood brings to light social patterns that reveal systems of social stratification, or the ranking of groups of people according to their access to and possession of the things valued in society such as wealth, power, and status. Looking through the sociological lens also reveals that U.S. society is economically stratified, with some Americans having a much higher level of income and wealth than others. In fact, annual income, which is the amount people earn from wages, investments, or selling property or goods, has fallen for most

Americans over the past decade. The median annual income is the midpoint of the incomes of all Americans, with half of incomes higher and half lower. In 2010, the median annual household income of the United States was $49,445. Adjusted for inflation, it was 6.4% lower than in 2007, and 7.1% lower than in 1999, the year of the highest recorded U.S. median income (DeNavas-Walt, Proctor, & Smith, 2011). However, annual income for the very wealthy has increased tremendously in recent years. Between 1975 and 2008, the share of U.S. income taken in by the top 0.1% of earners grew from 2.6% to 10.4% ((Not) spreading the wealth, 2011). By 2007, the top 1% took in almost 20% of all the income made in the United States (Congressional Budget Office, 2011a).

Figure 8-2 shows that the growth in income inequality in the United States is closely related to increases in compensation for top earners and stagnation of wages for the rest of the workforce. Between 1978 and 2005, the average pay for CEOs jumped from 35 times to almost 262 times the pay of the average worker (Sawhill & Morton, n.d.). The distribution of wealth is even more inequitable. In 2011, the top 20% of Americans held 84% of the wealth, while the bottom 40% held less than one-half of 1% of the total wealth in the nation (Norton & Ariely, 2011). Moreover, in 2010 those in the top 1% held more wealth at 35.6% than the entire bottom 90% of the population at 25% (Frank, 2010).

Inequality and Core Values

The growing gap in economic inequality between the very rich and everyone else strikes at a core American value: economic mobility, the ability to move from one social class to another. According to a 2011 survey, 7 out of 10 Americans believe that they have or will achieve the American Dream of upward mobility, rising in social class (Economic Mobility Project [EMP], 2011). Americans are far more likely than citizens of other countries to believe that they can influence their social class status through hard work. However, comparing parents' incomes with their adult children's incomes reveals that

Figure 8-2

Percentage change in income, adjusted for inflation, since 1979
Since 1979, top earners in the United States have seen marked, steady growth of income whereas the income of the rest of the workforce has remained stagnant.

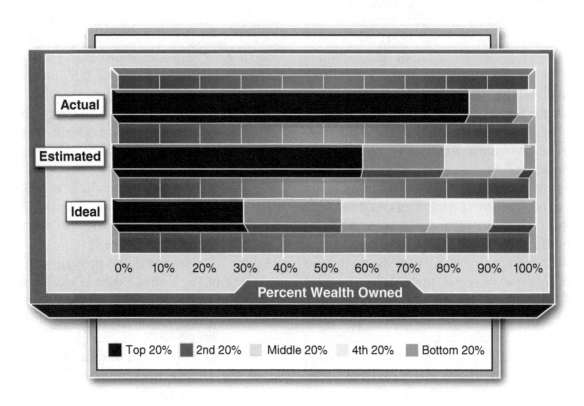

Maury Aaseng

Source: Based on data from the Congressional Budget Office, 2011, Trends in the Distribution of Household Income Between 1979 and 2007.

there is actually less upward mobility in the United States than in other developed nations, including Denmark, Norway, Finland, Canada, Sweden, Germany, and France (Sawhill & Morton, n.d.). And, as economic inequality increases, the ability to achieve upward mobility decreases. (Blanden, 2009).

Recognizing the growing economic divide, a majority (59%) of Americans now say that their children will have a harder time moving up the economic ladder than they did (EMP, 2011). This belief coincides with a dramatic recent increase in the percentage of Americans who believe there are "strong" or "very strong" conflicts between the rich and the poor in the United States. While 47% perceived this level of class conflict in 2007, 66% did in 2011 (Morin, 2012). The threat to the American Dream posed by increasing economic inequality could threaten the social cohesion and stability of the nation.

Inequality and Power Structure

Leaders throughout the world have reason to worry about rising economic inequality. The Arab Spring that began in 2010 and sparked revolutions in many Arab nations provides a recent example of the threat of economic inequality to national leaders. Satisfaction with the standard of living in Egypt and Libya fell during the years leading up

The Occupy Wall Street movement highlights the growing income gap between the top 1% of Americans and the rest of the country.

© Daryl Lang, 2014. Used under license from Shutterstock, Inc.

to the revolutions in those nations and increased dissatisfaction with old regimes (Breisinger, Ecker, & Al-Riffai, 2011). In the United States, the protesters of the Occupy Wall Street movement that developed in 2011 have, with their chants of "We are the 99%," focused a spotlight on the growing gap in income inequality between the top 1% of Americans and the rest of the nation, forcing politicians to begin talking about ways to curb inequality and provide more opportunities for upward mobility.

Politicians know that high levels of economic inequality, particularly in a nation with great wealth, can lead to feelings of relative deprivation, a sense among many citizens that others have what they do not. These feelings can prompt a sense of dissatisfaction and injustice, which can lead to political instability. To gain power or remain in power, political leaders feel they need to convince the public that they will increase opportunities for upward mobility.

Remedies for Inequality

A large majority of Americans (83%) say they want the government to take action to improve the economic situations of the poor and middle class. This desire for government to come up with remedies for the growing U.S. economic inequality spans political parties, with 91% of Democrats, 84% of independents, and 73% of Republicans

agreeing that the government should address economic inequality (EMP, 2011). According to a 2011 national poll (EMP, 2011, p. 4), Americans believe that the top five goals for government in helping people move up the economic ladder should be to

1. ensure all children get a quality education (88%),
2. promote job creation (83%),
3. ensure equal opportunity (79%),
4. let people keep more of their money (78%), and
5. provide basic needs to the very poor (75%).

A majority of Americans also maintain that the government should improve education, reduce the government debt, and retain jobs in the United States to prevent people from falling into the lower class (EMP, 2011).

21ST-CENTURY INEQUALITY IN THE UNITED STATES

Governments alone, though, cannot mitigate economic inequality. There are many interconnected and complex reasons for the current high level of economic inequality in the United States. Some relate to changes in the U.S. social structure and others to cultural influences.

Structural Forces

A social structure is a framework of established patterns of social interaction between people and groups, guided by accepted norms and shared values. Structural forces are fundamental patterns within a social structure that shape and influence our lives, as opposed to the individual and personal choices we make. Examples of structural forces include a society's use of a common language and the influence of large social institutions, such as schools or the economy. Over the past few decades, changes in one significant structural force, the global economy, have influenced the rise in levels of inequality in the United States and across the globe. These include

- the decline of unions,
- higher incomes for CEOs and lower tax rates for the wealthy,
- the move away from manufacturing to a service economy,
- supply-side economic policies,
- the Great Recession, the mortgage crisis, and the bursting of the housing bubble, and
- increasing unemployment.

Let's explore the influence of each of these structural forces on economic inequality in the United States.

The Decline of Unions

Modern labor unions emerged from the industrial revolution of the mid- to late 1800s, when workers commonly labored in unsafe conditions for low pay. Since the time of the first factories, workers have made attempts to band together to have the power to more effectively demand better working conditions and higher wages. Before unions, workers had no recourse when they were exploited by their employers. Just a few of the victories won by organized labor are the minimum wage, child labor laws, improved working conditions, and the 40-hour week. The bumper sticker, "Unions: the folks who brought you the weekend," sums up just one way unions have changed the lives of working Americans. Union workers tend to make more money and have better benefits than nonunionized workers. In 2010, the average weekly salary of a unionized worker was $917, compared to $717 for a nonunionized worker (Bureau of Labor Statistics [BLS], 2011c). In this sense, for many Americans a union job has been a ticket into the middle class.

The number of Americans in unions increased dramatically after the Wagner Act of 1935 protected nongovernmental workers' right to form

The efforts of organized labor unions have resulted in child labor laws, the minimum wage, 40-hour work weeks, and other regulations that have improved conditions for workers.

© Nic Neufield, 2014. Used under license from Shutterstock, Inc.

unions and to strike to try to achieve their goals. However, in the late 1940s legislative efforts began to curtail the rights of unions. For example, the National Labor Relations Act of 1947 placed restrictions on strikes and blunted some of the unions' power. Right-to-work laws, now in place in 23 states (including all Southern states), prohibit employers from requiring workers to belong to a union or pay union dues, even if the workers are represented by a union. One of the greatest political blows to unions occurred when President Ronald Reagan fired striking air traffic controllers in 1981, effectively destroying their union and delivering a chilling message to all unions.

Other factors over the past three decades have contributed to the decline of unions, including deindustrialization, automation, globalization, supply-side economics, and a political backlash from those who oppose taxpayers' contributions to public employee unions. For example, recent attempts have been made in such states as Wisconsin and Ohio to curtail the bargaining rights of public employee unions. In 1983, when comprehensive data was first compiled, one out of five Americans belonged to a union. Today, though, just slightly more than one in ten Americans is a union member (BLS, 2011c), and the percentage of unionized workers varies tremendously among states. For example, 1 out of 4 workers in Alaska and New York is unionized but just 1 out of 20 workers in Georgia and North Carolina (BLS, 2011c).

Higher Pay for CEOs and Lower Tax Rates for the Wealthy

While the wages of workers have declined or stagnated, the pay for the top 1% has increased dramatically since the 1960s. Figure 8-3 shows that the average CEO currently makes 243 times what the average worker earns.

Moreover, while many Americans complain about taxes, the federal tax rate for high-income

Americans is at a historic low. In 2011, the highest paid earners contributed 35% of their income exceeding $379,150 in federal taxes (Tax Foundation 2011). In 1945, the top tax rate was 94% in order to support the war effort, and it was never lower than 70% until the 1980s. Under President Reagan, the Tax Reform Act of 1986 lowered the tax rate dramatically, but also closed some loopholes that allowed many people and corporations to pay much less than the actual rate. Since 1986, more tax loopholes have been created, and demands to close them and make the system more equitable are increasing (Citizens for Tax Justice, 2011).

Today, the U.S. government taxes income at a much higher rate than it does wealth. Much of the income of wealthy Americans comes not from wages and salaries but from capital gains, defined as the income earned from investments.

Figure 8-3

Ratio of average annual CEO compensation to average worker compensation, 1965–2010
Since the 1960s, the gap between what CEOs and average workers typically earn in a year has increased dramatically.

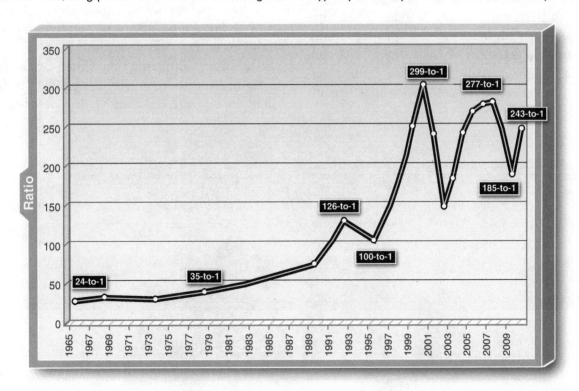

Maury Aaseng

Source: Adapted from Mishnel L. & Bivens J. (2011). Occupy Wall Streeters are right about skewed economic rewards in the United States. Economic Policy Institute Briefing Paper #331.

The reduction of the capital gains tax has therefore contributed to increased economic inequality in the United States. In 2011, the capital gains tax was at the historically low rate of 15%, down from 40% in the late 1970s. This means that all workers who earn wages or salaries of $34,500 a year or more pay a higher percentage of their income in federal taxes than wealthy Americans, whose incomes come primarily from stocks, bonds, and real estate profits (Mufson & Yang, 2011).

American billionaire and investment expert Warren Buffett famously pointed out in 2011 that he and others whose income is based primarily on investments have a lower tax rate than do their secretaries, who must pay the higher tax rate for wages and salaries. Since 1990, just one tenth of the wealthiest 1% of the population (0.1%) earned over half of all capital gains income in the United States, with the wealthiest 5% of the population earning 80% of capital gains income (Mufson & Yang, 2011). Only a very small percentage of the population earned capital gains income, and the same small number of people benefited from the dramatic decrease in the capital gains tax. The result is that, proportionally, the wealthy keep more of their money and contribute less tax revenue to provide human services and maintain infrastructure that benefits all Americans.

The Move Away from Manufacturing to Service

Deindustrialization, the reduction of industrial activity, or manufacturing, has played a major role in the increasing economic inequality in the United States. The percent of workers in manufacturing (excluding farming) dropped from 24% in 1973 to 10% in 2007 (Lee & Mather, 2008), in part because of globalization, the global distribution of the production of goods and services. With the rise of globalization and technology making it easier and cheaper to move goods and people across the globe, owners of corporations have used this new mobility to relocate their businesses outside of the United States in countries where labor is cheaper. For example, computer maker Apple Inc. has chosen to outsource manufacturing of many of its products, contracting with roughly 700,000 people in China and other parts of the world (Duhigg & Bradsher, 2012). As American businesses adapt to the global market, many American workers are left looking in vain for the decent-paying manufacturing jobs that previously allowed many Americans with just a high school education to attain a middle-class life.

In addition, although the United States has maintained some manufacturing jobs, it has shifted to a predominantly service-oriented

The transition to a service-oriented economy has contributed to the growing income gap in the United States.

economy. Service-oriented occupations are those in which workers provide their knowledge and time but not a tangible end product. The highest-paid workers in the service sector—lawyers, computer engineers, doctors—often have acquired a great deal of education, whereas and the lowest-paid—retail salespeople, nursing aides, security guards—require minimal training. The jobs that don't require a lot of skills or education typically do not pay well, certainly not as well as manufacturing jobs tend to pay. Thus, the move from manufacturing to service-oriented jobs has contributed to the expansion of the growing income and wealth divide.

The transition to a service economy also has led to a gap between eligible candidates and the jobs that are available. That is, despite high levels of unemployment, many companies struggle to find qualified workers for jobs in areas such as information technology and other skilled trades. To meet their personnel needs, business leaders have begun to advocate for restructuring education and on-the-job training systems (Manpower Group, 2011).

Another factor that has led to economic inequality in the United States is automation, the use of machines to produce goods or provide services. Automation in and of itself is not a bad thing—since the creation of the first factory, machines have replaced human effort, helped humans do their jobs more safely and efficiently, and made the American economy more productive. However, automation can hurt workers who lose or can't obtain jobs because of it. Thanks to automation, the amount of goods created in U.S. factories has continued to increase, despite fewer workers in manufacturing (Davidson, 2012). In this sense, automation can benefit factory owners at the expense of factory workers.

Recent advances in technology have sped up the automation process and allowed machines to take over more of the tasks that used to require human workers. For example, many jobs have been lost to computers that now can respond to phone calls, pay highway tolls, handle interactions with banks, and even tally up the cost of groceries. Similarly, computer programs exist

that can do the work once reserved for highly paid lawyers (Markoff, 2011). As a result, upper middle–class, middle-class, and low-wage workers have been pushed out of jobs that can be done by more efficient and cost-effective machines.

Finding the most cost-effective way to produce goods is a priority for business. Capitalist nations like the United States have economies based on private ownership and competition in free markets. These types of economies naturally favor owners rather than workers. Capitalism is driven by profits, and workers are just one of the resources that allow owners to operate profitable businesses. However, governments create laws and regulations that enforce limits and restrictions on businesses, sometimes prohibiting monopolies or unfair business practices and ensuring that workers are treated fairly. Likewise, on the global level, organizations, such as the World Trade Organization, set up agreements that establish trade rules among nations and promote the ability of "producers of goods and services, exporters, and importers to conduct their business" (World Trade Organization, 2012.).

In the United States and across the globe, there has always been a continuous struggle for power between those who want to limit government interference in the marketplace and those who advocate for more control. Many scholars now argue that global corporations, rather than nations, have the most power over the global marketplace (Derber, 2002; Johns, 2007). The recent growth of the global economy—with corporations gaining greater influence while individual nations struggle for control—allows businesses to easily move from one country to another in search of cheaper wages and less government interference. Businesses have developed a global perspective, which means they do not necessarily value Americans over citizens of other countries, both as employees and customers. Thomas Wilson, the CEO of Allstate, recently stated, "I can get [workers] anywhere in the world. It is a problem for America, but it is not necessarily a problem for American business. . . . American businesses will adapt" (Freeland, 2011, n.p.).

Supply-Side Economics

The reduction of government regulation associated with the supply-side economic policies of President Reagan in the 1980s helped speed up deindustrialization in the United States. Supply-side economic theory assumes that economic growth is stimulated by reducing taxes and freeing businesses of government regulation. The wealth thus created will be invested in things that increase "supply"—factories, new businesses, goods, and services. One key aspect of this theory is that if corporations receive tax cuts, they will reinvest that money to create more jobs for people, who will then spend their earnings creating more tax revenues and supporting the economy. Thus, the wealth of those at the top of the economic pyramid will "trickle down" to those below—hence critics of the theory referring to it as "trickle-down economics." In addition, it argues that if government policies lower the barriers to production, consumers will benefit from a greater supply of goods and services at lower prices.

However, decreased government regulation resulted in no strings being attached to the tax breaks. This allowed many corporations to keep their profits and establish factories outside the United States, where labor costs less, thus eliminating reinvestment in American workers and subsequently the U.S. economy. As a result, there were fewer jobs, lower wages, and reduced power of unions for American workers. When owners can simply say, "If you don't agree to these wage and benefit cuts, we will move this factory out of the United States," workers and their union representatives have little negotiating power.

The Great Recession and the Mortgage Crisis

In late 2007, a cascade of complex economic events converged, leading to a dramatic drop in American housing prices, the collapse of huge financial institutions, and downturns in global stock markets. These events, referred to as the Great Recession, or the Global Financial Crisis, peaked in 2007–2008 and continue to have a profound effect on the United States and the world, including lingering high unemployment and ongoing housing foreclosures. The Great Recession is the worst financial crisis since the Great Depression that began after the stock market crash of 1929.

One of the countless factors that led to this crisis was related to supply-side policies freeing businesses from regulation. In the midst of the Great Depression, in 1933, Congress passed the Glass-Steagall Act, which separated commercial banking (which accepts deposits and lends money) from investment banking (which issues securities and invests with credit). This law was designed to prevent banks from taking investment risks that could jeopardize their solvency. For decades, banks pressed for the repeal of the act, which finally occurred in 1999 under President Clinton. This freed commercial banks to again invest their clients' deposits and practice both investment and commercial banking. During the same period, under a push to provide home ownership to as many people as possible, government mortgage providers Fannie Mae and Freddie Mac lowered their standards and began issuing mortgages to people who could not afford them. Meanwhile, as government regulators turned a blind eye, other mortgage lenders followed suit and housing prices soared as more and more people bought homes.

In the absence of government regulation, mortgage lenders profited enormously by collecting fees from homeowners who were assuming mortgages they could not afford. But the original lenders did not hold onto these risky mortgages; instead, these residential mortgages became the basis for another level of investment. Lenders bundled these so-called "toxic mortgages," whose owners were likely to default, into a type of pooled securities called collateralized debt obligations (CDO). The lenders sliced these bundles into more CDOs and sold them to banks, who sold them to investment firms, which purchased insurance against possible losses on the bundled mortgages.

Companies that insured the investors who bought CDOs failed to maintain the resources needed to fund insurance claim payments for those they insured. Lax government rules and oversight allowed these insurance companies to

Government mortgage providers Fannie Mae and Freddie Mac were among the lenders whose practices helped lead to the housing bubble burst in 2008.

© Frontpage, 2014. Used under license from Shutterstock, Inc.

say they could insure far more than their resources on hand would allow. As a result, when homeowners defaulted on loans and investors filed claims to cover their losses on the CDOs, the insurance companies shirked their responsibility and the entire system crumbled.

At the same time, credit rating agencies, which rate securities so that potential investors will know the risks associated with them, also failed to sound an alarm. These credit rating agencies (Moody's, Standard and Poor's, and Fitch), in a clear conflict of interest, are paid by the banks to whom they issue credit scores. Without looking carefully into the problems with the CDOs, they granted them high credit ratings, leading investors to think their money was not at risk (Morgenson, 2008). When these CDOs started to fail, many investors lost money and some banks, such as Bear Stearns and Lehman Brothers, went bankrupt while others were saved through government bailouts to prevent further damage to the economy (Financial Crisis Inquiry Commission, 2011).

With banks reluctant to lend money, homeowners and new businesses could not obtain the funds they needed to keep the housing market and the overall economy healthy and functioning. At the same time, big businesses, fearful of further economic downturns, refused to risk major investments such as hiring new employees

(Leonhard, 2011). As a result, in 2011 the national unemployment rate doubled, standing stubbornly between 9 and 10% (BLS, 2011a), and consumer confidence, which indicates people's willingness to purchase goods and services, sharply decreased (Conference Board, 2011).

The housing crisis and the Great Recession caused a catastrophic drop in the wealth of Americans. Housing prices, which had peaked in 2006, dropped precipitously, as did home equity, pensions, retirement funds and other savings and investment assets. This bursting of the housing bubble had a dramatic impact on the level of economic inequality, particularly harming many working- and middle-class Americans. The wealth of this group most commonly relies on the value of their houses. Those who do not own a home tend to have few other assets. When houses declined in value with the fall of the housing market, much, or in some cases all, of the wealth of many Americans disappeared. When adjusted for inflation, the median net worth of U.S. households fell 28% from 2007 to 2009 (Kochhar, Fry, & Taylor, 2011). People with other types of wealth such as stocks were shielded from losses by the diversity of their assets. The result was greater economic inequality between people who could afford many assets and people whose only significant asset was their home.

These events in the United States resulted in huge declines in the stock market and the housing market and ignited a worldwide economic crisis. In April of 2009, the International Monetary Fund (IMF) declared that the global economy had not been in such dire condition since the end of World War II (Knowlton, 2009). By 2009, Europe was in the midst of its own, related, economic crisis. With the burst of its own housing bubble and huge debts in both banking and the governments of European Union nations, housing prices plummeted and borrowing money became much more difficult and expensive. Since the fall of 2009, the European Union has been struggling with enormous debts faced by Greece, Portugal, Ireland, Italy, and Spain. A series of negotiations and bailouts have attempted to stop this slide. Riots and strikes protesting austerity measures throughout the region illustrate the political dangers to leaders during times of rising inequality and relative deprivation.

Increasing Unemployment

The Great Recession continues to have a profound effect on the global economy. But in the United States, it has taken a much higher toll on people without a college education and on people of color. A 2010 study by the Brookings Institution concluded that during the Great Recession employment dropped much less steeply among college-educated workers than other workers. The employment-to-population ratio dropped by more than 2 percentage points from 2007 to 2009 for working-age adults without a bachelor's degree, but fell by only half a percentage point for college-educated individuals (Berube, 2010). The Bureau of Labor Statistics found in September 2011 that jobless rates for people of all races and ethnicities were much higher than before the Great Recession began. However, unemployment rates continued to be higher for Blacks and Hispanic-Latinos.

This situation has increased the inequality that already existed among Americans based on educational level and race. An analysis of 2008 government data by the Pew Research Center concluded that the median wealth of White households was 20 times that of Black households and 18 times that of Hispanic-Latino households. The study found that such "lopsided wealth ratios are the largest since the government began publishing such data a quarter century ago and roughly twice the size of the ratios that had prevailed between these three groups for the two decades prior to the Great Recession" (Kochlar et al., 2011). Bureau of Labor Statistics data continue to show a sizeable gap in jobless rates ranging among those with no high school diploma, high school graduates, those with some college, and those with bachelor's degrees.

Cultural Forces

Culture is comprised of the shared values, norms, and artifacts that characterize our society. *Values* are the ideas a society deems important, such as the importance of hard work. *Norms* are a society's guidelines for behavior and interaction, such as working hard to earn a good income. *Artifacts* are the tangible objects created by members of a society, such as a nice house or an expensive car that symbolize one's economic success.

Cultural forces since the end of the 20th century and beginning of the 21st century have made society in the United States increasingly materialistic, even as wages have stagnated, fueling an increased desire for *consumer goods*, or things created for people to use or consume, such as food, clothing, automobiles, and phones. Sociologists have noted that exposure to the lifestyles of wealthy Americans through television and other media has changed consumers' desires and their purchases (Schor, 1998). The result is that increasing numbers of Americans feel they must have what the wealthiest 20% of the population owns.

Sociologists have long noted the use of consumer goods as a way of signifying superiority over others. Through conspicuous consumption, people wear expensive jewelry and clothing, build expensive homes, and so forth in order to signal to others that they are wealthier and therefore more important (Veblen, 1994). The impulse to demonstrate superiority is encouraged by the

Cultural forces in the United States have fueled an increased desire for consumer goods.

© Monkey Business Images, 2014. Used under license from Shutterstock, Inc.

media, advertisers, and consumers themselves, who develop norms in which certain cars, clothes, and other goods acquire more social prestige and gratification than others. (One example might be driving a Porsche as opposed to driving a Ford.) This link between wealth and superiority is one way economic inequality can lead to social inequality, a situation in which individuals or groups in a society have unequal status. Social inequality is reinforced by the belief that some groups are better than others and therefore deserve more of what society values, such as material goods, nice housing, and good schools.

Credit Cards and Increased Inequality

Credit cards have enabled many Americans to fulfill their material desires and attain goods that they aren't able to purchase with their regular income. However, the overreliance on credit cards by many consumers has led to increased economic inequality as consumers, able to instantly acquire goods and services they cannot really afford, have to spend their income paying off debt and interest instead of saving and investing.

The widespread use of credit cards is a relatively recent phenomenon. Prior to the mid-1970s, banks were conservative about issuing credit cards, granting them to only relatively well-off consumers who were considered good credit risks. In 1978, at a time when wages for most Americans were stagnating, the U.S. Supreme Court made a ruling that transformed Americans' use of credit cards. The court ruled that state usury laws, which prevent banks from charging high interest rates, don't apply to nationally chartered banks based in other states. The court decided that nationally chartered banks can "export" the interest rates allowed in their own states to customers anywhere in the country. This helped credit card companies make profits by moving to states that allowed them to charge high interest rates. South Dakota and Delaware, for example, repealed their usury laws to lure credit card companies and jobs to their states (Stein, 2004). This sparked growth in credit card companies and the more widespread use of "plastic," allowing most people to acquire credit cards fairly easily. According to the American Bankers Association, in 1977 about 38% of American households had at least one credit card. Today, it's about 75%.

The Culture of Poverty

As the examples of Grace's family illustrate, people can follow the cultural norm of working hard, but if they do not have the education needed to attain a well-paying job in an increasingly service-based economy, their chances of moving up in social class are low.

People learn how to function and participate within their culture and in the world through socialization, the process by which individuals acquire the norms, values, and expectations of their family and society. Some sociologists maintain that growing up in a poor neighborhood can lead to children learning behaviors and attitudes that perpetuate an inability and, often, lack of desire to move up the economic ladder (Banfield, 1970; Mayer, 1997). The concept is known as the culture of poverty. In a poverty-stricken neighborhood, children may learn different norms and values than those taught in middle-class and wealthy areas. For example, a child raised by uneducated, underemployed parents and surrounded by similar families is naturally influenced by that experience. If the child's parents don't value working hard in school and none of the child's friends do, why should the child? If that child has never met anyone who has a well-paying job, why would that child believe he or she could, or even should, attempt to move up the social class ladder?

Sociologists who adhere to the perspective of the culture of poverty have a pessimistic view of structural efforts, such as job training and low-cost housing, to help people raised in such neighborhoods to rise out of poverty. Instead, they tend to argue that poor people must adopt and adhere to dominant values and norms, such as hard work and attaining and maintaining a job. If they do not, there is not much hope that, for example, even if they were given a job, that they would be able to keep it. Critics of the culture of poverty theory (e.g., Ryan, 1976; Steinberg, 2007) maintain that it is simply a means of "blaming the victim" and supporting social inequality.

Living in poverty while being part of a consumer culture that values material goods such as expensive homes and cars lead to discontent, hurt feelings, and a sense of deprivation for both adults and children. The American core values of fairness and the availability of social mobility to all clash with the values of our consumer culture. Adults may envy those who have more possessions, while children may feel removed from and disconnected to the experiences of those around them. This can bring about feelings of powerlessness and

unworthiness. As noted earlier, some adults use ownership of material goods as a means to feel superior to those who have less, while children use them as a means of signifying belonging to their peer groups (Pugh, 2011). Youngsters who do not have the same things as their peers can feel left out and isolated, the way Elizabeth and Grace imagine their classmates must feel when they receive holiday gifts from the PTA.

While some young people who grow up poor may feel hurt and isolated but adhere to the dominant cultural norms and values, others may develop an oppositional culture (Ogbu, 2003). They consciously embrace norms and values that provide them with a sense of belonging in their own subculture but prevent them from succeeding in the dominant culture. For example, they may deliberately fail their classes in school and challenge authority figures.

THEORETICAL PERSPECTIVES ON ECONOMIC INEQUALITY

Now that we have explored economic inequality in the United States and the reasons behind it, we have determined that it is a social pattern that affects broad categories of people and not just random individuals. Now we can begin to address the other three parts of the definition of a social problem. Does economic inequality violate the core values of our society? Does it negatively impact those in power? Can we, as a society, curb economic inequality if we choose to do so? An examination of different theoretical perspectives will help to answer these questions as each perspective provides its own view of economic inequality.

Functionalist Perspective

Sociologists who adhere to the functionalist perspective do not always see economic inequality as a social problem. In fact, many would argue that some level of inequality acts as a positive force in society. They believe that those who provide services most valuable to society and have the most training and talent to fulfill those

Functionalists believe that society can benefit from some level of inequality.

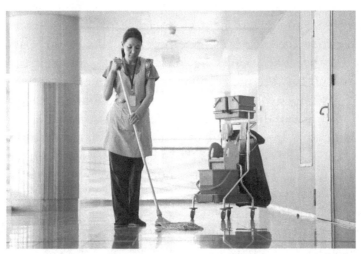

© Dmitry Kalinovsky, 2014. Used under license from Shutterstock, Inc.

services should be rewarded by being granted the highest ranks and greatest available rewards in society (Davis & Moore, 1945).

Likewise, some theorists believe that poverty serves positive functions. For example, having a class of poor people ensures the availability of a labor pool willing to do the dirtiest and most unpleasant work, such as housecleaning and yard work, at low wages. This frees the middle and upper classes, who can afford to hire someone to clean their house or mow their lawn, to pursue more pleasant activities. Some would argue that having an underclass creates service jobs for the middle class, such as social workers and police officers, and consumers for old or used products such as day-old bakery goods and used clothes, A class of poor provides examples of "deviants" who can be used to uphold traditional norms, making others feel superior because they are not "lazy," "spendthrift," "promiscuous," or have other stereotypical qualities that are ascribed to poor people (Gans, 1971).

However, Durkheim and other functionalists would be concerned about the negative impacts of economic inequality, when certain people are given greater access to good schools and other positive educational and socializing influences. These are examples of external inequality that harms society by preventing people from achieving their potential and contributing fully, possibly leading to a lack of social cohesion.

Functionalists such as Merton believe that while high levels of poverty can be beneficial for some groups in society, such as those seeking careers in social work and criminal justice, it hurts overall productivity. According to the Bureau of Labor Statistics (2011d), between September 2008 and September 2011, local governments eliminated 550,000 jobs, causing even those who normally benefit from high poverty to have difficulty finding jobs in their fields.

Both Durkheim and Merton would acknowledge that high levels of inequality violate core American values of fairness and the idea that hard work should be rewarded. Moreover, functionalists following in the steps of Durkheim and Merton recognize the need for those in power to address the threat to social cohesion and the possibility of civil unrest that often accompanies great inequality. Government leaders can mitigate the economic gap by implementing policies such as establishing progressive taxes, creating jobs, maintaining low interest rates and encouraging banks to issue government-backed loans.

Conflict Perspective

Viewing society as a collection of groups competing for power, conflict theorists are not surprised at high levels of economic inequality. In fact, they describe inequality as a normal result of a struggle for economic and political power in capitalist societies. They argue that those who control great wealth have managed to exert their influence over both economic and governmental institutions in order to enrich themselves at the expense of others (e.g., Derber 2009; Kalleberg, 2011). Weber might also find that the incredibly complicated economic institutions of the 21st century are set up in such a way that they are very difficult to dismantle and are designed to perpetuate the power of those who control them.

If Marx could see the level of economic inequality in the United States today, he might shout, "False consciousness!" The lack of awareness of the extent of inequality would trouble him greatly. He might also grind his teeth in frustration as many workers struggling to make ends meet turn against other workers who have better jobs rather than the owners of the means of production. If workers are not aware of the extent of economic inequality and who is behind it, how can they do anything about it?

However, conflict theorists are also aware that high levels of inequality can pose a threat to people in power. Inequality is an expected outcome when groups struggle for power, but when they unite and develop a class consciousness, workers can achieve greater equality. The Occupy Wall Street movement that sprang up in 2011 is an example of one attempt to unite the "99%" into one cohesive group. Those in power can also come to

realize that it is in their self-interest to mitigate extreme levels of inequality. It is no accident that social security, workers' rights, and other safety-net legislation were passed during the Great Depression. American leaders knew that to maintain power during a time when unemployment reached 25% and the Communist Party was actively supporting labor and civil rights efforts in the United States, they had to ensure that suffering citizens were given some relief and a reason not to rebel and overthrow the government (Piven & Cloward, 1993; Wormser, 2002).

Symbolic Interactionism Perspective

Maintaining a focus on interactions between individuals and a concentrated awareness of the power of socialization and symbols, theorists who use the symbolic interactionist perspective look at how inequality influences how members of different socioeconomic groups view themselves and each other. For example, they examine how media such as television and movies portray social classes and influence how people view themselves and those around them. In an era of high unemployment and increasing poverty, is conspicuous consumption now more likely to symbolize callousness than success?

Symbolic interactionist theorists also focus on the interactions that create and support

Symbolic interactionist theorists focus on the power of socialization and symbols. The use of symbols by the Tea Party movement is one example.

economic inequality. For example, through interacting with one another, people can maintain class hierarchies through a variety of intentional or unintentional means, including

- *oppressive othering*, defining another group as morally or intellectually inferior and thus not worthy of assistance;

- *fashioning superior selves*, when members of the elite portray themselves in ways that create the impression that they are of high status and should be respected;

- *defensive othering*, when a member of the same low-status group turns against others in the group to make himself seem of higher status;

- *trading power for patronage*, when the members of oppressed groups try to gain favor from the dominant group to aid themselves, while maintaining the system of inequality;

- *forming alternative subcultures*, which give a person status in a subculture but work to prevent her from effectively challenging the larger system of inequality;

- *boundary maintenance*, controlling access to people in power; and

- *cultural capital* and the passing down (or not) of the knowledge needed to interact effectively in high-status circles (e.g., knowledge of current events, knowing the difference between a water glass and a wine glass, experience and comfort talking to people in power) (Schwalbe, Godwin, Holden, Schrock, Thompson, & Wolkomir, 2000).

Politics is a common focus of symbolic interactionists, who observe that political leaders who seem unable to correct issues of inequality are considered inept and find it difficult to get reelected. Sociologists who take this perspective look at, for example, the growth of the Tea Party movement; its elaborate use of symbols, such as naming itself after the Boston Tea Party and flying flags that depict the "Don't Tread on Me"

motto from the American Revolution; and how it has moved the Republican Party farther to the political right (Williamson, Skocpol, & Coggin, 2011). They also study the attacks on and responding resurgence of unions (Acar, Chiles, Grainger, Luft, Mahajan, Peschanski, Schelly, Turowetz, & Wall, 2011) and the efforts of workers' associations such as the Coalition of Immokolee Workers to frame the struggles of organized, low-paid workers as a fight for economic justice (Coalition of Immokolee Workers, 2012). Symbolic interactionists are very aware that economic inequality, like every other aspect of society, is socially constructed, and they maintain that it can be addressed if enough people with enough power take action.

ECONOMIC INEQUALITY, POVERTY, AND HOMELESSNESS

The effects of the Great Recession have been far-reaching. However, although inequality is rising in many nations and geographic regions, it is decreasing on a global level. In the 5 years between 2005 and 2010, the number of the world's people living in poverty (defined as an income of less than $1.25 a day) dropped from more than 1.3 billion (25.7%) to less than 900 million (15.8%). According to a 2012 Brookings Institute Report (Chandy & Geertz, 2011), the rapid economic growth of developing nations such as China and India over the past decade has led to this dramatic decrease.

Certainly a decrease in poverty throughout the world is welcome progress. At the same time, there is a still a troubling number of people in the world who struggle with poverty and other inequality issues, such as homelessness. Let's take a look at how poverty and homelessness affects the United States.

Poverty in the United States

The United States has a higher poverty rate than most other similarly developed nations, with almost one in six Americans living in poverty. However, although the United States is the wealthiest nation in the world, what it considers the poverty threshold, the income level at which people are considered to be in poverty, is very low. This means that, in addition to the one in six Americans officially living in poverty, many people who are unable or barely able to afford a place to live and feed themselves earn too much to qualify as living in poverty. For example, in 2009 the U.S. Census defined an individual with an income of less than $10,956 a year to be in poverty (U.S. Census Bureau, 2011b). The Census Bureau describes how it measures poverty in the follow-ing way:

> The Census Bureau uses a set of money income thresholds that vary by family size and composition to determine who is in poverty. If a family's total income is less than the family's threshold, then that family and every individual in it is considered in poverty. The official poverty thresholds do not vary geographically, but they are updated for inflation using Consumer Price Index (CPI-U). The official poverty definition uses money income before taxes and does not include capital gains or noncash

benefits (such as public housing, Medicaid, and food stamps). (U.S. Census Bureau, 2011b)

Not surprisingly, the Great Recession led to an increased percentage of Americans living in poverty—the poverty rate rose from 12.5% in 2007 to 15.1% in 2010 (DeNavas-Walt et al., 2011). Many factors affect poverty rates. For example, the differences in poverty rates among racial groups are striking. Similarly, there are notable disparities in poverty rates among states. For example, the poverty rate among Whites is 16% in Arkansas, compared with 8% in New Jersey.

An issue closely related to poverty is food insecurity, the availability and access of enough food to support a healthy life. Many Americans face food insecurity, struggling with hunger, uncertainty about having enough food, or both. In 2010, 15.5% of American families did not have, "were uncertain of having, or (were) unable to acquire, enough food to meet the needs of all their members because they had insufficient money or other resources for food" (United States Department of Agriculture, 2011, n.p.). Figure 8-4 demonstrates

Figure 8-4

Prevalence of food insecurity, average 2008–2010

Food insecurity is found across the United States, but the level varies by state and region.

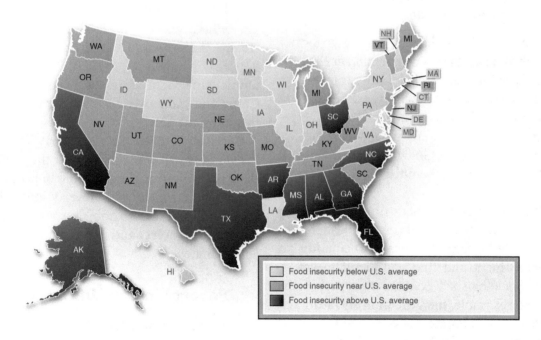

Maury Aaseng

Source: Based on calculations by ERS on current population survey food security supplemental data

HALF PRICE BOOKS ®

Half Price Books
1835 Forms Drive
Carrollton, TX 75006
OFS OrderID   28067762

SKU	ISBN/UPC	Title & Author/Artist	Shelf ID	Qty	OrderSKU
S375878991	9781524972004	The Sociological Vision Christopher Pieper	DB 50.05.4	1	

Thank you for your order, Tahera Stevens!

Thank you for shopping with Half Price Books! Please contact Support@hpb.com. if you have any
questions, comments or concerns about your order (680467588)

Visit our stores to sell your books, music, movies games for cash.

that food insecurity, like poverty, varies among the states and regions of the United States.

Homelessness in the United States

Another issue closely tied to poverty is homelessness, which has existed throughout the history of the United States. Cycles of increased homelessness have accompanied the nation's cycles of economic performance. In the preindustrial era, the homeless population was primarily made up of unemployed working men. In the "vagabond era" of the late 1800s, men hopped trains to travel to look for jobs, and the Great Depression saw an increase in working-class families without homes (Leginski, 2007). Homelessness hasbecome a much-discussed social problem in recent years due to the following factors identified by social scientist Christopher Jencks:

- outplacement, or the movement into mainstream society, of mentally ill patients formerly treated in psychiatric hospitals;

- steady increase in male long-term unemployment after 1970, due in part to a decline in low and semi-skilled jobs that paid a good wage;

- regulations against "skid row" housing, defined as cheap, single-room occupancy housing located in run-down buildings that do not meet safety codes, located above bars, and so on;

- the crack cocaine epidemic; and

- creation of more shelters for homeless people (Jencks, 1995).

According to a survey conducted by the U.S. Conference of Mayors (2010, p. 2), "[24] percent of homeless adults are severely mentally ill, 20 percent are physically disabled, 19 percent are employed, 14 percent are victims of domestic violence, 14 percent are also veterans, and three percent are HIV positive." Although homeless shelters are found in almost all urban areas of the United States, Jencks and other sociologists have helped promote the concept that shelters are not the solution to chronic homelessness among single men, who often suffer from mental illness or drug addiction. Jencks argues instead for providing more supportive services for people who continually circulate through homeless shelters, prisons, or hospitals (Urban Institute, interview of Cunningham, 2009).

Supportive housing services that concentrate on keeping homeless people housed, healthy, and employed actually costs less than the services the homeless population would otherwise use in emergency shelters, hospitals, and jails. (Urban Institute, interview of Cunningham, 2009; Culhane & Byrne, 2010). This pragmatic argument is not only supported by research but it also fits with a core value of Americans: the desire to look after those in need. The effort that began in 2000 to provide more services and supportive housing helped decrease the chronic homeless population of single adults in the United States. Further, 95% of the cost of supportive housing was found to be compensated for by the decline in the use of such services as hospitals, prisons, and emergency shelters (Culhane, Metraux, & Hadley, 2002; Urban Institute, interview of Cunningham, 2009).

Nonetheless, since the onset of the housing crisis and the Great Recession, homelessness rates are on the rise again. Families who simply cannot afford to put a roof over their heads represent a large percentage of the increase. Between 2009 and 2010, there was a 9% increase in the number of homeless families (U.S. Conference of Mayors, 2010), with unemployment most often reported as the cause of their homelessness. In addition, homeowners who faced increases in adjustable rate mortgages they could not keep up with and renters in foreclosed houses joined the ranks of the homeless (Urban Institute, interview of Cunningham. 2009).

Services to accommodate this population have not been sufficiently expanded, with 64% of the cities participating in a 2010 U.S. Conference of Mayors survey indicating that they had to turn away homeless families because they did not have

Between 2009 and 2010 the number of homeless families in the United States increased by 9%.

© Halfpoint, 2014. Used under license from Shutterstock, Inc.

the beds to accommodate them. As cities continue to face economic shortfalls due to the Great Recession and reduced federal aid, homelessness is bound to once again become a major social problem that affects many people, conflicts with our core values, and puts pressure on the leaders of U.S. society.

HOW SOCIOLOGISTS ARE ADDRESSING ECONOMIC INEQUALITY

In addition to local and federal government efforts to mitigate homelessness, nonprofit organizations—such as the National Coalition for the Homeless and the National Alliance to End Homelessness—and countless local organizations have attempted to address this social problem. Sociologists, too, have been tackling homelessness and other issues related to economic inequality. Let's explore how two sociologists, James Wright and Ruth Milkman, have used sociological tools to address two social issues related to economic inequality: attempts to move homeless populations from downtown areas near transportation and supportive services, and unjust labor practices that disproportionately harm the most economically vulnerable workers.

James Wright: Improving Facilities Rather Than Relocating Them

One of the many times sociologist James Wright used sociological tools to assist the homeless population in Orlando, Florida, came about when the city of Orlando tried to relocate the city's homeless population (Korgen, White, & White, 2011). As a member of the board of directors of the Coalition for the Homeless of Central Florida and a member of the board's Research and Evaluation Committee, Wright was in a good position to take action when the city attempted to move the site of the Coalition for the Homeless from the central business district to an area in Orlando that was out of sight and out of reach of the public transportation and other services heavily used by the homeless population.

Wright and his graduate students at the University of Central Florida conducted focus groups with homeless men and women to determine how the proposed move would affect them. They also conducted research identifying other cities that had tried to "revitalize" downtown business districts by removing services for homeless people and had either failed in their efforts to find other places for such services or, if they had managed to move the services, had not reduced the number of homeless people spending time downtown. These findings helped influence the final decision by Orlando's city government to let the coalition remain in the central business district and to create a new and improved facility for the homeless population on that site.

Ruth Milkman: Labor Laws and Inequality

Working Americans can thank Ruth Milkman for her research and advocacy work on such issues as immigrant labor organizing, minimum wage and overtime violations, and paid family and medical leave. With colleagues, she conducted a groundbreaking report, *Broken Laws, Unprotected Workers: Violations of Employment and Labor Laws in America's Cities* (Bernhardt,

Milkman, 2009), "exposing systematic and routine violations of employment and labor laws in core sectors of the economy."

This study revealed, among other findings, that all workers, no matter their race, gender, or citizenship status, may face unfair and illegal work practices, with low-wage workers most vulnerable. Over one quarter of low-wage workers surveyed were not paid even the minimum wage during the week prior to the survey, and over three quarters of participants who worked over 40 hours the week prior to the survey were not paid overtime wages as required by law. U.S. Labor Secretary Hilda Solis took note of the report and indicated that she was hiring more wage-and-hour investigators to tackle the issues of wage theft and other labor law violations (Greenhouse, 2009).

Box 8-1

Using the Sociological Lens: Arab Spring, American Autumn

Is the Occupy Wall Street movement an extension of the Arab Spring, or are the two completely different movements?

On December 17, 2010, a Tunisian street vendor named Mohamed Bouazizi set himself on fire in the ultimate gesture of protest. Bouazizi, like his fellow Tunisian citizens, had lived for two decades under the repressive leadership of President Zine El Abidine Ben Ali, where they lacked freedom of speech, freedom of the press, the right to democratically elect their own leaders, and suffered other injustices. On the day of his death, corrupt police confiscated property crucial to Bouazizi's business, while local authorities ignored his requests to have it back. Fed up, Bouazizi immolated himself. In doing so, he unknowingly gave rise to the revolutionary movement known as the Arab Spring, a populist uprising that has swept through half a dozen countries in the Middle East, causing regime change in at least two.

Less than a year later, on the other side of the world, shared issues of economic inequality and social injustice gave rise to an American protest movement known as Occupy Wall Street. Inspired by growing anger at economic disparity in the United States and taking its cues from the Arab Spring, the movement began on September 17, 2011, when at first dozens, then hundreds of protesters set up tents in Zuccotti Park, in the financial district of Manhattan. For months, protesters marched, chanted, and otherwise demonstrated their frustration with income inequality. Occupy sites sprang up in nearly every state, and sizeable demonstrations occurred in dozens of other countries, too. The movement became

immediately defined by its catchy, populist slogan, "We are the 99%," a reference to the prosperity of the top 1% of wealthiest Americans compared to the rest.

Both movements have featured calls for economic and social justice, and protestors in each demand an overhaul of the social frameworks that structure both Western and Arab societies. Yet how much the two movements have in common is a point of fascinating debate.

The Arab Spring and Occupy Wall Street are Twin Movements

According to data from the independent, nonpartisan, Congressional Budget Office and the White House, the richest 1% of Americans earn nearly 20% of the nation's income. They have seen their incomes grow by 275% since 1979, compared with 60% of Americans, who have seen their incomes grow by just 40%. The top 1% also, according to data from the University of California, Santa Cruz, and the Institute for Policy Studies, own 40% of the nation's wealth; 50% of its stocks, bonds, and mutual funds; and carry just 5% of the nation's personal debt. These eye-opening statistics are at the heart of the Occupy Wall Street movement, which demands redistribution of wealth, social justice, and economic equality for all Americans, no matter their class.

(continued)

Occupy Wall Street has been both praised and vilified for its populist approach to solving America's social problems. Because of its circus-like nature and tendency to oversimplify complex economic and social issues, Occupy Wall Street was often criticized for lacking a distinct message, and sometimes ridiculed for being immature and unrealistic. Yet the group's arguments reflected real and growing frustration found in the general population. An October 2011 poll taken jointly by CBS News and the *New York Times*, for example, found that although just 25% of Americans had a favorable impression of the Occupy Wall Street movement, 66% said they agreed with the movement's fundamental charge, that money and wealth are unfairly distributed.

By December 2011, the Pew Research Center recorded even higher dissatisfaction with economic equality. That month, more than three in four Americans—77%—said too much power is in the hands of just a few rich people and large corporations. Furthermore, 61% said the economic system unfairly favors the wealthy, while just 36% said the system is fair to the majority of Americans. Wall Street, too, remained unpopular: 51% of Americans thought Wall Street hurts America more than helps it, while just 36% thought the opposite.

In the following perspective, author Rebecca Solnit likens the spirit of the Occupy Wall Street Movement to the Arab Spring, arguing they are twin movements that share at their core a disenfranchised populace fed up with inequality and injustice. Tracing the Occupy Wall Street's birth to the shocking origins of the Arab Spring, Solnit links it to social justices movements of the past and makes an impassioned plea for a more economically equitable society.

Rebecca Solnit, "How the Arab Spring and Occupy Wall Street Started With One Tunisian Man," *Mother Jones*, October 18, 2011. http://motherjones.com/politics/2011/10/arab-spring-occupy-wall-street-protests

Occupy Wall Street Is No Arab Spring

Arab Spring protestors generally demand regime change, free and fair democratic elections, economic and social justice, and a bevy of human, political, and social rights. The movement was born after the death of Tunisian street vendor Mohamed Bouazizi, whose 2010 suicide provided a match that exploded the region's subjugated populace.

After Bouazizi's death, growing numbers of Tunisian protestors demanded justice, and then regime change. President Zine El Abidine Ben Ali sent police after them. Violent clashes grew increasingly intense until finally, after a month of unrest, Ben Ali was forced out of power on January 15, 2011.

The victory reverberated east, where politically and socially repressed citizens of other nations took note of what the Tunisians had accomplished. Weeks after Ben Ali resigned, protests began in Egypt, where conditions under dictator Hosni Mubarak, who held power for nearly 30 years, were even worse. The Egyptian protests were bloodier—hundreds were killed in violent clashes with police. In a dramatic, overwhelming outpouring, hundreds of thousands, possibly millions of people flocked to Cairo's Tahrir Square. They protested with one voice, demanding freedom, justice, economic opportunity, and democracy. After less than 3 weeks of aggressive demonstrations, Mubarak stepped down on February 11. Mubarak was one of the most iconic Middle Eastern leaders and Egypt a stable U.S. ally. The turn of events was astonishing.

The Arab Spring next bloomed in Bahrain, Syria, and Yemen, where in November 2011 Yemeni leader Ali Abdullah Saleh promised to step down after nearly a year of similarly fierce protests to his leadership. In Bahrain, tens of thousands of protestors gathered in Pearl Square, in the capital city of Manana. King Hamad temporarily avoided the fate of Ben Ali and Mubarak by responding to some of his protestors' demands. He dismissed members of his cabinet, made payments to Bahraini families, and released certain political prisoners. But thousands more have been arrested and dozens killed in the protests and uprisings that were ongoing through 2012. Hamad's hold on power is tenuous, as throngs of people flocked back to Pearl Square in mid-February 2012 to commemorate the 1-year anniversary of the uprising.

Protestors in Syria have been the victims of the worst of the Arab Spring's violence, as tyrant Bashar al-Assad clings to power. The United Nations human rights commissioner estimates more than 5,000 protestors (including more than 300 children) have been killed in Syria since the uprisings began in January 2011. Ruthless to his people and defiant of the international community's demands that he stop the violence, al-Assad is unlikely to step down and may go the way of Muammar Qaddafi, the former leader of Libya. When the Arab Spring spread there in mid-February 2011, Qaddafi had ruled with an iron fist for more than 40 years. Unlike in Tunisia and Egypt, most of the Libyan military sided with Qaddafi during the initial unrest, making large-scale protests like those in Tahrir Square and Pearl Square impossible. Instead, a civil war-like state erupted. Qaddafi was eventually forced into hiding in October and killed by rebels on October 20, 2011.

From Libya, to Syria, to Egypt, to Yemen, the Arab Spring is an ongoing movement that is reinventing the Middle East, though it remains to be seen whether it will be changed for better or for worse. In the following perspective, Ehab Zahriyah argues it is inappropriate to compare the Arab Spring with the Occupy Wall Street movement. Occupy Wall Street protestors, they explain, largely opposed economic injustices, such as gigantic CEO bonuses, widespread layoffs, and corporate greed. Arab Spring protestors, on the other hand, fought and are fighting to achieve basic human rights, democracy, and to be free from torture and intimidation. For Zahriyah, there is no reasonable comparison between the two.

Ehab Zahriyah, "Occupy Wall Street is No Tahrir Square," CNN.com, November 2, 2011. http://www.cnn.com/2011/11/02/opinion/zahriyah-occupy-tahrir-square/index.html

Chapter 9

Gender and Power

GENDER AS A SOCIAL CONSTRUCTION

Sex is a biological concept. Gender is a sociological concept. It describes the social and cultural differences a society assigns to people based on their biological sex. There is a set of social expectations (norms) for females and for males. These expectations are known as *gender roles*. Society expects certain behaviors of females, femininity, and certain behavior of males, masculinity. Gender therefore, may be described as a social construction. How we behave as fem ales and males is not pre-determined by our biology but is guided by society's expectations based on whether we are female or male. We learn about these expectations as we grow and develop a gender identity. Our gender identity reflects our beliefs about ourselves as females and males.

Femininity and masculinity are reflected in our language particularly adjectives, both positive and negative, that are used to describe females and males. Adjectives traditionally ascribed to women include: gentle, sensitive, nurturing, delicate, graceful, cooperative, decorative, dependent, emotional, passive and weak. Adjectives traditionally ascribed to men include: strong, assertive, brave, active, independent, intelligent, competitive, insensitive, unemotional and aggressive. The use of such adjectives contributes to the social construction of gender and perpetuates traditional gender roles.

Biology and Gender

Several biological explanations for gender roles exist. One explanation is from the related fields of sociobiology and evolutionary psychology (Workman and Reader, 2009) and argues an evolutionary basis for traditional gender roles. Scholars advocating this view reason that in prehistoric societies, few social roles existed. A major role centered on relieving hunger by hunting or gathering food. The other major role centered on bearing and nursing children. Because only women could perform this role, they were also the primary caretakers for children for several years after birth. Since women were frequently pregnant, their roles as mothers confined them to the home for most of their adulthood. Men, meanwhile, were better suited than women for hunting because they were stronger and quicker than women. In prehistoric societies, then, biology was indeed destiny: for biological reasons, men in effect worked outside the home (hunted), while women stayed at home with their children.

Evolutionary reasons also explain why men are more violent than women. In prehistoric times, men who were more willing to commit

From *Sociology: The Basics* by Marjorie Donovan. Copyright © 2014 by Kendall Hunt Publishing Company. Reprinted by permission.

violence against and even kill other men would win competitions for female mates. Such men were much more likely than less violent men to produce offspring who would then carry forward the violent tendencies.

If humans evolved along these lines, socio-biologists and evolutionary psychologists contend that natural selection favored societies with stronger men and more fertile and nurturing women. Such traits over time became fairly instinctual leading to different evolutionary paths for men and women. Men became more assertive, daring and violent than women, while women became more gentle, nurturing and maternal than men. Traditional gender roles for women and men make sense from an evolutionary point of view. This implies that existing gender inequality must continue because it is rooted in biology.

Critics challenge the evolutionary explanation on several grounds (Hurley, 2007; Begley, 2009). First, much greater gender variation in behavior and attitudes existed in prehistoric times than the evolutionary explanation assumes. Second, even if biological differences did influence gender roles in prehistoric times, these differences are mostly irrelevant in today's world since physical strength is not necessary for survival. Third, human environments over time have been too diverse to permit the simple biological development that the evolutionary explanation assumes. Fourth, evolutionary arguments implicitly justify existing gender inequality by implying the need to confine women and men to their traditional roles.

A second biological explanation for traditional gender roles centers on hormones and specifically on testosterone. One of the most important differences between boys and girls and men and women in the Unites States and many other societies is their level of aggression. Males are much more physically aggressive than females and in the United States and commit about 85%–90% of all violent crimes. Why? This gender difference is often attributed to higher levels of testosterone in males (Mazur, 2009).

Several studies have found that higher levels of testosterone appear to contribute to increased amounts of violence and aggression. A widely cited study of Vietnam-era male veterans found that those with higher levels of testosterone had engaged in more violent behavior (Booth and Osgood, 1993). This correlation however, does not necessarily prove that testosterone increased violence since some studies have suggested that violent behavior may increase testosterone levels.

Biological evidence for gender differences certainly exists but its interpretation remains very controversial. It must be carefully weighed against the evidence that supports cultural variations and how they affect experiences that contribute to gender socialization.

Culture and Gender

Anthropologists offer compelling evidence against a strong biological determination of gender roles. Anthropological studies of preindustrial societies demonstrate some striking gender variation from one culture to another. Anthropologist Margaret Mead (1935) studied cultural differences related to gender issues. Mead's work focused on three tribes in New Guinea: the Arapesh, the Mundugumor, and the Tchambuli. Gender roles varied among the three tribes. Both sexes displayed gentle and nurturing traits in the Arapesh tribe. Both men and women spent time with the children and exhibited behavior that would be considered "maternal." Distinct gender roles did not exist among the Arapesh because both sexes displayed behavior similar to modern female gender roles. Mead found the reverse among the Mundugumor. Both men and women were aggressive and competitive, even violent. Both sexes distanced themselves from the children. Mead's conclusion was that as with the Arapesh, the Mundugumor had no gender roles. Both sexes displayed behavior similar to modern male gender roles (Mead, 1935).

Mead's observation of the Tchambuli revealed very distinct differences from the other two tribes. She found that distinct gender roles existed among the Tchambuli. One sex was dominant, assertive and assumed leadership positions among the tribe. The other sex used make-up, dressed in elaborate clothing and even spent time giggling with other members of the tribe. Mead reported that she had found a society with gender roles similar to those found in the society of the United States, but there was an unexpected difference. In the Tchambuli women were the dominant, aggressive sex in leadership positions while men were submissive and focused on superficial details such as clothing and make-up (Mead, 1935).

Mead's research was of great interest among scholars because it challenged the biological view on gender that was very prevalent at the time. Today Mead's work is controversial. It is supported by some anthropologists and refuted by some anthropologists. Some argue that Mead may have applied an over simplified idea regarding gender roles among the three societies, (Scheper, 1987). Others defend Mead's work by citing numerous subsequent studies that also suggest that cultural forces powerfully influence gender roles (Morgan, 1989).

Sexual Orientation

Sexual orientation describes a person's preference for sexual relationships with individuals of the other sex (heterosexuality), one's own sex (homosexuality), or both sexes (bisexuality). The term also increasingly refers to transgendered individuals, those whose behavior, appearance, and/or gender identity fails to conform to conventional norms. Transgendered individuals include transvestites (those who dress in the clothing of the opposite sex) and transsexuals (those whose gender identity differs from the psychological sex and who sometimes undergo a sex change).

While most people learn stable sexual identities, over the course of one's life, sexual identity evolves. Heterosexual identity is thus strongly encouraged by the dominant culture, and young people growing up shape their sexual identity in this context. Sometimes, one's sexual identity may change. For example, a person who has always thought of himself or herself as a heterosexual may decide at a later time that he or she is gay or lesbian. In more unusual cases, people may actually undergo a sex change operation, changing their sexual identity in the process. In the case of bisexuals, a person might adopt a dual sexual identity.

Within the United States, the social construction of sexual identity is also revealed by studies of the "coming out" process. Coming out—the process of defining oneself as gay or lesbian—is a series of events and redefinitions in which a person comes to see herself or himself as having a gay identity. In coming out, a person consciously labels that identity either to oneself or others (or both). Coming out is usually not the result of a single homosexual experience. If it were, there would be far more self-identified homosexuals than there are, because researchers find that a substantial portion of both men and women have some form of homosexual experience at some time in their lifetime. A person may even change between gay, straight, and bisexual identities (Rust, 1993). This indicates, as the social construction perspective suggests, that identity is created not fixed, over the course of a life.

Sociological understanding of sexual identity has developed largely through new studies of lesbian and gay experience. Long thought of only in terms of social deviance, gays and lesbians have been much stereotyped in traditional social science, but the feminist and gay liberation movements have discouraged this approach, arguing that gay and lesbian experience is merely one alternative in the broad spectrum of human sexuality. Now there is a growing research literature examining different aspects of gay life (Nardi and Schneider, 1997; Seidman, 1994).

The institutional context of sexuality within the United States, as well as other societies, was historically one where homophobia permeated the culture. *Homophobia* is the fear and hatred of homosexuality. It is manifested in prejudiced attitudes toward gays and lesbians, as well as in overt hostility and violence directed against people suspected of being gay. Homophobia is a learned attitude, as are other forms of negative social judgments about particular groups. Homophobia is deeply embedded in people's definitions of themselves as men and women. Boys are often raised to be "manly" by repressing so-called feminine characteristics in themselves. Being called "fag" or a "sissy" is one of the peer sanctions that socialize a child to conform to particular gender roles. Similarly, verbal attacks on lesbians are a mechanism of social control, because ridicule can be interpreted as encouraging social conformity.

Homophobia plays an important role in gender socialization because it encourages stricter conformity to traditional expectations, especially for men and young boys. Slurs directed against gays encourage boys to act more masculine as a way of affirming for their peers that they are not gay. As a consequence, homophobia also discourages so-called feminine traits in men, such as caring, nurturing, empathy, emotion, and gentleness.

Because of homophobia in the culture, there are numerous misleading myths about gays and lesbians. One is that gay men have large discretionary incomes who work primarily in artistic areas and personal service jobs (such as hairdressing). This stereotype prevents people from recognizing that there are gays and lesbians in all racial-ethnic groups, some of whom are working class or poor, and who are employed in a wide range of occupations (Gluckman and Reed, 2007). Some lesbians and gays are also old people, even though the stereotype defines them as mostly young or middle aged (Smith, 2103).

Heterosexism refers to the institutionalization of heterosexuality as the only socially legitimate sexual orientation. Heterosexism is rooted in the belief that heterosexual behavior is the only natural form of sexual expression and that homosexuality is a perversion of "normal" sexual identity. Heterosexism is reinforced through institutional mechanisms that project the idea that only heterosexuality is normal. Institutions also structure the unequal distribution of privileges to people presumed to be heterosexual. Historically businesses and communities for example, rarely recognized the legal rights of those in homosexual relationships, although this is changing. Heterosexism is an institutional phenomenon although people's beliefs can reflect heterosexist assumptions. Thus a person may be quite accepting of gay and lesbian people (that is, not be homophobic), but still benefit from heterosexual privileges or engage in heterosexist practices that have the unintentional effect of excluding lesbians and gays, such as by talking with co-workers about their dating activities on the assumption that everyone is interested in a heterosexual partner.

The heterosexist framework of social institutions enforced situations in which gay and lesbian relationships lack the institutional support of heterosexual relationships. In the absence of such socially sanctioned institutions, lesbians and gays have invented their own rituals and communities to support these relationships. The absence of institutionalized roles for lesbians and gays affects the roles they adopt within relationships. Despite popular stereotypes, gay partners typically do not assume roles as the dominant or subordinate sexual partner. They are more likely to adopt roles as equals. Gay and lesbian couples are also more likely than heterosexual couples to both be employed, another source of greater equality within the relationship. Researchers have also found that the quality of relationships among gay men is positively correlated with the social support the couple receives from others (Smith and Brown, 2011).

Gender Identity

Gender identities are the conceptions we have of ourselves as being male or female. As such they are invisible, something that cannot be established by appearance. For most people, there is a good fit between their anatomy and their gender identity. Boys generally come to behave in ways their culture labels "masculine," and girls learn to be "feminine." But there are some individuals for whom this is not the case. The most striking examples are *transsexuals*—individuals who have normal sexual organs, but who psychologically feel like members of the opposite sex. In some cases medical science has found a way, through surgery and hormones, to reduce the incompatibility by modifying the person's anatomy to conform to the gender identity.

Learning plays a key part in the acquisition of gender identities. However, the exact nature of this learning has been the subject of considerable debate. According to Sigmund Freud and his followers, gender identity and the adoption of sex-typed behaviors are the result of an *Oedipus conflict* that emerges between the ages of 3 and 6. During this period, children discover the genital differences between the sexes. According to Freudians, this discovery prompts children to see themselves as rivals of their same-sex parent for the affection of the parent of the other sex. Such desires and feelings give rise to considerable anxiety. Freud said the anxiety is resolved through complicated psychological maneuvers in which children come to identify with the parent of the same sex. By virtue of this identification, boys acquire masculine self-conceptions and girls learn feminine self-conceptions. However, research that has tried to test Freud's theory has been either inconclusive or at odds with it. Additionally cross-cultural research suggests that the Oedipus conflict does not occur among all peoples.

Unlike Freud and his followers, *cultural transmission* theorists contend that the acquisition of gender identities and behaviors is not the product of an Oedipus conflict, but rather is a gradual process of learning that begins in infancy (Bandura, 1971). They suggest that parents, teachers, and other adults shape a child's behavior by reinforcing responses that are deemed appropriate to the child's gender role and discouraging inappropriate ones. Moreover, children are motivated to attend to, learn from, and imitate same-sex models as more like themselves. Children are given cues to their gender roles in a great variety of ways. Parents often furnish boys' and girls' rooms differently, decorating those of boys with animal motifs and those of girls with floral motifs, lace, fringe, and ruffles. The toys found in the rooms also differ. Boys are provided with more vehicles, military toys, sports equipment, toy animals, and mechanical toys; girls, more dolls, doll houses, and domestic toys (Caldera, Huston and O'Brien, 2009).

Cultural-transmission theory draws our attention to the part socialization plays in shaping the sex-typed behavior of children. However, the image we gain from the theory is one of essentially passive individuals who are programmed for behavior by adult bearers of culture. *Labeling theory* (also called cognitive-developmental theory) provides a corrective to this perspective by calling our attention to the fact that children actively seek to acquire gender identities and roles.

According to developmental psychologist Lawrence Kohlberg (1966, 1969; Kohlberg and Ullian 1974), children come to label themselves as "boys" or "girls" when they are between 18 months and 3 years of age. Once they have identified themselves as males or females, they want to adopt behaviors consistent with their newly discovered status. This process is called *self-socialization.* According to Kohlberg, children form a stereotyped conception of maleness and femaleness—an oversimplified, exaggerated, cartoon-like image. Then they use this stereotyped image in organizing behavior and cultivating the attitudes and actions associated with being a boy or a girl.

Both the cultural-transmission and labeling theories of gender-role learning have received research support (Maccoby and Jacklin, 1974; Bem, 1981; Serbin and Sprafkin, 1986). Increasingly, social and behavioral scientists are coming to the view that any full explanation of gender-role acquisition must incorporate elements from both theoretical approaches.

Gender Socialization

Gender socialization begins in infancy since most parents socialize their children into traditional gender roles without even knowing it (Snider, 2009). Parents typically describe their infant sons as big, strong and assertive while they refer to their infant daughters as pretty and delicate. Parents typically play more roughly with their sons and more quietly with their daughters. When infant daughters cry, they are comforted but infant sons are often allowed to cry for longer periods of time and they receive less comforting treatment.

Clues to proper gender roles surround children in materials produced by corporations (books, toys, games), in mass media images, in educational settings, and in religious organizations and beliefs. Agents of socialization play a major role in teaching children proper gender roles. Corporations, for example, produce materials that help to socialize children into proper conduct. Publishers produce books that present images of expected gender behavior. Language and pictures in preschool picture books, elementary children's books, and school textbooks are steeped in gender role messages, reflecting society's expectations and stereotypes.

Producers of toys and games also contribute to traditional messages about gender. Such toys fill rooms in the homes of children in the western world and it is usually quite clear which are boys' rooms and which are girls' rooms. Boys' rooms are filled with sports equipment, army toys, building and technical toys, and cars and trucks. Girls' rooms have fewer toys and most are related to dolls and domestic roles. Boys have more experience manipulating blocks, Tinker Toys, Legos, and Erector sets, all of which parallel masculinized activities outside the home in the public domain, from constructing and building trades to military roles and sports. Girls prepare for domestic roles with toys relating to domestic activities. Barbie dolls stress physical appearance, consumerism, and glamour. Only a few Barbies are in occupational roles. In contrast, the Ken dolls that Mattel designed to match Barbie (and have now been discontinued) were often doctors or other professionals.

In 2009, Mattel produced Barbie's online dream house, a virtual house that can be decorated and furnished. Barbie's house was designed with girls as the target market. A complementary target boy program features Hot Wheels cars with car races and uses virtual tools to customize cars. These models differed in more than simple appearance. The life lessons learned from such computer games reinforce gender stereotypes (Snider, 2009). Each toy or game prepares children through anticipatory socialization for future gender roles. Toys that require building, manipulating, and technical skills provide experiences for later life. Choices ranging from college major and occupational choice to activities that depend on visual-spatial and mathematical abilities appear to be affected by these early choices and childhood learning experiences (Tavris & Wade, 1984).

Television is also a very powerful agent of socialization. By school age typical U. S. children will have spent more time in front of a television than they will classrooms in the coming twelve years of school, a behavior that contributes to obesity in the United States (Randerson, 2008). Television presents a simple, stereotyped view of life, from advertisements to situation comedies to soap operas. Women in soap operas and ads, especially those working outside the home, are often depicted as having problems in carrying out their role responsibilities (Benokraitis & Feagin, 1995). See Box 9-1—The Boy Code—for additional information on gender socialization.

Gender Differences: Having v. Doing

Ideas regarding what is not "normal" for a particular gender are not based on biological traits; it is the product of social behavior. Childhood is the primary time for developing and understanding these standards. Children follow the cultural rules and try to meet the expectations of the gender that they perceive themselves to be. This results in the formation of gender identity. Once children learn the appropriate behaviors for their particular gender, they are more likely to fit in with peers and be accepted by family members and authority figures (West and Zimmerman, 2007).

In their work, *Doing Gender*, Sociologists West and Zimmerman suggest that there are distinctions between "doing gender" and "having gender" (West and Zimmerman, 2007). Specific body parts do not necessarily ensure that a child will be biologically forced to "do" that gender. "Doing gender" refers to the act of matching one's behavior to a certain set of gender-related standards. "Having gender" refers specifically to the biological characteristics that result in the attachment of labels, male or female. We all have a gender but the way we behave is the doing of gender. When little girls put on their mother's makeup or little boys pick up their father's tools, they are learning gender roles or doing gender. Gender constructs become so fixed that children who do not fit the model are often treated as outcasts and may experience negative sanctions including teasing, isolation, harsh words, and stigma. To avoid such informal sanctions, children usually conform to traditional gender expectations, at least in public situations.

As children reach school age, the lifelong process of gender socialization continues through activities separate from parents. Others in the community including teachers, religious leaders,

Box 9-1

The Boy Code

Boys and girls begin to conform to gender expectations once they are old enough to understand that their sex is permanent. They then become even more conscious of adhering to the norms of others in their gender category.

The so-called "Good Old Boy" network that has traditionally favored men in American society actually starts with "the boy code." Young boys learn the code from parents, siblings, peers, teachers, and society in general. They are praised for following the code and punished for violating it. William Pollack (1999) suggested that boys learn several stereotyped behavior models exemplifying the boy code:

1. "The sturdy oak"—men should be stoic, stable, and independent — a man never shows weaknesses.
2. "Give 'em hell"—from athletic coaches and movie heroes, the consistent theme is extreme daring, bravado, and attraction to violence.
3. "The big wheel"—men and boys should achieve status, dominance, and power—they should avoid shame, wear the mask of coolness, and act as though everything is under control.
4. "No sissy stuff"—boys are discouraged from expressing feelings or urges perceived as feminine—dependence, warmth , empathy.

The boy code is ingrained in society. By five or six years of age boys are less likely than girls to express hurt or distress. They have learned to be ashamed of showing feelings and of being weak. The gender straitjacket, according to Pollack, causes boys to conceal feelings in order to fit in and be accepted and loved. As a result some boys , especially in adolescence, become silent, covering any vulnerability and masking their true feelings. This affects boys' relationships, performance in school, and the ability to connect with others. It also causes young males to put on what Jackson Katz (2006) calls the "tough guise"—when young men and boys emphasize aggression and violence to display masculinity.

Pollack (1999) suggests that we can help boys reconnect to non-gendered norms by doing the following:

1. Giving some undivided attention each day just listening to boys.
2. Encouraging a range of emotions.
3. Avoiding language that taunts, teases, or shames.
4. Looking behind the veneer of "coolness" for signs of problems.
5. Expressing love and empathy.
6. Dispelling the "sturdy oak" image.
7. Advocating a broad, inclusive model of masculinity.

With the women's movement and shifts in gender expectations have come new patterns of male behavior. Some men are forming more supportive and less competitive relationships with other men, and there are likely to be continued changes in the broadening of "appropriate" behavior for men (Kimmel & Messner, 2009).

coaches, and other children become influential in the lives of young people. Many activities involve boys versus girls, we versus they, us and them and so forth. Even if parents are not highly traditional with regard to gender expectations, children still experience many influences at the micro level to conform to traditional gender notions.

Adulthood involves new forms of gender stratification in which men have traditionally had more networks and statuses as well as greater access to resources outside the home. This has resulted in women having less power because they depend more on husbands or fathers for resources. Consider the following example: When the question arises of who walks through the door first, the answer is that in most western societies, "she" does. The strong man steps back and defers to the weaker female, graciously holding the door for her (Walum, 2004). Yet when it comes to who walks through the metaphorical door to professions, it is the man who goes first. Women are served first at restaurants and other micro-level settings, but this seems little compensation for the fact that doors have traditionally been closed to them in other situations in society. See Table 9-1 for information on gender segregation in the workplace.

Gender stratification refers to males' and females' unequal access to a society's power, property, and prestige. Each society establishes a structure that, on the basis of sex and gender, permits or limits access to privileges. *Sex* refers to biological distinctions between males and females; *gender* refers to what a society considers to be proper behaviors and attitudes for its males and females. In the *"nature versus nurture"* debate, almost all sociologists take the side of nature.

Table 9-1

Gender Segregation in the Workplace for Selected Occupations (2010)

Occupation	Female Workers (%)	Male Workers (%)
Dental Hygienists	99.2	0.8
Speech-language Pathologists	98.0	2.0
Pre-school and Kindergarten Teachers	97.3	2.7
Secretaries and Administrative Assistants	96.7	3.3
Registered Nurses	91.7	9.3
Food Servers	74.0	26.0
Lawyers	32.6	67.4
Physicians	30.0	70.0
Dentists	28.2	71.8
Computer Software Engineers	20.8	79.2
Carpenters	1.9	98.1
Electricians	1.7	98.3

Source: Data from U.S. Census Bureau (2010). Statistical abstract of the United States 2010. Washington, DC: U.S. Government Printing Office.

Sociologists suggest that one is born a male or female but becoming a man or a woman is the result of social and cultural expectations that pattern the behavior of men and women. From birth, gender expectations influence how boys and girls are treated. Some researchers argue that biological factors (two X chromosomes in females, one X and Y in males) results in differences in male (more aggressive and domineering) and female (more comforting and nurturing) conduct. The dominant sociological position is that gender differences result from sex being used to mark people for special treatment. Symbolic interactionists stress that society interprets the physical differences: males and females take the relative positions that society assigns to them.

Globally, gender is the primary division between people. Because society sets up barriers to deny women equal access, they are referred to as a minority even though they outnumber men. Murdock (1935) surveyed hundreds of primitive societies and found activities to be sex-typed in all of them, although activities considered female in one society may be male in another (Murdock, 1935). Universally greater prestige is given male activities

regardless of the details. If caring for cattle is men's work, it carries high prestige; if it is women's work, it has less prestige. Although the origin of patriarchy (male dominance) is unknown, two theories have emerged, both assuming patriarchy to result from universal conditions.

1. As a result of pregnancy and breast-feeding, women were limited for much of their lives. They assumed tasks associated with the home and child care; men took over tasks requiring greater speed and longer absences, such as hunting animals. This enabled men to make contact with other tribes, trade with those other groups, and wage war and gain prestige by returning home with prisoners of war or with large animals to feed the tribe; little prestige was given to women's more routine tasks.

2. In prehistoric times, each group was threatened with annihilation by other groups, and each had to recruit members to fight enemies in dangerous, hand-to-hand combat. Men, who were bigger and

stronger, were coaxed into this bravery by promises of rewards, including sexual access to females. Thus, men were trained for combat; women were conditioned from birth to acquiesce in male demands. The drudge work was assigned to women since men preferred to avoid those tasks.

3. Either theory may be correct but the answer is buried in human history and there is no way of testing either.

4. A society's culture and institutions both justifies and maintains its customary forms of gender inequality. In the past, women in the United States did not have the right to vote, hold property, testify in court, or serve on a jury. If a woman worked outside the home, she handed her wages over to her father or husband. Males did not willingly surrender their privileges; rather, women's rights resulted from a prolonged and bitter struggle. While women enjoy more rights today, gender inequality still exists. Patterns of *gender discrimination* persist in everyday life. Females' capacities, interests, attitudes, and contributions are not taken as seriously as those of their male counterparts. Patterns of conversation reflect inequalities between men and women. Men are more likely than women to interrupt a conversation and to control a change in topics. Most victims of rape are females. Males are more likely to commit murder than females. Feminists use symbolic interactionism to understand violence against women. They stress that U. S. culture promotes violence by males. It teaches men to associate power, dominance, strength, virility and superiority with masculinity. Men use violence to try and maintain higher status.

5. Feminists advocate for a restructuring of social institutions to meet the needs of all groups, not just those who already have enough power and privilege to make social institutions work for them. The successes of the women's movement demonstrate that change is possible, but only when people are vigilant about their needs.

FEMINISM

Feminist theorists suggest that gender stratification is based on power struggles rather than biology. A distinguishing characteristic of most feminist theory is that it actively advocates a change in the social order. There are a range of feminist theories all of which argue for bringing about a new and equal ordering of gender relationships to eliminate the *patriarchy* and *sexism* of current gender stratification systems (Kramer, 2007).

Feminist theorists try to understand the causes of women's lower status and seek ways to change the systems to provide more opportunities, to improve the standard of living, and to give women control over their bodies and reproduction. Feminist theorists also feel that little change will occur until group consciousness is raised so that women understand the system that limits their options and do not blame themselves, or men, for their situations—a systemic social problem (Kramer, 2007).

As societies become technologically advanced and need an educated workforce, women of all social classes and ethnic groups around the world are likely to gain more equal roles. Women are entering institutions of higher education in record numbers, and evidence indicates they are needed in the world economic system and the changing labor force of most countries. Societies in which women are not integrated into the economic sphere generally lag behind other countries. Feminist theorists examine these global and national patterns, but they also note the role of patriarchy in interpersonal situations.

Feminist analysis finds gender patterns embedded in social institutions of family, education, religion, politics, economics, and health care. If the societal system is patriarchal, ruled by men, the interdependent institutions are likely to reflect and support the system. See Box 9-2 for information about Women's History Month and Box 9-3 for information on Betty Friedan, a leader of the modern women's movement who maintained that women and men must forge relationships as allies, not enemies.

Box 9-2

Women's History Month

National Women's History Month's roots go back to March 8, 1857, when women from New York City factories staged a protest over working conditions. International Women's Day was first observed in 1909, but it wasn't until 1981 that Congress established National Women's History Week to be commemorated the second week of March. In 1987, Congress expanded the week to a month. Every year since, Congress has passed a resolution for Women's History Month, and the President has issued a proclamation.

158.3 million

The number of females in the United States in 2011. The number of males was 153.3 million.
Source: Population Estimates: 2011, Table NC_EST2011_01
At 65 and older, there were 13.3 percent more women than men in 2011.
Source: Population Estimates: 2011, Table NC_EST2011_01

Jobs

57.7%

Percentage of females 16 and older who participated in the labor force, representing about 72.6 million women in 2012.
Source: U.S. Bureau of Labor Statistics, Current Population Survey, Table A-2

41.7%

Percent of employed females 16 and older who worked in management, professional and related occupations, compared with 35.1 percent of employed males in December 2012.
Source: U.S. Bureau of Labor Statistics, Current Population Survey, Table A-19

Military

204,973

Total number of active duty women in the military, as of Nov. 30, 2012. Of that total, 38,378 women were officers, and 164,021 were enlisted.
Source: U.S. Department of Defense, Selected Manual Statistics, annual, and unpublished data.

Earnings

$37,118

The median annual earnings of women 15 or older who worked year-round, full time in 2011. In comparison, the median annual earnings of men were $48,202.
Source: Income, Poverty, and Health Insurance Coverage in the United States: 2011, Page 7 & 11.

0.77

The female-to-male earnings ratio in 2011. The number of men and women with earnings who worked year-round in 2011 was not statistically different from the ratio in 2010.
Source: Income, Poverty, and Health Insurance Coverage in the United States: 2011, Page 12.

Education

31.4 million

Number of women 25 and older with a bachelor's degree or more in 2011, higher than the corresponding number for men (30 million). Women had a larger share of high school diplomas (including equivalents), as well as associate, bachelor's and master's degrees. More men than women had a professional or doctoral degree.
Source: Educational Attainment in the United States: 2011, Table 3

30.1%

Percent of women 25 and older who had obtained a bachelor's degree or more as of 2011.
Source: Educational Attainment in the United States: 2011, Table 3

11.3 million

Number of college students in fall 2011 who were women age 15 and older.
Source: School Enrollment in the United States: 2011, Table 5

Businesses

$1.2 trillion

Revenue for women-owned businesses in 2007.
Source: 2007 Survey of Business Owners

7.8 million

The number of women-owned businesses in 2007.
Source: 2007 Survey of Business Owners

7.5 million

Number of people employed by women-owned businesses in 2007.
Nearly half of all women-owned businesses (45.9 percent) operated in repair and maintenance; personal and laundry services; health care and social assistance; and professional, scientific and technical services. Women-owned businesses

(continued)

Box 9-2
Women's History Month *(continued)*

accounted for 52.0 percent of all businesses operating in the health care and social assistance sector.
Source: 2007 Survey of Business Owners

4

Number of states with at least 500,000 women-owned businesses in 2007 was California, Texas, New York and Florida. California had 1,039,208 women-owned businesses or 13.3 percent of all women-owned businesses in the United States, Texas had 609,947 or 7.8 percent, New York had 594,517 or 7.6 percent, and Florida had 581,096, or 7.5 percent.
Source: 2007 Survey of Business Owners

Voting

46.2%

Percentage of female citizens 18 and older who reported voting in the 2010 congressional election. 44.8 percent of their male counterparts cast a ballot. Additionally, 66.6 percent of female citizens reported being registered to vote.
Source: Voting and Registration in the Election of November 2010, Table 1

Motherhood

85.4 million

Estimated number of mothers in the United States in 2009.
Source: Unpublished data from the Survey of Income and Program Participation, 2008 1.9

Average number of children that women 40 to 44 had given birth to as of 2010, down from 3.1 children in 1976, the year the Census Bureau began collecting such data.
Source: Fertility of American Women: 2010 table 2 and Historical Table 2

The percentage of women in this age group who had given birth was 81 percent in 2010, down from 90 percent in 1976.
Source: Fertility of American Women: 2010 table 1 and Historical Table 2

Marriage

64.9 million

Number of married women 18 and older (including those who were separated or had an absent spouse) in 2011.
Source: Families and Living Arrangements: 2011, Table A1

5.1 million

Number of stay-at-home mothers nationwide in 2012.
Source: Families and Living Arrangements: 2012, Table FG8

Box 9-3
Focus on Betty Friedan (1921—2006)

"Man is not the enemy here, but the fellow victim."

– Betty Friedan

"It is easier to live through someone else than to complete yourself. The freedom to lead and plan your own life is frightening if you have never faced it before. It is frightening when a woman finally realizes that there is no answer to the question 'who am I' except the voice inside herself."

– Betty Friedan

"You can have it all, just not all at the same time."

– Betty Friedan

"The problem lay buried, unspoken, for many years in the minds of American women. It was a strange stirring, a sense of dissatisfaction, a yearning that women suffered in the middle of the twentieth century in the United States. Each suburban wife struggled with it alone. As she made the beds, shopped for groceries, matched slipcover material, ate peanut butter sandwiches with her children, chauffeured Cub Scouts and Brownies, lay beside her husband at night -she was afraid to ask even of herself the silent question- "Is this all?"

– Betty Friedan

Betty Friedan was born Bettye Naomi Goldstein in 1921 to Harry Goldstein, a Russian immigrant and owner of a jewelry store, and Miriam (Horowitz) Goldstein. Her mother gave up her position as editor of the women's page of the local paper to raise her family.

Bettye Goldstein majored in psychology and edited the college newspaper at Smith College. Under her guidance, the paper became a forum for the fight against fascism abroad and promoted the organization of unions at home. She graduated summa cum laude in 1942. Bettye, dropped what she thought was the pretentious "e" at the end of her given name when she became a psychology research fellow at the University of California in Berkeley. One year later she moved to New York to work as a reporter and she became involved in labor union activity. She worked for union publications as a labor journalist and pamphlet writer and developed an intense interest in working women's issues. In 1947, she married Carl Friedan. The marriage produced three children and ended after twenty-two years. Friedan received maternity leave and continued working after her first child was born in 1949, but she was forced to leave her job during her second pregnancy in 1953. She spent the next decade raising her two sons and a daughter. She continued to work as a writer for middle-class women's magazines.

In 1957, Betty Friedan surveyed two hundred of her Smith College classmates and found that many of them suffered from "the problem that has no name." They were supposed to be happy in their suburban paradises, with working husband and smiling children, but many were bored, depressed and anxious. She was not satisfied by the women's explanation that their unhappiness was their own fault so she continued to explore the matter. She received widespread response to an article she published in *Good Housekeeping* in September of 1960, entitled "Women Are People Too!" The reaction to the article helped her to realize that the malaise she found was not limited to women from prestigious eastern colleges.

The results of her research formed the basis of her book *The Feminine Mystique*, published in 1963, throughout which Friedan encouraged women to seek new opportunities for themselves. In *The Feminine Mystique*, Friedan described a type of depression experienced by many middle-aged, college-educated women, and she suggested its cause. She argued that the media and educators had created an image of women's proper role as appendages of their husbands and children: "as Tom's wife or Mary's mother." The effect of this "feminine

mystique" was that women denied their own desires for the sake of familial harmony. Their lack of excitement about their own lives made them smother their children and cling to their husbands. They were bored and ineffectual. The book quickly became a sensation, and created a social revolution by dispelling the myth that all women wanted to be happy homemakers, and marking the start of what would become Friedan's incredibly significant role in the women's rights movement (Friedan, 1963).

As a feminist revolutionary, Betty Friedan was considered by many to be the "mother" of the second wave of modern feminism. Her struggles against the "feminine mystique" and in favor of gender equality led to the establishment of a common cause and a fundamental transformation in the way American women view themselves. Betty Friedan did more though, than write about confining gender stereotypes. She became a force for change. She encouraged women to become more involved in the political process and co-founded the National Organization for Women in 1966. She served as its first president. She also fought for abortion rights by establishing the National Association for the Repeal of Abortion Laws (now known as NARAL Pro-Choice America) in 1969.

Friedan published *The Second Stage* in 1982, in which she presented a more moderate feminist position from her earlier work. Friedan later explored the later stages of a woman's life in *The Fountain of Age*, published in 1993, when she was in her 70s.

Betty Friedan died of heart failure on February 4, 2006, in Washington, D.C. She is remembered as one of the leading voices of the women's rights movement of the 20th century. The work that she started is still being carried on by the organizations that she helped to establish.

Selected Works by Betty Friedan –

The Feminine Mystique (1963, reprinted, 2001); *It Changed My Life* (1976); *The Second Stage* (1981); *The Fountain of Age* (1993); *Life So Far: A Memoir* (2000).

Sources: Friedan (1963, 1976, 1981, 1993, 2001), National Organization of Women (NOW) (2013).

Feminism and Sexism

"Just wait until your father gets home!" The statement suggests that Father is the supreme authority figure and that a severe punishment will occur upon his arrival. The threat was used historically to create fear in children. The statement indicates that a mother has less influence than a father on the behavior of children and reinforces an enduring stereotype that the man is the dominant member of the family. Such family

dynamics are common in a patriarchy, a social system in which men dominate and exert power and authority over women and children. In patriarchal societies, men manage public affairs in government, business, religion and education. No pure matriarchy exists even though some women may seem to have more power than men. In most cultures there are clear lines of male dominance in the social systems. Women, in general, have less power.

Income and Workplace Inequality and the Gendered Wage Gap

Such systems typically result in sexism, the belief that one sex is superior to the other. Patriarchal societies view women as weak and no match for a man's physical or intellectual prowess. Even in societies that give women the same civil rights as men, there are still different standards for women. Even after years of fighting for equal rights in the United States, women still earn less money than men. A man with a bachelor's degree earns about $71,000 annually while a woman with a bachelor's degree earns about $51,000 annually. Men with doctorates average $113,000 while women with doctorates average $82,000. The variations in salaries between men and women illustrate a gendered wage gap. The gendered wage gap primarily results from sex segregation in the workplace (see Table 9-1). While labor force participation has increased significantly for women in recent years, the workplace remains segregated by gender. Almost half of all women work in a few low-paying clerical and service –type jobs, such as retail or food, while men work in a much greater variety of jobs, including high paying jobs. Table 9-1 shows that many jobs are held primarily by either women or men. Part of the reason for this segregation is that socialization affects job choices for young people and women and men do not typically want to encounter difficulties including social disapproval that may result if they pursue a job that is traditionally assigned to the other sex. Compounding the problem, sex-segregated jobs often discriminate against applicants who are not the correct sex for the job. Employers may either consciously refuse to hire someone who is the wrong sex for the job or have job requirements and workplace rules that unintentionally make it more difficult for women to qualify for certain jobs. Such practices are of course, illegal, but they persist due to an institutionalized sexism that exists in societies. The sex-segregation that results contributes to the continuing gendered wage gap between female and male workers. Occupations dominated by women tend to pay lower wages and salaries and since women are concentrated in low paying jobs, their earnings continue to be much lower than earnings for men (Reskin and Padavic, 2002).

"The glass ceiling keeps women from reaching the highest level of corporate and public responsibility and the sticky floor keeps the vast majority of the world's women stuck in low-paid jobs" (Hunter College Women's Studies Collective, 2005). Men, on the other hand, face the glass escalator, especially in traditionally female occupations. Even if they do not seek to climb in the organizational hierarchy, occupational social forces push them up the job ladder to the higher echelons (Wingfield, 2009). Women around the world do two thirds of the work, receive 10% of the world's income, and own 1% of the world's means of production (Robbins, 2005). They make up more than 40% of the world's paid workforce but hold only about 20% of the managerial jobs, and for those, they are often compensated at lower pay than their male counterparts. Only 5% of the top corporate jobs are held by women. However, companies with women in leadership positions do realize high profits (Hunter College Women's Studies Collective 2005).

Sexual Harassment

Sexual harassment is a common workplace problem. It is defined by federal guidelines and legal rulings and statutes as unwelcome sexual advances, requests for sexual favors, or physical conduct of a sexual nature used as a condition of employment or promotion or that interferes with an individual's job performance and creates an intimidating or hostile environment.

Although men can be, and are, sexually harassed, women are more often the targets of sexual harassment, which is often considered a form of violence against women. This gender difference exists for at least two reasons, one cultural and one structural. The cultural reason centers on the depiction of women and the socialization of men. Women are depicted by mass media as sexual objects that exist for men's pleasure. At the same time our culture socializes men to sexually assertive. These two cultural beliefs combine to make men believe that they have the right to make verbal and physical advances to women in the workplace. When these advances meet the guidelines previously mentioned, they become sexual harassment.

The second reason that most targets of sexual harassment are women is more structural. Reflecting the gendered nature of the workplace and of the educational system, typically the men doing the harassment are in a position of power over the women they harass. A male boss harasses a female employee, or a male professor harasses a female student or employee. These men realize that subordinate women may find it difficult to resist their advances for fear of reprisals.

Title IX

In 1972, the Patsy T. Mink Equal Opportunity in Education Act, commonly known as Title IX, was passed in Congress. A revolutionary document, Title IX prohibits exclusion of any person from participation in an educational program on the basis of gender. The most extreme effect, and the one that gave the act its controversial reputation, was the allocation of funding to female extracurricular activities, particularly sports.

Before 1972, very few girls were involved in sports, partly because very few organized athletic programs existed for them. In the decades since Title IX was passed, the number of female athletes has increased dramatically. While women's participation in athletics has increased, the goal of equality has still not been met. Although girls have more opportunities now than they did forty years ago, they still fail to receive equal funding for sports programs for their schools. Even though women outnumber men on college campuses, they receive 45 percent of Division I scholarship money and only 32 percent of recruiting dollars on average. Even though Title IX requires equal treatment of male and female teams, it does not require schools to spend equal amounts of money on male and female athletes (National Women's Law Center). Many school districts are reluctant to invest in sports that have historically been of little interest to the public. Every dollar that is allocated to female sports has to be taken away from male sports.

Box 9-4

Consider the Theoretical Perspectives

Structural Functionalism—Functionalists view society as a system of many parts working together to form a whole. When studying gender, functionalists examine how different gender roles complement each other and help society run smoothly. If Mother does the laundry and Father mows the lawn, the house remains in good shape. Children watch and learn from their parents and step into these roles early in life. Girls are often expected to help their mothers with domestic chores while boys are primed to work outside the house (Parsons, 1942).

Gender roles can be rigid, but often complement each other. Does this help or hinder the lives of men and women?

Social Conflict—Conflict theorists are interested in the struggle for power between groups, especially economic power. In general, women are more likely to be poor than their male counterparts, a trend referred to as the feminization of poverty. This is a result of the job and wage discrimination present in the system. While it is true that globally inequality trends show that we are moving toward greater equality, studies show that

all nations continue to have gender inequality in all areas of life (Dorius and Firebaugh, 2010).

According to conflict theory, those with power often use it to dominate others. Even in today's world, the majority of societal power still lies in the hands of men. Can men benefit by keeping women in a subordinate position?

Symbolic Interactionism—Symbolic interactionists look at the micro-interactions of daily life and how they influence the ways in which we perceive an issue. Do we define certain tasks as "men's" or "women's" work? If a man prepares dinner for his family, does that make him less of a man? Gender roles in today's society are much more fluid than they were 50 years ago. What has changed? Over time, societal views on household labor have been modified. How does this affect the lives of present-day men and women?

How we define the roles of men and women determines how they act in society. What does it mean if a man stays home while his wife goes to work?

Chapter 10

Race, Ethnicity, and Power

On November 4, 2008, U.S. Senator Barack Obama of Illinois was elected as forty-fourth President of the United States. Obama, the first African American elected to the nation's highest office, beat his Republican opponent, John McCain, decisively and in doing so, garnered most votes numerically from white Americans. President Obama was re-elected in 2012 for a second term with an even larger margin of victory over his opponent, Massachusetts Governor Mitt Romney. In choosing him, voters saw not a black man but the candidate they thought best suited to lead the country. Consequently, his election served—among other things—as a referendum on race in this country. It marked an important turning point in the history of racial and ethnic relations, and, as such, offered a resounding repudiation of past values and practices by American society that will be explored briefly in the pages to follow.

DOMINANT GROUPS AND MINORITY GROUPS

What Is a Dominant Group?

A dominant group is a social category comprised of those in society who are dominant in power, prestige, wealth, and culture. Its members use this advantage to have their values and cultural orientation legitimized as society's dominant norms and the social policies that result from them (Schaefer, 2013).

The Historically Dominant Group in America: White Anglos   America was first settled predominantly by those of English, Scotch-Irish, and German descent. The United States originated largely from thirteen British colonies during the 1600s and 1700s. In the wake of a successful eighteenth-century revolt against British rule

(1776–1789), the next two centuries saw rapid industrialization and, with it, massive immigration by diverse racial and ethnic groups drawn by the prospects of a better life. Some, however, did not come as willing or paying passengers, but as commodities from Africa to be sold in commercial auctions, packed tightly in the bowels of slave ships. Others—white ethnics, Asians, and Hispanics—came voluntarily, but often found themselves, upon arrival, the victims of prejudice and discrimination which, in many cases, limited their life chances significantly (Table 10-1).

Regardless of whether immigration was voluntary are forced, however, it created a rich diversity of racial and ethnic groups in America. Given the values of freedom and individual rights and choice that formed the bedrock upon which the United States was founded, it was perhaps inevitable that the monopoly on power and policy established by the white Anglo establishment would eventually change. By working within the system of government set forth by the founding fathers, twentieth-first century Americans of all colors and creeds found themselves by the year 2008 at a tipping point in American history as the seeds of significant change planted during the 1950s and 1960s began to ripen and bear substantial fruit.

Societal Dominance Today: The Gathering Momentum of Change The laws and policies of the United States, even today, continue to be shaped largely by the Anglo-Saxon orientation of the original colonies. Such obvious examples as English language and legal traditions still dominate the norms of American culture. In addition, the upper classes who make up the affluent and powerful establishment and those wishing to emulate them exhibit an almost compulsive attraction to anything related to traditional English or European life from the architectural styles of their homes and their furnishings to the community developments they live in with names like Wimbleton Estates, Georgetown Colony, and Hampton Court.

Nonetheless, the United States today, in terms of both opportunities and racial and ethnic relations, is a far different place than it was just one-half century ago and is continuing to undergo significant if not dramatic change. Today, those from minority backgrounds increasingly are better represented in leadership positions. In the arts, Oprah Winfrey has dominated daytime talk TV for over well over two decades beginning in the mid 1980s and, in doing so, became the first African-American woman billionaire and one

Table 10-1
Ethnic Backgrounds of the U.S. Population, 1790*

Ethnic Background	Percent
English	60.1
Scottish, Scotch–Irish	14.0
German	8.6
Irish	3.6
Dutch	3.1
French, Swedish	3.0
Other	7.0

* Total may not equal 100 percent due to rounding. Estimates based on the first U.S. Census, 1790. They do not include the 20 percent who were slaves.
Source: Parrillo, V. N. (1985) Strangers to These Shores, 2nd ed., 119. New York: Wiley.

What Is a Minority Group?

A minority group is a social category of people distinguished by their physical or cultural characteristics whose members have experienced a historical pattern of prejudice and discrimination (Wirth, 1945). Minorities usually are smaller in number than the dominant or majority group, but not always. In South Africa, for example, nonwhites outnumber whites four to one. Historically, this country has been dominated by the white Afrikaner establishment, descendents of British colonists that from the nineteenth century until the 2000s, have dominated law and public policy. Although minorities in the United states have made tremendous strides in recent decades, it is important to examine sociologically their key characteristics, outline the history of racial and ethnic relations in America, and discuss some key racial and ethnic groups of today.

Key Characteristics of Minorities

Sociologists generally agree on the following five characteristics that distinguish a minority group from a dominant group (Wagley and Harris, 1964; Vander Zanden, 1983).

1. *Impaired Life Chances. Those belonging to a minority group have suffered disadvantages at the hands of those comprising the majority group.* Historically, minorities have not been accorded the same life chances as those in the Anglo-American majority, the "good things" in life. Even today, their members generally rank lower in terms of power, prestige, and wealth. Members of most minorities are more likely to live in poverty than those in the dominant group, are often more poorly educated, and remain underrepresented in positions of authority and influence in major institutions. In addition, they often represent the source of the advantages enjoyed by the majority. For one group to have tremendous privilege, another must be oppressed. Although such differential treatment has been reduced dramatically from one-half century ago, a certain amount of bigotry and discrimination still exists today, sometimes in new forms from different sources. For example, in the wake of the September 11, 2001 attacks on the United States by Islamic extremists, some Americans were subjected to prejudice and discrimination simply for being Middle Eastern or Muslim in ethnic origin or religion.

2. *Visible Characteristics Used as a Basis for Differential Treatment. Members of minorities are identifiable on the basis of visible physical and/or cultural characteristics and, as a result, are treated differently by the majority group.* Some minorities are identified primarily on the basis of physical attributes such as race, gender, or age. Others are defined by the dominant group primarily in terms of cultural characteristics including language, religion, family structure, dress, mannerisms, or even sexual orientation. Members of the dominant group historically saw minorities as deviant, condemned their norms and practices based on their cultural characteristics, and often made them the subject of jokes. And differences based on physical characteristics were often the basis for doctrines of supremacy leading to such attitudes as racism and sexism. Although times and norms have changed and most dominant group members today have left such attitudes and practices in the "dustbin of history," it would be inaccurate to say that bigotry and discrimination have been eradicated. They still exist, although they largely have gone underground and their practitioners and their actions—to the extent to which they still exist—are not socially accepted today in the American cultural mainstream.

3. *Strong Group Identification. Members of minority groups possess a strong sense of*

group identity. This feeling of identification is due partly to distinctive subcultural characteristics that give minority members characteristics in common with each other, such as similar language patterns, modes of dress, music, and value orientations. Historical patterns of oppression and persecution experienced by previous generations also acted to drive them together and caused sharpened distinctions between their group and others. This heightened self-consciousness resulted in a "stick together" attitude and intense loyalty to the group that remains with some minorities today, particularly among older generations.

4. ***Membership Based on Ascribed Status.*** *Minority group membership is an ascribed status.* Membership in most minorities is imposed by society on the basis of birth, not achievement. In Nazi Germany, for instance, Jews were persecuted mercilessly. It mattered not that some Jews looked just like non-Jew Germans or had adopted the Christian religion. They were still regarded as Jews because of their ancestry. In the United States, a person who appears white but who has even a single black grandparent is often viewed as black (Vander Zanden, 1983). For example, in the United States historically, particularly in the South, there was the "one drop rule." A person with any African ancestry—even though light skinned or sometimes Caucasian in appearance—was labeled as black and usually self-identified themselves in like manner. This traditional pattern of ascribed identity still exists to a significant degree today.

5. ***Ingroup Marriage.*** *Minority group members, by social pressure or choice, typically marry within their own group.* Societies in general tend to put pressure on people for "like to marry like." Such pressure, termed *endogamy* by sociologists, is felt by members of dominant and minority groups alike. This theme was explored in depth and with great sensitivity in the now-classic 1967 motion picture *Guess Who's Coming to Dinner?,* starring Spencer Tracy, Katharine Hepburn, and Sidney Poitier. In the story, a white liberal newspaper publisher (Tracy) comes face-to-face with his own supposedly progressive values when his daughter brings home her fiancée (Poitier) to meet her parents, who are surprised to discover that he is black.

Types of Minorities

Minority groups are difficult to classify precisely because many people fall into two or more historically disadvantaged groups. A black Jewish woman, for example, may find herself treated differently due to her race, ethnicity, gender, religion, or some or all of these factors. Of chief consideration, according to sociologist Louis Wirth, is that membership in a minority "carries with it the exclusion from full participation in the life of the society" (1945, p. 347).

Although minority membership can be based on a variety of discrete criteria including gender, age, religion, and sexual orientation, sociologists generally distinguish between two major overlapping types of minorities: racial minorities and ethnic minorities. A racial minority is a social category whose members have suffered social disadvantages because of visible physical characteristics (such as skin color). Racial minorities in the United States include Native Americans, African Americans, Asians (such as Japanese, Chinese, Filipino, Korean, and Vietnamese Americans), Hawaiians, and those of East Indian descent. An ethnic minority is a social category whose members have experienced social disadvantages mainly due to cultural characteristics such as language or national origin. There are many diverse ethnic minorities in the United States today. They include Hispanic Americans, such as those of Mexican, Puerto Rican, and Cuban descent, and white ethnics, such as Irish, Polish, and Jewish Americans.

The Nature of Discrimination

What Is Discrimination? Whereas prejudice is a judgmental attitude, discrimination refers to differential treatment of people based on their membership in a particular social category. Applied to minorities, such treatment at the hands of a dominant group is a negative and destructive force in society and often is based on prejudice. When established as a pattern, discrimination acts to reduce life chances for the group affected. The resulting deprivation, once visible, reinforces the prejudice that the minority group is inferior. This, in turn, breeds further discrimination and the circle is complete. According to Robert MacIver (1948), discrimination thus feeds on itself in a vicious cycle that he has illustrated as follows:

discrimination $\rightarrow$ lower income level $\rightarrow$ lower standards of living $\rightarrow$ lower education $\rightarrow$ lower earning capacity $\rightarrow$ discrimination (p.64).

Types of Discrimination There are several forms of discrimination that will be discussed briefly.

Individual Versus Institutional Discrimination First, sociologists recognize discrimination that occurs on both micro- and macrolevels of society. Individual discrimination is unequal treatment that occurs when individuals belonging to one group treat individuals of another group differently because of their group membership. During the era of legal segregation in the United States (1896–1954), African Americans, other minorities, and women at the interpersonal and community (micro) levels endured an incalculable number of small acts of ongoing discrimination in social relations on a daily basis, maintained and reinforced by those in the dominant group. Present-day examples would include a landlord who intentionally finds a way to refuse to rent apartments to people of Mexican or Middle Eastern Muslim descent, although they may be U.S. citizens. Institutional discrimination, by contrast, involves unequal treatment of certain categories of people as a result of inequities built into basic institutions. In this regard, the norms and values of the majority group take precedence over those of minorities in areas such as law, politics, education, business, and general customs. Black males, for example, were not allowed to vote in the United States until the 1860s, and American Indians and women did not gain suffrage until 1919 or later. While discrimination like this is direct and intentional, it sometimes takes indirect and often unintentional forms. The results, however, are the same.

A case in point was the minimum height requirement for police officers used by the Chicago Police Department during the 1960s. This had the effect of discriminating against otherwise qualified Puerto Ricans who, as a group, are shorter than white and black Americans. This height requirement was later changed in the wake of riots in the Puerto Rican community in 1966, which included charges of police brutality. Consequently, Puerto Ricans could then enter law enforcement and community relations were improved (Schaefer, 1985).

Reverse Discrimination Reverse discrimination is unequal treatment of individuals based on their membership in the dominant group. In 1978, for example, the U.S. Supreme Court ruled in *Regents of the University of California v. Bakke* that reverse discrimination did occur in the case of Allan Bakke, an older white male with an engineering background who was denied admission to medical school mainly due to a racial quota system established for minorities. The court ruled that the university abridged Bakkes's constitutional rights based on his charge of racial discrimination. However, the court also ruled that racial background could be use as one factor in establishing admission requirements (Schaefer, 2008).

Affirmative action programs mandated by the U.S. government have provoked much of the controversy involving charges of reverse discrimination, and several lawsuits have been filed and decided on by the courts in recent years. The original aim of affirmative action, as first put into effect through an executive order issued by President

John F. Kennedy in 1961, was for organizations and institutions receiving federal funds to actively seek minority applicants for employment and use their minority status as one factor in selection. However, in recent years, the original intent of affirmative action was modified and expanded, which resulted in controversial practices by organizations and several recent court rulings.

One example was the Gruttner case ruled on by the Supreme Court in 2003. This lawsuit was filed against the University of Michigan Law School by Betty Gruttner, a white woman who was not accepted into law school. Her attorneys argued that only about nine percent of white applicants with her LSAT admission test scores and grade point average records were admitted when she applied as compared with 100 percent of those with similar credentials who were African American. In a two-part decision, the court rejected Ms. Gruttner's claim regarding her own admission and ruled that the racial backgrounds of applicants could be used as a factor in admissions due to the need to encourage a diverse student body. However, the court—in the second part of its decision—set aside the school's policy for undergraduate admissions, which gave applicants points solely based on race or minority background. In the ruling of the court, race can be used as one factor in admission as long as several factors are considered that view each applicant mainly on their merits as an individual rather than their membership in a particular social category (Stout, 2003).

WHAT IS RACE?

Race can be a confusing concept that often means different things to different people. Even scientists use this term differently. In this regard, race can be seen from either a biological or sociological perspective.

The Nature of Race: Two Approaches at Definition

Race as a Biological Concept   From a biological perspective, *race* refers to a social category of people with certain visible physical features in common that are genetically inherited and passed on to future generations. There are numerous racial groups (called stocks or strains) throughout the world, with varying physical characteristics. Yet scientists have been unable to reach a consensus on how many such groups exist in the world or how they might be classified. No matter what "identifiable physical characteristics" are used as criteria—skin pigmentation, hair texture, facial features, blood types, etc.— different numbers and types of "races" appear.

Added to this is the complication raised by intermarriage between so-called races. In the United States, for instance, eighty percent or more of black Americans have white ancestry, at least fifty percent of Mexican Americans have both Indian (Native American) and white ancestry, and approximately twenty percent of white Americans have either African or Indian ancestry (Stuckert, 1976). Consequently, "race" as a clearly definable biological concept in science is a useless means of classification (Ferris and Stein, 2008)

Race as a Sociological Concept   What is important about "race," however, is how various individuals, groups, and cultures perceive it. This social meaning is of particular interest to sociologists. From a sociological perspective, race refers to a social category of people perceived and treated in a distinct manner on the basis of certain visible physical characteristics. As such, race as a concept represents a social invention used to assign meaning and value to people on the basis of so-called "racial" differences (Van den Berghe, 1978). Consequently, members of one "race" often see themselves as distinct from others. They assume that their physical traits are related to their intellectual ability and social fortunes, whether they be high or low, positive or negative. They expect to be treated a certain way by virtue of their "race" and are treated as expected in many cases.

In some societies, the racial background of the dominant group is often seen as superior to others, along with the life style or ethnicity that goes with it. Other racial groups and their life styles are similarly defined as inferior in the minds of some people in varying degrees. To some extent, the culture of the "majority race" is socialized into all offspring, including those of racial minorities. Because "race" and minority membership traditionally were ascribed, children of minorities historically were often left with a negative image of themselves because they could not become members of the dominant racial group.

When the concept of race is equated with expectations of success or failure, privilege or hardship, and self-worth versus self-deprecation, it can have a very negative impact on the self-image of minority children. In his autobiography *Nigger,* comedian and author Dick Gregory (1967) relates what it was like growing up in the inner city of St. Louis during the 1940s. Being poor, black, and fatherless, his experiences were not unlike those experienced by many poor and minority children of his time and even more recently.

> I never learned hate or shame at home. I had to go to school for that. I was about seven years old when I got my first big lesson . . . [and] learned to be ashamed of myself. It was on a Thursday. I was sitting in the back of the room, in a seat with a chalk circle drawn around it. The idiot's seat, the troublemaker's seat.

> The teacher though I was stupid. Couldn't spell, couldn't read, couldn't do arithmetic. Just stupid. Teachers were never interested in finding out that you couldn't concentrate because you were so hungry, because you hadn't had any breakfast. All you could think about was noontime, would it ever come? Maybe you could sneak into the cloakroom and steal a bite of some kid's lunch out of a coat pocket. A bite of something. Paste. You can't really make a meal of paste . . . but sometimes I'd scoop a few spoonfuls out of the paste jar in the back of the room. Pregnant people get strange tastes. I was pregnant with poverty; Pregnant with dirt and pregnant with smells that made people turn away; Pregnant with cold and pregnant with shoes that were never bought for me, pregnant with five other people in my bed and no Daddy in the next room, and pregnant with hunger. Paste doesn't taste too bad when you're hungry.

> The teacher thought I was a troublemaker. All she saw . . . was a little black boy who squirmed in his idiot's seat and made little noises and poked the kids

around him. I guess she couldn't see a kid who made noises because he wanted someone to know he was there (pp. 29–30).

Race: Myth Versus Reality

Because of the long and divisive history attached to "race" and the ways in which it has been used and misused against various racial minorities, it remains a sensitive and contentious subject even well into the twenty-first century. Just when many Americans—both dominant-group and minority-group members—begin to feel that their culture is about to transcend the typing and treating of people by so-called "racial" characteristics, there sometimes occurs a "racial incident" which brings old sentiments and resentments bubbling back to the surface in full focus and gives them renewed life. Charges of racism fly about with unbridled abandon, often from more than one side. And old wounds, once thought healed or nearly healed, are at least temporarily reinfected with bigotry, hate speech, and calls for justice and retribution as a reaction. To partially address such factors bearing on race and racial issues, we will discuss a few of the dominant myths that surround this subject.

Myth 1: The Notion of Racial Superiority Throughout history, conquering societies have used the physical characteristics of the people they conquered as a justification for subjugating or enslaving them as part of the spoils of war. When the Mongol hordes descended on the Roman Empire in the fifth century BCE, the physical features of the Caucasian Romans were used as an excuse by the invading Asiatics for enslaving them. In similar fashion, white colonists in America over one thousand years later during the 1600s and 1700s used the dark features of the Africans sold into bondage to them as a rationale for slavery. Even as recently as the late twentieth century, similar attempts have been made to justify a doctrine of racial supremacy.

However, scientists operating independently from one another in several disciplines have found no convincing evidence that any so-called "racial" group is superior or inferior to any other "racial" group regarding talents or characteristics of significance. Therefore, racial superiority argued for some groups over others in areas ranging from musicality and "natural" athletic ability to sexual prowess and intellectual capacity represent little more than cultural mythology.

Myth 2: The Concept of Pure Race Most of us represent an amalgam of different "racial" influences. African women brought to America as slaves were often impregnated by white planters and other white males because, as slaves, they had no power to resist or protest. The children born of such unions were legally considered slaves based on "the status of the mother." During the 1960s, the U.S. Supreme Court overturned state laws banning miscegenation (interracial marriage). Based partly on this but mainly the legacy created in the wake of the civil rights

movement, which was a cultural attitude of tolerance about race relations, bi-racial and/or ethnically mixed children have become normative in society's mainstream. Consequently, children today produced from racially mixed marriages do not grow up with the social stigma that was pervasive prior to the 1970s.

Myth 3: "Race" as a Meaningful Biological Concept in Science Biologists, geneticists, and biomedical researchers generally have joined with behavioral scientists in finding that "race" generally is not a meaningful biological concept in science. Beyond the problem of an agreed-upon and consistent classification system for "so-called races" and the complication of few if any people coming from a single "racial" background, there are few if any significant biological differences between alleged "racial groups." The

Tiger Woods claims a rich racial heritage that includes Caucasian (one-eighth), black (one-fourth), American Indian (one-eighth), Thai (one-fourth), and Chinese (one-fourth). He embraces all these ethnic influences and calls himself Cablinasian.

© Debby Wong, 2014. Used under license from Shutterstock, Inc.

Source: White, Jack E. 1997. "I'm Just Who I Am." Time. May 5, 32–36.

distinctions that do exist—skin pigmentation, hair texture, facial structure, eye folds, and so on—are cosmetic and superficial, not determinative. We are all *Homo sapiens sapiens* under the skin, with the same chromosomal characteristics, blood types, brain structures, and body architectures. Because of these considerations, the biological concept of race as a "pure type" is regarded as a social myth and is of little or no value to science (Montagu, 1972). Although physical "racial" differences do exist among humans, they are largely superficial and, by themselves, play no significant role in shaping intellectual capacity, biological potential, or social behavior. One finding from genetics is particularly interesting.

There actually is more genetic similarity between so-called racial groups than within them (Witherspoon et al., 2007). One consequence of this is that a person in need of an organ transplant who goes on the national organ recipient list is more likely to receive an organ from a person from a different so-called "racial group" than from his or her own. Consequently, there is a significant number of white Anglos walking around with African American hearts beating inside their bodies, African Americans with "white" kidneys or Asian livers, and Asian Americans with "white" or "black" corneas that better allow them to see. Other possible combinations are too numerous to mention. Such consequences stem from the fact that about eighty-five percent of genetic variations occur within populations or so-called racial groups (Barbujani, et al., 1997).

The Nature of Racism

When an awareness of racial differences includes a higher value placed on membership in one racial group as compared to another, then racism occurs. Racism is a doctrine—and acts stemming from it—that holds that one racial category is superior and all others, in varying degrees, are inferior. Therefore, racism includes both prejudice and discrimination in that it combines racial prejudice with the use of power to negatively affect how people are treated. The dominant or majority group benefits in several

ways from such an ideology (Nash, 1962). First, racism serves as a convenient moral justification for unequal treatment of a minority. Second, a racist doctrine, once institutionalized, is often viewed as normal by everyone, including oppressed minorities. This, in turn, acts to discourage them for questioning the "system." Finally, racial mythology tries to justify itself on the grounds that members of the "inferior race," being untalented and helpless people, would be much worse off if major social changes occurred and freedoms were allocated to them that they could not handle responsibly.

The historical treatment of blacks in America serves as a classic example of racism put into practice. During the summers of 1966 and 1967, racial unrest spread across America in a wave of riots and civil disturbances involving blacks and whites in dozens of cities. In places like Tampa, Atlanta, Newark, and Chicago many black communities erupted in violence that resulted in looting, arson, assault, and several deaths. By the end of July, 1967, President Lyndon Johnson had appointed a Commission on Civil Disorders to find the causes of these upheavals that were splitting the country into two polarized camps, one black and the other white. This is a brief excerpt summarizing the commission's findings:

> [T]he single overriding cause of rioting in the cities was not any one thing commonly adduced—unemployment, lack of education, poverty, exploitation—but . . . was all of these things and more, expressed in the insidious and pervasive white sense of the inferiority of black men. Here is the essence of the charge: "What white Americans have never fully understood—but what the Negro can never forget—is that white society is deeply implicated in the ghetto. White institutions created it, white institutions maintain it, and white society condones it" (*Report of the National Advisory Commission on Civil Disorders,* 1968, p. vii).

The Origins of Racism in America   To trace the origins of racism leading to the unrest of the 1960s and beyond, one must examine the early American experience. The first blacks in servitude were brought to the Jamestown settlement in Virginia in 1619 as indentured servants. By the 1660s, however, black slavery was becoming sanctioned by law and by 1700 had replaced indentured servitude as the primary source of cheap agricultural labor in the colonies (Quarles, 1969).

Slavery was justified by a doctrine of racial supremacy that consisted of several arguments. One was a biblical justification quoting various passages from the scriptures, including the Genesis account of Noah's curse on Canaan, which allegedly gave slavery God's sanction (Lincoln, 1968). A second defined the Negro as a subhuman, depraved beast. A third and somewhat more benign approach portrayed blacks as half-pathetic, half-comical creatures—simple-minded children that required constant supervision.

This last attitude toward the Negro became the basis for a stereotypical view of black people that continued well into the twentieth century. The following is fairly representative of the view of blacks offered by Thomas Dixon's racist novel *Leopard Spots* (1902) and other literary material of the early twentieth century:

> The Negro is an amoral creature . . . unable to discriminate between right and wrong. The power to make a free and intelligent moral choice has been denied to him by his Creator, leaving him a permanent cripple in the evolutionary struggle for existence. At his best he is a good child, for whom one may feel a genuine affection . . . akin to the love of a master for a loyal dog. But just as a dog must be told

what to do if he is to be of any use in a human society, so the Negro must be guided and controlled by his Anglo-Saxon superiors, on whose shoulders rests the burden of civilizing him, so far as his limited capacities will permit (quoted in Bloomfield, 1970, p. 118).

Even as late as the 1940s, popular American literature and motion pictures used images like Stepin Fetchit, a black movie character, to depict blacks as having rolling eyes, a shuffling gait, a whiny voice, and experiencing a never-ending series of predicaments brought on by simple-mindedness.

Racism and the Use of IQ Tests By the 1930s and 1940s, some forms of racism were much more subtle and indirect. One example is the manner in which IQ tests were used and interpreted. Although IQ tests were not designed with racist intentions, their use and abuse has had a discriminatory and stigmatizing effect on minority children and white children from lower socioeconomic backgrounds. In addition, supporters of white supremacy have used IQ test scores of minority children as "evidence" for racially biased arguments.

Psychological tests to measure intelligence or IQ (intelligence quotient) have been used in various applications—the military, education,

Movie and TV characters like Amos and Andy in the 1940s and 1950s portrayed blacks as simple-minded and in constant need of supervision by their white "superiors."

industry, law—since the early part of the twentieth century. Traditionally, IQ tests have been structured according to the pattern as established by L. L. Thurston (1938) to measure ability in three broad areas: verbal skills, spatial skills, and logical skills. IQ tests, such as the Standford-Binet and Wechsler, have been administered to several generations of American school children and have been shown to be good predictors of academic success (McCall, 1975).

The extensive use of IQ tests, however, has been highly controversial in recent years and has been criticized as invalid in assessing the abilities of minority children and those from lower socioeconomic backgrounds. Such children, including blacks and Hispanics, who historically have scored 10 to 15 points lower than white middle-class children, also have not done as well in school.

The term "IQ" or "intelligence test" is misleading because it implies that what is being measured in innate learning capacity. In truth, behavioral scientists are not in agreement as to precisely what intelligence is. Some see is as "adaptability," others "specific skills," and still others "scholastic aptitude" (Haber and Runyon, 1974). At best, IQ tests are imprecise measures of certain narrowly defined skills or abilities. Even these have not been measured directly but have been inferred from the behavior (scores) of children taking the tests. In partial recognition of this lack of clarity, a panel of experts appointed in 1975 by the American Psychological Association's Board of Scientific Affairs stated that IQ and other psychological tests "do not prove or disapprove anyone's capacity to learn" (Roediger, et al., 1984, p. 361).

In particular, the verbal and analogy sections of standardized IQ tests have been criticized for being culturally biased and representing little more than socialization keyed to a white middle-class cultural model. Many minority children and poor whites cannot be expected to "know" that cup goes with saucer, symphony with composer," or that silence is the "appropriate behavior" in church (Havighust and Neugarten, 1967; Vander Zanden, 1972). These things are not part of their cultural experience.

As a result of such test scores, an untold number of minority and poor children have been perceived as slow learners and tracked accordingly. Consequently, some teachers have exhibited a tendency to expend less time and energy on them than on "normal IQ" and "high IQ" children with more "potential." These children also have been more likely than their white middle-class counterparts to wear the label "mentally retarded" and to be placed in special education programs (Beeghley and Butler, 1974). At the same time, ironically, children of interracial and black parentage adopted by white middle-class couples with above average education, income, and IQs consistently score ten points above the national IQ average and twenty points above that of black children raised in poverty (Scarr and Weinburg, 1976). In summarizing the research on whether or not so-called "IQ" translates into life success, psychologist Don Hockenbury and science writer Sandra Hockenbury have stated that "[a]lthough intelligence is necessary for success in any field, the kind of intelligence that is reflected by high scores on traditional IQ tests is no guarantee of vocational success or professional eminence" (2006, p. 308).

Two Historically Dominant Forms of Racism   Sociologists generally recognize two major categories of racism, individual and institutional. Individual racism is unequal treatment that occurs when ideas and actions based on a doctrine of racial supremacy are applied to members of one racial category by members of another. The individual racist may do little more than talk, gossip, or joke about members of the "inferior race" with friends of like mind. However, sometimes such a person may put these attitudes into action, as in the case of the manager who tries earnestly to hire as few members of certain racial groups as possible. Institutional racism, by comparison, is unequal treatment of members of a racial category that results when ideas and actions based on a doctrine of racial supremacy are embedded into the structure of basic institutions (e.g., government, education, and the economic system). This particular type of racism, and the discrimination that results from it, historically took several specific forms. The era of legal segregation in America (1896–1954), for example, divided practically every aspect of life—neighborhoods, schools, businesses, transportation, churches, and even restrooms and drinking fountains—by racial category. The traditional practice of "ability grouping" and the tracking of minority children in school, based in large part on IQ test scores, could be considered as an additional illustration. Internationally, the apartheid policy practiced by the South African government until 1994, separating neighborhoods into "white," "black," and "colored," serves as an additional example of institutional racism from another part of the world.

The State of Racism Today: New Forms Due to such factors as the Civil Rights Act of 1964, affirmative action, the formation of the Equal Employment Opportunity Commission (EEOC), numerous supreme court decisions, and other reforms and mechanisms, racism, as manifested in racial discrimination, is illegal at federal, state, and local levels, and has retreated to the backwaters of American society. In addition, racism in America, once worn as a badge of pride by many and used to justify the enslavement of an entire people for two hundred years, is now socially unacceptable in almost all sectors of society. However, despite such beneficial changes, racism still remains today, although in anachronistic forms for the most part. Three of the more important of these will be briefly discussed here—hate groups, hate crimes, and reverse racism.

Hate Groups White racists still exist, the most extreme of which belong to small, but organized hate groups such as the Ku Klux Khan and the Aryan Brotherhood that have cells in all but four states. (Southern Poverty Law Center, 2008). Neo-Nazi groups tend to be prevalent in states such as New Hampshire, Michigan, and Minnesota. In addition, neo-Confederates have many cells in South Carolina and Georgia while the Ku Klux Klan has numerous active chapters in several states including Florida, Texas, Louisiana, and Arkansas. There are also anti-Semitic groups who focus hate on the Jews. As a final example,

numerous Black Separatist cells are active in states including North Carolina, Texas, and California; they focus their hate on what they stereotypically label as "white America." Many hate groups, such as white supremacist groups, have web sites from which they promote their pamphlets and other forms of propaganda aimed at blaming various contemporary problems facing America today on minorities and recent immigrants (Rivlin, 2005).

Hate Crimes In 1990, the Hate Crimes Statistics Act was enacted into law that called for the U.S. Department of Justice to develop an ongoing database on hate crimes. Hate crimes are ordinary crimes in which victims are chosen because of some characteristic they possess such as racial background, religion, ethnicity, or sexual orientation. As of 2005, national data compiled by the Justice Department as reported through local and state law enforcement agencies throughout the United States indicated that, out of eighty-eight hundred hate crimes and incidents reported, fifty-one percent were motivated by race, eighteen percent by religion, sixteen and one-half percent by sexual orientation, and nearly fourteen percent by ethnicity (Harlow, 2005). By 2006, the total number of reported hate crimes had increased to nearly 9100. However, by 2011 this trend had reversed itself and reported hate crimes had declined by 20.1 % (percent). See Table 10-2 for a breakdown of offenses by type and known offender's race.

Reverse Racism Members of the dominant group do not hold a monopoly on racism, particularly now in the twenty-first century. There is also *reverse racism* as exhibited by some African Americans, Asian Americans, and some members of other minorities. Reverse racism is a resentment and acts stemming from it focused on the group in power by some minority members driven by deep-seated bitterness at the wrongs done to their ancestors by the ancestors of the dominant group. Empowered by recently acquired rights and life chances, such racists try to invoke *white guilt* in members of the dominant group by using a technique that African

Table 10-2

U.S. Hate Crimes : 2011 (by Offense Type and Known Offender's Race)

Offense Type	Total Offenses	White	Black	Known Offender's Race*			
				American Indian	Asian/ Pacific Islander	Multiple Races/ Groups	Unknown Offender
Total (2006:9,080)	7,254 (-20.1%**)	3,101	902	43	64	207	2,374
Crimes against persons (2006:5,449)	4,623 (-17.9%**)	2,667	774	42	51	182	602
Crimes against property (2006:3,593)	2,611 (-27.3%**)	423	121	1	13	25	1,772
Crimes against society (2006:38)	20 (-47.4%**)	11	7	0	0	0	0

*In many instances, the offender's race or ethnic background was (were) unknown.

**Total offense type total/subtotals for 2011 (plus or minus in percentages) were in comparison with 2006 data.

Source: Hate Crime Statistics, 2011. U.S. Department of Justice, FBI, TABLE 3.

American scholar Shelby Steel (1990) has called *raceholding*. By intentionally invoking the "race card" in charging racism when most anything negative happens to themselves or to others in their social category, such individuals often try to avoid taking personal responsibility for their actions by scapegoating members of the dominant group whom they perceive as vulnerable. In doing so, they engage in a form of racism themselves.

In other cases, some such racists attempt to inflame emotions and exaggerate or even invent so-called racially motivated "incidents" or controversies out of thin air. The actions of Reverend Jeramiah Wright, President Barack Obama's pastor for twenty years, during the 2008 presidential campaign, provides a prominent example. The inflammatory rhetoric, comments, and hate speech emanating from Reverend Wright both from the pulpit and in speeches made in the network media and most notably at a National Press Club luncheon on April 28, 2008 where he was a keynote speaker, were astounding in their apparent display of hatred toward the United States, its leaders, and the majority of its people. Among other things, he suggested that the United States was a terrorist nation that brought the September 11th attacks on itself and that the HIV virus was concocted by the U.S. Government as a form of genocide aimed at eradicating people of African descent (Halloran, 2008).

In commenting directly the next day after Wright's Press Club speech, then presidential candidate Barack Obama soundly denounced his former pastor of twenty years and characterized the reverend's rhetoric as "divisive," "destructive," and comforting to those in society who feed off of hate. In doing so, the man who six months later would be elected as the first African American president informed the American people that Wright's world view was a contradiction of who he was and what he represented as a person (The Associated Press, "Obama Denounces Former Pastor," April 29, 2008, pp. 1–2.)

Racism in Perspective Racism—like sexism, ageism, anti-Semitism, homophobia, and other forms of bigotry—is a form of dehumanization.

Its purpose, used by those who practice it, is to objectify those seen as powerless by labeling, ridiculing, or reviling them in various ways that reduce them as individual human beings and negatively impact on their life chances. In this sense, racism is used as a psychological weapon by those seeing themselves as having power against those whom they resent and wish to exploit or harm—for whatever reason or reasons—and perceive as powerless. Up until the later decades of the twentieth century, which were marked by the end of legal segregation and enabling civil rights reforms, racism and other forms of bigotry in America appeared in blatant, overt forms used by many members of the group in power—the white Anglo establishment—to dominate and belittle minorities and women and keep them "in their place."

However, the last half century has witnessed seedbed changes in the fabric of American culture, and racial bigotry has declined to relatively insignificant levels when compared to the benchmarks of the past. Particularly among the college educated and those Americans who grew up in the postsegregation world, racism and racist expressions have all but disappeared in social discourse in most sectors of society. White racists still exist but in much smaller numbers than in the past. There are also racists that have emerged from other racial and ethnic groups, who harbor deep-seated resentment toward members of today's dominant group for past social policies and acts that harmed their parents, grandparents, and certainly ancestors. Many sociologists would agree that in a progressive, enlightened society, there is no place for racism in any guise or for any other form of bigotry, regardless of who espouses it or the group on which it is focused.

RACIAL MINORITIES

Native Americans

American Indians, or Native Americans, were the first to settle in North America and also the first to be dominated and placed in a minority position by European immigrants. It is estimated that in the year 1500 there were approximately ten million indigenous people north of the Rio Grande River. They were divided into so many different tribal groups that approximately seven hundred languages were spoken. However, by 1850, they numbered only about 250,000, decimated by a loss of food supply and exposure to such "white man's diseases" as influenza, measles, and smallpox (Schaefer, 2008, pp. 167–168). In 2013, it was estimated that there were about 3.0 million Native Americans (or American Indians) living in the United States (including Alaska) based on updated 2010 census data and projections (U.S. Census Bureau. 2012b). According to the Bureau of Indian Affairs, the number of Native Americans in 2011 within states with federal reservations ranged from about 2,400 people in Vermont (one reservation) to over 330,000 in California (twenty reservations).

Native Americans under Colonial Rule At first, these original Americans were seen by many European colonists as "noble savages," well meaning but ignorant in the ways of civilization. Early missionaries, after some contact with Indian groups, declared that these native inhabitants were the "Ten Lost Tribes of Israel" (Deloria, 1970, p. 13). Even today, children in elementary schools are taught stories—partly mythical and highly romanticized—of Squanto and the Pilgrims and how the Indians and the early white settlers shared in the feast of the first so-called "Thanksgiving" in a spirit of goodwill. However, by the eighteenth century, Native Americans—who had their own strongly held cultures and ethnocentric pride and who wanted nothing to do with the white man's civilization, including his religion—had been redefined by many in the dominant group as heathens or beasts.

As European settlers demanded more and more territory for permanent settlement that had been used by Native Americans for centuries, confrontations between the two groups escalated and became increasingly hostile. The English authorities responded in the 1750s by declaring members of some Indian tribes vermin by official proclamation and calling for their extermination.

It was the English and not the Indians—as commonly portrayed in nineteenth-century American literature and twentieth-century motion pictures—who introduced scalping to America. In 1755, for example, a proclamation was issued at Boston sanctioned by King George II that called for all Penobscot Indians to be destroyed and a bounty of forty pounds sterling each was to be paid for the entire scalps of all adult males and twenty pounds for the scalps of all females and children under twelve years (Deloria, 1970).

Yet at the same time, some Indian groups were highly respected by the colonists. The Iroquois, for instance, consisted of a league of six tribes—the Cayuga, Mohawk, Oneida, Onondaga, Senaca, and Tuscarora—which collectively were regarded as very civilized. Portions of their system of government served as a model for some provisions incorporated into the U.S. Constitution. For example, the method used by a joint Senate–House conference committee to arrive at a compromise bill from separate bills passed in each legislative body is based on an Iroquois concept (Parrillo, 1985).

Native Americans after the Formation of the United States With the formation of the United States and the end of English rule, Native Americans as a group did not fare well during the nineteenth and early twentieth centuries. Under the onslaught of Western expansion and the continuing demand for Indian territory, the U.S. Government entered into numerous treaties with various tribes for the settlement of their lands However, many of these treaties were broken by the government, and the pressure to move from one reservation to another, sometimes with the threat of force, destroyed much of the traditional culture and food sources of many tribes.

In 1871, the government ceased to make treaties with the Indians and, instead, made them wards of the U.S government under the administration of the Bureau of Indian Affairs (BIA). The BIA did little on the Indians' behalf, and most Native American groups were left to their own resources. The destruction of the American buffalo (bison) by American sportsmen and hide hunters, for example, pushed the Plains Indian tribes to the brink of starvation. Some tribes reacted with violence and fought back in numerous encounters with settlers and the U.S. military forces, but to no avail.

Native Americans in Recent Times and Today Today, Native Americans represent the poorest of all American minorities. Not granted full citizenship until 1924, they have suffered under many confusing and often contradictory shifts in government policy throughout the twentieth and into the present twenty-first century. Most of these policies have not helped them to better their social and economic position. Indicators of poor life chances abound. Overall, thirty-eight percent live below the poverty line and, on reservations, the figure is forty-eight percent. Fifty-five percent of those on reservations live in substandard housing, seventy percent must haul drinking water at least a mile to their homes, and fifty-eight percent of their children receive less than an eighth grade education (Vander Zanden, 1983).

Nonetheless, some improvements are being made, most notably what sociologist Richard T. Schaefer (2008, p. 178) calls *pan-Indianism*. Similar in many respects to the political organization of blacks during the civil rights movement of the 1960s, pan-Indianism involves attempts by Indian groups to develop coalitions between several tribes to deal effectively with common problems. One perceived common problem is the insensitivity of the federal government, which many Native Americans feel treats them and their tribes as captive colonies. The most successful of the pan-Indian groups in recent years has been the Council of Energy Resource Tribes (CERT). By 1986, CERT had membership and representation from forty-two tribes. This coalition was able to negotiate a deal for the Navajos with Atlantic Richfield Company (ARCO) which brought in an estimated $78 million in revenues by 2006. If pan-Indianism is to grow into a consistent social force, fragmented and isolated Indian tribes must overcome their differences and learn to work together as a force for social change.

African Americans

The largest racial minority in the United States consists of African Americans who, as of 2012, numbered 44.5 million and accounted for 13.1 percent of the population (*The World Almanac Book of Facts*, 2013).

A Cultural Experience Rooted in Slavery The black experience in this country is rooted in slavery, which lasted for more than two hundred years. The period of what has been called "the peculiar institution" might have been much shorter had Thomas Jefferson had his way. When Jefferson wrote the first draft of the declaration of Independence in Philadelphia during June of 1776, he included a paragraph denouncing the slave trade and slavery which was blamed on King George III (England was the primary slave trafficker at the time). If retained, this clause would have established the foundation for emancipating the slaves. Jefferson already had a plan for this called "the Jeffersonian solution." However, the Continental Congress deleted the paragraph from the final draft (Lincoln, 1968). The trafficking in African slaves, first sanctioned in the Virginia Colony in 1661, became an institutionalized practice in America that was to last over two hundred years before being brought to an end, largely as a result of the Civil War fought between North and South in which the issue of slavery was a major precipitating factor.

The Decades after the Civil War In the aftermath of the Civil War (1861–1865), the Thirteenth, Fourteenth, and Fifteenth Amendments to the Constitution abolished slavery and gave males of African descent full citizenship and voting rights. Many of these freedoms were short-lived, however. The Ku Klux Klan, a white supremacist organization, brutalized black communities from the middle 1860s through the 1870s in an attempt to keep blacks from voting and engaging in other forms of participation in "white" society. During this period, assaults, murders, and nightly cross burnings were relatively common. In a backlash of institutional racism, several states began passing "Jim Crow" laws (named after a blackface minstrel dancer). Jim Crow laws were statutes passed by Southern states after the Civil War that denied blacks access to public facilities used by whites (e.g., restaurants, hotels, restrooms, rail cars, etc.).

The African American Experience: 1900 to 1954 The first half of the twentieth century did not bode well for the life chances of African Americans. The Jim Crow policy was upheld in 1896 by the U.S. Supreme Court in *Plessy v. Ferguson*, which stated that "separate but equal" facilities for blacks was reasonable accommodation for their needs (Woodward, 1974). This ruling ushered in a sixty year period of legally sanctioned racial segregation in which blacks sat at the back of the bus, prayed in separate churches,

For Portuguese, English, and Dutch merchants and ship owners during the 1600s and 1700s, the African slave trade was a lucrative business. As shown in the print above, most slavers were "tight packers" who tried to cram as many slaves as possible into the holds of their ships to maximize profits. Forced to lie side by aside in their own excrement with only two feet or so of crawl space, one out of every eight slaves died during the fifty days it took to make the Atlantic passage (The Bettman Archive).

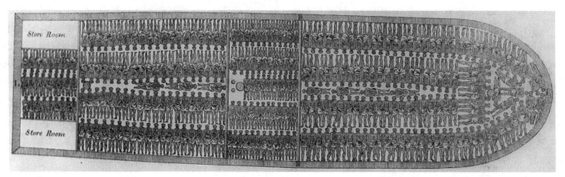

Courtesy of Library of Congress

attended separate schools, and were set apart from white society in practically all aspects of social life. The Supreme Court finally set this policy aside in 1954 in *Brown v. the Board of Education,* which overturned the "separate but equal" doctrine as it applied to school facilities as unconstitutional. This, in part, helped set the stage for the Civil Rights movement of the 1960s.

Changing Life Chances: 1955 to the Present— Trends, Problems and Remaining Challenges

The period from 1955 to the present has been marked by social reforms and many institutional changes that have impacted significantly on African Americans as a consequence. In the wake of such events as the March on Selma and Dr. Martin Luther King, Jr.'s "I have a dream" speech in the 1960s, many changes came about for black Americans, some very positive and others not so positive.

Positive Trends Groundbreaking federal legislation, including the Civil Rights Act of 1964, accompanied by vigorous enforcement of desegregation laws, reduced racial segregation in most communities. Federal programs in the areas of education, occupational training, housing, and urban renewal created unprecedented opportunities not only for African Americans but other minorities as well (Farley, 1977, 1984). Research conducted during this period indicated that attitudes in the white community also changed significantly and both prejudice and acts of discrimination declined (Farley, 1977, 1984). During the past half century, life chances for African Americans in general have improved considerably. The black middle class rose from less than ten percent of the total American population to thirty-four percent of black families with annual earnings of $50,000 or more by 2000 (U.S. Census Bureau, 2002). This was facilitated in large part by a percentage growth among African Americans. This trend continues today, particularly due to a greater number of African Americans who attend and graduate from college (Schaefer, 2013).

And the number of elected black officials— including members of Congress and mayors of several major cities—increased to nearly 7,000 by the late 1980s as compared to less than 100 in 1955 (Gelman, et al., 1988). By the beginning of the 2000s, the number of black elected officials had increased over fivefold from under 1,800 in 1970 to over 9,000 in 2001 (Bositis, 2003).

Today, the black middle class is a growing phenomenon. Middle class African Americans accounted for over thirty-four percent of the black population in 2000 and could reach forty-forty five percent or more by 2020.

© MONKEY BUSINESS IMAGES, 2009. Used under license from Shutterstock, Inc.

Problems and Challenges Despite the rise of the black middle class and an apparent decline of "race" as an important social concept to most Americans, there are still major problems and challenges facing the African American community. Racism in thought and deed still occurs and some forms of artificial segregation and denied opportunity still exist. However, the challenge today and in the future for both the black community and American society as a whole has more to do with class than race. (Wilson and Aponte, 1985). The poor are much more likely to be victimized by crime and to experience disorganized fractured families than are those occupying the more affluent classes. In addition, their children are only about half as likely to pursue postsecondary college degrees or technical education (Lareau, 2002).

For those who are marginally middle-class or with aspirations for the same, economic setbacks in recent years have created obstacles to achieving upward socio-economic mobility. The three year period from June, 2009 through June, 2012 saw median annual household income for blacks decline during the recession much more than for other groups. While whites and Hispanics saw an income decline during these years of 5.2 and 4.1 percent respectively, African American households saw their annual income decline by 11.1 percent according to U.S. Census Bureau figures. In terms of dollars lost, annual average income for black households declined from $36,567 in 2009 to $32,498 in 2012 (Trice, 2012).

Much of the challenge facing the African American community today is related to the family and demographic factors that impact on it. While affluent, college-educated African Americans usually move to the suburbs or gated urban areas, the underclass tend to be trapped in inner city neighborhoods which are in decay due to a lack of industry and jobs and a stagnating tax base which means poorly funded schools. Add to this the fact that only thirty-five percent of black children live in a two-parent home (compared to nearly seventy-six percent for white children) and just over fifty percent of black children live in a home maintained by a single mother, the consequences and implications for the life chances of black children are daunting (U.S. Bureau of the Census, 2006a). For example, twenty-eight percent of black, female-headed households live in poverty (Ibid.). Such dynamics contribute to high teenage pregnancy rates for girls and high rates of crime for adolescent males who (1) lack pro-social male success models in the inner city and (2) have little access to legitimate jobs, which are scarce and low paying. The cumulative impact of such family related dynamics tends to be felt most acutely by African American children, 37.4 percent of whom live in poverty (U.S. Census Bureau, 2012c).

Factors such as teenage pregnancy, coupled with lack of opportunity because of residual racism, low education, and the lack of job skills together create a vicious cycle that poor blacks find difficult to break. Consequently, African Americans as a whole have made tremendous strides since the 1950s, but several social conditions require change before they will be able to participate with realized life chances equal to those in the dominant group.

Asian Americans

Collectively, people of Asian descent represent the fastest growing minority group in America whose numbers had quintupled from three and one-half million in 1980 to nearly seventeen and one-half million by 2012 (U.S. Census Bureau, 2004b; Kivisto and Ng, 2008; and U.S. Census Bureau, 2010, 2012). They represent several countries and regions of the world, most notably China, Japan, the Philippines, Korea, India, and Southeast Asia. Due largely to a greater participation in education than other Americans—eighty-five percent graduate from high school and fifty percent earn college degrees—Asian Americans are often referred to as the "model minority." While about twenty percent of white Americans are represented in managerial, professional, and executive occupations, the numbers for Americans of Asian descent—Asian Indians (forty-seven percent), Chinese (thirty percent), and Japanese (twenty-eight percent) for example—are significantly higher (Thompson and Hickey, 2008). If current immigration trends continue, Asian Americans are expected to triple in number to nearly thirty-three and one-half million by 2050 (U.S. Census Bureau, 2004).

The first immigrants from Asia came in the nineteenth century, predominantly from China and Japan. As late as 1970, three-quarters of all Asian Americans were from these two countries. However, with the dramatic influx of Filipinos, Koreans, East Indians, and Vietnamese in recent years, those of Japanese and Chinese descent now constitute only about one-third of all Asian Americans.

Chinese Americans Of all Asian Americans, those of Chinese descent (nearly twenty-two and one-half percent) comprise the largest group (American Community Survey, 2005). As the first Asians to emigrate to the United States, the Chinese came mainly to California in the 1840s to escape economic problems and unrest in their own country (Kitano, 1985). At first, these new immigrants were accepted because they helped to alleviate an acute labor shortage in menial occupations. During the gold rush days of 1849 and 1850, there was a severe scarcity of women who traditionally did cooking, laundry, and other domestic chores. Although most Chinese immigrants were male, they were glad to do this work. They later worked as laborers in the mines and on the railroads.

As more and more Chinese came to the West Coast over the next several decades—at least three hundred thousand by 1880—their numbers, coupled with their very different racial and cultural characteristics, resulted in tremendous anti-Chinese sentiment. Many Californians, driven by fear that these strange, hardworking people would take their jobs, subjected the Chinese to scorn and racial slurs and beat and killed many of them. The Chinese, in reaction, found themselves forced to retreat to segregated communities called "Chinatowns." Californians, and later, leaders in Congress were so fearful of unchecked Chinese immigration—often called "the Yellow Peril"—that Congress passed the Chinese Exclusion Act in 1882, which banned further immigration for ten years. This exclusion was later made permanent and was not repealed until after World War II. Today, Chinese Americans are most likely of all Asian immigrants to complete college.

Because of a combination of war hysteria and racial bigotry, 110,000 persons of Japanese descent, most of whom were U.S. citizens, were forcibly relocated in 1942 to an American version of "concentration camps." Once relocated, they remained in these camps as prisoners of the U.S. military for the duration of World War II. Today, greater opportunities coupled with a strong work ethic have resulted in Japanese Americans and others of Asian descent becoming among the most upwardly mobile of minority groups.

Photograph by Ansel Adams from the Manzanar War Relocation center photography collection, courtesy of the Library of Congress Prints and Photographs Division.

Japanese Americans The immigration patterns of those who came to this country from Japan were somewhat different from the Chinese. When the Japanese government ended its two-hundred-year-old prohibition against foreign travel in 1865, some Japanese citizens began to emigrate to the United States. However, they did not arrive in significant numbers until about 1900 (Parrillo, 1980). Unlike the Chinese immigrants—who were almost exclusively single males—the Japanese came as married couples. Once in the United States, they established families and tried to assimilate into the American cultural mainstream. In addition, because jobs were difficult to obtain in the large cities and unions and their members considered Asians as a threat because they would work for lower wages, most Japanese Americans settled in rural outlying areas. There, they worked on farms, and some ultimately became successful tenant farmers and small farm and vineyard owners.

U.S. policy changed however, on December 7, 1941, when the Japanese bombed American naval installations at Pearl Harbor. The resulting war hysteria—many Americans feared a Japanese land invasion of California—resulted in the classification of Japanese Americans as a possible threat to national security. Consequently, 110,000 people of Japanese descent, 70,000 of whom were native-born, American citizens, were uprooted from their homes and businesses and schools and were relocated to detention camps in other states. There they remained for the duration of the war (Parrillo, 2009). They lost their homes and farms, and were not paid reparations after the war. In an ironic twist, the most highly decorated allied fighting unit in the European theater during World War II was the 442 Regimental Combat Team, a unit of Japanese American soldiers.

In August of 1988, forty-three years after the end of the war, President Ronald Reagan signed into law a bill designed to make reparations to the survivors of the forced imprisonment.Under this legislation, the U.S. government agreed to pay each of the estimated 62,000 Japanese American detainees still alive a reparation payment of $20,000 (Molotsky, 1988).

Asian Americans Today In recent years, Asian immigrants have come in large numbers from Indochina, a region in Southeast Asia. During the decade following the fall of South Vietnam in 1975, more than 840,000 immigrants, mainly refugees from countries including Vietnam, Laos, and Thailand (Rumbault, 1986). A large number have also immigrated from the Philippines.

Since the end of World War II, Asian Americans have become increasingly successful. Their families typically are tight-knit and stress self-discipline, hard work, and appreciation of education as the primary means of gaining upward mobility. Because of these values, Asian Americans, including more recent arrivals from the Philippines and Indochina, are among America's most successful minority groups. Japanese Americans, for example, have a higher per capita income than any other racial minority (Wilson and Hosokawa, 1980). Asian students are more likely to take college preparatory classes in math and science while in high school, devote more time to study, and are overrepresented in the freshman classes at the nation's leading universities in comparison with other Americans (Zigli, 1984; Butterfield, 1986; Parrillo, 2009).

ETHNICITY AND ETHNIC MINORITIES

The Nature of Ethnicity

Ethnicity refers to the specific cultural heritage that distinguishes one social category of people from others. In some societies, almost all inhabitants share essentially the same ethnicity. By comparison, the United States is a pluralistic society with citizens from dozens of different ethnic backgrounds. Nonetheless, those of European heritage, and particularly those of Anglo-Saxon descent, comprise the dominant or majority group today and have dominated both law and custom throughout American history. As a result, those with different ethnic backgrounds historically were seen as out-groups and often were denied equal life chances. Consequently, several groups became ethnic minorities that are regarded differently and treated unequally because of their cultural characteristics such as customs and country of origin.

It should be mentioned that racial minorities, as previously discussed, also have a distinctive ethnicity. However, the source of their unequal treatment has more to do with their visible physical characteristics than distinctive cultural attributes. The relocation of Japanese Americans into detention camps during World War II serves as a good example. The United States at that time was at war with the Axis Pact, which included Germany and Italy as well as Japan. While it is true that many German Americans were harassed during this time and some last names such as Mueller became Miller and DiBennedettos became Bennett, there was no serious attempt to systematically quarantine these groups of Caucasians. Only the Japanese Americans, because of their racial visibility, were perceived as potential enemies requiring involuntary relocation and detention.

Nonetheless, several ethnic minorities have been regarded and treated differently primarily because of their cultural backgrounds and characteristics. A brief discussion of some of these groups follows.

Hispanics

Today, the largest U. S. ethnic group is comprised of Hispanics who, by 2012 had grown in number to more than fifty-three million, which is two and one half times their U.S. population in 1980 (U.S. Census Bureau, 2012). People of Hispanic background, most of whom are Spanish speaking, originally came to the United States from different countries with distinct cultural traditions. When racial background and ethnicity are considered, they represent the largest American minority, having surpassed African Americans in number as of 2001 as a result of both high fertility rates and rates of immigration (Parrillo, 2009).

Hispanics represent a diverse social category of people whose origins are such places as Mexico, Puerto Rico, Cuba, and various Central and South American and Caribbean countries. They share, however, certain characteristics in common including language, the Roman Catholic faith, and strong ethnic identification. Many Hispanics are found in large cities like Los Angeles, Houston, and Miami, and most are concentrated in two states, California and Texas. Other states including Arizona, New Mexico, New York, and Florida also have large Spanish-speaking populations.

Mexican Americans The nearly thirty-four million Mexican Americans (by 2012) represents the largest Hispanic group in the United States, about sixty-four percent of all those of Latino origin (Thomas and Hickey, 2008; Gonsalez-Barrera and Lopez, 2013). This estimate does not fully account for illegal immigrants from Mexico who number several million more (Kandel and Massey, 2002; Kivisto and Ng, 2005). Those of Spanish descent first migrated to what is now the American Southwest in the 1500s. Isolated Spanish missions designed to bring Christianity to various Indian groups grew to become settlements of significant size devoted to agriculture. When Mexico ceded one-third of its territory to the United States in 1848 following the Mexican-American War, many Mexican citizens suddenly found themselves living in the United States, which did not recognize their claims of land ownership that, in some cases, were granted much earlier by the King of Spain. Following political and economic unrest in Mexico during the late 1800s and early 1900s, many Mexicans came to America as agricultural workers or *braceros* who were in high demand because they accepted low wages.

During the late twentieth century and the first years of the new century, unstable political and poor economic conditions in Mexico have produced a flood of illegal immigrants desperate to earn a subsistence living. Both these people and U.S. citizens of Mexican descent have faced many problems, including the language barrier and economic and social discrimination. For example, until the 1960s, it was not uncommon for Mexican Americans to be denied service at restaurants and other businesses owned by white Anglo Americans.

Since the 1960s, however, the Chicano political movement has helped make Mexican Americans a more viable political force. Leaders have included Cesar Chavez, who organized Mexican migrant farm workers in the 1960s, and Henry Cisneros, former mayor of San Antonio who by the late 1980s had gained a national following. More recently, politicos such as Governor Bill Richardson, a Mexican American candidate for the Democratic presidential nomination in 2008, have been an influential force in addressing issues impacting on the life chances of Hispanics and other minorities. Political activism by Hispanics and others have allowed Mexican-American children who, until the late 1960s were not allowed to speak Spanish on school property, to have bilingual education to help them more readily acquire formal learning and, if designed properly, to become literate in English as well.

Nonetheless, Mexican Americans as a group remain significantly behind other Americans in terms of life chances. As of 2006, nearly twenty-four percent were living below the poverty line as compared to eighth and one-third percent for white non-Hispanics. Their plight is related to the fact that many first-generation Mexican Americans speak little or no English and just over thirty percent of twenty-two to twenty-four year olds (in 2005) had not finished high school (Parrillo, 2009).

Puerto Ricans   Governed by Spain for several hundred years, Puerto Rico was ceded to the United States by Spain in 1898 as a result of the Spanish-American War. At first there was little migration of these new Americans to the mainland even after they were granted citizenship in 1917. However, the collapse of the sugar industry after World War II coupled with such factors as low airline fares and the promise of jobs triggered one of the largest voluntary migrations in recent history. During the 1950s, one-half million Puerto Ricans—one of every six—left their native land and came to the mainland, most settling in New York City initially (Kitano, 1985). Because the majority were unskilled, poorly educated, and faced problems such as the language barrier and discrimination by labor unions, in

housing, and in other areas, they were relegated to an underclass position.

Although increased opportunities in recent decades have made it possible for a larger number of Puerto Ricans to join the middle class, serious obstacles remain. In terms of positive life chance indicators, thirteen percent of Puerto Ricans were completing college in 2001 as compared to just over ten and one-half percent of all Hispanics and almost seven percent of Mexican Americans. However, Puerto Ricans, whom today live mainly in New York, New Jersey, Pennsylvania, and Florida, have obstacles to overcome that are similar to those of Mexican Americans and Hispanics as a whole. More than forty-three percent of their families are headed by a single parent as compared with thirty-two percent for Hispanics in general and thirty percent for Mexican Americans. Due to these and other factors, they have the highest unemployment rate (just over eight percent) of all Hispanics and represent the poorest of all Hispanic groups with nearly twenty-six percent (as of 2000) living below the poverty line (Therrien and Ramirez, 2001).

Cuban Americans   Of all Hispanics, Cuban Americans are closest to the American mainstream in annual family income and life chances. The majority—more than 910,000—have come to the United States since 1959 to escape communism under Fidel Castro. Once here, they have settled mainly in Miami, New York, and other major cities. Most of these people and their descendents are middle class, many with technical skills or college degrees (Parrillo, 2009). In terms of life chance indicators, twenty-three percent of Cuban Americans (as of 2000) complete college degrees, more than double that of Hispanics (just over ten and one-half percent) as a whole. In addition, just over seventeen percent live below the poverty line as compared to nearly twenty-three percent for Hispanics as a total group (Schaefer, 2008).

Although Cubans have faced both prejudice and discrimination, their class characteristics and education (as a group) have made it easier for them not only to survive but to prosper in a country with an urban business economy. Consequently, they have furnished positive role models for other Hispanics. According to sociologist Vincent B. Parrillo (2009),

[T]he Cuban impact on Miami, now dubbed "Little Havana," has been significant. About 52 percent of all Cuban Americans live in Miami-Dade County, where Cuban influence has transformed Miami from a resort town to a year-round commercial center with linkages throughout Latin America and has turned it into a leading bilingual cultural center. Over 57 percent of Miami-Dade County is now Hispanic with, including 657,000 Cubans, 80,000 Puerto Ricans, 38,000 Mexicans, and 522,000 others from Central and South America (p. 410).

White Ethnics

Those of largely non-Protestant European origin, termed "white ethnics," began emigrating to the United States in significant numbers a full half century before the following words included in a poem by Emma Lazarus were inscribed on the base of the Statue of Liberty in 1886:

. . . Give me your tired, your poor,
Your huddled masses yearning to breathe free,
The wretched refuse of your teeming shore

They came primarily from Eastern and Western Europe for a variety of reasons, some out of desperation. Many Irish arrived during the 1840s in the wake of the potato famine in Ireland that ravaged the country causing economic devastation and, for some, starvation. Some Jews came to escape religious and political persecution in Europe. But mainly they came—the Italians and French, the Slavs, the Greeks, Poles, and others—to seek a better life in the emerging giant of a country called America.

Most white ethnics came to the United States in a great "second wave" between the 1870s and 1920s. The majority were poor and unskilled. Because of their meager resources, they settled mainly in eastern cities at or near their ports of entry. There, in places like New York and Chicago, they worked—men, women, and children—fourteen to sixteen hours a day, six or seven days a week, as laborers in industrial "sweat shops" and at other unskilled and semi-skilled occupations. Many, because of low wages, were forced to live in vermin-infested tenements or "flophouses" in ethnic ghettos, where whole families of six or eight often lived in one or two rooms.

Although these people provided American industry at that time with a seemingly inexhaustible supply of cheap labor and were exploited before protective legislation began in the 1930s, they were not welcomed with open arms. Quite

White ethnic families often occupied one or two rooms in "flop houses" when they came to America early in the twentieth century.

the contrary, they were subject to prejudice, discrimination, and racism for a variety of reasons. First, the sheer numbers of these "foreigners" struck at the ethnocentrism of Anglo-Saxons citizens who felt their culture threatened by the strange ways and customs of the newcomers. Many Protestants, for example, rioted against Irish Catholics in the 1840s because of religious intolerance and later exhibited anti-Semitism toward the Jews. Others displayed racism against some newcomers because their swarthy Mediterranean complexions differed from those of lighter-skinned Caucasians from Northern Europe. In addition, these people were for the most part poor and unskilled and the more affluent considered them inferior. An editorial writer in 1886, for example, referred to them as "the very scum and offal of Europe" whom he described as

"bad-smelling, . . . foreign wretches, who never did an honest hour's work in their lives" (quoted in Parrillo, 1985, p. 156).

Despite these obstacles, white ethnics as a whole have fared better than most minorities. Because they were Caucasian and understood the need to learn English, many of the first and second generations tried to assimilate into the American cultural mainstream with some success. In addition, many white ethnics changed their family names in order to "fit in" with the dominant Anglo-Saxon culture. As illustrated in Table 10-3, this pattern still exists to some degree.

Jewish Americans Jewish Americans represent one example of a white ethnic group that came to this country. Although a few Jews from

Table 10-3

Original Names of Selected White Ethnic Entertainers

Alan Alda: Alphonso D'Abruzzo	Ben Kingsley: Krisna Banji
Pat Benatar: Patricia Andrejewski	Cheryl Ladd: Cheryl Stoppelmoor
Tony Bennett: Tony Benedetto	Huey Lewis: Hugh Cregg
Joey Bishop: Joseph Gottleib	Jerry Lewis: Joseph LeVitch
Bono: Paul Hewson	Madonna: Madonna Louise Veronica Ciccone
David Bowie: David Robert Jones	Barry Manilow: Barry Allan Pincus
Nicolas Cage: Nicholas Coppala	Marilyn Manson: Brian Warner
Michael Caine: Maurice Mickelwhite	George Michael: Georgios Panayiotou
Tom Cruise: Thomas Mapother IV	Helen Mirren: Ilynea Lydia Mironoff
Danny Devito: Daniel Michaeli	Demi Moore: Demetria Guynes
Kathy Lee Gifford: Kathi Epstein	Bernadette Peters: Bernadette Lazzaro
Pee Wee Herman: Paul Reubenfeld	Joan Rivers: Joan Sandra Molinsky
Wynona Judd: Cristina Ciminella	Meg Ryan: Margaret Hyra
Elton John: Reginald Dwight	Winona Rider: Winono Horowitz
Carol King: Carole Klein	Jane Semour: Joyce Frankenburg
Larry King: Larry Ziegler	Randy Travis: Randy Trawick

As illustrated above, many white ethnic entertainers of North and East European and/or Jewish ancestry—for whatever reasons—have chosen to change their name, often to an anglicized version.

Source: The World Almanac and Book of Facts. 2008. New York: World Almanac Books, 227–228.

Table 10-4

National Population by Racial or Ethnic Origin United States: 2010

Racial or Ethnic Origin	Percent of Population	Change: 2000–2010
White	72.4%	+5.7%
Hispanic or Latino	16.3%	+43.0%
Black or African American	12.3%	+12.3%
Asian	4.8%	+4.8%
American Indian or Alaska Native	0.9%	+18.4%
Native Hawaiian or Pacific Islander	0.2%	+35.4%
Other origins alone	6.2%	+24.4%
Two or more origins	2.9%	+32.0%

Source: U.S. Census Bureau, 2010; http://www.census.gov/2010census/data/

Spain and Portugal arrived as early as 1654, the most significant Jewish migration to America occurred around the turn of the twentieth century. Most early Jewish immigrants came voluntarily to seek a better life. However, some also came to escape religious persecution and political expulsion in Europe. By the 1930s however, most Jews entering the United States were refugees fleeing from the tyranny of Germany's Third Reich.

Today, the United States is home to the largest concentration of Jews (forty-one percent) in the world. The largest concentration of America's nearly five and one-half million Jewish citizens reside in and around New York city, the center of Jewish culture in America (Schaefer, 2008). Contrary to myths and stereotypes held by some, Jewish identity is neither racial nor religious, but largely ethnic. Jews share a common cultural identity or "peoplehood," based at least partially on centuries of tradition and custom. Because most Jewish people who emigrated to America had been urban dwellers in Europe engaged in industrial occupations, they adapted readily to the American economic system and, as a group, have prospered.

One problem faced by Jewish people is anti-Semitism, prejudice and discrimination focused on people of Jewish culture or faith. The most extreme expression of Jewish persecution was the *Holocaust,* a systematic, state-sponsored attempt (1939–1945) by the Nazi German government to eliminate all Jewish people from the European continent. By the end of World War II, over six million European Jews had been exterminated in killing factories or concentration camps with their remains either buried in mass graves or cremated (Thio, 2008). This included two-thirds of Europe's entire Jewish population and ninety percent of all Jews from Austria, Germany, and Poland who were murdered (Schaefer, 2008). Although nothing this extreme has ever happened in America, numerous anti-Semitic incidents still occur in the United States each year. During 2006, for example, there were over fifteen hundred such episodes including eighty-one on college campuses, some perpetrated by anti-Semitic hate groups (Parrillo, 2009).

White Ethnics Today   In addition to the Jews, many other white ethnics had also been urban dwellers in Europe. Consequently, the transition to an industrial economy in the United States was relatively smooth for many of them, especially for those who have emigrated during the past several decades. Ethnic groups including the Irish, Italians, Germans, and Poles have made strong efforts to assimilate and today have family incomes competitive with most Americans (Greeley, 1976). Jewish Americans, for example, have higher median incomes than Americans in general, and almost twice as many, proportionally speaking, complete four years of college. Third generation white ethnics today are showing an ethnic pride that their parents and grandparents did not exhibit, because of the cultural climate in decades past. In 1960, John F. Kennedy, an Irish Catholic was narrowly elected president, although his Catholicism was an issue for more conservative Protestants. During 1988, Governor Michael Dukakis, the son of a Greek immigrant, was nominated by the Democratic Party to run for the same office. In 2004, a Jewish U.S. Senator named Joseph Lieberman was the Democratic Vice Presidential nominee (who ran with John Kerry) and an Austrian American named Arnold Schwarzenegger became Governor of California.

RACIAL AND ETHNIC RELATIONS IN PERSPECTIVE

The manner in which specific racial and ethnic minorities relate to the dominant group and culture is perhaps best illustrated by a polar typology as shown in Figure 10-1. On one side of the continuum are patterns of exclusion in varying degrees, which result in discrimination and denied or impaired life chances. On the other are differing degrees of participation and acceptance.

Patterns of Exclusion

As we have seen throughout this chapter, minority groups often have been excluded from social participation in varying degrees. The most extreme form of exclusion is genocide, an intentional and systematic attempt by one group to exterminate another. Throughout much of human history, there have been attempts at genocide at both micro (local) and macro (societal) levels. For example, the ancient Hebrews tried to eradicate the people of Canaan. During the colonial period in American history, both the colonists and Indians, on occasion, engaged in local massacres of one another. In addition to the *Holocaust* previously discussed, there have been others. Prominent examples include the murder of thirtymillion people by Soviet Union dictator Josef Stalin, Cambodia dictator Pol Pot's extermination of two million people—one-quarter of the country's population—from 1975–1980, and "the killing of hundreds of thousands of people in the Darfur region of the Sudan" in the 2000s (Macionis, 2007, pp. 313–314). A precondition for such barbarism is the dehumanization of the enemy (Duster, 1971).

Segregation involves the involuntary separation of a minority group from the dominant group in terms of general social contact and participation. There are two basic forms. *Defacto segregation* is separation "in fact" as established by social custom. *Dejure segregation* is separation mandated by law, such as that practiced in the United States during 1896–1954 and the apartheid system established in South Africa until abolished in 1994.

The least extreme form of exclusion is accommodation, a process in which members of a minority group attempt to coexist with the dominant group without making a significant effort to adopt the norms and values of the dominant society. Some, including Jewish and Cuban Americans have been able to gain relative prosperity while maintaining a strong ethnic identity,

Figure 10-1

Minority Exclusion and Participation: A Continuum

Degrees of Exclusion ———————————— ± ———————————— Degrees of Participation

(genocide → / segregation → / accommodation → / assimilation → / pluralism)

which includes a high value placed on economic independence and higher education. Others, including poor Mexican Americans and Puerto Ricans, have not fared so well, in part because they still cling to portions of orthodox Catholicism and the agricultural ethic that both encourage high rates of fertility. These factors combined with others—such as low levels of formal education—add up to a formula for continuing poverty.

Patterns of Participation

Minority groups may exhibit varying degrees of participation with or without the consent of the dominant group. Two of these patterns, diffusion and assimilation, were discussed earlier and will be mentioned only briefly here. *Diffusion* is cultural change brought about through direct contact of two cultures in which certain traits of one are borrowed from the other. In the context of minority relations, diffusion often is the first step toward full participation, in that members of a minority often will, for example, learn the language and acquire the skills valued in the larger society that are needed to improve their general life chances. *Assimilation* is a process whereby an immigrant or minority group changes its cultural patterns to conform and adapt to the ways of the dominant culture.

The key challenge for many minorities is not full assimilation but pluralism. Pluralism refers to equal social participation by diverse groups in society based on tolerance and mutual respect for each other's cultural distinctions in a climate of cooperation. In an atmosphere that is truly pluralistic, no one has to sacrifice their cultural heritage and identity but must learn to appreciate the richness that other cultural traditions can offer in enriching their own lives.

Usually the most complete level of participation is reached with some people who engage in amalgamation, the process through which members of the dominant group and a minority group combine to form a new group through intermarriage. State laws forbidding racial intermarriage were struck down as unconstitutional by the Supreme Court in 1967.

Chapter 11

Who Gets How Much and Why: Economic Institutions

The American economic recession of 2008–10 had an immediate impact on society. Millions of individuals lost their jobs, while millions of families lost their homes. It also had an impact on corporations: large and venerable companies such as Bear Stearns and Lehman Brothers went out of business completely, and many others, like General Motors, had to file for bankruptcy protection. The recession also changed politics in the country: the economic situation at least contributed to the change of political party control of the presidency in 2008 (the election of Democrat Barack Obama over Republican John McCain) and the 2010 change of political party control of the House of Representatives (to a Republican majority). However, if Don Peck is correct, the worst recession since the Great Depression of the 1930s will leave a much deeper and more enduring mark on American society. In his article in *The Atlantic* (2010), he predicts a "new jobless era" for Americans that will lead to long-term or permanent modifications to institutions like marriage, to the career paths of young people who entered the job market during those bad years, and to the psyche

of the nation, with effects on spending and saving habits, on decisions about buying a house or having children, and on confidence in politicians and employers. Likewise, Trent Hamm of MSN Money (2011) argues that every individual in a society is affected by these economic social realities but none today more so, perhaps, than the old and the young. Elderly and retired people, whose wage-earning years are behind them, are particularly vulnerable to swings in the economy. And the young, including those who are about to join the workforce, face a unique challenge: Hamm insists that "it is much more difficult today for young people to establish themselves financially" than it was for the previous generation, because real wages are actually lower than they were in 1970 and falling, because the price of homes and educations is higher, and because the cost of participating in the workforce—for instance, owning a computer, cell phone, and Internet connection—is greater. Hamm concludes, "in order to have housing and an education comparable to what a young person had in 1970, they must spend 50% more on housing and 30% more on education, and do it all while earning less money. That doesn't even include the extra expenses needed to compete." These facts will no doubt shape the economic and social experiences of a generation.

When most people think of "the economy," they imagine money and banks and corporations and "the market." Sometimes these items and institutions almost seem to exist independent of humans, to float along in some abstract realm and yet to possess a reality that is natural, necessary and self-evident (that is, there is no other way to do it), and coercive (that is, we human beings have no choice in the matter). When sociologists think about "the economy," they see instead a web of human actions as well as the concepts, values, meanings, and practices that humans have invented and then institutionalized—made into institutions and perpetuated as institutions—and that they have enforced on themselves and on each other. In a word, "the economy" is eminently and thoroughly social.

In one sense, it is obvious that an economy is social: economic behavior is something that humans engage in together. People buy from and sell to each other. They work in groups, and they mostly consume in groups. But the social nature of economic activity goes much deeper. People produce, distribute, and consume goods and services within a dense system of social relationships, and those relationships simultaneously shape and are shaped by economic processes. These relationships include everything from the family to government and religion; much of the educational system is geared toward participation in the economy (acquiring the skills to get a job), and other social variables such as age, gender, and race relate significantly to the economy as well.

So while it is perhaps possible to approach "the economy" as an autonomous and self-governing thing (and the public and some scholars do approach it in that way), sociologists—using their famous "sociological imagination"—try to identify and describe the complex network of beliefs and behaviors through which people create and sustain that thing called "the economy." This network is often transparent or taken for granted,

and as individuals we often occupy a position in it that is so low or peripheral—so far from the sites of power—that we cannot easily see it and its functioning. However, at times like the economic crisis of 2008–10, the internal intricacy of the economy, its effects on us as individuals, and its fragility as a social formation become much clearer.

WHAT IS A SOCIOLOGY OF THE ECONOMY?

According to Richard Swedberg (2003b), the term "economic sociology" was first used in 1879 by British economist William Stanley Jevons, who envisioned a new social science of the economy as "doubtless a portion of what Herbert Spencer calls Sociology, the Science of the Evolution of Social Relations" (1879: 22). Swedberg further finds that the notion and phrase were adopted by the pioneers of modern sociology such as Durkheim and Weber. So the economy was one of the initial subjects of interest to sociology, especially the questions of how economic and social relations change over time and how the contemporary economy first appeared and currently operates.

While today's sociology tends to focus more squarely on the nature and processes of present society than on the evolutionary history of society, both these perspectives share a fundamental sociological motivation. As Mark Granovetter has phrased it, sociologists are curious to explain how "individual actions, conditioned by incentives, trust and cooperation, power and compliance, and norms and identities that affect these . . . actions, come to be shaped by and themselves reshape larger institutional configurations" (2002: 49), including those configurations that we collectively call "the economy."

We can think of economics or the economy, then, as a configuration of institutions by which humans transform the natural world and its resources into goods and services that are useful to humans. This transformation is always and essentially a cooperative, collective, and therefore social process that occurs in three phases. In the first phase, production, human activity is applied to the natural world to extract and convert resources into usable forms. This is followed by the second phase, distribution, in which products are moved from the location of production to the location of eventual use. Finally, consumption is the actual use of the products of economic activity.

Most of the social-scientific attention to the economy has been directed toward the production phase, for a number of reasons. Until recently, with the globalization of mass production, production was seen as the main economic "problem." Economists have themselves sometimes called their discipline "the dismal science" because it has been defined first and foremost by the fact of scarcity. In other words, human desires seemed to surpass human productive capacity, so there was never enough for everyone. Thus,

Karl Marx was the founder of materialist/communist sociology and a hero and inspiration to many scholars and politicians, as indicated by this commemorative Russian stamp.

production was the problem that needed solving. Additionally, production was believed to be the most influential aspect of the economy on other parts of the economy, as well as on the society more widely. Understanding production would lead to an understanding of the economy and the society in general. Finally, distribution and especially consumption were not viewed as being *as social* as production. In other words, while production obviously required collective action, consumption was relatively nonsocial, as simple as putting food in your mouth. (Of course, as we will discuss below, consumption is highly social and much more complicated than that.)

While there is lively debate within sociology and other social sciences about the dynamics of the economy, one influential analysis breaks production down into two more elementary components—the means of production and the relations of production. The means of production include the particular human (and thoroughly social) forces that are applied to the physical world to begin the process of transformation. In addition to the natural world and its resources (water, wood, metal, crude oil, plants, animals, etc.), Karl Marx, the originator of this analysis, emphasized *labor* above all other inputs. Labor, or in a word "work," is bodily engagement with the material world, that is, effective action on the world, whether that means hunting it, farming it, digging it, drilling it, chopping it, or what have you. This is usually not a solitary activity.

The means of production include other forms of energy than human muscle power, such as draft animals, wind and water power, steam, electricity, and nuclear; in general, the greater the input of energy, the greater the production. In addition to power are tools and technology, which also enhance productivity. These can be as simple as a digging stick or a bow and arrow or as sophisticated as a robotic factory. Related to tools are knowledge and skills, also an entirely social factor as these abilities must be discovered, shared, taught, and usefully employed. Finally, capital of some sort may be and usually is added to the system. Capital in the most basic sense is any resource or wealth "re-invested" in the economy to generate more economic output. Thus, capital includes seeds from the previous harvest that are planted to provide another harvest, as well as money from previous activities that is spent to acquire more resources, labor, tools/technology, or knowledge/skills to use in future activities.

According to Marx, the precise forms of the means of production generate specific relations of production, or the social arrangements by which economic activity and its outcomes are organized. Most fundamentally, all economies involve more than one kind of work, so a division of labor emerges, with different categories of individuals (ages, genders, races, etc.) performing different tasks. Also central to the society that arises from the means of production is the amount of surplus produced and how that surplus is controlled. Significantly, surplus (which represents "wealth") is virtually always unevenly shared, so that as the level of surplus increases, the inequality between "rich" and "poor" also increases, leading to the appearance of "classes." Also, surplus contributes to cultural concepts like "ownership" and "property." Further,

inequalities in wealth tend to breed inequalities in power and status, in the form of rank systems, hierarchies, and governments. Other social consequences of the means of production might be master/slave relations, apprenticeship, and clientship (where weak "clients" attach themselves to more powerful "patrons"), not to mention landlord/renter and boss/employee relationships.

Finally, on top of the "base" of the means of production and its productive relations, Marx placed the layer of "ideology," roughly what we mean by "culture" today. A society's ideology consists of its beliefs and values, its symbols and meanings, and its higher-level pursuits and institutions like art and religion, together with its institutions of perpetuation and control like education and law. But for Marx these were not innocent effects of the economic base but rather systems intended to preserve that base and its (mostly unequal) social arrangements. In other words, the ideology of a society was not merely ideas but a comprehensive model for thought, a worldview—and more sinister, a worldview that actually misrepresented, that disguised, the true

Box 11-1

Engels on the Economy and Family

Friedrich Engels, a collaborator of Karl Marx, applied the means/relations of production model to the nineteenth-century "bourgeois" family, linking family, marriage, and gender to economic practices and particularly the role of private property. Building on the cross-cultural evolutionary thinking of Lewis Henry Morgan, Engels pictured different forms of family as appropriate to economic systems: "group marriage" was associated with hunting and gathering societies, while farming societies tended to generate the "pairing family." With civilization, especially its urban industrial version, came the monogamous patriarchal family. The key to this historical progression was the accumulation of wealth and the formulation of the concept of private property, which fell under the exclusive control of males. Writes Engels:

Monogamy arose from the concentration of considerable wealth in the hands of a single individual—a man—and from the need to bequeath this wealth to the children of that man and of no other. For this purpose, the

monogamy of the woman was required, not that of the man, so this monogamy of the woman did not in any way interfere with open or concealed polygamy on the part of the man . . . And when, with the preponderance of private over communal property and the interest of its bequeathal father right and monogamy and gained supremacy, the dependence of marriages on economic considerations became complete. The *form* of marriage by purchase disappears; the actual practice is steadily extended until not only the woman but also the man acquires a price—not according to his personal qualities but according to his property. That the mutual affection of the people concerned should be the one paramount reason for marriage, outweighing everything else, was and always had been absolutely unheard of in the practice of the ruling classes; that sort of thing only happened in romance—or among the oppressed classes, who did not count." (1972 [1884]: 139–42) nature and cause of those relations and inequalities. A good example from a Marxist perspective would be the Hindu caste system, which purports to explain why some people are in higher or lower castes. The ideological reason for caste position (which determines one's occupation and social status) is religion: based on one's spiritual condition or purity, one is born into a certain level of society. However, the economic reality, from a means-of-production point of view, is that the upper castes monopolize the most prestigious positions (and usually the wealth and power) and seek to convince the lower castes that they "belong" in their inferior station through the caste ideology. A similar analysis of Christian ideology has been offered, with the dominant classes seeking to convince the subordinate groups of society that poverty is a virtue and they will be rewarded with treasures in heaven—just not on earth.

Production

Every society in the history of humanity has had an economic system. Yet, as already mentioned, a sociological approach to the economy is a recent development, and that approach has tended to focus on production. Hence, the earliest contributors to an economic sociology stressed production and how it shapes and is shaped by social relations. Among these thinkers were Adam Smith, Karl Marx, Émile Durkheim, and Max Weber.

Adam Smith

Adam Smith (1723–90) was not only one of the first scholars to propose a model of economy and society, but he also showed how strongly both of these issues are related to what we can and must call "morality," that is, how people should live or what the good way of life is. Before he penned his great economic opus, Smith was a moral philosopher, writing *The Theory of Moral Sentiments* in 1759. Like many social theorists after him (including Durkheim), Smith considered society to be a moral system, relying on certain shared sentiments like compassion and justice and simple "fellow-feeling."

In his seminal work, *The Wealth of Nations* (full title: *An Inquiry into the Nature and Causes of the Wealth of Nations*), published in 1776, Smith painted a very different picture of the nature of economic society and of the glue that holds it together. In one of its most famous lines, he asserted:

> It is not from the benevolence of the butcher, the brewer, or the baker that we expect our dinner, but from their regard to their own interest. We address ourselves, not to their humanity but to their self-love, and never talk to them of our own necessities but of their advantages (2005: 19).

Here, Smith not only offered an economic and social theory but a psychological and moral one as well. The most basic fact of the economy/society is a division of labor, different individuals engaged in different kinds of productive activities (the butcher, the brewer, the baker, etc.). The most basic fact of psychology and morality for Smith is *self-interest*: individuals do what they perceive to be in their own best interests. Additionally, Smith assumed that social actors are rational. Given sufficient information and the freedom to choose, they will make the best decisions to reach their individual goals. This will result in the exploitation of opportunity and in competition. Say that a person owns some land and grows corn. If the demand (and hence price) for corn increases, the farmer will do what he/she can to take advantage of this opportunity—buy more land, hire more laborers, invent better techniques, and so on. And other people will also enter the corn-growing business, leading to competition, which will be won by the farmer who can grow the best or cheapest corn.

The upshot of the perspective is that, without any governmental regulation (and without any real concern for the consumers) the economic system should achieve its optimal state. Members of society, both producers/sellers and consumers/buyers, react rationally and self-interestedly to the "information" that the economy transmits in the form of *prices* (what modern economists call "market signals"). It is as if an "invisible hand" were steering the economy, when in actuality the performance of the economy is nothing more than the aggregate of all of the individual, self-interested actions of its members. If, then, individuals are free to act in their own interest, the collective outcome should be the best possible state of the economy and society. In a word, greed is good—a moral assertion if there ever was one.

Karl Marx

Marx did not have nearly as optimistic a view of the economy and society as Smith. Marx agreed that humans tend to act in their own interests. However, he also recognized that these interests are not entirely individual but also collective, and that collectivities (groups, especially "classes") differ in their power to achieve those interests.

Like Smith and probably all other scholars of the economy, Marx's economic theory was a social theory. For him, production—understood more broadly as "productive activity," transformative work on the material world, or simply "labor"—was the fundamental social force. Production not only brought society into existence, but it literally brought human beings into existence, constructing socially and historically specific kinds of people. As described earlier, he distinguished the means of production from the relations of production. Together, these factors constitute the "mode of production" (*Produktionsweise* or "way of producing"), and any particular mode of production leads to a particular social formation or society. Over history, various social formations or types of societies have appeared, including

- "primitive communism," such as prehistoric tribal societies which were (allegedly) essentially classless

- "Asiatic mode of production," including ancient civilizations like Mesopotamia and Egypt, which exploited labor to create great works like the pyramids

- "antique mode of production," like ancient Greece and Rome, where private property existed and was the basis for social stratification

- "feudalism," exemplified by the European Middle Ages, during which workers were "serfs" tied to the land

- "early capitalism," before the rise of modern industry and the fully formed

institutions of "the state" and "the corporation"

- "late capitalism," the form of society characteristic of Marx's time as well as our own

- "communism," the predicted future society in which private property and class inequality would be abolished, along with institutions specific to the capitalist mode of production, such as the state, religion, and the bourgeois family.

Marx gave most of his attention to the contemporary capitalist mode of production, describing its functioning and its failures. He believed that it operated on the basis of "surplus value," that is, workers produced more value than they were paid in wages (in other words, Smith was wrong that prices were reflective of the cost of labor). The owners of the means of production (the bourgeoisie) thus extracted this surplus value from the workers (the proletariat) to enrich themselves. But more significantly, Marx found two more evils in the capitalist mode of production. First, because workers did not control the products of their labor, they were profoundly alienated from their own efforts. Skilled craftsmen and artisans of earlier periods had put themselves into their labor and seen themselves in the outcomes of that labor, but capitalist workers experienced their labor and its outcomes as foreign or "alien" to themselves. In an important way, workers lost part of themselves in their labor. Second, because the bourgeoisie was always trying to maximize surplus value, it was motivated to develop new techniques and technologies, to experiment continuously with social arrangements and to undermine everything that stood in its way. Marx referred to the "creative destruction" inherent in capitalism, an irresistible force that respects no tradition and holds nothing sacred. As a result, institutions like the family or religion were constantly overthrown and/or twisted to the purposes of the economy and its dominant class.

Émile Durkheim

Durkheim's perspective on the economy focused on labor, which he also viewed as constitutive of society and as a moral phenomenon, although he did not share Marx's jaundiced opinion. In his book *The Division of Labor in Society* (first published in 1893 under the title *De La Division du Travail Social*), he described modern society as a system of mutually dependent specializations. Large complex societies like our own contain many kinds of people and, even more important, many tasks to perform. Therefore, people must specialize. Some are farmers, some are teachers, some are doctors, and some are janitors. Society needs all these specialties, and they need each other. So, modern societies are integrated by this division of labor; it generates a certain kind of social order or social solidarity that Durkheim called "organic." Organic solidarity results from individuals, groups, and classes acting like organs in the body social, each providing a valuable function for each other. He contrasted this to mechanical solidarity, supposedly characteristic of premodern societies, in which individuals were more or less identical and performed more or less identical tasks.

Like Smith and Marx, Durkheim's economic theory is a total theory of society and personhood. While mechanical solidarity produced a clear social order, individuals were not completely individualized. Individual consciousness was not differentiated from group consciousness, or what he called "collective representations." True individuality was only achieved under conditions of organic solidarity. Additionally, mechanical societies, he asserted, often depended on political repression, while organic societies are more free and voluntary. It is also the type of social relationship appropriate to modern societies with their greater physical density—measured by spatial concentration of the population, the rise of cities, and the increase in the amount and efficiency of communication—and therefore with greater social and "moral" density. However, Durkheim also understood that the division of labor could have negative consequences: the economic diversity of the society could lead to such a degree of social and moral diversity that disintegration could occur, related to the famous Durkheimian concept of "anomie," the breakdown or disappearance of shared social sentiments and norms. But most of the time, Durkheim insisted, organic societies function successfully not only because the various occupations and classes need each other but because society produces the kinds of individuals who are prepared for—socialized for—their particular roles in the system.

In modern societies and economies, the division of labor creates mutual dependence among those people who work to produce food and those people who perform other economic tasks.

U.S. Census Bureau, Public Information Office (PIO)

Distribution

After the crucial work of production is done, economies must distribute the goods and services produced. While the question of distribution preoccupied important theorists like Smith and Marx and Durkheim less than the question of production, it is still plain to see that distribution is a fundamentally social phenomenon, too. First, humans must organize themselves into relations and chains of distribution, as simple as sharing between two friends or kin and as complex as shipping crude oil around the world. Second, these distribution relations and systems exist in the context of and exert their influence on wider social relations and systems. Third, insofar as goods and services are *unevenly* distributed, this situation creates social differences and social inequalities with powerful consequences for individuals, groups, and society as a whole.

Types of Distribution Systems

The most famous and persuasive analysis of economic distribution came in Karl Polanyi's *The Great Transformation* (1944). Like many other great social thinkers, Polanyi was interested in the evolution of society. It is certain that societies have not always used the processes of distribution that economists and the modern general public most associate with distribution, namely money and stores and all the institutions that we collectively call "the market." In short, distribution is not synonymous with markets. In premodern societies, markets either did not exist or were minor aspects of the economy; in some tribal societies, a market-day might be held once every few days but was hardly the heart of the circulation of goods.

Polanyi identified other, equally valid methods to circulate products. In the absence of writing, formal distribution institutions, and elaborate management of the economy, distribution could be carried out via reciprocity or redistribution. Reciprocity refers to social norms and relations of sharing or give-and-take. For Polanyi, the key to reciprocity as a means of distribution is the "symmetry" of society, in which roughly equal individuals or groups exchange goods within relationships or networks of exchange. This is one of the crucial elements of reciprocity: as Polanyi acknowledged, reciprocity tends to take place between trading partners or friends and kinfolk. These bigger, more enduring, and more significant social bonds provide the necessary conditions—especially trust, affection, and the guarantee of long-term interaction—that make reciprocity possible.

Reciprocity has often been further divided into three subtypes. In generalized reciprocity, individuals or groups offer their goods without calculating the value of those goods and without an expectation of receiving comparable goods at any specific time in the future; in other words, generalized reciprocity is not the same as "lending" or "selling." The assumption is that when the receiver has goods to share, she/he will offer them, but there may be no long-term balance of giving and receiving. Balanced reciprocity refers to the effort to maintain a short-term equality between the value of goods given and received, while negative reciprocity names a form of distribution in which each party tries to outdo the other in getting more for what is given.

It is obvious that reciprocity is not a kind of circulation found only in "primitive" or kin-based societies. In modern, complex societies people still enter into social and nonmarket relationships with each other. Friends give each other

Gift-giving continues to be an important practice in modern family and other personal relationships.

© Yuri Arcurs, 2012. Under license from Shutterstock, Inc.

Box 11-2

Marcel Mauss on 'The Gift'

Marcel Mauss, a collaborator and nephew of Durkheim, contributed an important study of distribution in his book *The Gift*, originally published in Durkheim's journal *L'Année Sociologique* in 1923–24 under the title *Essai sur le don: Forme et raison de l'échange dans les sociétés archaiques,* or "An Essay on the Gift: The Form and Reason of Exchange in Archaic Societies." Mauss argued that gifts are far from trivial socially and that they are not quite as voluntary as we often think. First, gift-giving is part of the social whole, tied to other aspects of our relationships with those on whom we bestow gifts. In many circumstances, gifts are a social expectation, even an obligation: you would not attend a birthday party or wedding without bringing a gift. Further, any act of gift-giving is part of a larger relationship and even of the overall system of reciprocity (here, he used "gift" in the sense of, say, the way that a hunter would share food with his entire family or community). Most important, a system of gift-exchange creates two other kinds of social obligations beyond the obligation to give: there is also an obligation to receive and an obligation to reciprocate. It would be somewhere between inappropriate and antisocial *not* to give a gift at moments that are socially demarcated as gift-giving occasions; it would be a failure of social etiquette. However, when a gift is offered, it would be equally rude and antisocial to refuse or reject the gift; one must often actually praise the gift publicly. Finally, accepting the gift is also accepting a kind of social "debt." While one does not construe a gift as a loan to be repaid with interest, one does enter into a gift-based relationship, and when the appropriate gift-giving occasion comes, one is expected to make an offering of generally comparable value. It would be extremely rude to accept a birthday gift and then not offer a gift on the giver's birthday. Thus, gift-giving or reciprocity is a powerfully integrative process in society, as well as a powerful commentary on persons and relationships.

gifts, family members share food and other wealth, and neighbors may host parties or look after each other's pets. They usually do not seek financial compensation, nor do they closely count the amount of goods and services rendered to make sure they are all even. Indeed, in such relationships it would be rude to calculate the value of gifts or favors and to demand perfect equality.

Unlike the symmetry of reciprocity, redistribution is founded on a basic asymmetry, or what Polanyi calls "centricity." Here, a central person, group, or institution collects wealth or surplus from a number of contributors or followers, who sometimes give voluntarily and sometimes are compelled to give; the center then acts as the redistributor, making decisions as to who should receive or how the wealth should otherwise be used (for public services, for war, for the benefit of the center, etc.). This system naturally confers a kind of prestige and power on the center. It is not only a center of distribution but a center of politics, too. Honor is conferred on the center, as well as on those who ally themselves with the center, and the center has at least a measure of persuasive power, if not coercive power, over the participants in the system.

Polanyi maintained that all economies and societies up to and including medieval feudalism operated on the principles of reciprocity or redistribution (or simply on the principle of the household). However, a third distribution system existed even in some premodern tribal societies as well as in most ancient societies, although it may not have been as pervasive and dominant as it is today. This is the market, or what has been called "market exchange." In its simplest form, a market is nothing more than "a meeting place for the purpose of barter or buying and selling" (59); again, many tribal and ancient societies possessed such a place, but it was one among many social settings for trade and exchange, and it did not dominate the society.

A market is thus a social institution, and when a society contains many interrelated markets, it is appropriate to refer to a "market system." The market system may be a collection of specialty and general markets, urban and rural, local and regional and international, private and public, free and regulated. A market economy, however, is something else altogether. A market economy is "an economic system controlled, regulated, and directed by markets alone" (68), which is impossible without other changes in society that mark Polanyi's great transformation. (Of course, a society directed by markets *alone* is probably if not certainly an impossibility.) A market economy, and the alteration of a society into a market society, entails all sorts of other social changes. The first is commodification: the components of the economy must be reconceived as commodities, a commodity being something that has been produced specifically for sale on a market. It is something to which a "price" can be attached and that is intended for market exchange. Potentially—and actually—anything can become a commodity, can be "commoditized," such as food, clothing, cars, etc. Even land, labor, and money itself can be a commodity, although Polanyi regards their commodification as "fictitious."

The market needs more than a reinterpretation of goods and services as market commodities. It also needs a certain kind of social and political context and support, as well as a certain kind of market person. The wider society, especially the government or state, must provide the conditions for stable markets (see below). Even more, the state must see to it that "nothing must be allowed to inhibit the formation of markets, nor must incomes be permitted to be formed otherwise than through sales. Neither must there be any interference with the adjustment of prices to changed market conditions—whether the prices are those of goods, labor, land, or money" (72). Finally, a competent market person is like Adam Smith's rational self-interested actor: she/he is assumed and expected to behave in particular ways, not the least of which is to offer everything (including one's time and energy) to and to obtain everything from the market.

Consumption

The consumption phase of the economy has, until recently, received the least attention from sociologists. One plausible reason is that consumption has not been seen as a social "problem" in the same way as production or distribution. It is easy to consume but much harder to produce or distribute. Gregory goes so far as to assert that

the "consumption sphere is very much a subordinate sphere under capitalism, and as such was not subjected to any systematic analysis by the classical economists. . . . The methods of consumption under capitalism are disorganized relative to the methods of production" (1982: 75–76). And unfortunately Marx himself in *The Grundrisse* stated (erroneously) that consumption falls outside the domain of economy, although he also wrote that consumption is a kind of production, just as production is a kind of consumption (since resources get consumed when goods are produced). So it should be clear that consumption is eminently economic, too.

Equally, consumption is eminently social. First, people tend to consume in groups. They eat together, shop together, and use all manner of goods and services together. Additionally, people consume according to their group membership and social characteristics. Men consume different things than women (most men do not consume make-up or lingerie, at least not for themselves), the young consume differently than the old, and rich differently than poor. There are also regional and historical variations in consumption. There are norms and rules about who may consume what (for example, "sumptuary laws" attempted to restrict extravagant or luxurious expenditure on clothing, food, and other items) or with whom. In the traditional Hindu caste system, members of different castes might not be able to dine together. Even what counts as consumable diverges between societies. Muslims abjure eating pork, while some Hindus are discouraged from eating beef, and some societies eat insects or other things that Americans might not regard as "food" at all. There are rules about how and when to consume, such as standards for fasting and feasting. And consumption varies according to seasonal and ceremonial/ritual occasions (in mainstream America, cake for birthdays and turkey for Thanksgiving).

These observations suggest that consuming has more than practical or "use" value. Consumables have social value or meaning as well. Even food, according to the famous culture theorist Roland Barthes, "is not only a collection of products that can be used for statistical or nutritional studies. It is also, and at the same time, a system of communication, a body of images, a protocol of usages, situations, and behaviors" (1997: 21). That is, like all other parts of culture, consumable goods are *symbols* with social significance and effects. Any object—food, clothing, a house, a car—"sums up and transmits a situation; it constitutes information; it signifies."

One of the first social thinkers to comment on the cultural significance of consumption was Thorstein Veblen, whose 1899 *Theory of the Leisure Class: An Economic Study of Institutions* introduced the concept of conspicuous consumption. Veblen claimed that consumption was a means to display social status; that is, goods and services (a Rolls Royce or a live-in maid) were "status symbols" or indicators of one's status. (Of course, "status" in this sense need not refer only to high status; certain symbols mark one's low status, such as having an old, beat-up car or eating cat food.) There are two things in particular that the privileged classes can enjoy and flaunt—ostentatious goods and "conspicuous leisure." The rich and privileged can obviously buy and use more, better, and more flamboyant things. But they also display their freedom from ordinary labor with their conspicuous use of their time. They travel and vacation; they play tennis and golf in the middle of the day; they go on adventures like around-the-world balloon voyages or rides in spacecraft.

At least as important, Veblen believed that the "leisure class" served as the arbiters of taste and style in society. The lower classes watched and emulated the upper class, getting their image of proper behavior from the latter. Upper-class speech patterns (accents, grammar, etc.) were elevated as superior and sophisticated; upper-class trends in clothing, food, music, art, and so forth were assumed to be the epitome of fashion. Evidence for this process today is how ordinary people imitate the look of the modern leisure class—especially movie stars and other entertainment figures—such as buying copies of the clothing they wear or imitating their hairstyles.

David Brooks recently proposed that the leisure class is not what it used to be. For one thing, almost all Americans today enjoy some of the fruits of leisure, and other countries actually offer more in the way of vacation time and retirement benefits than the United States does. According to Brooks, not only are more members of society participating in the lifestyle of the leisure class, but that class is also comporting itself differently from the past. His term for the "new upper class" is Bobos, a contraction of "bourgeois" and "bohemian." The Bobos, he declares, "define our age. They are the new establishment. Their hybrid culture is the atmosphere we breathe. Their status codes now govern social life. Their moral codes give structure to our personal lives" (2000: 11).

The two main differences between the Bobos as the new elite and past elites are the education levels and the occupations of the Bobos, which are closely related. Bobos are highly educated, and many of their habits are formed at prestigious institutions like Harvard, Yale, and Princeton. They are also members of information professions—doctors, lawyers, scholars, computer programmers, and the like. This new elite establishment "is a large, amorphous group of meritocrats who share a consciousness and who unselfconsciously reshape institutions to accord with their values" (44). The key to the bohemian quality of their bourgeois lifestyle is the mixture of affluence with the sensibility of "a free-spirit rebel" (42). While they are clearly well-to-do, they do not value ostentation, viewing the old style of wealth with its top hats and gold gilt as tacky and snobbish. However, they happily display their prestige and sophistication by consuming designer brands of clothing and coffee, "all-natural" foods, and gym memberships, and generally partaking of "utilitarian pleasure." They also collect and consume experiences, whether "cultural tourism" or spiritual quests, and show off their youthful and athletic physiques.

Emerging social phenomena like the Bobo lifestyle illustrate Zukin and Maguire's point that consumption "is a social, cultural, and economic process of choosing goods, and this process reflects the opportunities and constraints of modernity" (2004: 173). In their survey of the sociology of consumption, they find that consumption practices illustrate the connections among "economic and cultural institutions, large-scale changes in social structure, and discourses of the self"—and these practices are not only reflective of these things but constitutive of them. That is, how and what we consume is not only a product of who we are but also *produces* us as the kind of people we are, in the kinds of relationships we have.

From Walter Benjamin's early studies of the Paris Arcades to George Ritzer's recent work on "cathedrals of consumption" (see below), changes in consumption—especially the rise of mass consumption—tell the tale of "the development of an institutional field . . . made up of consumer products, texts, and sites. New retail stores, advertisements, popular magazines, and daily newspapers all brought consumers into contact with goods and tended to make the consumer a powerful role model" (176). Add to that list new media like the Internet, and you can see how consumption pervades and shapes modern life—not to mention the modern person *as* consumer

in the first place. Growth and change in consumption also obviously reflect "qualitative changes in demographics, new trends of social and geographical mobility, and the growing appeal of standardized goods as badges of both democratization and social status" (177).

Perhaps the most fundamental product of modern consumption practices is the consumer himself/herself, what some social theorists have called "the choosing self." If the production end of the market did not create an autonomous individual actor, the consumption end would. Zukin and Maguire stress "the process of individualization, in which identity shifts from a fixed set of characteristics determined by birth and ascription to a reflexive, ongoing individual project shaped by appearance and performance" (181). An essential component of this modern self is what we consume. We literally construct and display our individuality with our food, our cars, our homes, and our clothes (and most overtly with our slogan-bearing t-shirts). Along with this

Box 11-3
George Ritzer: The New Means of Consumption

Not all Americans or citizens of modern industrial societies participate in "production" in the conventional sense—what are often called "primary" sector (agriculture or raw-material extraction) or "secondary" sector (manufacturing) jobs—but we all participate in consumption. Indeed, Ritzer notes the obvious, that consumption "plays an ever-expanding role in the lives of individuals around the world" (2005: 1). For this reason, Ritzer calls for more attention to the "new means of consumption," which he defines as "the settings or structures that enable us to consume all sorts of things" (6) or, more thoroughly and sinisterly, "those things that make it possible for people to acquire goods and services and for the same people to be controlled and exploited as consumers" (50). As sociologists, we can readily perceive that these means of consumption involve many interrelated social factors and relations such as "advertising, marketing, sales, individual taste, style, and fashion" (6). For this culture of consumption to operate, it must have its sites or locations, which proliferate dramatically in contemporary capitalism. Ritzer calls these sites "cathedrals of consumption" because they provide not only goods and services but also *entertainment, meaning,* and even what he—following Weber—calls *enchantment,* a certain

magical or almost religious quality. He offers a long list of such cathedrals, including fast-food restaurants and other franchises, chain stores, shopping malls, discount stores (like Costco and Wal-Mart), superstores or "big box" stores (such as Toys-R-Us or Staples), catalogs, electronic shopping outlets (including Home Shopping Network, Amazon, and eBay), casinos, and cruise ships/vacation spots. Once the logic of consumption is diffused throughout a society, other institutions offer opportunities for or are re-interpreted as consumption, not the least of which are hospitals and healthcare facilities (which include gyms and other athletic clubs), museums, schools and colleges, and even churches. This preoccupation with consumption not only changes what we have but how we relate to each other. For instance, the need to make consumption more rational and efficient (which largely means *cheaper*) has commonly meant that "face-to-face relationships have been reduced (e.g., at the drive-in window of a fast-food restaurant) or eliminated completely (e.g., in cybermalls, on home shopping networks, and at self-service storage centers)," not to mention automated customer-service systems (37). All of this Ritzer regards as the relentless march of capitalism and modernization.

focus on the consuming self comes a conscious awareness and choice of "taste" and "lifestyle" (182). In the process, we become members of and declare our allegiance to various consuming communities.

After all, consumption is as much social as personal. First, as they remind us, and as exhortations to spend and buy after 9/11 and in the midst of the recession of 2008–10 demonstrate, "consumption is presented not as an option but as a duty of the consumer-citizen" (Zukin and Maguire, 183): when we consume, someone else gets or keeps a job. So, our consumption habits are not entirely our own private business; indeed, the "illusory nature of consumer freedom is further supported by academic studies of marketing, public relations, and consumer research." Finally, consumption pressures and practices do not merely constrain us but actually construct us. Among the psychosocial consequences of modern consumption are "encouragement of self-expression through consumption practices, tolerance of visible signs of luxury and comfort, and the shifting of goods and services (such as housing, transportation, medical care, and meals) from collective provision by the work unit to individual provision on the open, and often

unregulated, market. These changes expand the means of sociability that are both available and desirable to consumers—at the cost of increasing social inequality" (190).

COMPARATIVE ECONOMIC SYSTEMS

The three major phases of economics can and do vary independently, but they are also regularly organized into "economic systems," which are further attached to power structures and even government in modern societies. Marx himself noted, as mentioned earlier, that a number of historical economic systems had existed, from tribal "communism" without classes to feudalism. However, for most citizens of the modern world, three systems predominate and compete, although (a) each of them is diverse, (b) none of them does or probably could exist in its "pure" form, and (c) one of them has come to triumph and dominate over the others. These three systems are capitalism, socialism, and communism. What is particularly interesting sociologically about each system is the social relations and values it promotes, the social institutions it creates, and the type of person it socializes.

Capitalism

Capitalism evolved out of the feudal order of premodern Europe, fed significantly by the wealth extracted from colonialism. It is based on three premises or social concepts/relationships:

1. Private property

2. Profit motive

3. Market as a means of distribution and decentralized decision making

The most fundamental premise of capitalism is private property, a concept often absent from traditional societies (which is why Marx claimed them as "primitive communists"); however, existence of private property is not automatically the same thing as a formal system of capitalism. It

Modern practices of consumption depend on sites of consumption like the mall, where goods are on display and consumers make decisions by "shopping."

took European societies a long time to convert the basics of private property into an organized capitalist economy, not least because the powerful Catholic Church of medieval Europe condemned *usury* or the practice of charging interest to lend money (Islam has a similar rule today). This is why non-Christians, particularly Jews, were often left to occupy non-Christian roles like trade and banking.

In one of Max Weber's most acclaimed books, *The Protestant Ethic and the Spirit of Capitalism*, he maintained that a change of norms and values, closely tied to religion, had to occur before capitalism could coalesce. Further, other changes in society were required. Property that was not private had to be privatized, as with the "enclosure" of formerly public or "common" land. Property laws had to be established, with courts to enforce them. Equally important, institutions had to be invented or expanded, such as the "bank" and the "corporation" (see below). As early as the fourteenth century, rich cities like Florence, Italy possessed large and powerful banks, often owned by prominent families. The Bank of England was not founded until 1694. Merchants and traders throughout Europe organized fraternal and self-protective "guilds" (akin to labor unions today; see below). And the "joint-stock company" (co-owned by multiple investors who bought "stock" in the company) or the "chartered company" (licensed to do business by the local royalty) became a major factor in large-scale, expensive, and risky ventures like overseas trade. Some significant early chartered companies in England were the Muscovy Company (1555), the British East India Company (1600), and the Hudson's Bay Company (1670); other countries followed suit, for instance Holland with its Dutch East India Company (1602).

These grand institutions transformed the previous "petty capitalism" or small-scale marketing and trading into a large-scale and increasingly integrated enterprise, supported by governments and borne eventually by the wage-laborers in the emerging industrialization of Europe and early America. Industrialization altered the nature of work—and social experience more generally—in many ways (which is a major theme throughout this book), for instance, separating work from home, centralizing it in a specialized location (the factory or later the office), and creating new roles (e.g., "the worker"). Thus, the first phase of the economy to be modified by capitalism is production, including and especially the relations of production; for Marx, the key development was the rise of two distinct classes.

But capitalism also affects distribution and consumption. For distribution, the market becomes the dominant practice, leading to a market society. Individuals approximate Adam Smith's ideal market actor, exercising their freedom and interest to sell their goods or time for maximum profit. Indeed, Richard Swedberg (2003a) insists that the true uniqueness of capitalism lies in its sole preoccupation with profit, and the market or competitive exchange is the perfect mechanism for this goal. Finally, capitalism also reconfigures consumption, first by seeking mass consumption to absorb its mass production and pursuit of mass profits and second by offering continuous innovation as well as advertisement to build new markets. Goods and services also take on new meanings as they circulate in the system of social symbols. All of this together leads to perhaps the essential mandate of capitalism, which is *growth*. Individuals and corporations are driven to produce and sell more goods and increase their profits.

Proponents of capitalism hail it for encouraging creativity, stimulating competition, and enriching the society generally (the idea that "a rising tide lifts all boats"). Critics of capitalism accuse it of creating class inequalities and centralizing wealth within an elite, eroding values and destroying institutions, and generating damaging economic cycles of boom and bust.

Socialism

Socialism in its familiar form rose largely as a reaction against capitalism and its perceived social effects. Instead of individual ownership and the profit motive, it promotes

- Collective ownership
- "Social good" or social justice
- Centralized planning

It does not necessarily oppose markets nor does it exclude industrialization, but it does not leave all economic decisions in the "invisible hands" of the market.

As frequently oppositional, socialism has tended to take the form of a social movement. One of its earliest expressions, before the advent of fully modern capitalism, was a group called the Levellers in mid-seventeenth-century England, who demanded more freedom and justice for the lower and middle classes of society (a "leveling" of social differences). Even more radical were the Diggers, a movement of lower-class and landless folk who sought to occupy and work land communally. One of the most influential figures in early socialism was Robert Owen, an industrialist who criticized the poverty of the nineteenth century and, in response, established communities where not only land ownership but also residence and even childrearing were communal. In the United States he organized New Harmony, Indiana, and others like John Humphrey Noyes and his Oneida Community (New York) started similar socialist experiments.

Marx rejected the "utopian socialism" behind such efforts, and twentieth-century socialism abandoned the ideal-community approach in favor of the governmental approach. Thus, modern socialism tends to designate government ownership and control of some or all means of production (land, factories, etc.), with central decision making and an emphasis on collective social goals like equality or justice instead of individual or corporation enrichment. The government (or "state") typically acts as a redistributor, reducing the extreme effects of capitalism through high tax rates and state provision of many social services such as education, health care, or retirement insurance.

Advocates of socialism claim that it promotes fairness, meets basic human needs, and acts more rationally than capitalism. Enemies of socialism feel that it threatens individual freedom, discourages innovation, and deprives individuals of the benefits of their own efforts.

Communism

The communism envisioned by Marx, and attempted by countries like the Soviet Union and the People's Republic of China, differed from modern socialism by advocating not only the elimination of all private property and of all class distinctions *but of the very government or state itself.* Marxist communism (which he regarded as "scientific socialism" and as the inevitable destination of capitalist societies) was to result in a perfectly level society, without classes at all. Since no individual would own anything, no one could be richer or more powerful than others. The state (as well as religion, he believed) would "wither." The state would be replaced by committees or councils (*soviet* in Russian) of workers, which would make decisions on behalf of and in the interests of those workers. Religion would also vanish completely, since the fulfillment of real economic needs would render wishful or imaginary fulfillment unnecessary.

Communism further entailed the promotion of new values and attitudes and even a new notion of personhood—the new communist man. Citizens were supposed to abandon other characteristics and identities (of race, nationality, ethnicity, gender, or religion) and identify simply as workers, as equal comrades. They were also expected to reject private property and accept "collectivization," the transfer of people to group- or state-run cooperatives. Communist regimes used extensive re-education and "criticism" techniques to achieve this new mentality and often persecuted, if not exterminated, objectors. Russian communism glorified the industrial worker, while Chinese communism upheld the peasant villager as its model. These and other systems used arts and film to promote communist identity and ethics. The state that was supposed to wither away, meanwhile, became a huge bureaucratic apparatus, managed by a single modern "party" (the Communist Party) that claimed to rule in the name of "the people." These governments thus regarded themselves as democratic (democracy, "the rule of the people," being based on *who* holds power, not on *how* they acquire power).

Champions of communism believed that it would achieve complete equality, free humanity from the tyranny of politics and religion, and release the potential of every individual. Detractors feared its potential for totalitarianism, its aggressive revolutionary stance, and its stifling of individuality.

In the real world, of course, the pure forms of these ideal systems do not exist. As indicated, even the pro-capitalist United States has had its experimental socialist communities, and the Great Depression of the 1930s ushered in elements of institutional socialism in programs like Social Security and AFDC (Aid to Families with Dependent Children), with Medicare added in the 1960s. Thus, in virtually every capitalist society, pure (sometimes referred to as *laissez-faire* or "let them do it") capitalism has given way to welfare capitalism in which the government acts to regulate the economy, smooth out the boom-and-bust cycle, and guarantee a decent standard of living for its citizens. As governments have become increasingly unable to keep these promises, and as powerful interests have challenged them, a new phase of corporate capitalism in which the interests of corporations predominate has emerged. Critics like Naomi Klein in her book *The Shock Doctrine* (2007) call it "disaster capitalism" or "casino capitalism."

Meanwhile, formerly socialist or communist systems have either collapsed (as in the Soviet Union) or survived in name only (as in the People's Republic of China), with increasing amounts of capitalistic and market practices entering their economies. In yet other locations, societies have attempted their own local variations on economic systems, like Julius Nyerere's "African socialism" for Tanzania, allegedly based on traditional African village beliefs and values.

SOCIOLOGY OF THE MARKET

Despite the survival of reciprocity and redistribution within specific social relationships, and notwithstanding the ideological debate over "socialism" in the United States, there is little room to doubt that the market is a pervasive and dominant form of global economic activity. And while Polanyi and others have argued that a self-regulating or (presumably) autonomous market "demands nothing less than the institutional separation of society into an economic and political sphere" (74), sociologists understand—and Polanyi appreciated—that this "disembedding" of the market, or of the economy in general, from society is impossible. Sociology claims and finds that economic concepts, practices, relations, and institutions of every kind are thoroughly social in that they require certain kinds of social arrangements while also producing certain kinds of social arrangements. In a word, even markets are effectively embedded in society—and the more embedded, the better for the markets.

Fligstein and Dauter (2007) and Lie (1997), for instance, have summarized the contributions of sociology toward the description and analysis of markets. As Lie reminds us, "We live in the age of the market. The category of the market dominates everyday discourse and political reality" (1997: 341). Indeed, market thinking can be and is applied to many and potentially all aspects of life: "Jobs, spouses, and commodities are all said to be obtained in their respective markets." However, as best illustrated by Adam Smith and the classical tradition of economic theory, this market phenomenon is seen as self-generating, asocial, and almost independent of humans. It is "shorn of social relations, institutions, or technology and is devoid of elementary sociological concerns such as power, norms, and networks" (342).

Social theorists like Talcott Parsons and Amitai Etzioni, on the other hand, stressed the social nature of economics generally and markets specifically. Parsons, a modeler of grand social systems, saw the economy as a subsystem of the wider social system, and Etzioni explicitly advocated a "socioeconomics" that would go beyond the "utilitarian, rationalist, and individualist" perspective of conventional economic theory (1988: 1). Instead, a socially informed economics assumes "that individuals act within a social context, that this context is not reducible to individual acts, and, most significantly, that the social context is, to a significant extent, perceived as a legitimate and integral part of one's existence, a We, a whole of which the individuals are constituent elements" (5). As Lie put it, aspects of social life such as "duties, trust, cooperation, and other integrative principles and mechanisms [serve] not only as descriptive tools but also as prescriptive principles" (Lie 1997: 347), with their own explanatory and even moral force (see below).

One of the key concepts to which Lie referred, which was suggested by Polanyi and has been elaborated by Mark Granovetter, is "embeddedness."

Box 11-4
Of Markets and Morals

Etzioni's work on socioeconomics explicitly insisted that economics is a moral problem, and Adam Smith agreed: economics is part of the larger question of "the good." What is a good life, how should we organize ourselves, and what kind of society do we want? Fourcade and Healy explore the morality of the market, both in the sense of the moral principles that are expressed in it and of the moral actors (the sorts of individuals) that it produces. Their questions are, "Upon what kind of moral order does capitalism rest? Conversely, does the market give rise to a distinctive set of beliefs, habits, and social bonds?" (Fourcade and Healy 2007: 285). By asking such questions we discover that markets are "cultural phenomena and moral projects in their own right." Sociologists begin by realizing that market actors are involved in day-to-day social relationships with one another, relationships based on trust, friendship, power, and dependence. For the modern sociology of markets, unstructured, haphazard, one-shot, anonymous social exchange is not a market. Instead, markets imply social spaces where repeated exchanges occur between buyers and sellers under a set of formal and informal rules governing relations between competitors, suppliers, and customers. These fields operate according to local understandings and formal and informal rules and conventions that guide interaction, facilitate trade, define what products are produced, indeed are constitutive of products, and provide stability for buyers, sellers, and producers (Fligstein and Dauter 2007: 113).

They first note four views on the morality of markets. In the "liberal dream" (what today we might prefer to call the "neoliberal" or "conservative" or "globalization" dream) markets are believed to generate the best possible outcome, the greatest collective happiness, and the most civil type of society. At the very least, markets spawn virtue and harmony, if only because "each individual's hunger for profit will be kept in check by a similar drive among other individuals" (Fourcade and Healy, 287). The result is people who are "polite, serviceable, and honest." At most, as champions of the market such as Milton Friedman and Friedrich von Hayek assert, markets maximize freedom. They liberate individuals from

institutional (especially governmental) control and encourage creativity and innovation. However, others see markets as corrosive. In the "destructive markets" view, markets reduce people to their lowest motives (self-interest and profit) and discourage higher principles like cooperation and altruism. Everything becomes a commodity, and wealth becomes its own reward. Such a system also depends on desire, envy, and even waste and obsolescence. Finally, markets in this way of thinking are not freeing. People are coerced into unequal economic and social relations (e.g., Marxist "classes"), are compelled to sell their labor, and are often misled by an elite that *does* benefit from the system but does not share those benefits (the much-vaunted "trickle-down" theory of economic growth). The third view of markets sees them as essentially feeble, having little moral significance. Different societies can and do operate markets differently, so there is no single "market culture" or "market morality"; further, markets are fundamentally voluntary, and their effects may be good, bad, both, or neutral. Fourth, Fourcade and Healy advance the "moral markets" standpoint, that "markets are culture, not just because they are the products of human practice and sense making, but because markets are explicitly moral projects, saturated with normativity" (299–300). For instance, market practices establish moral qualities of and moral boundaries between individuals, groups, and societies. They promote notions of a person's social worth or status, of property as private and market-able, of the market itself as a moral force (e.g., "fair trade"), and of the individual as a free, rational agent. Also, markets "turn out to be filled with explicit moralizing, whether concerning the creditworthiness of nations, their degree of corruption and cronyism, or the extent of corporate social and environmental responsibility" (300). In conclusion, the market "is saturated with moral meaning. . . . It involves more or less conscious efforts to categorize, normalize, and naturalize behaviors and rules that are not natural in any way, whether in the name of economic principles (e.g., efficiency, productivity) or more social ones (e.g., justice, social responsibility)" (300).

As Granovetter emphasized as early as 1985, "economic action is embedded in structures of social relations" (1985: 481) and cannot be understood in isolation from those relations. He argued that theories like those of Adam Smith not only expect individualism to prevail in the economy but *prefer* that it does: "social atomization is prerequisite to perfect competition" (Granovetter, 484). However, economic action, as a particular form of social action, is never so totally undersocialized; rather, the perspective of embeddedness leads us to appreciate "the role of concrete personal relations and structures (or 'networks') of such relations in generating trust and discouraging malfeasance" (486), which is a basic precondition of economic life.

Fligstein and Dauter further identify three sociological approaches to markets, centering on networks, institutions, and performativity (that is, how social actors employ knowledge, situations, and institutions to construct and perform their actions). Yet, all three of these perspectives "rely on viewing markets as social arenas where firms, their suppliers, customers, workers, and government interact, and all three approaches emphasize how the connectedness of social actors affects their behavior" (Fligstein and Dauter 2007: 107). In short, the ideal rational, self-interested, atomized market actor, engaging in a series of discrete and episodic market interactions, does not exist. What exists is socialized individuals participating in socialized markets that are set within—and regulated and reproduced by—other (and more general and not necessarily "market") social values, practices, and relations. First among these is government. Markets do not appear spontaneously but must be created and managed. Markets can also cause disorder and even chaos, so "governments would have to intervene in markets to stabilize them and to provide social protection for workers and rules to guide the interactions between groups" (109).

Thus, Fligstein and Dauter conclude that, while individuals do participate in market activity, these activities—and the actors themselves—already evince "a great deal of social structure" (112).

> Market actors have to find one another. Money has to exist to allow market actors to get beyond

bartering nonequivalent goods. Actors have to know what the price is. Underlying all exchange is that both buyers and sellers have faith that they will not be cheated. Such faith often implies informal (i.e., personal knowledge of the buyer or seller) and formal mechanisms (i.e., law) that govern exchange. Furthermore, market actors are often organizations, implying that organizational dynamics influence market structures. For sociologists, market exchange implies a whole backdrop of social arrangements that economics does not even begin to hint at. (113)

And these arrangements extend beyond the market into other facets of social life; in fact, these arrangements tend to originate in general social life and *extend into* the market.

CONTEMPORARY QUESTIONS IN THE SOCIOLOGY OF THE ECONOMY

While sociology has classically concerned itself with certain questions, as the economic realities of contemporary societies have changed, so have the concerns of sociology. These new orientations are reflected in the research that sociologists currently conduct. This final section of the chapter surveys some of the recent topics and insights found in sociology in the last few years.

Sociology of Contemporary Business and Entrepreneurship

Sociologists have turned their attention to describing and explaining the practices and structures of contemporary business institutions and practices. As Patricia Thornton shows, there is a lively sociology of entrepreneurship, which has paid attention to "the influence of firms and markets on how, where, and why new enterprises are founded" (1999: 19). Lisa Keister, similarly, finds that financial markets, money, and banking are within the purview of sociology, since "a financial market is a social system. . . . Underlying research in each of these areas . . . is the notion that financial relations are social relations and that a financial market is a structure of ongoing and relatively stable exchange ties among buyers and sellers of financial resources" (2002: 39–40). Even a fundamental concept like property rights can be illuminated by sociology. Carruthers and Ariovich suggest five social dimensions of property rights, including "the objects of property (what can be owned), the subjects of property (who can own), the uses of property (what can be done with it), the enforcement of rights (how property rules are maintained), and the transfer of property (how property moves between different owners)" (2004: 23).

As mentioned above, a key, if not the key, to modern economies is the corporation, which is not an entirely new institution but an increasingly important and dominant one. In a sense, the corporation is the ultimate example of Max Weber's notion of modernity, which he characterized as bureaucratic, rational-efficient, urban, and secular. The corporation is unique even among modern institutions for being a "legal person," that is, for having a legal identity of its own, separate from the humans who work and make decisions for it. A corporation has its own assets and liabilities, enters its own contracts, and can sue or be sued in its own name; thus, individuals—whether investors or managers—cannot necessarily be held responsible for what the corporation does. This is sometimes referred to as "limited liability" precisely because it does limit the liability of individuals with regard to corporate actions. In fact, American law recognizes the "limited liability company" as a business structure akin to a corporation, in which owners (legally recognized as "members") have, according to the Internal Revenue Service, "limited personal liability for the debts and actions of the LLC."

Corporations fall within the sociology of organizations, and one question that sociologists can ask and have asked is how corporations are organized and governed. Gerald Davis defines corporate governance as "the structures, processes, and institutions within and around organizations that allocate power and resource control among participants" (2005: 143). He further stresses that the operation of a corporation should be seen as more than merely a "nexus of

contracts" as classical economic theory would suggest, but includes "networks, power, and culture." Neil Fligstein's more detailed study of the history of corporate governance in the United States likewise argued against understanding the actions of corporate executives as driven solely by rational-efficient interests but as

determined by a legal framework and a self-conscious version of the world that make both old and new courses of action possible and desirable. Like everyone else, managers tend to see the world in a certain way and the framing of action often takes place in a context where the action taken was the only and obvious one. New courses of action require risk takers with alternative conceptions of the world. (1990: 4)

Among the formal aspects of corporate structure are "interlocking directorates" or individuals who hold positions of power in multiple corporations or institutions, as well as more informal and personal relationships and networks. Especially in times of uncertainty or transition, social relations, knowledge, and trust are often essential in the decision making of firms.

Sociologists have investigated important developments in the United States and other economies like the expansion of corporations like Wal-Mart. According to Melissa Rossi (2005),

Corporations like Wal-Mart are powerful forces in the economy and the wider society.

© pcruciatti, 2012. Under license from Shutterstock, Inc.

Box 11-5
The 'Wal-Mart Effect'

Charles Fishman has proposed the term "the Wal-Mart effect" for the impact that the company has on our lives, our society, and our world.

> Wal-Mart shapes where we ship, the products we buy, and the prices we pay—even for those of us who never shop there. It reaches deep inside the operations of the companies that supply it and changes not only what they sell, but also changes how those products are packaged and presented, what the lives of the factory workers who make the products are like—it even sometimes changes the countries where those factories are located. (2006: 5)

The retailer, Fishman continues, "has even changed the way we think about ourselves—as shoppers, as consumers. Wal-Mart has changed our sense of quality, it has changed our sense of what a good deal is. . . . The Wal-Mart effect touches the lives of literally every American every day." While this is no doubt true, and Wal-Mart has come under savage criticism for

it, the company hardly invented large-scale sales nor is it alone in its influence on modern life.

Long before Wal-Mart, Montgomery Ward (founded in 1872) and Sears, Roebuck, and Company (founded in 1893) brought department-store and mail-order shopping to America a century earlier, and corporations from Pfizer and Monsanto to Halliburton and Exxon-Mobil shape our world. Further, as a recent article in *The Atlantic* (Schell 2011) discusses and Fishman admits, Wal-Mart's effects have not been all bad: The company has established ambitious waste-reduction and product-quality standards not only in the United States, but also in China, the site of many of its suppliers and retail stores. In China, shoppers actually trust Wal-Mart more than their own local and smaller shops, and through its power to influence manufacturing and government itself, "In Wal-Mart, the Chinese government has found a source of public education, control, and regulation—at no extra public cost" (Schell 2011: 89).

Wal-Mart is the largest retailer in the world, employing over a million people (possibly 2 million by 2012) and generating more than a quarter of a billion dollars in annual sales. Almost 9 percent of all American consumer spending occurs in Wal-Mart, and it sells 14 percent of all American groceries, 26 percent of all American toothpaste, and 36 percent of all American dog food. At the same time as it provides huge savings to its customers, it pays low wages, offers few employee benefits, and actually destroys other jobs: "the opening of every Wal-Mart results in the loss of some two hundred local jobs" (2005: 156), between the elimination of retail competition and the pressure on suppliers to move their manufacturing to other countries.

Many people have noticed not only the aggressive growth of Wal-Mart in recent years but the sometimes equally aggressive resistance to that growth, premised on the destruction of local businesses or the suppression of wages. Ingram, Yue, and Rao performed a statistical analysis of the protests against Wal-Mart and discovered that the greatest obstacle to Wal-Mart's

expansion has been protests by local activists: Between 1998 and 2005, Wal-Mart encountered 563 protests against proposed new stores, and 65 percent of those protests succeeded in blocking the store openings (2010: 53). The authors then tested a number of hypotheses and determined that Wal-Mart was less likely to open new stores when local protests were led by organizations, when protests had already been successful in neighboring communities, and when the targeted communities were inhabited by liberals and Democrats. Not surprisingly, Wal-Mart was more likely to increase donations to a community after protests against its plans erupted.

Globalization and Economic Transition

One of the most prominent economic-social developments of our time is the increasing economic and social integration of the world's many countries and societies, which has been labeled "globalization." Globalization is, of course, not an entirely new phenomenon: societies have traded with, provided resources and labor for, and otherwise interacted with each other from the beginning, and European colonialism started the process of the integration of global societies over five hundred years ago. But in terms of the current extent and pace of the circulation of goods, ideas, labor, money, and even people around the world, globalization today is unprecedented. The American Forum for Global Education has defined globalization as "the acceleration and intensification of interaction and integration among the people, companies, and governments of different nations" (Rothenberg 2002–2003: 1).

Globalization is thus a shift in the nature of social relations and interactions, with a number of important consequences. Most obviously, it brings people into contact with others who would have less or no contact otherwise; it also exposes people in one society to the effects of natural and social forces (hurricanes, wars, economic recessions, or mere changes in taste) in distant societies. It has consequences for work and wages (see below). Rothenberg in particular mentions three "tensions" inherent in globalization: the tensions between individual choice versus societal choice, between the free market and government intervention, and between local authority and supralocal authority. Some commentators, like Benjamin Barber, see globalization—which is, in a large sense, simply the extension and integration of market forces globally—as spawning counterglobalization and antiglobalization reactions, at the most extreme, what Barber (1995) calls "jihad." Jihad is not specifically Islamic here but rather any exclusionary, often violent, cultural rejection of the blurring or altering of social identities and boundaries.

Another related phenomenon of the last two or three decades has been economic transition, particularly from nonmarket (mostly communist) to market societies across vast areas of the world. The two biggest examples are the former Soviet Union and China. The transition from communism to market capitalism happened first and most suddenly and traumatically in the USSR, following the fall of the communist regime in 1991. Inviting Western experts to aid in the transformation, Russia undertook a rapid process of economic and social change, which more than a few observers have likened to shock therapy (see especially Naomi Klein [2007]). But according to Grigory Yavlinsky, Russia discovered the hard way that markets are not merely economic phenomenon but also social ones that require an entire system and foundation of social institutions to organize and stabilize them: "In the last ten years, Russia has learned that an open society has one more enemy: capitalism that is not limited by laws, civil institutions, tradition, belief, trade unions—by anything at all. It is capitalism that drives itself by the wild will for profit at any price" (Forbes and Popov 2008). China has pursued a different path, with more gradual transition under tighter government control, but even there the consequences for wealth and inequality, gender relations, rural-to-urban migration, and general social unrest have been undeniable.

The Sociology of Work

Many years ago E. P. Thompson (1967) wrote an influential essay about the impact of industrialization on the experience of work, in which he described the changes to the workers' sense of time and to their work-discipline—alterations that some workers, like the famous Luddites, often resisted with violence. At least since then, sociologists have been acutely attuned to the social construction of work. At the macro social level, one of the most prominent developments has been the relative and absolute decline in employment in the primary and secondary sectors of the economy in the United States and similar countries. According to the U.S. Bureau of Labor Statistics, work in nonfarm goods-producing activities (including mining and logging, construction, and manufacturing) has actually dropped while the working population has more than doubled over the past fifty years.

One of the effects of these employment shifts has been the deindustrialization of many economies, including the United States. The International Monetary Fund (IMF), which commented on the trend as early as 1997, defines deindustrialization as the decline in

Table 11-1

Employees on Nonfarm Payroll by Major Industry Sector, 1961–2010 (in thousands)

Year	Total Workers	Workers in Goods-Producing	Workers in Mining and Logging	Workers in Construction	Workers in Manufacturing
1961	54,105	18,647	728	2,908	15,011
1971	71,335	21,602	658	3,770	17,174
1981	91,289	24,118	1,180	4,204	18,624
1991	108,375	22,588	729	4,780	17,068
2001	131,826	22,873	606	6,826	16,441
2010*	129,818	17,755	705	5,526	11,524

Source: U.S. Department of Labor

* Midrecession

manufacturing as a share of total employment, and as such, it is evident for the United States in the statistics presented in Table 11-1. It has also been experienced in Europe, Japan, Taiwan, South Korea, and Singapore—all highly industrialized economies until recently. The IMF found in 1997 that the most industrialized economies in the world had fallen from 28 percent of their workforce in manufacturing in 1970 to 18 percent of their workforce in 1994, with only 16 percent working in manufacturing in the United States (Rowthorn and Ramaswamy 1997: 2). Some have seen this as the general decline of the economy, and no doubt many people have lost jobs and many regions have been negatively affected. However, while sociologists Brady, Beckfield, and Zhao agree that there has been "an unmistakable decline in manufacturing employment in all affluent democracies" (2007: 321), neither they nor the IMF find cause for alarm, since much of the shift is based on improved technology, increasing worker productivity, and the transition to "white collar" jobs in service, management, or information industries. Some of the job shift, though, reflects competition from low-wage countries like China, as well as the down-shifting to lower-wage work in retail, food service, or health-care careers.

One of the subjects for sociological attention has been the rise of so-called "nonstandard employment relations." Nonstandard employment relations refers to work situations "that depart from standard work arrangements in which it was generally expected that work was done full-time, would continue indefinitely, and was performed at the employer's place of business under the employer's direction" (Kalleberg 2000: 341). Particular forms of such work relations include part-time employment, temporary employment, and contract work. At the time of his research, Kalleberg calculated that one-fifth of American workers worked part-time, many by choice; however, since 1970 "virtually all of the increase has occurred among those who would prefer full-time work (i.e., 'involuntary' part-timers), who currently make up about one quarter of part-timers" (344). Interestingly, he also concludes that "the growth in part-time work in the United States since 1979 appears to have been due to the expansion of industries that typically employ many part-timers (services, retail trade, finance, insurance, real estate) rather than to the substitution of part-time for full-time workers within industries that occurred mainly in the 1970s. . . . The growth of part-time employment has similarly accompanied the expansion of the service sector in other industrial countries" (344).

Not surprisingly, part-time workers tend to earn less per hour than full-time employees, even when their education and skills are comparable.

Temporary or short-term employment is another nonstandard work relationship, in which workers may have fixed or open-ended employment periods or may be hired on an on-call basis (like substitute teachers, for instance). Some of these jobs fall within the concept of "contingent work," defined as "any job in which an individual does not have an explicit or implicit contract for long-term employment or one in which the minimum hours worked can vary in a nonsystematic manner" (Polivka and Nardone 1989: 11). Also, numerous people work as independent contractors, essentially self-employed and providing their specialized services to consumers or corporations for a fixed period, sometimes on the clients' premises and sometimes not. Finally, Valenzuela notes the increase in day labor in recent years, by which he means "the practice of searching for work in open-air, informal markets such as street corners or in formal temp agencies" (2003: 307). The growth of day labor is linked to three macrosocial processes—globalization, the informal or "underground" economy, and immigration—and has tended to associate with certain kinds of work, primarily agricultural and manual labor. There have also been strong gender, class, and ethnic associations with day labor (mostly male, low socioeconomic status, and immigrant or nonwhite).

The Dynamics of the Workplace

Sociology is particularly well suited to examine the social nature of the workplace. Since the workplace is a site of human interaction, it is a specific case of more general processes of group dynamics, social networks, and organizational culture. One immediate issue is the gender and race composition of the workplace. For instance, it is a truism that particular genders, races, and ethnic groups are disproportionately represented in some jobs than others, as well as in various

levels of work or management. According to the U.S. Bureau of Labor Statistics, for example, in 2010 women comprised 78.3 percent of the workers in personal care and service occupations, while African Americans, Asians, and Hispanics filled 14.8 percent, 7.8 percent, and 14.6 percent, respectively. Women also disproportionately fill sales and office jobs (62.9 percent) and administrative support jobs (73.9 percent), while women, African Americans, and Hispanics were seriously underrepresented in management positions (women 38.2 percent, African Americans 6.4 percent, and Hispanics 7.6 percent).

As Reskin, McBrier, and Kmec (1999) point out, the demographics of the workplace reflect various social realities of the wider society. Some of the factors that they relate to gender and race compositions of workplaces include the composition of the available labor pools (further related to differences in skill, education, credentials, and "social capital" in general); statistical discrimination and hiring discrimination; relative numbers, group power, and threat; and labor costs and group status. And even when they are hired, disparities remain in the authority that various groups can exercise in the workplace. Ryan Smith (2002) identifies a number of variables that lead women and minorities to have lower workplace authority—and, significantly, he identifies "authority" as a multivariate phenomenon, not a simple duality of powerful and powerlessness. Among the contributors to the lower authority of women and minorities are inequalities in training, education, and experience; lack of seniority; inconsistent work history; union or non-union status; "homosocial reproduction" or the tendency for workforces to draw on members of the social groups already represented in the workforce; and "social closure" or the intentional exclusion of job candidates from certain gender and race categories. One of the emerging issues of recent years, given the increase of labor participation by women, is sex and romance in the workplace, including but not limited to sexual harassment (see Williams, Guiffre, and Dellinger 1999).

Labor Unions as Social Action

The workplace is a site of labor but also a site of association—the sharing of interests, the formation of relationships, and the creation of identity. It is often a site of struggle and resistance, as Marx reminded us. Collective action by laborers against their working conditions is nothing new in history: there were major peasant revolts in 1381 and 1524 over wages, taxes, and wealth inequality. In the premodern era, skilled craftsmen attempted to secure their status by forming "guilds," sometimes semireligious organizations with oaths that bound members by pacts of mutual support and agreements that regulated their trades, such as apprenticeship and prices.

The arrival of the industrial era put new pressures on and raised new challenges for labor. Machines could do the work of many men: with a steam engine, three semiskilled men and two children could produce the same amount as twenty-seven skilled textile craftsmen (Sale 1996: 23). Obviously, work was simultaneously deskilled, and wages dropped: an English weaver who earned 15–20 shillings per week in 1790 made only 10 shillings in 1811 and 5 shillings by 1820. Finally, many men had no work at all or else only sporadic work. Working and living conditions in factory cities were often grim, and many contemporaries—including the early sociologists—claimed to witness the rise of a vile and cruel new social order.

Some of the first collective behavior of laborers came in the form of rioting and sabotage of factory buildings and machines. For a short period from 1811 to 1813 (with a few spasms over subsequent years), a group calling themselves Luddites attacked factories in England, trying to stop the factory system and the erosion of their skilled craft way of life; they were met with political opposition and physical force and eventually subdued. (The term luddite is still applied today to someone who resists new technologies.) Indeed, even before these outbreaks, England had passed laws in 1799 and 1800 criminalizing "combinations" or associations of workers that sought better pay or working conditions. As the nineteenth century advanced, and with it industrialization, Marx and Engels not only predicted but assumed and hoped that industrial laborers would recognize their common cause and organize as an urban proletariat. Class would become more than a dominant identity but the only identity, surpassing nationality or race or religion. The final line of their 1848 "Communist Manifesto" was "Workers of the world, Unite!"

While socialist and communist parties aimed to alter the basic institutions of economics and society, workers also struggled with more day-to-day problems. In the United States as in Europe, craftsmen tried to form associations to stem the unskilled factory system; one example was the Mechanics' Union of Trade Associations in Philadelphia. As early as the 1830s labor groups were using the strike or work stoppage as a tactic. Employers had their tactics, too, including lockouts, firings, intimidation, and even guns. However, the organizational model of craft unions gave way to the model of the "industrial union" or the labor union of today. According to Wolfgang Streeck's major summary of the sociology of unions, early industrial or labor unions "aimed at organizing all workers in a workplace or industry; in fact, given the already existing unions of the skilled, they mostly remained organizations of unskilled laborers" (2005: 267). Such institutions are "*cartels* of sellers of labor. . . . Enabling workers to speak with a

Labor unions are a particular form of economic organization and action.

© Michael-John Wolfe, 2012. Under license from Shutterstock, Inc.

collective voice, unions replace individual with collective contracts and thereby correct the imbalance of power that distorts individual bargains between workers and employers" (263). They intervene in the labor market, for instance, to limit the amount of labor that an employer can extract from any worker (by working-hour or vacation rules), to protect jobs, and to establish standards for employment contracts. Some examples of important unions in American history are the Knights of Labor, the American Federation of Labor, the Industrial Workers of the World, and the Committee/Congress for Industrial Organizations, as well as industry-specific unions such as the United Mine Workers, the United Automobile Workers, and the American Association of University Professors.

The United States and many capitalist-industrial societies have never been very supportive of labor unions, regarding them as socialist or communist, or at least as an obstacle to production and wealth. The heyday of unions in the United States was the 1950s, when almost one-third of workers were union members; in parts of Europe, union growth continued into the 1970s and 1980s reaching two-thirds in Norway and 90 percent in Sweden. Sociologists have dispelled some stereotypes about union members, such as that they were only the lowest and most troublesome of workers. Toimi Kyllonen found in 1951 that union members came from all wage and skill levels, in fact more often from higher wage, skill, and rating levels (that is, they were frequently the best workers in the factory). Even more interesting, union members tended to be more socially active in general, with strong family ties and busy social lives, including card-playing, fishing, and church attendance. Union membership was one of their many social activities.

There has been an unmistakable decline in union membership and union action in recent decades in the United States, for which Dan and Mary Ann Clawson offer a number of explanations: "(a) demographic changes, (b) the role of the union itself as an institution, (c) the state, especially the legal system, (d) globalization and neoliberalism, and (e) the employer anti-union offensive" (1999: 97). Among the demographic changes are increased immigration and the changing nature of work itself, with fewer manufacturing and more service jobs. Sometimes the tactics of unions and their growing bureaucracy have turned workers against them. Finally, both the government and corporations have acted to weaken unions; the most interesting and important steps in recent years have been the promotion of "right to work" laws (which forbid mandatory union membership in the industry) and the attacks on public employee (e.g., teachers, police officers, etc.) unions in states like Wisconsin. Interestingly, according to the U.S. Bureau of Labor Statistics, public-sector union membership was much higher (36.2 percent) in 2010 than private-sector membership (6.9 percent), with an overall rate of 11.9 percent, down from 12.3 percent in 2009. Rates vary by race (black 13.4 percent, white 11.7 percent, Asian 10.9 percent, Hispanic 10 percent), by gender (men 12.6 percent, women 11.1 percent), by region (states in the Mid-Atlantic and Pacific areas above the national average, states in the South below it), and industry (education, training, and library professions 37.1 percent, sales 3.2 percent). Union members earned on average almost one-third more than non-union members.

Chapter 12

Health, Illness, and Who Decides

In 1968, Dr. Sheldon Korones founded a special neonatal intensive care unit at the Regional Medical Center in Memphis, Tennessee. Dr. Korones was angry then—and he remains angry—about the staggering infant mortality rates in the African American community. The overall infant mortality rate in the United States hovers at over 6 per 1,000 births (which is inordinately high compared to other rich industrial societies), but that rate varies dramatically by race, from less than 6 for whites to more than 13 for blacks. In some areas of the country, the infant mortality rate for black babies approaches 17—almost three times the national average and equivalent to countries like Jordan, Bulgaria, and Surinam. According to certified midwife Shafia Monroe, the causes of this disparity include premature and low-weight birth, poor nutrition, poor prenatal health and healthcare, high blood pressure among mothers, and accidents. Other contributors are poverty, high stress levels in mothers, violent neighborhoods, racism, lack of access to the healthcare system, poor housing, and exposure to environmental hazards such as lead, cigarette smoke, and other pollutants. A high proportion of the babies, up to 80 percent, are born to young and unwed mothers. As a result, too many black babies in Memphis and other parts of the country end up in the neonatal ICU, and too many do not leave it alive. Mothers too poor to keep their babies alive are often too poor to give those babies a burial, so many of the infants go to the County Cemetery in Memphis, a "potter's field" for poor graves. Among the poor black residents of the city, who have consigned thousands of babies to the field, it is often called Babyland.

The health of its members is a primary concern of every society, although different societies define health in different ways, commit different amounts of resources to the problem, and organize their systems of healthcare in different manners. So, while health is a physical phenomenon, it is also a social process: the ideas, values, and practices of a society shape its health circumstances, and those health circumstances feedback on society in terms of social costs and consequences. Sociologists have become interested in the roles, norms, behaviors, and institutions that comprise the health conditions in society. These include the lifestyle and choices of individuals, as well as the ways in which health varies along with other social variables such as age, gender, race, education, income, and so forth. They also include the medical systems—knowledge, technology, roles and interactions, and institutions—that provide medical care (often unequally) to members of the society.

Sociologists recognize that, like education, health and medicine are social phenomena intimately coupled to the wider society. Further, health and medicine are not a single institution but a network of institutions, some involved directly in the provision of care and some not. In addition to doctors and hospitals, depending on the society, the structure of health and medicine also implicates pharmaceutical companies, insurance companies, medical schools, medical researchers, medical journals and conferences, professional associations (like the American Medical Association), medical supply companies, hospices, and a constellation of specialists from surgeons to nutritionists and nurses and therapists, not to mention employers and the government as well as family members who are often primary caregivers. Health and medicine surely not only affect us all but touch every aspect of society.

FROM SOCIAL MEDICINE TO SOCIOLOGY OF MEDICINE

Given the central role of health in the lives of all members of society, one would expect health and medicine to be a major preoccupation of sociology from its earliest days. Surprisingly, in his text on medical sociology, William Cockerham concludes that "Unlike law, religion, politics, economics, and other social institutions, medicine was ignored by sociology's founders in the late nineteenth century because it did not shape the structure and nature of society. . . . Durkheim, Marx, Max Weber, and other major classical theorists did not concern themselves with the role of medicine in society" (Cockerham 2004: 13). This is not to say that the founders of sociology had nothing of relevance to say about health or medicine, nor that their ideas offered no useful insights for thinking about health and medicine, but the formal sociological study of health and medicine emerged relatively late and arose from different sources than most other subdisciplines of sociology.

For instance, Marx's collaborator, Friedrich Engels, produced a short but important document in 1845 on "The Condition of the Working Class in England." At the time only 24 years old, Engels decried the physical living conditions of the urban laborers of the industrial revolution. The air of London was already polluted and poisonous, he insisted. Garbage and sewage presented serious health threats:

> All putrefying vegetable and animal substances give off gases decidedly injurious to health, and if these gases have no free way of escape, they inevitably poison the atmosphere. The filth and stagnant pools of the working-people's quarters in the great cities have, therefore, the worst effect upon the public health, because they produce precisely those gases which engender disease; so, too, the exhalations from contaminated streams. (1892: 97)

Housing was cramped and squalid, packed in among the "tanneries, bonemills, and gasworks," exposing residents to contaminants even at home. Meanwhile on the job, they performed dangerous tasks at rapid pace with minimal breaks or safety standards and virtually nothing in the way of health insurance; their low wages did not allow them to eat well, leading to malnutrition and susceptibility to infectious diseases, which was rampant in the fetid water and decaying refuse. Vices like gambling and drinking

added to their misery. As a result, Engels described the denizens of urban industrial London as "pale, lank, narrow-chested, hollow-eyed ghosts, whom one passes at every step, these languid, flabby faces, incapable of the slightest energetic expression" (98). He even provided some basic statistics on the mortality rates in the factory towns, which were sometimes twice as high as in a "healthy agricultural district."

Durkheim actually did conduct a study not only relevant to but indicative of sociological interest in health. After his 1893 *The Division of Labor in Society* and 1895 *Rules of the Sociological Method*, his next major publication, in 1897, was *Suicide: A Study in Sociology*. In this work he did two crucial things. First, he overtly redirected the investigation of suicide (and by extension, other behaviors) from individual and psychological causes to collective and social causes. Second, for the purpose of making suicide a social question he introduced the concept of "social suicide rate," defined as "the rate of mortality through suicide, characteristic of the society under consideration" (1951: 48). Thus, with substantial statistical information, he could argue that each society has a stable suicide rate that cannot be explained by personal/psychological variables.

Durkheim proposed a number of social causes and social types of suicide. The types he identified were egoistic, altruistic, and anomic. In short, egoistic suicide was more likely when the individual was too detached from society and its integrative functions. This was further related to gender (men more likely than women), class (upper class more likely than lower class), and marital status (single more likely than married, but early marriage and widowhood also increased the likelihood). His conclusion was that "suicide varies inversely with the degree of integration of the social groups of which the individual forms a part" (209). Altruistic suicide, ironically, occurred when the individual was too tightly controlled and defined by society, which he called "insufficient individuation" (217). In such situations, social values like duty overrode the value of individual life, as in the soldier, the classical Japanese *samurai* who committed ritual suicide, the Hindu widow who accompanied her husband

into death, and political followers or servants who died with their leader. Finally, anomic suicide (resulting from Durkheim's critical concept of *anomie* or social disorder) was driven by crises like economic downturns or family dissolution (i.e., divorce or the death of a spouse). All in all, Durkheim asserted, "the social suicide-rate can be explained only sociologically" (299).

Finally, Max Weber provided a concept that has great resonance for modern medical sociology, namely the concept of "lifestyle," along with its allied concepts "life conduct" and "life chances." Weber argued that one's location in a class system—one's access to wealth, power, and prestige—contributed to a particular style of life, and this lifestyle included the opportunities or "chances" of the individual as well as his/her behavior or "conduct." For instance, a person in a socially disadvantaged race or class or gender category might have less chance of getting a good job and quality medical care, while she/he might have a greater chance of being exposed to dangerous working or living conditions. Equally, depending on their position in society, individuals would make different behavioral choices, such as smoking or drinking or taking drugs or eating poorly, that negatively affect their health. The obvious implication is that health is a product of socially defined life chances and life conduct, which are themselves products of class-based lifestyles.

However, as promising as these starts were, the original impetus for attention to the social contribution to health came principally not from academic sociology but from the medical community itself and the interest in "social medicine" and the reform of society through medical knowledge and practice. This concern for "public health" was shared by non-Marxists, as in physician James Kay's 1832 *The Moral and Physical Conditions of the Working Classes Employed in the Cotton Manufacture in Manchester*, as well as the famous 1842 Chadwick Report or *Inquiry into the Sanitary Conditions of the Laboring Population of Great Britain*. As George Rosen has expressed it, in line with Engels' observations above, the industrial revolution "changed the living conditions of millions of people: ill health, poor housing, dangerous and injurious occupations, and excessive morbidity and mortality could not be overlooked and investigations of the causes and possible remedies of these social problems were undertaken, often by medical men" (1979: 31). By 1848, the great pathologist and medical reformer Rudolph Virchow could declare, "Medicine is a social science" (quoted in Bloom 2002: 11).

The search for the social causes of health and illness, thus, emerged out of a recognition of the relationship between hygiene and environment on the one hand and health on the other. By 1894, Charlie McIntire used the term "medical sociology" in an essay entitled "The Importance of the Study of Medical Sociology," in which he defined the new field as

> the science of the social phenomena of the physicians themselves as a class apart and separate; and the science which investigates the laws regulating the relations between the medical profession and society as a whole; treating of the structure of both, how the present conditions came about, what progress civilization has effected and indeed everything related to the subject. (1894: 425–26)

In 1909, James Warbasse wrote a text titled *Medical Sociology*, but the sociology of medicine really began to advance as the institutional structure of medicine was forged. For instance, medical schools themselves prior to 1900 were informal and mostly private and for-profit, as well as over-abundant. Bloom reports that 400 medical schools were opened during the nineteenth century, but by 1905 they had been consolidated into 155. In 1927 a group of doctors, social scientists, and concerned citizens founded the Committee on the Costs of Medical Care in Washington, D.C. to study the economics of medicine and to promote public health and preventive medicine. Interestingly, much of the focus during that era was on mental health rather than physical health, largely on the premise that the new urban lifestyle was bad for the mind. Perhaps the most important piece of work to come from this emphasis was Robert Faris and Warren Dunham's *Mental Disorders in Urban Areas* (1939). Hailing from the University of Chicago, which also produced Robert Park and Louis Wirth, Faris and

Dunham contributed to the "urbanism hypothesis of mental illness" that related crime, violence, suicide, depression, and other dysfunctions to life in the big city.

The University of Chicago was one of the pivotal institutions in the formation of medical sociology, along with Yale University's Institute of Human Relations. Equally important were medical associations like the National Institutes of Health (founded 1930), including the National Institute of Mental Health (founded 1949), the Russell Sage Foundation (which became active in the area of medicine after 1948), and the Medical Sociology section of the American Sociological Association (ASA, founded 1959). By 1980 the ASA's Medical Sociology section had grown to be the largest of the specialties of the professional association, with 8 percent of all member sociologists belonging to the section.

TALCOTT PARSONS: THE FUNCTIONALIST APPROACH AND THE 'SICK ROLE'

No individual did more to bring health and medicine into the center of sociological interest than Talcott Parsons. In fact, his mammoth and seminal *The Social System* (1951) devoted almost one-tenth of its space to "the case of modern medical practice." The first salient point that Parsons made is that medicine "is a 'mechanism' in the social system" (432) and, as such, can and should be investigated in the same way as all other facets of society. This includes the rules and roles of participating in the system, as well as the norms and institutions that structure the system. And just as every element of society had its function in his view, the function of the medical system was "coping with the illnesses of its members" (432). Thus, the structure of medical behavior involves minimally two key roles: the medical practitioner, who plays the "healer" role, and the patient or ill person, who plays the "sick role."

This is Parsons' second, more original, and more controversial contribution. Illness, from

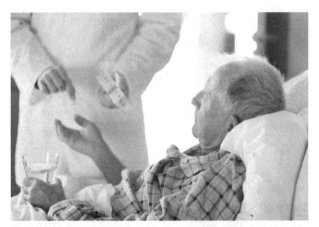

© Yuri Arcurs, 2012. Under license from Shutterstock, Inc.

Parson's functionalist perspective, "is a state of disturbance in the 'normal' functioning of the total human individual, including both the state of the organism as a biological system and of his personal and social adjustments" (431). In a way, Parsons saw sickness as a kind of deviance and the sick person as a kind of deviant. In particular, he identified four aspects of the "institutionalized expectation system relative to the sick role" (436):

1. "Exemption from normal social responsibilities, which . . . requires legitimation by and to the various alters involved and the physician often serves as a court of appeal as well as a direct legitimatizing agent."

2. "The sick person cannot be expected by 'pulling himself together' to get well by an act of decision or will. In this sense also he is exempted from responsibility—he is in a condition that must 'be taken care of.'" (437)

3. "The state of being ill is itself undesirable with its obligation to want to 'get well.'"

4. "The obligation . . . to seek *technically competent* help, namely, in the most usual case, that of a physician and to *co-operate* with him in the process of trying to get well."

Box 12-1

The Social Scientist in the Sick Role

Sociologists often describe norms, roles, and institutions from "outside," that is, without actually being a member or part of those social realities (on the other hand, sociologists frequently do participate in the groups or subcultures they discuss). In the case of sickness, all of us, even social scientists, eventually succumb to some ailment, and Robert Murphy reported on the decline of his own health with the sober objectivity of a scholar. In *The Body Silent* he told how he was diagnosed with a tumor on his spinal column that led to progressive weakness and dependence. He also maintained a dialogue with the health concepts and practices of an indigenous people, the Mundurucu of the Amazon rainforest. His first experience of illness was as a "breach of order, an assault upon both flesh and thought"; his tumor "infringed upon both symbolic coherence and real systems of motor control" (1990: 33). After the awareness of the breach of the order of his personal and social life came the experience of losing a part of his self. Just as sociologists since Charles Cooley and George H. Mead understood that the self is a social construction, so the self can be reconstructed and deconstructed. A critical aspect of the deviance of illness is the diminution of the self, resulting in a reduced or "damaged self." Murphy the sick person, the wheelchair-ridden person, the dependent person, could not do what Murphy the healthy person used to do. Especially as a man, Murphy found this threatening to "the cultural values of masculinity: strength, activeness, speed, virility, stamina, and fortitude" (94–95). Worse yet, he discovered that illness carries a sort of stigma, a judgment of inferiority. Wellness, he said, is "an unmarked category" (103), largely taken for granted, while sickness or disability is a negative category, a kind of "embattled identity" similar to all other undervalued categories. The social experience of other people changed for him, too. He felt resented by healthy people, as if he were a traitor to the ideal of good health—and perhaps a reminder to healthy people of their own fragility. Old friends did not know how to relate to him; some stopped relating at all. He made new friends and contacts in the disabled community. He also found himself asked (and forced) to submit to the handling of doctors, nurses, and physical therapists and *to make their lives easier* by not showing too much emotion and by being passively obedient. Finally, he felt his effect on his wife and family, who now had to rearrange their lives to accommodate his. "Such shifts within the family structure often create strains so deep that it self-destructs. . . . When [marriages] are additionally freighted with the problems of the handicapped, they frequently dissolve" (207).

In other words, the person who plays—or has been assigned—the sick role does not have to perform his/her usual social activities; she/he can stay home from work or take a day off from school. Further, she/he is not responsible for his/her actions. If it is the illness or injury that causes certain behavior, then the individual cannot be held accountable for it (see the discussion of "medicalization" below). The sick person also submits himself/herself to the authority of a medical specialist and should do his/her part to get well, including following the doctor's orders, taking the medicine, observing the diet, or what have you. In a word, the sick role is a kind of freedom from social norms as well as a kind of surrender to a different set of norms: "the sick person is helpless" (440).

Twenty-four years later Parsons revisited his sick-role concept to address some of the criticisms that had accumulated against it. He stressed that "deviance" was never his main interest but rather the asymmetrical relationship between the physician and the patient.

> The most general basis of the superiority of health agency personnel generally, and physicians in particular, seems to me to rest in their having been endowed with special responsibilities for the health of persons defined as ill or as suffering threats to their future health who have come under their jurisdiction, that is, who have become in some sense patients of the individual physician or of the health-care organization in which he performs a role. This is to say in very general terms that the physician has been institutionally certified to be worthy of entrusting responsibility to in the field of the care of health, the prevention of illness, the mitigation of its severity and disabling consequences, and its cure insofar as this is feasible. (1975: 266–67)

This insight suggests strongly that the medical expert or the wider medical system is of as much importance to the sociologist as is the sick individual. Finally, Parsons drew a surprising but reasonable parallel between the medical system and the education system. In both, the asymmetry of the deficient person (patient or student) in a subordinate relationship with a competent authority (doctor or teacher) is supposed to make the deficient person "better" but only if she/he submits to the superior knowledge and power of the authority. In a way, both doctors and teachers "operate on" their submissive charges.

Parsons was not unaware of the role of the medical specialist and also paid attention to it in his 1951 discussion. His comments on the "situation of the physician" and on the "institutional pattern of medical practice" are often overshadowed by his thoughts on the sick role. However, he also launched sociology into an analysis of the actions of, including the training of, medical professionals, highlighting the significance of technical knowledge and skill, the limits of medical knowledge and control (hence "uncertainty"), and the norms and ideals to "do everything possible" but to "do no harm." Last but not least, he remarked on the structure of the medical institution, from the norms of confidentiality and neutrality/objectivity (some would even say impersonality) and of trust to the violation of ordinary norms of privacy and touching. Ultimately, in Parsons' approach, "both the sick role and that of the physician assume significance as mechanisms of social control" (477).

THE STATE OF MEDICAL SOCIOLOGY TODAY

As has been mentioned, medical sociology or the sociology of medicine is currently a large and vibrant field. According to Katherine Rosich and Janet Hankin's recent summary of fifty years of work, the sociology of medicine has evolved into a subdiscipline that studies

> the social dimensions of health and disease, and the social aspects of health care functions and processes (i.e., operations of health care organizations and providers, and patterns of health service delivery) as well as the behaviors of health-care providers and patient–provider relationships. Sociological research also investigates power relations among various stakeholders in medicine (e.g., challenges to the traditional authority of the physicians), and the social movements that have evolved around health-related issues (e.g., disease-focused activism).

Sociological research thus provides an essential and unique view of the social causes and consequences of illness in society. (2010: S2)

These issues raise further questions about the "persistence of health inequalities" that are deeply rooted in society, including social stresses and strains that affect health as well as social relationships that influence health behaviors and outcomes (S3)—not the least of which are class and race. Also, as we will see below, medical sociology interrogates the healthcare systems of the United States and other countries, to learn how public access to and use of healthcare differs and changes, how technological advances and cost increases impact the system, and how the medical profession itself adjusts to these forces.

Social Epidemiology: Health and Social Networks

Sociologists know, and the medical community understands, that individuals get sick or injured but (a) the causes and consequences of illness and injury are often social and (b) illness and injury are distributed unevenly through a group, resulting in what Durkheim above noted as a characteristic social rate or incidence. The ways that a disease or pathogen—or anything else, including an idea or a fashion—spreads through a population is the subject of epidemiology (from the Greek *epi* for "upon, among" and *demos* for "people"). According to Nancy Krieger, the perspective of the social epidemiology of health and illness insists "on explicitly investigating social determinants of population distributions of health, disease, and wellbeing, rather than treating such determinants as mere background to biomedical phenomena" (2001: 693). That is, there are discoverable social reasons why some people enjoy or suffer certain health conditions, and health or illness are shared and transmitted by social relationships and interactions. Some of the social factors related to the transmission and distribution of health and illness cited by Krieger are race and racial discrimination, sex and sexism, age and life-course processes, socioeconomic status

and poverty, deprivation, stress, and scientific/technical knowledge.

The most obvious way in which social contact and interaction affects health is in terms of infectious diseases. For instance, increased travel has allowed bacteria and viruses to spread more widely and rapidly, and the human incursion into new ecosystems has brought humans in contact with new diseases, like Ebola. Living conditions can cause the spread of diseases like typhus, diarrhea, and cholera, and the overuse of antibiotics can actually strengthen bacteria and give rise to new strains of drug-resistant germs. And certain diseases are transmitted in particular ways, such as HIV and AIDS, which are primarily spread through blood transfusions and sexual contact. It has been noticed that AIDS, for instance, has been carried through societies in Africa and Asia by male truck drivers or migrant workers who frequent prostitutes along their routes.

In their review of social networks and health, Kirsten Smith and Nicholas Christakis specify a number of social mechanisms that affect health, such as "(a) the provision of social support (both perceived and actual), (b) social influence (e.g., norms, social control), (c) social engagement, (d) person-to-person contacts (e.g., pathogen exposure, secondhand cigarette smoke), and (e) access to resources (e.g., money, jobs, information)" (2008, 406). They identify both dyadic (two-person networks) and superdyadic (multiple-person networks) as critical to social epidemiology. Among the most important dyads is the marital couple, whose health and habits profoundly influence each other. But individuals also share health-related variables and outcomes with a wider assortment of people, partly because we tend to interact with others similar to us and partly because the people we interact with have significant impacts on us. In Christakis' book-length study of networks, he and co-author James Fowler (2009) find that physical health conditions like obesity and smoking are strongly affected by our social networks, as well as mental health conditions like depression and suicide.

Finally, Bruce Link (2008) explores the "social shaping" of the health of a population in terms of its knowledge and, even more important, its

Box 12-2
Science, Health, and Social Morality

We often like to think that health is an objective good and that any scientific advance that improves health is necessarily desirable. However, science is not socially neutral, and members of society often have beliefs and values that prevent the adoption or use of available medical methods. In some parts of Africa, it is believed that HIV is not spread by a virus at all or that sex with a virgin will cure a man of AIDS. In Western and American society, moral authorities have often opposed the use of certain pain-reducing or life-saving medical procedures. In 1722, Reverend Edward Massey preached a sermon in England "against the dangerous and sinful practice of inoculation," arguing that disease was a judgment of God (like the plagues sent upon Job) and that disease prevention was "a diabolical operation which usurps an authority founded neither in the laws of nature or religion [and which tends to] promote the increase of vice and immorality." His was no lone voice. A pamphlet circulated around the same time condemning

vaccination as contrary to scripture, and in 1840 the British government actually outlawed smallpox inoculation. In Boston in 1721 a doctor was threatened with prosecution for offering such treatment, and in 1798 the Anti-Vaccination Society was formed there to stop the practice for "bidding defiance to Heaven." In 1847 using chloroform to relieve the pain of childbirth was also denounced as weakening "God's primeval curse on woman"—that is, women were supposed to suffer during childbirth because of Eve's alleged misbehavior. Such thinking persists today. Seth Asser and Rita Swan (1998) calculated that over 90 percent of the children who died from parental medical neglect would have had a good or excellent prognosis if they had received medical treatment. However, the parents elected not to seek medical treatment for their children on the basis of their religious beliefs, and the law in most U.S. states allows parents to exercise their religious freedom even if it endangers the life of a child.

acceptance or adoption of knowledge about causes and cures of sickness. He gives two main examples: the slow adoption of pasteurization (which kills bacteria in milk) when it was first introduced and the reluctance that some people have about vaccination. In regard to the latter, one reason people have given for resisting vaccination is its purported relationship to autism (although there is no good science to support that claim), while others have objected to particular vaccines, like the HPV or human papillomavirus vaccine, for "moral" reasons (e.g., that it might encourage casual sex).

Sociology of Medical Professionals

One of the perennial subjects of sociological investigation is the roles that individuals play in their institutions and interactions, as well as how they acquire those roles. As we have seen, Talcott Parsons was among the first to direct attention to the role of the physician (as well as to the role of the patient) in the social performance of health. Of course, medical doctors are hardly the only professionals involved in the healthcare system. There are also nurses, physician assistants,

orderlies, nutritionists, physical therapists, pharmacists, midwives, assisted-living caretakers, not to mention all the professionals in the mental health industry. At any rate, sociologists have developed a number of interests in the medical profession itself, including the knowledge-training and more general socialization of doctors, the nature of medical discourse (how doctors talk), and doctor-patient interaction.

Not long after Parsons' epochal work, Robert Merton, George Reader, and Patricia Kendall (1957) edited a volume called The Student-Physician on the social organization of the medical school, on the premise that it (like any school) is a social setting with its norms and roles and, most importantly, its socialization functions. Not only must medical students learn medical knowledge, but they must learn to play the role of a doctor, both in front of patients and in front of other doctors. This was soon followed by Howard Becker, Blanche Geer, Everett Hughes, and Anselm Strauss' 1961 study Boys in White: Student Culture in Medical School, in which the authors characterized medical school as a long process of ritual initiation, with uniforms (the white lab coat), discipline, ceremonies, and ordeals.

In training for medicine, great emphasis is laid upon the learning of basic sciences and their application in the diagnosis and treatment of the sick. But science and skill do not make a physician; one must also be initiated into the status of physician; to be accepted, one must have learned to play the part of a physician in the drama of medicine.

As in other dramas, learning the lines is not enough. One must learn what others expect of him and how they will react to his words and actions. (1961: 4)

© Golden Pixels LLC, 2012. Under license from Shutterstock, Inc.

In fact, Becker and his colleagues argued that the future doctor must first learn how to be a medical *student* before he (and, in the twenty-first century, increasingly she) can learn how to be a medical *doctor*.

More recently, Donald Light has taken a fresh look at medical education, particularly in the context of changing systems and expectations for medicine. Focusing on the experience of the individual medical student, Light suggested that

"suffering is the most pervasive attribute in most sociological studies of medical school, internship, and residency. . . . [O]ne reads page after page about physicians in training who are exhausted, demoralized, assaulted, insulted, and, finally, skilled at 'working the system'" (1998: 314). Yet, he claimed that little effort had been made "to discover why the schedule is so exhausting; the answers will be different for medical students than for residents in hard-pressed hospitals. One key lesson imparted to aspiring doctors, Light feared, "is to get rid of patients: dispense with them as quickly as possible or you will drown. Equally important is the deep-seated tradition of hierarchy: senior residents are arrogant toward new residents, new residents toward interns, interns toward fourth-year students, and ultimately physicians toward patients."

At the institutional level, Light argued that teaching has increasingly been replaced in medical schools with research and clinical practice, which in turn shifts the attention of the schools away from learning and toward grant-writing, experimentation, and invention. He even quoted one "leading academician" who urged "that we stop using the term 'medical school' at all: 'There's not a single faculty member who is hired to teach medical students. We should call them 'medical centers' where medical students get trained along with everything else" (309). Even so, Light concluded, "important research has yet to be conducted on the institutional dynamics and the political economy of medical education" (310).

Once a doctor earns his/her degree, the familiar practice of medicine begins, and sociologists have also been keen to study the social interaction between doctors and patients as each performs their requisite role. For instance, in 1976 Patrick Byrne and B. E. L. Long published their report *Doctors Talking to Patients* on medical consultations in England, in which they found a distinct social structure to the dialog between doctors and patients. John Heritage and Douglas Maynard recently surveyed thirty years of research on physician-patient interaction, stressing for example, as in the case of medical education, the bureaucratic and ceremonial quality of this behavior, "involving formality, politeness, and control of emotions" (2006: 358). They further found that doctor-patient interactions are even more structured than most social behavior, "beginning with an opening sequence, progressing through problem presentation, history taking, physical examination, diagnosis, and treatment recommendations, and then on to a closing sequence"—all sometimes in a few minutes (363). These discoveries have led sociologists to analyze the micro-interactions, the ethnomethodological practices, and especially the conversational behavior of physicians and patients.

© Vasilry Kovai, 2012. Under license from Shutterstock, Inc.

As one last example, Renee Anspach also studied the language behavior of doctors in another medical setting, the "case presentation," that is, the formal presentation of patient case-histories by physicians-in-training. These occasions are full of stress, as the presenters are being evaluated by superiors, so the case presentations are situations of "presentation of self" as well as of presentation of clinical data. The case presentation is also "an arena in which claims to knowledge are made and epistemological assumptions are displayed, a linguistic ritual in which physicians learn and enact fundamental beliefs and values of the medical world" (1988: 357). Therefore, the presentation process "tends to follow an almost ritualized format, characterized by the frequent use of certain words, phrases, and syntactic forms and by a characteristic organization" (360). Key to this

professional-verbal behavior are certain social features such as depersonalization of the patient, the use of the passive voice, the recognition of "technology as agent," and what Anspach called "account markers." "If physicians imbue the physical examination and diagnostic technology with unquestioned objectivity, they treat the patient's reports with an ethnomethodological skepticism—that is, as subjective accounts with only tenuous links to reality" (368). The "consequences of medical discourse" then include the minimization of responsibility, "passive persuasion," a "surrender of subjectivity," and ultimately "socialization to a world view"—namely, a medical-scientific worldview.

The Medicalization of Society

The mention of a medical-scientific worldview raises the issue of precisely what this worldview includes and how extensively it exists even outside of the formal medical setting. One of the more interesting and disconcerting things that sociologists have noticed is a tendency toward the medicalization of society. Once a medical science and a medical worldview appear, they have a propensity to spread into many aspects of social experience. Peter Conrad is one of the leading sociologists of medicalization, writing in 1976 *Identifying Hyperactive Children: The Medicalization of Deviant Behavior* and in 1980 with Joseph Schneider *Deviance and Medicalization: From Badness to Sickness*. In his words, medicalization "describes a process by which nonmedical problems become defined and treated as medical problems, usually in terms of illnesses or disorders" (Conrad 1992: 209). That is, some formerly nonmedical issue—usually some behavior or idea or experience—gets assigned to the category of "medical problem," which includes "defining a problem in medical terms, using medical language to describe a problem, adopting a medical framework to understand a problem, or using a medical intervention to 'treat' it" (210).

Medicalization is an instance of the more general sociological issue of labeling or categorizing. The crucial point is that it is not objectively obvious what question is "medical" and what is not.

Societies create categories or labels like "medical," establish the norms and roles and practices pertaining to the "medical" category, and then add items to or remove items from that category. Medicalization is further a topic in the more general sociological approach to deviance (recall that Parsons viewed the "sick role" as a kind of deviance). The question becomes, Is some particular sort of deviance "medical" or not, and if so, what "treatment" or "cure" should it receive, and *who gets to decide and to administer the treatment*?

As Conrad reminds us, many behaviors have been medicalized recently, and many new medical conditions have been proposed to name and describe them. Among the forms of medicalized deviance, he listed "madness, alcoholism, homosexuality, opiate addiction, hyperactivity and learning disabilities in children, eating problems from overeating (obesity) to undereating (anorexia), child abuse, compulsive gambling, infertility, and transexualism, among others. Natural life processes that have become medicalized include sexuality, childbirth, child development, menstrual discomfort (PMS), menopause, aging, and death" (213).

A number of consequences flow from the phenomenon of medicalization. One is the increasing scope of medicine. If obesity or alcoholism or homosexuality is a medical condition, then it is one more area for medical professionals to intervene—and more medical services to offer (that is, sell) to clients or patients. Another is the extension of the features of the sick role to more people and their behaviors. If alcoholism is an illness rather than a choice or a character flaw, then the alcoholic is not entirely responsible and is to some degree "out of control." Third and related to this, medicalization often means moving a behavior from the category "moral failure" to "medical condition," now not to be punished or condemned but to be medicated and cured.

In another essay, Conrad and co-author Valerie Leiter (2004) describe four cases of medicalization and their specific medical interventions: male impotence or "erectile dysfunction" and Viagra, "social anxiety" and Paxil, shortness and human growth hormone, and infertility and in-vitro fertilization. Harvey Molloy and Latika Vasil discuss the more contentious question of Asperger Syndrome and by implication autism and argue that Asperger Syndrome—a psychological "condition" characterized by lack of empathy, poor verbal skills, repetitive speech, and general inability to perform social relationship—may not be a "medical problem" so much as a personality difference. They further warn of the dangers of viewing differences as disabilities (see below for a discussion of deafness as a "culture") and the attempt of medicalization "to help to rehabilitate or 'normalize' the child" (2002: 659).

It should be clear that medicalization is an interesting illustration of the social construction of medical categories and conditions, but it is also a powerful instance of *social control* and *social jurisdiction*. That is, medicalization gives "medicine jurisdiction over virtually anything to which the label 'health' or 'illness' could be attached" (Conrad and Leiter 2004: 159). In other words, medicalization gives the medical profession authority over more aspects of social life. Michel Foucault, it will be remembered, stressed the "techniques of the self" that impose institutional control over persons, and some of his main examples were medical, as in his famous *The Birth of the Clinic*, subtitled *An Archaeology of Medical Perception* (first published in French in 1963) and *Madness and Civilization: A History of Insanity in the Age of Reason* (first published in 1964). He stressed the power of the medical professional, exercised initially through the "medical gaze" or the right to look at us in indiscrete and impersonal ways, but embodied in many deep practices, from taking our clothes away to slapping a label (diagnosis) on us to keeping records on us to strapping us down to a bed. Indeed, Rodney Coe's (1978) discussion of hospital practices mentioned three specific kinds of control: control over resources (like clothes and medicines, as well as information), restriction of mobility, and what he called "stripping" or the removal of the markers of the patient's pre-medical self and the imposition of a new self in the form of hospital gowns and wrist bracelets.

Two last words on medicalization are in order. First, as Conrad states, medicalization is never entirely complete, and it is always contestable; members may resist the encroachment of the medical worldview into their lives. Second, there is always the possibility of "demedicalization," such that conditions previously thought to be medical are reconceived in some other way. For instance, Conrad and Foucault both mention the preoccupation in nineteenth-century Western society with masturbation, as if it would cause any number of medical conditions; for a time, professional psychology also categorized homosexuality as a medical disorder but has since removed it from that category.

HEALTH AND MEDICINE IN AMERICAN SOCIETY

Health and medicine are chief concerns for sociologists, as well as for the general public, for all of the reasons previously mentioned, as well as others. Every American, indeed every human, will more than likely eventually need some kind of medical care, and the medical industry is a huge, influential, and expensive sector of the society and economy. It has recently and over the years been a subject of contentious political action, too, and it cannot be forgotten that the health conditions and outcomes in American society vary extensively along such social lines as race, gender, class, and age.

At the macrosocial or institutional level, healthcare is big business in the United States. According to the federal Centers for Medicare and Medicaid Services, in 2009 U.S. healthcare costs hit $2.5 trillion, which is 17.3 percent of the entire gross national product. Healthcare costs are also rising quickly, and at the current rate it could consume $4.5 trillion or 19 percent of GDP by the year 2019. Americans spend more per capita on healthcare than any country in the world, as depicted in Table 12.1.

Unfortunately, for this expense the United States does not buy the best health in the world. For instance, the United States does not have the best infant mortality rate or the longest life expectancy (see Table 12.2). In fact, there is no correlation internationally between healthcare spending and major health indicators. Countries that spend much less per capita than the United States (like Japan, Switzerland, or even Cuba) achieve equal or superior life expectancies (http://ucatlas.ucsc.edu/spend.php).

Further, some conditions detrimental to health are more common in the United States and are increasing. One of these is childhood obesity, which has nearly doubled in the past twenty years (see Figure 12.1).

Table 12-1

Per Capita Health Expenditures, in U.S. dollars, by Selected Country, 2009

Country	Expenditure
United States	7,960
France	3,978
Canada	4,363
England	3,487
Germany	4,218
Israel	2,165
Mexico	918

Source: OECD Health Data 2011

Table 12-2

Infant Mortality Rate (per 1,000 Live Births) and Life Expectancy, for Selected Countries, 2011

Country	Infant Mortality Rate per 1,000 Births	Life Expectancy
United States	6.06	78.54 years
England	4.62	80.05 years
Spain	3.39	81.17 years
New Zealand	4.78	80.59 years
France	3.29	81.19 years
Japan	2.78	82.25 years
Cuba	4.19	77.70 years
Croatia	6.16	75.79 years

Source: CIA Factbook

Figure 12-1

Obesity among Children in United States, 1988–2008

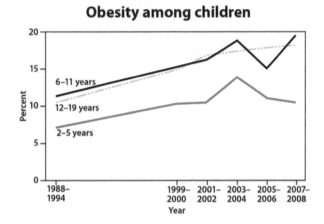

Source: CDC/NCHS, Health, United States, 2010, Figure 13. Data from the National Health and Nutrition Examination Survey.

Among adults, more than half of Americans are overweight or obese. Not surprisingly, chronic conditions like diabetes are also on the rise. In young adults ages 20 to 44, the incidence of diabetes went from 3 percent to 4 percent since 1988, and in the elderly over age 65, there was a dramatic increase from 20 percent to 27 percent. Many more people are on drugs for depression and anxiety, and the increase has been particularly pronounced for women: 12 percent of women ages 18–44 were taking antidepressants in 2008 and a staggering 22 percent of women ages 45–65. Men and women in every age category took more statin drugs—up to twice as many—in 2008 as a decade earlier. At the same time as more Americans need medical attention, more of them have to delay or do without this attention, especially if they are uninsured but even if they have private health insurance.

Finally, as a measure of the overall health of a society, sociologists and medical professionals use the concept of morbidity, the incidence or prevalence of a disease or of all diseases. The following are some key data on morbidity in the United States, according to the U.S. Department of Health and Human Services report *Health, United States, 2010*:

- Annual deaths per 100,000: 760.2 (2007) versus 869 in the year 2000

- Heart disease is the leading cause of death, followed closely by cancer

- 9.9 percent of all Americans claimed to suffer from fair or poor health in 2009

- 11.9 percent of Americans over the age of 20 had diabetes in 2007–2008

- 32.6 percent of Americans over the age of 20 had high blood pressure

- 33.7 percent of Americans over the age of 20 were obese

- 20.6 percent of Americans over the age of 18 smoked cigarettes

- 37.8 percent of Americans ages 18–44 used a prescription drug in the previous month, 64.8 percent of people ages 45–64 used a prescription drug, and 90 percent of elderly citizens used some prescription drug

- 5 percent of children under age 18 had an asthma attack in the previous year, 11 percent had a skin allergy, and 6 percent had three or more ear infections

- 9 percent of school-age children were diagnosed with attention deficit disorder and 6 percent with serious emotional or behavioral problems

History of Public Health in the United States

As in many other Western societies, health became a public concern and a cause for political action in the United States in the mid-nineteenth century. A major motivation was the Civil War (1861–65), during which millions of Americans died, were injured, or were exposed to dangerous conditions. The Sanitary Commission was established in 1861 to promote hygiene and health in the military camps of the North. Agents of the Commission inspected camps and military hospitals and also coordinated the handling of food. According to John Haller, insurance companies were interested in the work of the Commission, as it provided useful and valuable information with which they "could work out statistical averages on the physical condition of the population" (1971: 20).

Two other driving forces behind the official curiosity about public health were the urbanization of the society, which really began in the mid and late nineteenth century, and the racial attitudes of the white majority. Cities were sites of health concern as in Europe, where diverse populations were crowded into unhygienic living conditions. However, "hygiene" meant more than physical well-being to the "scientific racism" of the era. Medical professionals also operated with racist assumptions about the fitness and capabilities of the races, which they set out to investigate through a variety of physical measures. Much attention was paid to the skull and face, since brain size and facial features were believed to be prime indicators of the mental and moral status of races, but "along with measuring the proportions of the skeleton, physicians began to study muscles, viscera, vessels, and nerves for comparative analysis" (Haller 1971: 39). For many men of science at the time, the differences in bodies proved the inequality of the races.

At any rate, the discovery of microorganisms and the social-epidemiological linking of germs to health threats like cholera and tuberculosis led to efforts to provide clean water, adequate drainage and sewerage, latrines, and trash collection. By the early twentieth century, awareness of the importance of health issues for society led to the concept of public health, which C. E. A. Winslow defined in 1920 as "the science and art of preventing disease, prolonging life and promoting health through the organized efforts and informed choices of society, organizations, public and private, communities and individuals" (1920: 23). Some of the steps to improving public health were aimed at the medical profession itself. Back in 1847 the American Medical Association had been founded to raise the standards of medical education and medical practice, and by

Figure 12-2

Americans Who Delayed or Did Not Receive Needed Healthcare in the Past 12 Months Because of Cost.

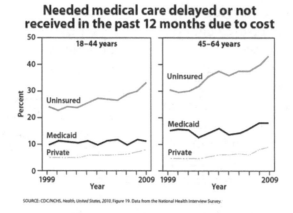

Source: CDC/NCHS, *Health, United States, 2010*, Figure 19. Data from the National Health Interview Survey.

Table 12-3

Disabilities among American Population, by Percentage

Age Group	Hearing Difficulty	Vision Difficulty	Cognitive Difficulty	Ambulatory Difficulty	Self-Care Difficulty	Independent-Living Difficulty
All	4.0	4.2	4.6	4.7	4.6	4.6
Under 5	5.1	5.2	n/a	n/a	n/a	n/a
5–14	4.6	4.6	5.0	5.1	5.0	n/a
15–64	3.6	3.9	4.2	4.3	4.3	4.4
Over 64	4.5	5.3	5.9	6.0	5.9	6.2

Source: American Community Survey 2008

the 1910s American hospitals were incorporating antiseptics and other cleanliness procedures.

Meanwhile, in 1912 Theodore Roosevelt, a central figure in the Progressive movement, promised national health insurance during his presidential campaign but lost his election bid. President Warren Harding also proposed a Department of Education and Welfare in1923, but no action was taken. The first tentative step toward the national institutionalization of public health came during the Great Depression, when the Laboratory of Hygiene was reorganized into the National Institute of Health (today the National Institutes of Health, www.nih.gov). The NIH has since grown to twenty-seven centers, specializing in everything from cancer to arthritis to deafness to drug abuse, not to mention the National Institute of Mental Health and the National Institute of Minority Health and Health Disparities. However, despite the fact that President Franklin Roosevelt's 1935 "New Deal" proposals also considered national health insurance, such insurance was not offered in the final legislation.

World War II was the impetus for much of the current public health infrastructure. For instance, the Centers for Disease Control (www.cdc.gov) was established in 1942, originally as the Office of National Defense Malaria Control Activities. The U.S. Public Health Service came into existence in 1944 out of older and less coordinated policies like the National Quarantine Act of 1878. The NIH, CDC, and other agencies like the Agency for Toxic

Substances and Disease Registry, and the Food and Drug Administration (FDA) fall under the authority of the Public Health Service. The FDA, emerging from the Food, Drug, and Cosmetic Act of 1938, regulates food safety, pharmaceuticals, tobacco products, medical devices, and cosmetics. The National School Lunch program also began in 1946 to offer free or low-cost lunches to school children, on the premise that learning as well as health were enhanced by nutrition. Interestingly, the National School Lunch program was and is administered as an agricultural program rather than an educational program, because part of its original motivation was to buy up farm surplus so as to support food prices.

The second major wave of public health institutions and laws appeared in the 1960s and 1970s. Central to these developments was President Lyndon Johnson's "Great Society" vision, which succeeded in the only attempt (until President Barack Obama's healthcare legislation of 2010) to provide some type of national healthcare coverage. In 1965 Johnson won the battle to create Medicare and Medicaid, which offered medical services to the elderly and the poor and disabled. As it dawned on people that the environment was crucial to public health, the Environmental Protection Agency was inaugurated in 1970, tasked to promote clean air, water, and soil, to control hazardous waste, and to protect endangered species. Finally, the Cabinet-level Department of Health and Human Services was established in 1979 when the former Department of Health, Education, and Welfare was divided into two offices, HHS and the Department of Education. HHS oversaw Social Security until 1995, when that agency was spun off into an independent institution.

Health Disparities in the United States

One of the abiding problems in the United States, and one of the abiding subjects of sociological research, is the disparity in health conditions and outcomes between various groups and regions in the society. For instance, a June 2011 study concludes that, depending on the county, life expectancy in 2007 ranged widely, from 65.9 to 81.1 years for men and from 73.5 to 86 years for women. For African Americans the numbers were worse, with a range of 59.4 to 77.2 years for men and of 69.6 to 82.6 years for women. More troubling, the vast majority of counties actually fell further behind the international standard for life expectancy in developed countries. The counties with the lowest life expectancies are heavily concentrated in the South. The report warns that "The U.S. has extremely large geographic and racial disparities, with some communities having life expectancies already well behind those of the best-performing nations. At the same time, relative performance for most communities continues to drop" (Kulkarni, Levin-Rector, Ezzati, and Murray 2011: 3).

Health Disparities and Class

Sociologists have drawn a strong connection, as suggested by Schnittker and McLeod, between health inequalities and socioeconomic inequalities. Bruce Link and Jo Phelan have gone so far as to call socioeconomic conditions "fundamental causes" of the differences in health conditions and outcomes (Link and Phelan 1995; Phelan, Link, and Tehranifar 2010). In their (widely held) view, the difference in "money, knowledge, prestige, power, and beneficial social connections" (2010: S28) impacts health in a number of ways:

First, it influences multiple disease outcomes, meaning that it is not limited to only one or a few diseases or health problems. Second, it affects these disease outcomes through multiple risk factors. Third, it involves access to resources that can be used to avoid risks or to minimize the consequences of disease once it occurs. Finally, the association between a fundamental cause and health is reproduced over time via the replacement of intervening mechanisms. (S29)

Fred Pampel, Patrick Krueger, and Justin Denney unpack the relation between socioeconomic variables and health variables still further. First, they note that socioeconomic status means more than using income "to purchase good health" (2010: 349). Rather, social and economic differences appear to affect the odds of engaging in unhealthy habits like smoking, poor diet, excess weight, and less physical exercise. They then specify nine means by which socioeconomic status can shape health-related behavior (353–60):

1. most directly, deprivation, inequality, and stress

2. fewer benefits of health behaviors, that is, the fact or perception that healthy behavior does not really make a difference in one's life or is not worth the extra cost and effort

3. other latent traits, such as the effects of family structures or schools

4. "distinctions" in the style or taste of different classes, such as cultural preferences for thinness or a smoke-free life

5. lack of knowledge of and access to information about health risks

6. efficacy and agency, that is, the ability to gather and process information and to solve problems, giving the person a sense of control over his/her life, behavior, and medical treatment

7. aids for healthy behavior, such as the capacity to afford quit-smoking products, gym memberships and weight loss programs, and healthier foods

8. community opportunities, like access in the neighborhood to gyms and fitness

Box 12-3
Social Psychology of Health Disparities

In a recent review of health disparities, Jason Schnittker and Jane McLeod discussed some of the mechanisms responsible for inequalities in health status. First, they distinguish between what they call "downstream" and "upstream" mechanisms, downstream referring to processes "through which social experiences 'get under the skin' and create disparities in physical and mental health" and upstream referring to "basic social processes that are not reducible to any particular proximal risk factor" (2005, 76). Research into downstream or psychosocial factors tends to emphasize "stress, coping, health behaviors, and their physiological correlates" but gives less attention "to their structural origins or to the possibility that social structures may modify their effects on health." Scholars who focus on upstream forces "redirect attention from psychosocial risk factors to the distribution of knowledge, power, and resources as they are implicated in health disparities" (76–77). The authors proceed to argue that "knowledge, power, and resources influence health not only through their direct effects on the material conditions of life, but also as they derive symbolic importance in social interaction, and as they define the contexts for individual responses to those conditions" (77). Among the crucial social-structural variables that affect health is certainly socioeconomic status, especially income: "persons near the top of the income distribution enjoy mortality risks approximately half of those near the bottom" (77). They also suggest that perceived social status or prestige is an important input; for instance, "Subjective status has been associated with obesity, depression, and susceptibility to respiratory infection" (83). Racism cannot be ignored as a contributor to health disparities. Schnittker and McLeod insist that "racism affects health through multiple pathways" such as "(*a*) economic and social deprivation, (*b*) toxic exposures and other hazardous conditions, (*c*) targeted marketing of commodities that harm health, (*d*) inadequate medical care, (*e*) personal experiences of racially motivated discrimination or violence, and (*f*) health-damaging self-perceptions" (86).

centers, health-food stores, and parks, bicycle trails, and recreation centers, as opposed to cigarette and liquor stores and fast-food restaurants

9. social support, social cohesion, and peer influence

Socioeconomic status is, of course, a complex concept, including many particular subvariables. Of all of them, Pampel, Krueger, and Denney hold out education as the most influential: for instance, "high school dropouts have odds of smoking and not exercising that are, respectively, 3.7 and 4.9 times larger than for college graduates" (351). Irma Elo in her current analysis of social class and health concurs:

> educational. attainment is perhaps the single SES indicator that most consistently exhibits a significant association with various measures of health and all-cause and cause-specific mortality in a wide variety of settings: Those with higher levels of schooling have better health and longer lives. In the United States, life expectancy at age 25 in 2000, for example, was estimated to be seven years higher for individuals who had attended at least some college (56.6 years) than for those with a high school education or less (49.6 years). (2009: 557)

The reasons for the strong correlation between education and health are manifold: knowledge and decision-making skills, typically higher income, safer occupation, and better access to medical technology, not to mention medical insurance, healthy middle- and upper-class lifestyle, freedom from financial stress including the financial resources to handle a medical crisis, and better housing conditions and neighborhoods. Interestingly, since the health of children is related to the education of their mothers, and since health during childhood can affect health throughout life, higher-educated women set the terms of health not only for themselves but for the next generation of middle- and upper- income members.

Health Disparities and Race

As mentioned already, health circumstances differ profoundly by race in the United States. Schnittker and McLeod explain that African Americans, for example, are less healthy, die younger, and have higher incidences of hypertension, diabetes, asthma, and AIDS, as well as some cancers (2005: 78). We have already seen that the infant mortality rate is much greater for African Americans, too. Hispanics, as is often the case, are intermediate. They suffer equal or lower rates of heart disease and cancer as non-Hispanic whites but higher rates of diabetes, tuberculosis, and homicide. The Office of Minority Health of the Department of Health and Human Services published the following results for 2005:

- African American men were 1.3 times as likely to develop new cases of lung and prostate cancer as non-Hispanic white men and 2.4 times as likely to die from prostate cancer.

- African Americans were twice as likely to have diabetes and 2.2 times as likely to die from the disorder.

- African Americans, at approximately 13 percent of the population, represented almost half of the HIV and AIDS cases; the AIDS rate among black women was *22 times* as high as non-Hispanic white women.

- Sudden Infant Death Syndrome (SIDS) was 1.8 times more common among African Americans as among non-Hispanic whites.

- African Americans were 1.7 times as likely to have a stroke, and African American men were 60 percent more likely to die from a stroke.

The situation for Hispanics, again, was more mixed as compared to whites and African Americans:

- Hispanic men were actually less likely to have prostate cancer, and Hispanic women were one-third less likely to have breast cancer and twice as likely to have cervical cancer.

- Mexican-Americans in particular were twice as likely to have diabetes, although they were less likely to die of heart disease.

- Hispanic men were 2.5 times as likely to die from HIV/AIDS as non-Hispanic white men, and women were 3 times as likely to die as their white counterparts.

Table 12.4

Top 10 Causes of Death, by Race, 2007

White	Black	Hispanic	Asian	Native American
Heart disease	Heart disease	Heart disease	Cancer	Heart disease
Cancer	Cancer	Cancer	Heart disease	Cancer
Lung disease	Stroke	Accidental injury	Stroke	Accidental injury
Stroke	Accidental injury	Stroke	Accidental injury	Diabetes
Accidental injury	Diabetes	Diabetes	Diabetes	Liver disease
Alzheimer's	Homicide	Liver disease	Flu or pneumonia	Lung disease
Diabetes	Kidney disease	Lung disease	Lung disease	Stroke
Flu or pneumonia	Lung disease	Homicide	Suicide	Suicide
Kidney disease	HIV/AIDS	Perinatal condition	Kidney disease	Kidney disease
Suicide	Septicemia	Flu or pneumonia	Alzheimer's	Flu or pneumonia

Source: U.S. Department of Health and Human Services

■ Both Hispanic men and women were less likely to die of a stroke.

Much of the difference in health status can be attributed to socioeconomic status. Much of the remaining difference is related to lifestyle and to discrimination and (social and physical) environment.

Health Disparities and Gender

Despite the fact that women and men die from many of the same causes (primarily heart disease, cancer, stroke, and lung disease), sociologists and epidemiologists have noticed some important health differences between the genders. According to the Society for Women's Health Research:

■ Chronic pain conditions like rheumatoid arthritis, migraine, and fibromyalgia are more common in women.

■ More women die from strokes and heart disease each year than men.

■ Women are 2–3 times more likely to experience depression than men.

■ Women are twice as likely to catch a sexually transmitted disease as men, and HIV is one of the top ten killers of women ages 25–54; among African American women ages 24–34, it is the #1 killer.

Also, as an apparent contradiction, women on average live several years longer than men yet appear to suffer from more illness than men. In assessing the literature on gender and health, Jen'nan Read and Bridget Gorman suggest that much of the difference in gender mortality relates to lifestyle:

> At younger ages men tend to engage in more health-damaging behaviors than women (like heavy drinking, illegal drug use, and until recently, smoking) that adversely affect their well-being and increase their risk of death via accidental injuries and homicide. These behaviors also have a cumulative impact that negatively affects men's health at later stages of life by elevating their likelihood of premature death from life-threatening conditions (e.g., heart disease, cancer). In contrast, women are more likely to suffer from nonfatal, chronic conditions such as arthritis and disability that do not necessarily result in their death but do depress their quality of life. (2010: 373)

In addition, "across a wide array of risky behaviors (including illegal drug use, drunk driving, and lack of seatbelt and helmet use), men participate at higher levels than women. As a result, they experience more unintentional injuries than women, contributing to their elevated rate of premature mortality" (374–57).

At the same time, statistics suggest that women are less healthy than men. Some of the difference is attributable to women's longer lives. Since they outlive men, they suffer more long-term degenerative diseases, such as heart disease and cancer. Women's historically lower socioeconomic status, including (until recently) education, could mitigate some of the behavioral advantages affecting female health. But some social scientists like Constance Nathanson have seen more at work than this. She argued that cultural norms impact women's health in unique ways, including "(1) women report more illness than men because it is culturally more acceptable for them to be ill; (2) the sick role is more compatible with women's other role responsibilities; and (3) women have more illness than men because their assigned social roles are more stressful" (Nathanson 1975: 57). Juanne Clark went further to mention a number of more pestilent cultural attitudes that plague women, such as the "myth of female frailty," which holds that women are weaker and more in need of professional intervention than men. Additionally, many aspects of women's lives and bodies have been especially medicalized (see above), like pregnancy, childbirth, and the menstrual cycle. At its worst, this has led to the "belief that female reproductive organs are expendable equipment, dangerous and dysfunctional outside of childbearing" (1983: 64).

Finally, women are under singular pressure in American society to conform to certain standards of beauty, which negatively impact their health. Naomi Wolf described in her book *The Beauty Myth* (1991) how cultural images and ideals damage the physical and mental health of women. One of the main effects of this social pressure, other than unnecessary and often unhealthy cosmetic

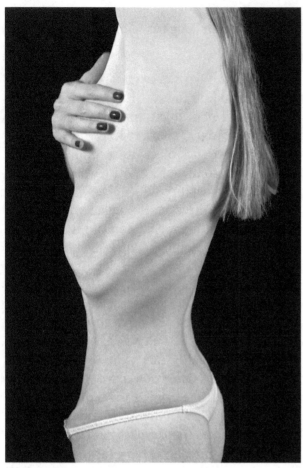

© Baloncici, 2012. Used under license from Shutterstock, Inc.

surgery, is eating disorders and body dysmorphic disorder, in which women dwell on or invent imperfections in their body and appearance (i.e., their own body-image is inaccurate). According to the National Eating Disorders Association, up to 10 million females have a life-threatening eating disorder like anorexia or bulimia, while 25 million struggle with binge eating. Almost half of the cases of anorexia occur in teenage girls, and more than half of all teenage girls engage in unhealthy weight-loss activities such as fasting, skipping meals, vomiting, or taking laxatives.

EMERGING ISSUES IN THE SOCIOLOGY OF MEDICINE AND HEALTH

In the twenty-first century, healthcare is more advanced than ever, but it is also prohibitively expensive for many people and largely unavailable for a significant portion of the American population. The problem is equal if not greater in other countries. Yet, other societies have arrived at different solutions to their health and medical challenges, depending on their wealth, the political system, and their culture. Finally, there are efforts to rethink the status of conditions like deafness, which are a "disability" to many but an identity, even an "ethnicity," to others.

Comparative Healthcare Systems

As noted, the United States has the most expensive healthcare per capita in the world, without the best health outcomes in the world. Indeed, a 2007 analysis of six developed countries (Australia, Canada, Germany, New Zealand, the United Kingdom, and the United States) found that the United States ranked last overall in quality of care, access, efficiency, equity, and healthy lives and last in almost all the individual measures. The report concluded:

> The most notable way the U.S. differs from other countries is the absence of universal health insurance coverage. Other nations ensure the accessibility of care through universal health insurance systems and through better ties between patients and the physician practices that serve as their long-term "medical home." It is not surprising, therefore, that the U.S. substantially underperforms other countries on measures of access to care and equity in health care between populations with above-average and below-average incomes. (Davis et al. 2007: vii)

Countries have arrived at a myriad of mechanisms for providing healthcare to their people and for financing that care. Recently the American Public Broadcasting System (http://www.pbs.org/wgbh/pages/frontline/sickaroundtheworld/countries/models.html), in association with its documentary *Sick Around the World*, has summarized the main options as:

- the Beveridge model (named after British National Health Service designer William Beveridge), in which the government provides and pays for the medical system in the same way that it provides and pays for the police and library systems

- the Bismarck model, invented in Germany but also used in France, Japan, and other countries, in which employers and workers pay into one of many "sickness funds" (similar in ways to insurance plans), but the sickness funds cover everyone in the society, are not-for-profit, and are tightly regulated by the state

- the National Health Insurance model, as in Canada, in which doctors and hospitals act as private-sector health providers but the government is the single payer for healthcare costs; all citizens pay into the government program, and the state negotiates prices with medical professionals and drug companies, keeping prices lower

- the out-of-pocket model, in which individuals pay personally for whatever medical attention they receive

The United States, curiously, has elements of all these models in its complex, uncentralized healthcare system, adding to cost and inefficiency. Some sectors of the healthcare system are thoroughly socialized, like the Veterans Administration. In other areas, citizens pay into social programs like Medicare, while individuals also buy fee-for-service healthcare either with or without health insurance.

In their review of comparative medical systems, David Mechanic and David Rochefort (1996) found that sociologists had attempted to categorize the healthcare approaches of various countries. M. G. Field, for instance, suggested that there were five types (anomic, pluralistic, insurance/social security, national health service, and socialized—with all systems moving toward socialized), while Milton Terris found three types (public assistance, health insurance, and national health service). In public assistance systems, which are common in poorer and more rural societies, for "the great majority of the population, whatever medical care is available is provided through a . . . system for the poor which includes government hospitals and health centers financed by general taxation" (Terris 1978: 1125). Unfortunately, these facilities are often overcrowded and underfunded, with insufficient staff earning low salaries. Health insurance systems are associated with capitalist industrialized societies and usually involve some combination of private and governmental insurance. Further, "practically all national health insurance programs in the industrial nations are based on fee-for-service private practice" in which healthcare providers "are independent entrepreneurs" (1126). The national health service model was the least common at the time of Terris' research, found in only fourteen countries. In this system, the government provides medical services through state-run hospitals and clinics financed by taxes. "Practically all services are included and provided free of charge" (1126), since citizens have already paid for them.

For many observers, the key division comes down to fee-for-service medicine as opposed to "socialized" or publicly funded and provided service. Each approach has its advantages and disadvantages. In a fee-for-service world, patients can shop around for the best care for the price; they are free to make their own healthcare decisions, including which doctors or hospitals to use. However, healthcare, as in the United States, can be prohibitively expensive, effectively denying many individuals their "freedom" to choose. If you cannot afford the fee, you cannot have the service. Also, as a purely "market" version of medicine, medical professionals may be inclined to sell services that are not entirely necessary and may be pressured by other aspects of the market, such as pharmaceutical and insurance companies. Socialized/public medicine ideally makes healthcare available to all citizens, but critics have condemned the long waiting periods and lower quality of care. Additionally, as in any collective arrangement, individuals may pay into a system they do not use (while, on the other hand, they may use more than they ever pay for). Interestingly, even in the 1970s Terris noted a trend "unmistakably toward the national health service" which he claimed had "demonstrated not only its superiority in terms of quality and cost effectiveness, but has shown that it is unnecessary to submit to the blind forces of the medical marketplace" (1130).

Beyond that, Mechanic and Rochefort have asserted that all the world's healthcare systems were "converging" on similar solutions because of the similar conditions and problems they faced. Among the factors favoring convergence were the development and dissemination of medical knowledge and technology, changing patterns of disease and illness, the rising costs of medical care, the aging of the world's population and the attendant shift in medical priorities, and the commoditization of healthcare, that is, medical care becoming a "product" in a sort of global healthcare "market" in which the patient becomes a (hopefully informed, self-interested, and rational) "consumer."

The important sociological question still remains as to why the United States has resisted universal health coverage, despite the fact, described above, that attempts have been made for a century to implement it. As Jill Quadagno proposes, there are clear political and cultural reasons. Much of the American public has "anti-state" values, desiring to keep the government small and out of personal affairs when possible, as well as a distaste for anything that smacks of "socialism." Additionally, she notes that the political system itself, with power and authority divided across various branches and levels of government and without "a working class movement and labor-based political party" (2004: 26), has been unable to muster the unity to implement a national system. But she also highlights some interest group elements in the struggle, finding that the diverse social "stakeholders" in the system—the doctors and their professional organization (American Medical Association or AMA), the insurance companies, the pharmaceutical companies, even the labor unions, and of course, the political parties—have acted to undermine healthcare reforms.

For instance, when President Truman promoted national health insurance in 1945, the AMA not only supported candidates who opposed the plan but

also ran half page ads of a photo showing Senator Pepper [a proponent of the plan] with the African American singer, Paul Robeson, who was a member of the Communist party. Racism and the Red Scare provided a potent framework for defaming national health insurance and demonizing its proponents. In 1945, 75 percent of Americans supported national health insurance; by 1949 that figure had declined to only 21 percent. (Quadagno, 30)

Similar tactics were employed to derail President Bill Clinton's efforts in 1993 and President Barack Obama's successful legislation in 2010.

Disability or Culture? Deafworld

Finally, sociologists appreciate that there is a difference between health as a "fact" and health as an experience and an "identity"—and that all these facets of health are socially constructed. Many people, for example, would no doubt regard deafness as a medical condition, indeed a disability. And it is true that most people acquire deafness or hearing loss as a result of accident or injury. Nevertheless, a significant number of hearing-impaired people do not consider themselves "disabled" at all, but rather, as members of a deaf minority, even of a distinct community or subculture that has been called Deafworld. Harlan Lane (2005), one of the preeminent scholars of deafness, insists that Deafworld qualifies as a social identity and community—even as an "ethnicity"—because it possesses a shared name and sense of community, as well as a culture (norms, values, knowledge, arts, and customs), the most important item of which is its *language* of American Sign Language, a social structure and set of

© Vladimir Mucibabic, 2012. Under license of Shutterstock, Inc.

institutions like schools for the deaf (the leading one being Gallaudet University), and history.

As with the social construction of health and illness in general, the social construction of deafness illustrates the politics of the body, or what Foucault called biopolitics. Owen Wrigley, in his aptly named *The Politics of Deafness*, for instance, reminds us that deafness is part of the biopolitics of nature; "it involves the politics of being 'normal,' the politics of difference and deviance, the politics of identity" (1996, 220). In earlier Western history, figures like John Bulwer back in 1648 "suggested deaf children were the result of their parents' sinfulness and little better than 'Dumb Animals'" (2), and the U.S. Census from 1830 until 1900 categorized the deaf among "defectives" (3). However, the deaf founded their own national organization, the National Association of the Deaf, in 1880, and by 1924 they held the first World Games for the Deaf, followed by the American Athletic Association of the Deaf in 1945. Since that time they have opened a National Theater for the Deaf (1967), as well as many schools, clubs, and other social groups, including an international network of websites (www.deaf-websites.com).

Harlan Lane, Robert Hoffmeister, and Ben Bahan concluded in their major study of Deafworld that "Deaf people themselves, who surely should know whether they have a disability or not, typically find they do not have a disability" (1996: 410). Instead, they often find themselves disadvantaged in a majority-Hearing world, one that excludes and "medicalizes" them. This is why many inhabitants of Deafworld reject medical "cures" for deafness like cochlear implants—and even "assimilation" practices like lip-reading—since they feel that such "treatments" are an assault on their deaf identity and culture.

Chapter 13

The Pictures in Our Heads: Media as a Social Force

As we grow and develop as individuals, many forces play a role in shaping how each of us comes to think, what we believe, and how we feel and act in various situations. All of our experiences, our family, friends, education, cultural background, and the communities in which we live and work are all sources of influence. Mass communication, and the multitude of mass media messages to which we are exposed over the course of our lifetimes are also power shaping influences.

Given the ubiquity of mass media and the messages they provide, it is not surprising that scholars have been interested in studying mass communication. Over the last century, scholars have undertaken a number of studies aimed at determining *how* mass communication influences us, and *what* consequences that influence has.

Not surprisingly, early studies of mass communication reflected linear thinking about the way mass media operate. Accordingly, researchers focused their attention on the classic mass media—radio, television, newspapers and magazines which tended to have large, anonymous, and quite heterogeneous audiences.[1] The thinking then was that mass media were extremely powerful forces, so much so that some scholars were "alarmed by the ubiquity and potential power of the mass media."[2] One scholar at a conference expressing this perspective in the extreme stated that 'the power of radio can be compared only with the power of the atomic bomb.'[3] Given this way of thinking, it was natural for studies to focus on message producers and mass media in an effort to identify, in many cases, to isolate influence of the message sources, media, and messages on message receivers.[4]

---

[1] Charles Wright, *Mass Communication: A Sociological Perspective,* New York: Random House, 1959.

[2] Paul F. Lazarsfeld and Robert K. Merton, Mass Communication, Popular Taste, and Organized Social Action. From *The Communication of Ideas,* 1948, ed. by Lyman Bryson. Reprinted in *Mass Communication and American Social Thought: Key Texts 1919–1969,* John Durham Peters and Peter Simonson, eds., Lanham, MD: Rowland and Littlefield, 2004, p 230.

[3] Ibid.

[4] Harold D. Lasswell, "The Structure and Function of Communication in Society," In the *Communication of Ideas,* ed. by Lyman Bryson. Champaign, IL: University of Illinois Press, 1960, 117–130.

The multitude of mass media messages we see are powerful influences in our lives. © Olly/Shutterstock

These studies produced a number of interesting results that advanced our understanding of mass communication's influence. Perhaps the great contribution of these studies was to heighten our understanding of the complexity of the mass communication process, and the challenges of studying it. Researchers found that it was very difficult to isolate the influence of sender, message and receiver in their studies. Moreover, it was also to isolate the influence of the entire process of mass communication from the influence of other social influences like families, friends, schools, and communities. For example, as we shall see, researchers determined that in many cases the influence that mass media and their messages had for receivers depended upon the reactions of friends, relatives, or other individuals.[5] While the linear model implied that media and messages had a direct influence on message receivers, researchers found that in many cases audience members were influenced by people who they looked up to—which researchers termed, *opinion leaders,* who *mediated*—came between sender and ultimate receivers in the mass communication process. This insight meant that it would be very difficult to differentiate the influence of media messages, from the influences of family, friends and other opinion leaders who helped influenced audience

members' exposure to the media and their interpretation of the messages.

Over time mass communication researchers began to broaden their study of the influence process to include message consumers and the message consumption process. Accordingly, they focused attention on message receivers, and how their individual needs, attitudes, knowledge, beliefs, backgrounds, culture and social networks influenced what messages they exposed themselves to, how they interpreted those messages, and what ultimate influence these decisions had.[6]

This research added clarity to our understanding of the many factors and richness to our understanding of the complexity of mass communication, and also called attention to further challenges that are present in efforts to identify exactly how mass communication influences us, when that influence takes place, how particular media and messages have an influence, with whom, and with what consequence.

As mass media have grown and evolved, new, more interactive ways of thinking about how mass communication works and its impact have emerged. Traditional mass media have been joined by newer media such as cable and the internet which often cater to smaller, less diverse, and sometimes less anonymous audiences. These new media of mass communication cater to audiences that are described as *demassified.*

The audiences of media receivers for some newer media are more selective and as a group, they are sometimes less heterogenous. In the case of radio, for example many talk radio programs appeal to groups with particular political orientations—either Republican or Democratic, conservative or liberal. In so doing, such programming provide information to these groups that helps inform them, but often in a way that supports, reinforces, and validates the particular points of view, values, and biases that audience members bring to the listening experience. These

[5] Elihu Katz and Paul F. Lazarsfeld, *Personal Influence: The Part Played by People in the Flow of Mass Communications,* New York: Free Press, 1956.

[6] David Berlo, *The Process of Communication: An Introduction to Theory and Practice,* New York: Holt, Rinehart and Winston, 1960.

Many talk radio programs appeal to those who support either the Republican or Democratic party.
© Gary Hathaway/Shutterstock

outcomes occur with great regularity with many internet websites and blogs that attract individuals with similar needs, perspectives, or goals.

As media continue to evolve and become increasingly demassified, the typical approaches to thinking about and studying the effects of traditional mass media are evolving—and newer ways of thinking about and studying influence are emerging. These approaches will benefit an understanding of the complex and interactive relationship that exists between messages senders, media and consumers.

Pioneers in Media Research

Pioneering researchers from the early 20th century created theories that laid the groundwork for much of how we conceptualize the effects of media today. Charles Horton Cooley was one of the first social psychologists to establish such theories on the effects of mass media. In works such as *Human Nature and Social Order* (1902) and *Social Organization* (1909), Cooley attempted to explain the role of communication in society. In his studies, Cooley unveiled two opposing ideas. On one hand, Cooley saw new media as a way to encourage individuality by supporting ideas and customs that follow a person's self-interest. For

example, if a person has political views that are not popular in his or her community, media can introduce that person to other like-minded individuals and give validation to unique ideas. On the other hand, new media limits the distribution of new ideas and customs, therefore leading to assimilation. For example, the type of language used in a widely distributed newspaper may, over time, become accepted as the universal dialect for a region, and all local dialects may disappear. Cooley explains that people have an innate desire to be alike and new media gives people information on how others talk, dress, and feel.

Cooley solved his paradox by determining that there are two different kinds of people: one that embraces isolation and one that is drawn to choice. Additionally, Cooley feels modern media fosters isolation and obliterates choice. Meaning, over time media will gradually eliminate the things that make us unique as individuals, communities, races, and nations. This process creates a universal understanding that although individuals may look, dress, or behave differently, we are all still extremely similar. For example, by watching a television show with homosexual characters such as *Will & Grace*, viewers can learn that homosexuals deal with the same life issues as heterosexuals. This type of effect can have a positive impact on society, as it promotes tolerance and acceptance. However, it can also have a negative effect. Since we learn about such a large variety of people, we only have the capacity to develop a superficial understanding and concern for other people. We are unable to learn about others in detail because we are overloaded with information.[7] Therefore, while a syndicated sitcom may help heterosexuals learn to view gay men and lesbians as equals, heterosexuals may never take the time to learn about the personal and political issues such as gay rights that are important to the gay community. Cooley's theories were mostly based on the effects of print media. However, his studies inspired other researchers as new types of media emerged.

---

[7] John Downing, Denis McQuail, Ellen Wartella, *The SAGE Handbook of Media Studies*, Thousand Oaks: California, 2004.

MEDIA AS MESSAGE

In addition to theories suggesting that mass communication products have a *direct* effect on consumers, there are others proposing that this influence is significant but *indirect*. One such group of theorists has focused its research efforts on the impact of the media themselves rather than on the messages they convey. These researchers have been termed the "medium theorists," and together form what could be called *the technological school*. Proponents of the technological school do not dismiss the idea that particular messages may have various effects on particular individuals, audiences, or behaviors. They contend, however, that the most substantial impact of mass communication lies in the more general and indirect effects of different communication technologies (including writing, printing, and electronic media) on modes of thought, patterns of human interaction, and the structure of societal institutions. Because of its origins, this line of thought is sometimes also called the Toronto School.

This emphasis can be summed up by the saying that "the medium is the message." Marshall McLuhan, author of this memorable phrase, was one of the earliest, and certainly the most widely known, of the medium theorists, and he and his mentor, Harold Innis, did much to highlight this point of view. Innis argues that Western culture has been deeply influenced by the spatial bias and cognitive processes associated with print media, which he believes has promoted cultural complexity, but also confusion and alienation.

By saying that "the medium is the message," McLuhan was attributing to any particular medium (books, television, and now the Internet) the power not only to shape and influence the message itself, but also the power to determine how the audience would interpret that message. If you think about the producers' side of the mass media, when putting together their media products TV journalists and documentarians will be much more influenced by the power of the image than will be newspaper journalists working on the same story. In this sense, much of a journalist's message is shaped by the medium he or she is working in. On the other hand, the medium is the message also means that, as audience members, our perception of a message, or a news story to stay with the same example, will be extremely influenced by the medium through which that message is reaching us.

McLuhan shared with Innis the conviction that communication media are extensions of the human mind and body. He considered modern electronic media to be a sort of extension of the human nervous system, an extension that circles the globe and establishes a network of interpersonal involvements that he referred to as a "global village," an aphorism that has been widely used to describe the Internet, which was adopted and popularized only decades after McLuhan coined that emblematic phrase.

Joshua Meyrowitz and Manuel Castells are other thinkers who have made major contributions to the technological school of thought in media effects. Meyrowitz's book *No Sense of Place* (1985) examines the influence of electronic media on the construction of particular kinds of cultural environments in which our roles and behavior patterns are played out. In Castells' massive three-volume book *The Information Age* (1997), Castells deals with the social, political, economic, and cultural impact of the so-called information society on our daily lives. In the trilogy's second volume "The Power of Identity," he focuses particularly on how new media and new technologies are changing the ways in which we organize and define ourselves.

How does the media used help shape the message?
© Moshimochi/Shutterstock

AGENDA-SETTING THEORY AND MASS COMMUNICATION

Agenda setting describes a very powerful influence of the media—the ability to tell us what issues are important. For example, if the media choose to highlight declining wages and lower standards of living for the current generation of adults, then concern over the economy becomes an important issue, regardless of the level of importance we placed on it before the media attention. Books addressing the issue start to sell across the country. Suddenly, people are concerned about loss of leisure time compared to previous generations. Entertainers joke about children in their thirties moving home to live with their parents.

Agenda setting has been the subject of attention from media analysts and critics for years. As far back as 1922, the newspaper columnist Walter Lippman was concerned that the media had the power to present images to the public. Because firsthand experiences are limited, we depend on the media to describe important events we have not personally witnessed. The media provide information about "the world outside"; we use that information to form "pictures in our heads" (Lippman, 1922). Political scientist Bernard Cohen (1963) warned that "the press may not be successful much of the time in telling people what to think, but it is stunningly successful in telling its readers what to think about." Prior to the early 1970s, the prevailing beliefs of mass communication research were that the media had only limited effects. Most research assumed the following sequence: the media generate awareness of issues through presentation of information; that information provides a basis for attitude change; the change in attitude includes behavior change. Most research looked for attitude and behavior change and found very limited influence. A study by Max McCombs and Donald Shaw (1972) in Chapel Hill, North Carolina, changed the emphasis of research efforts and stimulated a flurry of empirical investigations into the agenda-setting function of the mass media.

McCombs and Shaw focused on awareness and information. Investigating the agenda-setting function of the mass media in the 1968 presidential campaign, they attempted to assess the relationship between what voters in one community *said* were important issues and the *actual* content of media messages used during the campaign. They first analyzed the content presented by four local papers, the *New York Times,* two national newsmagazines, and two national network television broadcasts. They ranked importance by looking at the prominence given a story (lead, frontpage, headline, editorial, etc.) and the length. The researchers then interviewed 100 undecided voters (the assumption being that voters committed to a candidate would be less susceptible to media influence). McCombs and Shaw concluded that the mass media exerted a significant influence on what voters considered to be the major issues of the campaign. In addition to pioneering an entire line of research, McCombs and Shaw provided an excellent example of the thinking on which this textbook is premised. They believe that effective scientific research builds on previous studies. As a result, their study of the next presidential election (Shaw & McCombs, 1977) extended the scope of the original study, the objectives, and the research strategies. The study took place in Charlotte, North Carolina, and extended the analysis over time using a panel design. One of the interesting objectives added to this study was the investigation of what types of voters would be more likely to depend on the media. The researchers looked at two factors—the relevance of information to an individual and the degree of uncertainty—in determining need for orientation. Voters with a high need for orientation would be more likely to be influenced by the media in determining the importance of issues when issues were relevant and uncertainty was high. Just as McCombs and Shaw expanded their focus, other researchers have extended investigations of agenda setting to issues including history, advertising, foreign, and medical news.

Despite the extensive outgrowth from the original hypothesis, critics charge that there is insufficient evidence to show a causal connection between the order of importance placed on issues by the media and the significance attached to those issues by the public. McQuail (1984, p. 276) argued that, at least for the time being, agenda-setting theory remains "within the status of a plausible but unproven idea." The direction of influence still needs to be resolved. Do the media influence the opinions of the audience or reflect public concerns? Are both dictated by actual events? Do external or internal forces have more influence on media content? What roles do the elite media play? That is, if the *New York Times* runs a story, can the *Washington Post* afford to ignore it? How much power do special interest groups, the president, senators, or chief executive officers of large corporations have to pressure the media to present their views? Is credibility a balancing factor? The media are in business; does profit and loss play a larger role than a culture that prides itself on presenting unbiased reports? Other research could look at internal processes. What effects do deadlines, space restrictions, and the use of official sources have? The number of variables offer new opportunities for research on this topic for years to come.

CULTIVATION THEORY

The cultivation theory of mass communication effects was developed by George Gerbner and his associates at the Annenberg School of Communication at the University of Pennsylvania. The theory has been tested by numerous empirical studies. Cultivation theory asserts that television influences our view of reality. A causal relationship is suggested between television viewing and perceptions of reality—thus situating the theory in the law-governed approach to mass communication. Cultivation theory (Gerbner, Gross, Morgan, & Signorielli, 1980, 1986) asserts that television is primarily responsible for our perceptions of day-to-day norms and reality. Establishing a culture's norms and values was once the role of formal religion and other social initiations. Previously the family, schools, and churches communicated

standardized roles and behaviors, serving the function of enculturation. Television now serves that function. It has become the major cultural transmitter for today's society (Gerbner & Gross, 1976a, 1976b). "Living" in the world of television cultivates a particular view of reality. Some argue that television provides an experience that is more alive, more real, and more vivid than anything we can expect to experience in real life!

The Interaction of Media and Reality

One of the authors read an article in a local newspaper that illustrates the tendency to confuse a real event with images absorbed from television. A reporter had stopped his car at the intersection of a rural road and a larger highway. He noticed a car speeding on the highway at approximately 100 miles per hour. As the car reached the point where the reporter was stopped, it suddenly tried to make a left turn without slowing down. It clipped a light pole and flipped over on its back, wheels still spinning. No one else was in sight. The reporter described staring forward, not believing what he had just seen. He recalled his mind saying to him very clearly, "What you are seeing isn't real, You are just watching a movie." For almost ten seconds he just sat there, waiting to see what would happen next. Of course, nothing happened, and he realized that it was up to him to help. He fell prey to two fears as he approached the car—one artificial (induced by previous television images) and one very real (which contradicted other images received). Television portrayals of overturned cars invariably end with fires and explosions. With televised accidents, no "real man" thinks twice about rushing to a scene where someone may be dead or horribly mutilated. The reporter was very afraid on both counts. Television is so pervasive that the line between illusion and reality is blurred. We sometimes mistake a real event for a televised one; we probably make the opposite mistake more frequently. This phenomenon provided the basis of the research into cultivation theory.

Heavy versus Light Television Viewers

George Gerbner's participation in two national studies provided the foundation for cultivation theory. He contributed a content analysis of television programming to the National Commission on the Causes and Prevention of Violence in 1967 and 1968 and for the Surgeon General's Scientific Advisory Committee on Television and Social Behavior in 1972. Gerbner and his colleagues tracked the incidents of violence portrayed during a randomly selected week of fall prime-time programming plus children's weekend programming. They compiled the percentage of programs marked by violence, the number of violent acts, and the number of characters involved in those acts. They found violent acts portrayed in 80% of prime-time programming; children's shows were the most violent of all. Older people, children, women and minorities were the most frequent victims—despite the fact that three quarters of characters portrayed on television were white middle-class males.

Building on this work, the researchers surveyed viewers to determine the number of hours spent watching television daily, the programs selected and why, attitudes about the probability of being a victim of crime, perceptions about the numbers of law enforcement officials, and general attitudes about trusting other people. Gerbner and his associates classified people as heavy viewers (four or more hours daily) and light viewers (two hours daily or less).

Cultivation theory predicted that heavy viewers would perceive the world as more dangerous because of repeated exposure to violent television portrayals. Persistent images of danger and violence color views of reality and create the perception of a mean world. Heavy viewers overestimated their chances of being involved in a violent crime. They also overestimated the number of law enforcement workers in society.

Individuals frequently confuse media-constructed reality with actual reality. Gerbner and Gross (1976b) reported that in the first 5 years of its broadcast life, the television show *Marcus Welby, M.D.* (a fictional doctor portrayed by Robert Young), received over a quarter of a million letters from viewers. Most of the letters contained requests for medical advice! Television is highly effective in the cultivation process because many of us never personally experience some aspects of reality but the pervasive presence of television—constantly available for relatively little expense—provides a steady stream of mediated reality. We may have limited opportunities to observe the internal workings of a real police station, hospital operating room, or municipal courtroom. Thus, the media images become our standards for reality. Have you noticed that the New Year's Eve parties we actually attend *never* seem quite as exciting as the New Year's Eve parties we see on television?

The theory predicted uniform effects for all heavy viewers—regardless of factors such as gender, education, socioeconomic group, or media preferences (for example, reading newspapers versus viewing televised newscasts). As the primary source of socialization, television's messages provide a symbolic environment that transcends demographic differences. The only factor that seemed to have an independent effect on perceptions was age. Respondents under thirty consistently reported that their responses were more influenced by television than those of people over thirty (Gerbner & Gross, 1976b). Because people thirty and under have been "weaned" on television, the influence of media messages may be especially potent.

Refinement of Cultivation Theory

In response to criticisms that cultivation theory ignored the contributions of other variables (see next section), Gerbner and his associates introduced the factors of mainstreaming and resonance (Gerbner, Gross, Morgan, & Signorielli, 1980). Mainstreaming refers to the power of television to present uniform images. Commercial sponsors want to appeal to the broadest possible range of consumers, so television presents mainstream images. Differences are edited out to present a blended, homogenous image acceptable to a majority of viewers. Differences in perceptions of reality due to demographic and social factors are diminished or negated by the images projected on television. Ritualistic patterns reinforce sameness and uniformity. Resonance describes the intensified effect on the audience when what people see on television is what they have experienced in life. This double dose of the televised message amplifies the cultivation effect.

Criticisms of the Theory

Despite the large data set supporting the theory, the cultivation effect has encountered several challenges. Hughes (1980) reanalyzed data used in the original research and failed to support the core assumptions of cultivation theory. He suggested that the measures of heavy viewing only relate to total exposure to television, not specifically to what is watched. Certain personality characteristics related to the selection of television programs were not controlled in the earlier studies. He also reported that television may actually cultivate realistic and functional perceptions of the world. Hirsch (1980) found that if other variables are controlled simultaneously, very little effect remains that can be attributed to television. In his review of the original data, he found that even people who did not watch television perceived the world as violent and dangerous.

Conversely, it has been argued that major assumptions of cultivation theory may be correct, but the procedures used to study it may be incapable of uncovering the effect. Hawkins and Pingree (1982) reviewed 48 research studies conducted on the cultivation effect. They concluded that modest evidence supports the influence of television viewing on perceptions of reality. In fact, covering laws researchers find fault with the admission by Gerbner and his associates that the measurable effects of television are relatively small. Although the creators of the theory point to the cumulative effect of repeated exposure to limited influence (something like the steady drip of a faucet that eventually overflows the pail), scientific research relies on observable effects in laboratory settings that control for other influences. Cultivation researchers used self-reports of viewing habits; they did not observe respondents in a carefully controlled setting.

Potter (1986) concluded that the cultivation effect may be more complex than is currently stated; the amount of exposure to television may be less important than the attitudes and perceptions of individuals exposed. His conclusions match the criticisms from the rules perspective that fault cultivation theory with treating all viewers as helpless to withstand the manipulated images of reality projected by television. The interactions of audiences, television, and society are complex and cannot be reduced to simple cause and effect.

Cultivation theory links heavy television viewing with a distrustful view of a violent world. The final criticism questions the meaning of that link. The research has demonstrated a correlation between certain behaviors and certain attitudes, but has it proven the direction of influence? Do people who are distrustful watch more television because they have few friends? Cause and effect have not been established. There is no doubt that the controversy surrounding the media's influence on our perceptions and behavior will continue to rage. We can expect more research from scholars of mass communication in this area. New findings will refine and advance our efforts to theorize about the effects associated with the mass media.

A Modern Look at Media Effects

Towards the end of the 20th century, some researchers started to look at media effects from a new angle. They began to examine not just how the public is affected by the media, but how the pubic *thinks* they are affected by the media. Born in the early 1980s, the third-person effects hypothesis states that people tend to believe media messages influence others more than themselves. It claims that as audience members, we resist the idea that we can be directly affected by messages, and instead tend to believe that other people are always more influenced than we are. This hypothesis is still very favored in mass communication research, and many studies have been published that tend to confirm it. Born out of the third-person effects hypothesis, a more recent model, called the indirect-effects model states that people tend to perceive the effect that media messages have on others and then react to their perception. For example, we would hear so much about a popular show such as *Dancing with the Stars* or *American Idol*, that even if we are not fans we would assume that those shows are very influential on audiences, and might be tempted to "jump on the bandwagon" so that we won't be left out.

IMPORTANT ISSUES IN MEDIA EFFECTS

In psychological theory, social learning involves learning behavior that is controlled by environmental influences rather than by inherent or internal forces. Modeling is a typical result of social learning. Modeling is a type of learning that occurs when an individuals observes the actions of others to gain information on how to behave. You probably participate in modeling on a daily basis. In class you may notice your peers diligently taking notes. Regardless of whether or not you use class notes to study, you may start taking notes simply because it seems like appropriate behavior for the setting. While it seems bizarre, many of the choices you make every day are based on modeling the behavior of others rather than making an internal decision. For example, you look out the window of your home and notice that most people outside are wearing jackets. Without going outside to test the temperature for yourself, you decide that since everyone is wearing jackets it must be cold and you put on a jacket before leaving the house as well.

Children are active participants in modeling. American psychologist Albert Bandura was one of the pioneers of modeling theories. He conducted numerous studies showing that when children observe the actions of others they learn many forms of conduct. Behaviors such as sharing, aggression, cooperation, social interaction, and disappointment are picked up from the individuals in their environment.

Bandura's Bobo Doll

In 1961, Albert Bandura conducted an experiment to study the effects of viewing violence on children. Bandura used 36 boys and 36 girls enrolled in Stanford University Nursery School whose ages ranged from 3 to 5 years old. The subjects were divided into eight experimental groups and 24 subjects were put into a control group. The experimental groups were shown a video that displayed an adult model hitting, throwing, and kicking an inflatable doll called a Bobo doll, as well as using aggressive language. After viewing the video, the children were left in a room by themselves with the same BoBo doll and other toys. The children were told all of the toys were there for them to play with. The study showed that the majority of the children who were exposed to the aggressive video played with the Bobo doll and repeated much of the same violent behavior and language displayed in the video. Other parts of Bandura's study showed that the Bobo doll video encouraged some subjects to participate in other aggressive acts such as gun play and harsh language.[8]

---

[8] Albert Bandura, Dorothea Ross, Sheila A. Ross, "Bandura: Transmission of Aggression Through Imitation of Aggressive Models" 1961 *Journal of Abnormal and Social Psychology,* 63, 575–582.

Violence

Bandura's insights into the learning habits of children led him and many other psychologists to question the effects of the media, specifically television, on the behavior of children. If children learn to be aggressive or introverted from the people in their environment, it is possible that they can learn similar behavior from the people on their television set.[9] Research on the effects of violence in the media has been controversial. Two types of theories have been proposed. One suggests that a child's urge to participate in violent behavior can be diverted by watching violent behavior on television. In other words witnessing violence lessens the drive to commit violence. Under this theory, a young girl who watches a cartoon character play a violent prank on another character will be less likely to play a violent prank on a classmate. The second theory suggests that viewing violent behavior actually increases the drive to participate in violent activities. Following Bandura's idea of modeling, children model their behavior after the images they see on TV. Under this theory, the same little girl that witnessed the prank simulated in a cartoon would be more likely to initiate a similar prank on a classmate.

Violence in the media, especially on television, has been a concern since the medium became popular, in the 1950s. A great deal of effects research has focused on violence in the media, where researchers have gone back and forth between a more critical position, which says that media violence has a great influence on causing aggressive behavior on consumers; and a "limited effects" position, which is still concerned with the impact of violent messages but sees their influence as more moderate.

In the late 1960s two governmental commissions—the National Commission on the Causes and Prevention of Violence, and the Surgeon General's Scientific Advisory Committee on Television and Social Behavior—undertook a series of research studies. On the basis of laboratory experiments and field studies, the Surgeon General's committee concluded,

Do you believe that witnessing violent behavior on television leads to aggressive behavior?
© GeoM/Shutterstock

somewhat cautiously, that viewing violence on television contributes to violent or aggressive behavior in viewers. Just how much this influence really amounts to is still a point of disagreement for specialists. In general, most studies have supported that there is a causal relationship between watching violent programming and acting aggressively.

In the past 15 years, the discussion about violence in the media has gained even more strength on the basis of the popularity of video games and hip-hop music. In the early 1990s, Congress once again focused its attention on violent rap lyrics, denouncing artists such as Ice-T for what they saw as the aggression and incitement contained in lyrics for rap songs such as "Cop Killer." In the late 1990s, the attention shifted to the violence in video games. Incidents such as the Columbine and Arkansas school shootings led parents, educators, and other groups to argue that the extreme violence contained in some video games was influencing children to behave more aggressively. Several states have passed laws that ban the rental or sale of violent video games to minors, and the Supreme Court in 2010 will consider whether the California version of this law violates the Constitution.

Violence in the media is a compelling and contentious subject for both consumers and researchers. Some feel the media is often used as a scapegoat for other causes of violence in our society. It is often easier to blame a popular video game for an increase in firearm-related deaths than blame the government's policy on gun

---

[9] social learning. *Encyclopedia Britannica* at http://www.britannica.com/EBchecked/topic/551304/social-learning. Accessed October 31, 2008.

control. Still no person can deny that there is a substantial amount of violence in the media today. The average child under the age of 14 is exposed to 11,000 murders on television in his/her lifetime.[10] According to The National Television Violence Study, nearly two out of three TV programs contained some violence, and average about 6 violent acts per hour.[11]

Many theories have been developed to explain the various effects of mediated violence on audiences. The catharsis theory claims media outlets such as television can ease children's urges to participate in violent behavior. According to the theory, mediated violence allows aggressive people to discharge their anger vicariously through the media images, therefore lessening aggressive behavior. The concept of the catharsis theory dates back to Aristotle and the ancient Greeks. In his work *Politics,* Aristotle stated that viewing tragic plays allows people to release emotions related to negative feelings such as grief, rage, and fear.

A study done by the American Academy of Pediatrics focused its attention on violent video games, noting that the most popular video games tend to have "behavioral scripts" in which players not only are rewarded for their violent actions, but also learn to act in a way that goes from choosing a violent scenario to resolving that conflict through the use of violence. Video games have been accused of encouraging children and young teens to commit real-life crimes, and in some cases they are used as a form of defense in court (see Grand Theft Causes Grand Crime?).

While the judicial system is not ready to accept violent video games as the primary cause

Do you think violent video games influence a person's behavior?
© Paparazzit/Shutterstock

of violent behavior, many professionals are. David Walsh, a child psychologist, believes that exposure to violent video games can cause teenagers to participate in violent behavior. He supports his beliefs with research conducted by the National Institutes of Health, which shows the brains of teenagers are not fully developed. According to Walsh, the impulse control center of the brain, the section that helps us think ahead, control urges, and consider consequences, is under construction during the teenage years. When this low level of control is combined with a continuous flow of violent images, Walsh believes teenagers are capable of violent behavior without fully understanding the consequences. Walsh admits that other risk factors such as a troubled upbringing can contribute to violent behavior, but violent video games heighten the impulses of those troubled teenagers.[12]

---

[10] Daniel Chandler, "Television Violence and Children's Behavior" December 22, 2004 at http://www.aber.ac .uk/media/Modules/TF33120/tv-violence_and_kids.html.

[11] The Kaiser Family Foundation, Key Facts, Spring 2003 at http://www.kff.org/entmedia/upload/Key-Facts-TV-Violence.pdf.

[12] "Can a Video Game Lead to Murder?" *CBS News,* March 6, 2005 at http://www.cbsnews.com/stories/2005/ 03/04/60minutes/main678261.shtml.

Grand Theft Causes Grand Crime?

Shortly after the shoot 'em up video game Grand Theft Auto released its third edition, the same violence glamorized in the video game emerged in real life on the streets of Fayette, Alabama. On June 9, 2003, 18-year-old Devin Moore was charged with three counts of murder for allegedly shooting two police officers and a dispatcher while fleeing a police station. Moore was in the process of being booked for auto theft when he grabbed an officer's gun, fired fatal shots, and escaped in a stolen police cruiser. After he was arrested and arraigned, Moore pleaded not guilty by reason of mental defect. He blamed the combination of the abuse he endured as a child and the influence of playing Grand Theft Auto for his violent behavior.[13] On August 2005, a jury determined Moore was guilty as charged. While the jury did not believe that the video caused Moore to murder three people, the victims' relatives did. Attorney Jack Thompson filed a civil lawsuit on behalf of the relatives of the shooting victims against Sony Corp., the makers of Grand Theft Auto. The wrongful death suit claimed that Sony and other video game retailers were liable for the deaths of the officers because they created and distributed a game that encourages violent behavior. After a lengthy process, the civil case was dismissed.

A more recent study focused on violent images in music videos, especially music videos made available online by cable channels such as MTV, BET, VH1, and Country.com. The study found that 185 out of 951 videos analyzed (16.4%) contained acts of violence. Although the proportion found was relatively low, the author of the article was troubled by the kind of violence portrayed, where 76% of all violent acts were assisted by the use of weapons. The study also found that hard rock (72% of videos) and hip-hop/rap (48% of videos) were the musical genres where violence was more often committed.

The vast majority of studies analyzing violence in the media point toward three general areas of concern:

1. **Increased levels of aggressiveness.** Children and teenagers, especially boys, who are exposed to heavy levels of media violence, tend to perceive real-life violence as the natural, accepted way to resolve conflicts. Most of these children also tend to act more aggressively when they are playing or having other types of social interaction.

2. **"Mean world" syndrome.** A steady diet of violent media over a long period of time tends to cultivate in users the perception that the real world is a "mean and violent" place, which might lead to feelings of anxiety, alienation, and depression.

3. **Desensitization.** Refers to the widely tested hypothesis that constant exposure to violent messages might lead to a loss of sympathy for victims, less proactive involvement in preventing/stopping violence, and a general perception of violence as a normal occurrence.

Sex and Pornography

The production and consumption of sexually explicit material such as books, magazines, and videos is a worldwide business of enormous dimensions. The Internet and other digital technologies such as DVDs added new ways to make pornographic material even more widespread and accessible. But while many consumers enjoy a regular diet of such material, others find it distasteful, obscene or corrupting.

With a wide range of views concerning what is offensive and what is not, what is pornographic and what is simply erotic, what has artistic merit and what does not, it is obviously difficult to formulate definitions or a widely accepted concept of obscenity. Even the courts have a very hard time determining clear limits or legal concepts that could be applied across the board.

---

[13] AP, "Teen Charged in Alabama Cops Shooting" *CBS News*, June 9, 2003 at http://www.cbsnews.com/stories/ 2003/ 06/07/national/main557477.shtml.

Such concerns have led Congress to dedicate a whole section of the Telecommunications Act of 1996 to the issue of pornography on the Internet. The courts have subsequently struck down some of these rules as unconstitutional and in conflict with the protections warranted by the First Amendment.

Despite the legal ramifications, the discussion rages on about the potential harmful effects of pornographic messages in the mass media. Research on the functions and effects of sexually explicit material in the media began in earnest with the establishment in 1970 of the Presidential Commission on Obscenity and Pornography. Since that time a good deal of study has been done on the various aspects of this issue, including the influence of pornography on the image and treatment of women and on the relationship between the sexes, on the physiological effects of viewing such material, and on the possible relationship between pornography and violent crimes such as rape and murder and other forms of aggressive behavior.

More recently, a great deal of criticism has focused on the depiction of women on hip-hop lyrics and music videos. Many feminists and other media critics have argued that those lyrics and videos often degrade women and present them as subservient to men. Others have focused their attention on popular video games, which they accuse of objectifying and stimulating violence and aggressive behavior toward women, many times presented in a very sexual manner.

Analyses of the content of pornographic materials have provided some evidence that messages of the supremacy of men over women are often present. Other research indicates that viewing pornography can contribute to attitudes of increased acceptance of violence toward women. Other studies, however, show that sexually explicit material portraying men and women as partners or equals can educate and help to reduce antisocial attitudes. Although some studies indicate a relationship between high rates of availability and/or consumption of pornography and high rates of rape, a causal relationship has never been found, so it would be premature to say, on the basis of this research, whether, or how, one causes the other.

A study done recently showed that 83% of the most popular TV shows among teenagers in 2001–2002 had sexual content, while on average each hour of programming contained 6.7 scenes with sexual references. In the same study, only 1% of shows containing sexual behavior focused on the risks or negative aspects of it, while only 3% of scenes analyzed discussed sexually transmitted diseases or pregnancy. A similar study argues that exposure to high dosages of sexual content might not only stimulate sexual behavior in children, but also artificially age them, accelerating their developmental stages and making children act between 9 and 17 months older than their actual age.

Ethics and Antisocial Behavior

Other concerns with potentially harmful effects of media come from those who worry that some messages might be eroding traditional ethical values, thus stimulating antisocial behavior. Some media critics argue that negative media messages are so pervasive that they might be creating a sense of alienation and frustration in younger generations, manifested in a disregard for commonly accepted cultural traditions and societal rules, and leading to apathy, cynicism and nihilism. Religious leaders often raise similar concerns.

Other critics note that pervasive and widespread media use might lead to a society that places excessive importance on materialism, appearances, and the consumption of material goods. These critics see the preponderance of commercial media messages as an indication that mass communication has lost its power to educate and socialize, or at least that younger generations are being socialized into a community that sees them only as potential buyers. Many media literacy programs have been developed and adopted by educators concerned with these potentially harmful media effects.

STEREOTYPES

In general, research suggests that media messages tend to reflect and perpetuate gender and ethnic stereotypes, for example. Scientists want to know how much of these stereotypes affect our perception of reality. Many of the men and women characters appearing on television present somewhat stereotyped male and female images. Various studies have shown that children, who are heavy television viewers, when asked whether certain activities or occupations would be associated with women or with men, gave answers more in line with television stereotypes than did lighter viewers.

Research also indicates, however, that programs with characters in atypical occupational roles can educate children away from the traditional sexual stereotypes. Additionally, it has been found that boys almost always choose male characters as ideal role models, and that girls sometimes choose female characters but also often choose male ones.

A similar situation happens with ethnic stereotypes. Content analyses of television programming have shown the lack of ethnic diversity on mainstream television programs, as well as the presence of harmful ethnic stereotypes, or yet the association of particular ethnicities with certain occupations. Studies have shown that people who are heavy television viewers, or who rely heavily on television for information about the world, tend to associate some ethnic minorities to stereotypical behaviors presented on television.

EDUCATION AND SOCIALIZATION

Questions concerning the educational, cultural or social impact of mass media have been discussed and debated for centuries. In ancient Greece, Plato warned that writing weakens the mind and destroys the memory. In the fifteenth century, similar complaints were leveled against printing, though many people defended it as an unprecedented means for distributing and increasing knowledge. From the birth of electronic media on, the focus has been on television.

Studies have shown that people who spend a great deal of time watching television have lower Intelligence Quotients or IQs than people who spend less time doing so. However, more recent studies have shown that children who spend a limited amount of time watching television (two hours per day, on average), actually perform better academically than children who do not watch TV at all. It is uncertain from both sets of studies if there is a causal relationship between television viewing and intellectual performance. Our understanding of the relationship between reading behavior and TV viewing also remains uncertain. Some studies have found a positive correlation over time among younger viewers, while other studies have shown that adults who spend no time reading watch much more television than those who read. Similarly, the nature of the connection between viewing and both academic performance and educational aspiration has not yet been unraveled; so many factors—such as grade level, gender, television content, and type of school subject—seem to be implicated in this complex relationship.

On the positive side, researchers have also studied the effects of so-called educational programming, such as *Sesame Street*, and found that not only the content of these programs can help children strengthen certain cognitive abilities such as problem solving, reasoning, language, and arithmetic skills, but also that the form or style of presentation can stimulate the development of other important mental operations. The

What effects can educational programming have on children?
© Dmitriy Shironosov/ Shutterstock

research also suggests that the educational impact of television viewing is affected by the nature of the family and social relationships prevailing in the child's environment.

Quite a bit of media research has examined the ways in which people, including children, use communication messages in the socialization process. Researchers have investigated the influence of media such as television, music, movies, and videogames on the development of personal identity and on the association of certain attitudes and behavior patterns with particular sexes, ages, races, and occupations. If so much of what we know about the world comes from the media, researchers are interested in finding out how much impact the content of these messages have on the socialization process, our personalities, and the development of our worldviews.

Chapter 14

"The Sacred Canopy:" Understanding Religion Sociologically

When Sathyanarayana Raju was 11 years old, he fell ill and lost consciousness for days. When he awoke, he began speaking Vedanta (Hindu) philosophy, singing in the ancient language of Sanskrit, and reporting on the places and gods he had seen (Srinivas 2010: 55–56). Soon he was materializing out of thin air treats like candy and milk as gifts to the local villagers and claiming affiliation with—and eventually reincarnation as—a deceased Muslim Sufi holy man named Shirdi Sai Baba. He insisted that people call him Sai Baba. At this point he was still a local *guru* or religious guide, and people traveled to his home village of Puttaparthi for his mystical healing powers. But his reputation continued to grow as he demonstrated additional spiritual abilities, including "simple healings with or without sacred ash, magical materializations of fruit, sweets, ash, pictures, watches"—and ultimately miracles like "teleportation, telekinesis, mind-reading, appearance in dreams to give guidance, speaking many languages, and resurrecting people from the dead" (61). His village became a destination for pilgrimages and

audiences with the great man. In 1957 around age 30 he declared himself a *guru-avatar*, a manifestation of divinity; by the 1960s he claimed that he combined within himself early Vedic religion as well as later traditions like the Upanishads, the Bhagavad Gita, and yoga. He asserted that he was literally the god Shiva as well as Shiva's female consort Shakti. He further integrated Islamic mysticism and, by the 1970s, "the cosmic Christ" (69). By the late twentieth century, Sathya Sai Baba was the center of an international religious movement, with a magazine, local chapters around the world, thousands of followers, and a religious center at Puttaparthi, which serves as a global pilgrimage site. Just as Sathya Sai Baba was transformed into a sacred person, the former barren village has transformed into a sacred city where devotees can experience his power and take home souvenirs of their visit.

For many people, religion is a highly "traditional" and "personal" matter, but from a sociological point of view, religion is dynamic—as the case of the Sai Baba illustrates—and entirely social. People learn religion from society, particularly from the other individuals with whom they associate; people practice religion collectively; and religion is shaped by and shapes the wider society and culture. Appropriately then, since its earliest days sociology has been fascinated with religion, and this fascination has grown and changed as the discipline of sociology has grown and changed.

THE EVOLUTION OF A SOCIOLOGY OF RELIGION

As noted in previous chapters, the initial approach of sociology to the study of social ideas and institutions stressed history and change, and the study of religion was no different. Auguste Comte (1798–1857), for instance, lived through the exciting and traumatic days of Napoleon, the 1848 revolutions throughout Europe, and the industrial and urban revolutions. It seemed clear to him that society changed over time, in a specific way: society, he posited, had passed "successively through three different theoretical conditions: the Theological, or fictitious; the Metaphysical, or abstract; and the Scientific, or positive" (2009: 1). That is, religion was characteristic of the first phase of social evolution. The metaphysical phase referred to later philosophical speculation, while the scientific phase was just beginning. Comte further speculated that the religious/theological stage had passed through three substages, first "fetishism" or the belief in multiple natural powers and spirits, then "polytheism" or the belief in many gods, and finally "monotheism" or the belief in one god. Significantly, while Comte lumped religion among the many fictitious elements of human history, he also seemed to feel that even modern scientific humans needed it, since he proposed a "positive religion," a scientific religion, a religion of Humanity that would be complete with its own doctrine, worship, and morality. (The 1789 French Revolution, which tried to purge society of religion, also offered its own version of a religion of reason.)

Karl Marx also concluded that society evolved over time, although his theory placed the material/economic conditions of society at the forefront of that change. So, each particular historical mode of production led to a particular "social formation," including an ideological dimension of beliefs and values and philosophies. Religion belonged to this ideological level; in other words, religion was an effect of more basic and more "real" material causes. Religion, like all ideological/symbolic systems, both represented (or sometimes *mis*represented) social-economic realities and legitimated those realities. A good example would be the Hindu caste system, which provides spiritual explanations for the economic or occupational inequalities of society and why individuals find themselves in their specific caste groups. Moreover, the system explains why it is *just* or *appropriate* for people to be in those levels and what they can do to improve their lot—but not in this life. And since most socie-ties had developed exploitative class relations by the time of Marx, he saw religion as a pernicious distraction from the practical problems of the world. This led to his most famous dictum on religion:

> Religious distress is at the same time the expression of real distress and the protest against real distress. Religion is the sigh of the oppressed creature, the heart of a heartless world, just as it is the spirit of a spiritless condition. It is the opium of the people.

> The abolition of religion as the illusory happiness of the people is to demand for their real happiness. The demand to give up illusions about the existing state of affairs is the demand to give up a state of affairs that needs illusions. The criticism of religion is therefore in embryo the criticism of that vale of tears, the halo of which is religion (Marx and Engels 1975: 38).

Once the social and economic injustices of the world were righted, Marx fully expected that religion would wither and vanish.

Émile Durkheim wrote one of his most substantial books on religion, also illustrating the historical/evolutionary approach to social institutions. In *The Elementary Forms of the Religious Life*, first published in 1912, Durkheim attempted to expose the core or essence of religion by identifying what he thought was the minimal form of religion, which he claimed to find in "primitive" societies like those of the Australian Aboriginals. Aboriginal societies, based on nomadic hunting and gathering, had no priests, no scriptures, no church buildings, and no high doctrine. What they did have, according to Durkheim, was a spiritual relationship between society and the natural world, as well as certain ritual practices. This spiritual relationship Durkheim called "totemism," in which natural species are associated with human individuals or groups, like clans or lineages. Thus, the natural world becomes a symbolic reflection of the social world. More fundamentally, Durkheim viewed the essence of religion to be the experience of "the sacred," that which is powerful and special and set apart from ordinary life. But where did this notion of the sacred—and therefore the origin of religion—come from? In other words, where would a sociologist locate that which is more powerful than the individual, which exists before the individual, which survives after the individual, and on which the individual wholly depends? Durkheim's answer was the social group itself: "this power exists, it is society" (1965: 257). The group is a "social fact" and an inescapable one, consisting of the society as a whole and its subgroups like the family, the clan, the village, etc. Durkheim concluded that "the god of the clan, the totemic principle, can therefore be nothing else than the clan itself, personified and represented to the imagination under the visible form of the animal or vegetable which serves as totem" (236).

Weber also found religion to be an irresistible topic for social analysis. His two most important publications on religion are *The Protestant Ethic and the Spirit of Capitalism*, written in 1904 and 1905, and *The Sociology of Religion*, first published in 1922. *The Protestant Ethic* presented a challenge to the Marxian interpretation of religion, in which religion is a passive artifact of the economic base of society. Weber argued that religion, like other belief and value systems, could have practical effects on the world. His argument was that the beliefs and attitudes of early Protestantism (especially Calvinism) resulted in a set of behaviors that were conducive to early capitalism, such as hard work, frugality, individualism, and the evaluation of people in terms of their material success. Weber's deeper interest, then, was "the part which religious forces have played in forming the developing web of our specifically worldly modern culture, in the complex interaction of innumerable different historical factors" (1930: 90).

Weber's second book, *The Sociology of Religion*, is a yet grander attempt to organize the changes in the social forms of religion over time. In it, he considers the initial rise of religion (originally "this-worldly" and magically motivated), the appearance of concepts like "god" and social roles like magician and priest, and religious ideas like taboo, sin, and salvation. Later chapters turn to more conventionally religious subjects like the congregation, preaching, class and caste differences, asceticism and mysticism, and even politics, economics, sexuality, and art. While his gaze was focused primarily on Christianity, his closing chapter comments on "the attitude of the other world religions to the social and economic order" (1956: 262). In short, Weber explored the relationship between diverse aspects and forms of religion and their social setting.

SOCIOLOGICAL DEFINITIONS OF RELIGION

How one defines a term has profound consequences for how one *understands* a phenomenon and how one *studies, especially counts,* that phenomenon. For example, if religion is defined as the belief in god(s), then only belief systems with god(s) would count as religions, in which case there would be fewer religions than under other definitions, such as the belief in spiritual beings. And, if religion is defined, as Rudolf Otto did in his *The Idea of the Holy*, as an emotional experience of mystery and awe; or as Sigmund Freud did, as a projection of unconscious drives; or as William James did, as "the feelings, acts, and experiences of individual men in their solitude, so far as they apprehend themselves to stand in relation to whatever they may consider the divine" (1958: 34), then the recommended approach would be a psychological/mental one. However, even if religion emanates from emotional or unconscious sources, it is still constructed, organized, and practiced collectively and socially, and before individuals feel and act in solitude they must learn the socially correct feelings and actions. These facts call for a sociological definition of and approach to religion.

Sociologists have offered two main kinds of definitions of religion, known as functionalist and substantive. Functionalist definitions highlight what a phenomenon like religion *does*, how it works, and how it interconnects with other aspects of society. Most functionalist definitions of religion tend to stress its integrative function. Georg Simmel was one of the most emphatic in declaring that "without it society would disintegrate" since religion provides the foundation for "obedience" and the "easy-going, uncritical faith in the power, value, superiority, and goodness of those in authority" (1905: 366). Durkheim's celebrated definition of religion

also has a functionalist quality, although it suggests a substantive essence to religion: "a unified system of beliefs and practices relative to sacred things, that is to say, things set aside and forbidden—beliefs and practices which unite into one single moral community called a Church, all those who adhere to them" (1965: 62).

Other functionalist perspectives promote the meaning-creating function of religion. The anthropologist Clifford Geertz suggested one of the most often-quoted definitions of religion in all of the social sciences: "(1) a system of symbols which act to (2) establish powerful, pervasive, and long-lasting moods and motivations in men by (3) formulating conceptions of a general order of existence and (4) clothing these conceptions with such an aura of factuality that (5) the moods and motivations seem uniquely realistic" (1973: 90). The point of the definition is that religion's key purpose is to establish mental moods and behavioral motivations in its followers, to transform them into certain kinds of people. Sometimes this function depends on religion's purported explanatory function, its ability to answer the questions of life.

Box 14-1
Peter Berger on the Ideological Uses of Functional Definitions

Peter Berger, whose *The Sacred Canopy* (1967) is an important contribution to the sociology of religion, came to express some grave reservations about functionalist definitions. He thought that the trend toward functionalist definitions was a symptom of the failure to take religion seriously, even of an antireligion bias, in sociology—what he called "assassination by definition" (1974: 126). More precisely, he insisted that such definitions belie "the interest in quasiscientific legitimation of the avoidance of transcendence" (128). What he meant is that the "specificity of the religious phenomenon is avoided by equating it with other phenomena. The religious phenomenon is 'flattened out'" (129). This can be seen in functionalist definitions like those of Simmel or Geertz or Yinger, which make no mention of anything uniquely religious and which could just as easily apply to nonreligious concepts as well. Any number of things could provide meaning or social order or victory. For Berger, religion was not the same as other, potential integrative or meaningful systems. It "introduces an additional

dimension to experience; once this has happened, there continues to be the awareness that the stage of everyday action is 'hollow,' that there is another level 'beneath' it, and that the figures located there may 'surface' at any moment. Needless to say, this awareness (even if at the time it is only held dimly) accentuates the precariousness of everyday life and all its works" (131). If he is correct, then purely functionalist approaches to religion fail or refuse to acknowledge and address the experience and importance of religion to members of those religions, to "understand" (in the sense of Weber's famous *Verstehen*, to get inside the heads of those who believe and do) religion, and to see how it differs from other aspects of society. No doubt, functionalists are eager to sidestep the problem of the "truth" of religion, but Berger warned us that "whatever religious apparitions the future may bring forth, it would be regrettable if the scientific study of religion were systematically blinded to them by its own conceptual machinery" (133). In a word, definitions make a difference.

Milton Yinger recommended a functional definition along those lines:

> Where one finds *awareness of and interest in the continuing, recurrent, 'permanent' problems of human existence*—the human condition itself, as contrasted with specific problems; where one finds *rites and shared beliefs relevant to that awareness which define the strategy of an ultimate victory*; and where one has *groups organized to heighten that awareness and to teach and maintain those rites and beliefs*—there you have religion. (1969: 91, emphasis in the original)

Substantive definitions, on the other hand, privilege the substance or essence of religion, especially that which makes it uniquely religious. Even functionalist definitions tend to indicate some key characteristic(s)—for Geertz symbols, for Durkheim the sacred, for Yinger rites and beliefs. But substantive definitions favor these features over the alleged functions. The early comparative mythologist James Frazer thought of religion as "a propitiation or conciliation of powers superior to man which are believed to direct and control the course of nature and human life" (1958: 58–59). For Anthony Wallace, ritual was the key to religion, making it "a set of rituals, rationalized by myth, which mobilizes supernatural powers for the purpose of achieving or preventing transformations of state in man and nature" (1966: 107). Others place the seat of religion in myths or spiritual beings or religious institutions.

Whether or not it escapes all of the objections of Berger, one definition that seems to communicate the comprehensively social nature of religion comes from Robin Horton, who over a half-century ago proposed that

> in every situation commonly labeled religious we are dealing with action directed towards objects which are believed to respond in terms of certain categories—in our own culture those of purpose, intelligence, and emotion—which are also the distinctive categories for the description of human action. . . . The relationship between human beings and religious objects can be further defined as governed by certain ideas of patterning and obligation such as characterize relationships among human

beings. In short, Religion can be looked upon as an extension of the field of people's social relationships beyond the confines of purely human society. (1960: 211)

That is, religion is *more society*, including nonhuman and superhuman beings ("objects") in perfectly social relationships with humans.

MEASURING RELIGION: RELIGIOSITY

Two conclusions that Yinger reached were that "religion" refers to a class of social phenomena, not to any particular species like Christianity or even monotheism, and that we should try to think about and describe religion as much as possible as members themselves do. We should, he wrote, "ask our respondents to 'speak their religion'" (1969: 91) without imposing our preconceptions and categories on them and thus listen carefully to how religion "sounds." This requires, then, the development of appropriate and sensitive tools and techniques to measure religion in order to answer questions such as "(a) the distribution of beliefs and commitments, (b) trends in beliefs and attachments, and (c) predictors of religiosity" (Sherkat and Ellison 1999: 365). Only in this way can sociologists investigate people's religious beliefs and behaviors, how those beliefs and behaviors are related to other social variables, and how those beliefs and behaviors change over time and circumstances.

One central sociological concept is religiosity, loosely defined as the quality of being religious. But what exactly does that mean, and how can sociologists study and measure it? Sociologists, for instance, have often turned to the available quantitative statistics of religious participation, such as church attendance and/or church membership (which are, by the way, not identical). The polling service Gallup (Newport 2011) calculated that 41.6 percent of Americans attended church, synagogue, or mosque at least once a week in 2009. Based on that information alone, we might conclude that Americans are not a very religious people, but such a conclusion would be dubious in a variety of ways. First, religious attendance is not the only way to measure religiosity; second, there are many variations within those attendance numbers. For instance, some states enjoy two or three times the rate of church attendance as others: New England states like Vermont, New Hampshire, Maine, and Massachusetts registered less than 30 percent attendance (Vermont only 23 percent), while southern states like Mississippi, Alabama, South Carolina, and Louisiana, not to mention Utah, recorded levels above 50 percent (Mississippi the highest level, at 63 percent).

In other Western/Christian countries, the results are similar but worse. According to data on the Church of England, attendance during the 1970s dropped by 30,000 persons per year, and in the 1980s the decline continued but slowed to 10,000 per year. By 2009, only half as many people attended Anglican services as 40 years before (Church Society 2011). Some commentators have considered the decrease so dire that they have called England and other European societies "post-Christian."

Another potential measure of religiosity is religious identity, which itself could mean a number of things, including whether one avows an identity as religious (i.e., calls oneself "Catholic" or "Protestant," etc.) or whether one considers religion important in one's life. Here, the data are not quite as negative but still show a nonreligious trend. A 2010 Gallup poll indicated that the percentage of Americans claiming no religious identity had grown more or less steadily since 1948 from 5 percent to 16 percent (Newport 2010). Meanwhile, in terms of the importance of religion in life, since 1958 those who believed that religion could answer life's problems dropped from 82 percent to 58 percent, while those who regarded religion as "old-fashioned and out of date" had risen from 7 percent to 28 percent.

Commenting on the British religious scene, Grace Davie (1994) suggested the useful concept of believing without belonging. It is entirely possible, and probably common, for people to possess religious beliefs but not to belong to or participate regularly in collective religious activities. For instance, many people may call themselves

© bikeriderlondon, 2012. Under license from Shutterstock, Inc.

Christians and even believe some or all Christian doctrines but attend church sporadically, perhaps only on special days like Christmas and Easter. Others may get their religion in other nonchurch ways, such as religious television programming or the Internet. Some may regard themselves as "spiritual" rather than "religious" (see below). So measuring "belonging" in terms of church membership or attendance might not reflect the actual condition of "believing" at all. Even worse, it is conceivable that some percentage of people who belong do not believe—that they attend religious services for other reasons than personal acceptance of its doctrines. Worst of all, Lewis and Huyser de Bernardo (2010) suppose that there might be a certain amount of "belonging without belonging" going on, in which sociologists assume that people who either attend or identify with a religion really "belong to" the religion in a straightforward way. Instead, in studying evangelicals in the United States, they conclude that "there may be more than one way of being an evangelical" (113) and thus more than one kind of religious identity or belonging for evangelicals.

The Dimensions of Religiosity

Because religiosity can mean more than one thing, sociology has attempted to disaggregate the components of religion. As noted, Davie distinguished believing from belonging. Mockabee, Monson, and Grant add a third element—behaving—to the mix, suggesting that these "three aspects of religion—beliefs, belonging, and behavior—can be used in combination to measure religious commitment (or 'religiosity')" (2001: 675). Adding behavior opens a new set of possible data, including things like prayer, Bible reading, participating in church activities, and so forth, and sociologists have regularly measured such behaviors. However, Mockabee, Monson, and Grant offer a serious warning: these "commonly used religious commitment items such as frequency of church attendance and Bible-reading measures are highly normative in the Evangelical Protestant tradition. . . . Thus religious commitment scales can be 'biased' in favor of evangelicals" (675–76). Indeed, church attendance and Bible reading would be utterly inappropriate measures of Muslim or Hindu religiosity, so there is a likely bias not only toward Protestant religiosity but toward Christian religiosity in general in such studies. So, not only definitions but also measurements and tests can influence our data and conclusions. For this reason, the authors call for "tradition-specific" variables and weights for the variables.

Becoming Religious: Religious Socialization

The next obvious sociological question is how people become religious, how they acquire religious beliefs, and how they commit to those beliefs. Since humans are not born with a particular religious knowledge or commitment, these must certainly be learned, and they are learned from other people in social situations and institutions. In other words, becoming religious is a special case of socialization, a matter of religious socialization.

One familiar approach to the question of becoming religious is the concept of "conversion." In a classic study, A. D. Nock described conversion as "the reorientation of the soul of an individual, his deliberate turning from indifference or from an earlier form of piety to another, a turning which implies a consciousness that a great change is involved, that the old was wrong and the new is right" (1933: 7). Conversion, then, is understood as a total, sudden, irreversible, personally profound or emotional, and basically doctrinal change of religious

orientation. This is once again a standard Christian ideology, but the evidence does not support this view. Instead, change of religion is often partial, gradual, reversible, mundane, and based on a number of matters, including whom one does or wants to spend time with.

For these reasons, sociologists are less likely to talk about conversion and more likely to talk about affiliation and disaffiliation. Affiliation is the condition, or more accurately the process, of associating and identifying with a particular religion or religious community, while disaffiliation is losing or breaking such an association or identification. According to Sherkat and Ellison, sociological research has discovered religious affiliation to be a function of "(a) family and denominational socialization, (b) gender, (c) social status, and (d) life course events and aging" (1999: 367). For instance, "parents influence their children's religious beliefs and commitments both directly through the socialization of beliefs and commitments and by channeling other social relationships" (367). Obviously, children who are raised unaffiliated (what the Barna Group calls "unchurched") are more likely to be unaffiliated in adulthood: a survey by the Pew Forum on Religion and Public Life (2009) reported that 46 percent remained unaffiliated as adults. Yet that means that the majority, 54 percent, subsequently "converted to" or affiliated with a religion—39 percent with a Protestant church (22 percent evangelical), 6 percent with the Catholic Church, and 9 percent with another religion.

© Zunjeta, 2012. Under license from Shutterstock, Inc.

Box 14-2

Acquiring a Religious Identity

Joining a religion is at least as much as matter of developing a new identity as believing a new creed. Two studies illustrate this point. Lori Peek recently took the relatively unorthodox approach of investigating the religious identities of young Muslims in the United States. Most of her subjects were born into Muslim families, but as they became more conscious of and committed to their religion they went through three identity-building stages. In the first stage, religion was merely ascribed: "they engaged in very little critical reflection when they were children regarding the meaning of 'being Muslim' because their religious identity was taken for granted as part of their everyday lives" (2005: 224). Some actually ignored or actively concealed their Muslim identity because of social pressure and stigma. For many, though, young adulthood, especially college, was a time of intensification of religious identity, during which their religion came to be not ascribed but *chosen*, almost as if they were affiliating or "converting" for the first time. In college, they made Muslim friends and participated in Muslim student associations, which "offered an organizational and social setting in which the interviewees could collectively examine specific aspects of the religion of Islam and the meaning of being Muslim" (228). Gradually, as they "learned more about Islam and drew closer to the religion, they became more likely to reject or downplay other aspects of their identity" (230). Finally, they arrived at the stage of *declared* religious identity, in which they not only explicitly but publicly avowed their religion, feeling "the increasing importance of positively representing Muslims and Islam to others" (232) as well as a greater tendency "to approach others and offer information about their religion" (233).

Susan Harding's study of fundamentalist Baptist conversion raises other critical points. In this case, becoming a Baptist is similar to—indeed, effectively is—learning a new language, a way to talk and think about your experiences. The two key acts of conversion and of membership are preaching and witnessing, both verbal skills of "speaking the Gospel." Witnessing, that is, describing one's conversion and religious experience, "aims to separate novice listeners from their prior, given reality, to constitute a new, previously unperceived or indistinct, reality, and to impress that reality upon them; make it felt, heard, seen, known, undeniably real" (1987: 169). The process of conversion begins when a nonmember (that is, a "sinner," one of the "unsaved") begins to listen to the Word and "is completed when sinners are 'saved,' or 'born-again,' 'regenerated,' 'washed in the blood of Christ'" (170). The technique involves telling stories (personal and biblical) and moves through a series of stages: "equating his present listener with the listeners in his stories; defining the listener as lost; defining the speaker as saved; transforming his narrative listeners into speakers; exhorting his present listener to speak" (170). If the process works, "the Holy Spirit penetrates the conscious mind and becomes 'another voice,' 'a real person,' who begins to recast their inner speech. After salvation, the voice of the Holy Spirit 'guides' converts, gives them 'discernment,' and seems to alter the very chemistry of desire" (174–75). The convert is thus "under conviction," but as a convert you "do not believe in the sense of public declaration, but you gradually come to respond to, and interpret, and act in the world as if you were a believer" (178). In other words, speaking is believing, and one must learn to speak.

Moreover, even people raised in a religion are likely to change their religious affiliation at least once in their lives. In the same study, only 47 percent of people had not changed their childhood affiliation; another 9 percent had changed but returned (in other words, a *double* conversion, out and back again). A full 44 percent did not belong to their childhood religion, with 5 percent being raised Catholic but changing to Protestant, and 15 percent being raised Protestant but changing to a different Protestant sect. And just as childhood affiliation is not permanent, so a "conversion" is not permanent. Around one-third of people (depending on their starting faith) claimed to have undergone two religious changes, and between 21 and 32 percent (depending on their starting faith) had experienced three or more changes (with the highest number being former Protestants who ended up unaffiliated).

The reasons that people give for changing their religion are diverse and vary depending on what religion they are changing from. Understandably, many people assert that they stop believing in the teachings of their original religion (an "ideological" change), but others mention finding another religion that "they like more," unhappiness with the worship services, or dissatisfaction with their priest or pastor.

As indicated, people not only disaffiliate from religion but also affiliate or re-affiliate, which

Christians often call "returning to the fold." In an article by that title, Wilson and Sherkat examined the social factors that correlate with leaving and returning to religion. They determined that two important variables in the life of the child are his/her relationship to parents and the religiosity of the family: "Those who were close to their parents as teenagers and had already developed religious habits are less likely to have dropped out" (1994: 154). Additionally, women were less likely to disaffiliate than men, and individuals who married and started families early (by age 25) were also less likely to leave the fold. This latter observation suggests that there may be a significant life-cycle and social-stage aspect to affiliation and disaffiliation, too. Young adults are prone to leave their religion, but this departure is not usually final. Instead, when they get older and especially when they marry and have children, they are likely to re-affiliate with a religion—although not necessarily the one they left. Interestingly, the Pew Forum also found that people who convert to a religion are more inclined to take that religion seriously, to engage in its religious activities, and to express absolute certainty in its dogmas than those who were merely born and raised in it.

TYPES OF RELIGIOUS ORGANIZATIONS

The question of religious firms and religious economies suggests another line of investigation for sociology: the different types of religion or forms of religious organization. As in so many other areas of society, Weber was one of the first to notice and name crucial distinctions. For Weber, a church differed from a sect. A church is a hierarchical organization, inclusive of its society, which most crucially claims its members by ascription: If an individual is born into that society, she/he is a member of that church. A sect, according to Weber, is more democratic or at least individualistic, more exclusive (not all members of society are members of the sect), and more "achieved," that is, it must seek members and convert and confirm them. Thus, the key difference is the mode of

membership: Individuals do not choose a church (it commandeers them), but individuals do choose a sect.

It became apparent immediately that not all religious organizations fall neatly into these two categories and that mode of membership is not the only variable distinguishing them. Ernst Troeltsch (1931) added the criterion of the relationship between the religious organization and the wider society, regarding a church as a well-integrated institution, either providing the society with its dominant beliefs and values or compromising and adapting its beliefs and values to the socially dominant ones. A sect, in distinction, is not integrated into society and may struggle with the societal beliefs and values or suggest new beliefs and values of its own. Significantly, he also suggested a third type, "mystical," to which we return below.

Troeltsch's model is still static, but Richard Niebuhr (1929) suggested a more dynamic model by putting church and sect at the opposite ends of a spectrum of religious organization, with diverse forms in between. Central to these was the denomination or a particular, often new branch within a religion. Every new religion begins as a sect, but if it survives, grows, and institutionalizes it may *become* a church or it may remain on the greater "tree" of a church to *become* a denomination (literally "name from" or "call by name"). In most analyses, Catholicism would qualify as a church, while congregations like Baptists, Methodists, and Lutherans would be denominations of the Protestant category, and groups like Mormons would have been sects in their early days, although Mormonism (Church of Jesus Christ of Latter-Day Saints) is accepted as a Protestant denomination by many people today (but not accepted as even Christian by others).

Finally for our present purposes, Milton Yinger (1957) advanced a model containing six religious types: cult, sect, established sect, class church/denomination, ecclesia, and universal church. A cult would be the newest and socially strangest of religions, while a sect could actually take three forms (accepting, avoiding, and aggressive). An established sect is more institutionalized and "normalized" but still independent, such as Christian Science. An ecclesia is fairly organized and socially accepted but a more "local or national" religion than a church, such as the Church of England, while a universal church would be translocal and potentially global, like Catholicism.

As valuable and fertile as this categorical thinking is, it should be obvious that it is difficult to encompass the variety of religions within a short list of types. Not all religions have all or only the characteristics of their supposed type, and of course, religions change their organization (and their beliefs, values, and practices) over time. The Church of England, for instance, was originally a national church or ecclesia, but it is global today, perhaps qualifying it as a universal church; with diocese and parishes in the United States, Asia, and Africa, there are more Anglicans *outside* England than *inside*. Further, as mentioned, every religion begins its life as a sect—or even a cult—and settles into the role of denomination, ecclesia, or church. Finally, a branch of a church (like Protestantism from Catholicism) can itself sprout branches (like Methodism, Baptism, Quakerism, etc.), which can sprout yet more branches (e.g., there are more than twenty branches or subdenominations of Methodism in the United States). So classifying religions is and appears set to remain a difficult task.

WORLD RELIGIONS

Until a couple thousand years ago, there were innumerable religions in the world, but all of them were "local" in the sense that they belonged to a particular group of people and were associated with a particular territory. These local or tribal or traditional religions reflected the nature of the societies where they were found. As examples of Durkheim's "mechanical solidarity" or Ferdinand Tönniës' *"gemeinschaft,"* such societies were small, autonomous, preliterate, and kinship-based. Durkheim referred to such societies in his *Elementary Forms of the Religious Life* as "moral communities," held together by the common beliefs and values—and especially the common rituals—of their socially embedded religion.

For Australian Aboriginals, who were Durkheim's paradigm of such societies, there was and could be no thought of extending or imposing their religion on other societies, since it applied to them as a people and to their land, their ancestors, and the indigenous plants and animals. Lacking literacy and a specialized class of religious functionaries and interpreters, religion was not highly self-conscious or systematized.

However, as societies changed, so did religion. Larger societies, more diverse and pluralistic societies, richer and more stratified societies, and more centralized societies called for new religious ideas and organization. Literacy, especially the possession of a religious "document" and the existence of a literate class of priests and scribes, made religion more self-conscious and systematic, as well as more rigid. Most importantly, perhaps, religion became detached from any single people or place and became "portable." According to Yinger, such religion was, for the first time, *universal* or at least universalizable, applicable to any—and ultimately and ideally to all—individuals and societies. Such a universal religion would be a product of its social circumstances: "a universal religion will be invented only in a particular sociocultural context. There must be extensive social differentiation, religious specialists, culture contact, and a long period of frustration of major needs and aspirations" (Yinger 1970: 474). In other words, a new, cosmopolitan social experience would call for a more cosmopolitan religion, a world religion.

A world religion does not, even today, actually achieve universal human membership (there are, after all, many rival world religions), but it has the potential if not the aspiration to do so. Being free of "place," it can and does circulate throughout the world, finding and converting members in many, perhaps every, country. More important, because of its written documents (its scriptures, its canon), it attempts to impose orthodoxy on its members (with little success, sociologically speaking, as new interpretations and new cults/sects/denominations continually arise). Because a world religion is initially an unprecedented phenomenon, it necessarily must gather its first recruits through "conversion," and because it is constantly spreading into additional societies and encountering competition from other religions (world and local), it must constantly seek to acquire members through conversion. The result is something like Stark's ideal of a religious economy.

As Table 14-1 indicates, there are many more world religions than the famous five (Christianity, Islam, Judaism, Hinduism, and Buddhism), and new potential world religions are invented regularly (see the discussion of new religious movements below). Some of the other, large religions are comparatively localized (Shinto is a predominantly Japanese religion, while Cao Dai is based in Vietnam), although migration and diaspora (the dispersion of members of a society across a region or the globe) as well as print and electronic media

have led to the establishment of communities of all of these religions throughout the world. Other, even smaller religions, like the Unification Church (known popularly and pejoratively as "Moonies" after their leader Reverend Sun Myung Moon) or Scientology, are also international.

Judaism and Hinduism are the oldest of the major world religions, each originally a tribal/local religion—Judaism among the ancient Hebrews, Hinduism among the ancient people of India. Each has a written literature—for Judaism, the Torah as well as commentaries such as the Talmud, and for Hinduism, the Vedas as well as later texts like the Upanishads and the Mahabharata. Each has key historical figures (such as Adam, Abraham, and Moses for Judaism, or Rama and Arjuna for Hinduism), but

Table 14-1

The Top 15 World Religions, by membership

Religion	Members
Christianity	2.1 billion
Islam	1.5 billion
Hinduism	900 million
Chinese traditional	394 million
Buddhism	376 million
Sikhism	23 million
Juche (North Korea)	19 million
Judaism	14 million
Baha'i	7 million
Jainism	4.2 million
Shinto	4 million
Cao Dai	4 million
Zoroastrianism	2.6 million
Tenrikyo (Japan)	2 million
Rastafarianism	600,000

Source: www.adherents.com

(In addition, 1.1 billion secular/nonreligious people constitute the third-largest religious identity in the world, and 300 million people still practice tribal/indigenous religions.)

not a single known founder. And both are still, although their members can be found all around the world, relatively "national" religions, associated with the Hebrew and Indian people today and not actively seeking converts.

Buddhism, Christianity, and Islam are all historically more recent religions and can be tied to the careers of individual founders. Buddhism originated in the sixth century BCE in the teachings of the north Indian prince Siddhartha Gautama. As an offshoot or reform movement from Hinduism, it incorporates many similar ideas (like karma and reincarnation), but offers a more immediate (in this lifetime) escape from the cycle of rebirth through the achievement of enlightenment. It also formally rejects the caste system, making salvation available to all. Buddhism eventually spread to central Asia and China, and then on to Japan, where in each location it adapted to local culture, producing Tibetan Buddhism in central Asia and Zen Buddhism in Japan.

Christianity also began as an offshoot or reform movement, in this case of Judaism. Its original form was a "Jesus movement" elaborating the Jewish idea of a messiah or anointed leader who would reestablish the kingdom of Israel. Jesus came to be understood by his followers as more than a rabbi (teacher) or prophet but the actual incarnation of God, whose death and resurrection ushered in a new world. Paul contributed greatly to the early doctrine and organization of Christianity as more than a Jewish sect, and the adoption of Christianity as the official state religion of the Roman Empire by Constantine in the third century CE secured the survival and commenced the institutionalization of Christianity as a universal or "catholic" church. Many of the structures and trappings of the Catholic church reflect its imperial origins.

Islam was the last of the major Western or "Abrahamic" religions to appear, called Abrahamic since it (along with Judaism and Christianity) recognizes Abraham as the starting point of the historical relation or "covenant" with God. All three religions include many of the same characters and events, including Adam and Eve and Moses. Islam even accepts Jesus as a prophet but not the son of God. Islam's central figure is Muhammad, who around 610 CE began to receive divine messages that Muslims believe were the actual text of the Qur'an. At first seeking to replace the polytheism of Arab culture with a strict monotheism dedicated to Allah (from the Arabic al-Lah or "God"), Muhammad met resistance from the local tribes and fled to Yathrib or Medina, where he became a political leader or arbitrator. His ongoing revelations, as well as recorded acts and sayings collected in the *hadith*, provide the basis for a body of laws known as *sharia*. In 630 CE he and his followers captured Mecca and established it as the sacred city of Islam, although he died soon after in 632.

All three Abrahamic religions continued to adapt and divide over the years. The primary divisions within Judaism include Orthodox, Reform, and Conservative, in addition to ultra-orthodox groups like Hasidism and Haredim. Christianity split after a millennium into Western/Catholic and Eastern/Orthodox churches, with a single international Catholic organization but multiple national Orthodox churches (e.g., Russian Orthodox, Greek Orthodox, etc.). Five hundred years later, in the early sixteenth century, "protesters" against the Catholic Church inaugurated the Protestant movement, in the form of Lutheran, Calvinist, and then hundreds of sects and denominations. (It is worth noting, then, that "denomination" is a distinctly Christian concept.) Islam, too, split early into two major traditions: Sunni and Shi'ite. Sunnis, the majority of Muslims globally, are regarded as the "traditionalists" who

---

Blue Mosque in Istanbul, Turkey

© Xuanlu Wang, 2012. Under license from Shutterstock, Inc.

accept political institutions in addition to religion, while Shi'ites or "partisans" (*shi'a* means partisans, specifically the party of Ali, Muhammad's kinsman and successor) tend to insist that only a direct descendant of Muhammad should have authority over the *ummah* or community of Muslims. Other traditions like the mystics known as Sufis also emerged.

RELIGION IN AMERICAN SOCIETY

The world is a highly diverse and often fractious place when it comes to religion, and virtually all major religions are present in the United States. Although first settled by Protestants from England (after Catholics from Spain explored the southern regions of North America), many religions were active in the American colonies from their first days— English Catholics (largely in Maryland), English Anglicans (especially in Virginia), English "puritans" or fundamentalist Protestants (particularly in New England), and Quakers (in Pennsylvania), not to mention Jews, Dutch Protestants, and French Catholics. African slaves brought with them their own religious traditions, which mixed with Christian traditions to create new syncretistic belief systems. By the early 1800s, large numbers of Irish Catholics were arriving, as well as Chinese non-Christians (Buddhists and Confucians) in the mid-1800s and numerous Eastern European Catholics, Orthodox Christians, and Jews by the later 1800s. Many African slaves were Muslims, carrying that religion to America, and new immigrants from Africa and Asia added to the Islamic population; there was a Muslim Union Society in New York, founded by a Sudanese immigrant named Satti Majid, as early as 1904.

The United States has also produced its share of homegrown sects, denominations, and churches. Methodism was not started in America, but its founder John Wesley planted it here in 1735. From the mid-1800s a vast array of new religions bloomed in the United States, -including

Mormonism, Christian Science, Seventh Day Adventism, Jehovah's Witnesses, and the group known as the Shakers (the United Society of Believers in Christ's Second Appearing). Communities like the Amish maintained their separate subculture in areas in the East and Midwest. In the twentieth century, religions like Hinduism and Buddhism took root, while new sects such as Scientology and TELAH (The Evolutionary Level Above Human, or "Heaven's Gate") appeared.

As can be seen from these data, Christians collectively still comprise most of America, but the Christian category includes great diversity. Catholics are the single largest church, at around 25 percent; all Protestant sects and denominations total just over 50 percent; and non-Christians make up the remaining almost 20 percent. But there are important changes going on within the Christian category. What are often called the "mainstream" or traditional Christian denominations like Methodism and Baptism have diminished noticeably, while nontraditional identities like "evangelical" and "Pentecostal" have exploded. Also, the non-Christian groups have nearly doubled over the past two decades, with Muslims and Buddhists doubling, as well as the number of people who identify with no religion.

Most Americans are Christians, and Christianity is a monotheistic (one-god) religion, yet Paul Froese and Christopher Bader find that American Christians' ideas about their god are surprisingly diverse. The researchers go so far as to posit that American Christians hold four kinds of images of God, depending on how judgmental the deity is and how engaged in the world, he is a/an (1) Authoritative God, "a God who is both engaged in the world and judgmental," (2) Benevolent God, "a God who is engaged, yet nonjudgmental," (3) Critical God, "a God who is judgmental but disengaged," and (4) Distant God, "a nonjudgmental and disengaged God" (2010: 24). Perhaps this is one more reason why America needs a nonsectarian "civil" god. But Froese and Bader also find that these four versions of God make a difference in regard to other social and political attitudes and behaviors. For instance, believers in an Authoritative God are more likely than other believers to be politically

Table 14-2

Religions in the United States, 1990 and 2008: Christian Denominations

	Number, 1990	%, 1990	Number, 2008	%, 2008
Total U.S. adult population	175,440,000		228,182,000	
Total Christian groups	151,225,000	86.2	173,402,000	76.7
Catholic	46,004,000	26.3	57,199,000	25.1
Baptist	33,964,000	19.4	36,148,000	15.8
Protestant—no denomination	17,214,000	9.7	5,187,000	2.3
Methodist/Wesleyan	14,174,000	8.0	11,366,000	5.0
Lutheran	9,110,000	5.1	8,674,000	3.8
Christian—no denomination	8,073,000	4.6	16,834,000	7.4
Presbyterian	4,985,000	2.9	4,723,000	2.1
Pentecostal/Charismatic	3,191,000	1.8	7,948,000	3.5
Episcopalian/Anglican	3,042,000	1.7	2,405,000	1.1
Mormon	2,487,000	1.4	3,158,000	1.4
Churches of Christ	1,769,000	1.0	1,921,000	0.8
Jehovah's Witness	1,381,000	0.7	1,914,000	0.8
Seventh-Day Adventist	668,000	0.4	938,000	0.4
Assemblies of God	660,000	0.4	810,000	0.4
Congregational/United Church of Christ	438,000	0.2	736,000	0.3
Church of God	590,000	0.4	663,000	0.3
Evangelical	546,000	0.3	2,154,000	0.9

Source: American Religious Identification Survey. Reprinted with permission.

Table 14-3

Religions in the United States, 1990 and 2008: Non-Christian and None

	Number, 1990	%, 1990	Number, 2008	%, 2008
Total Other Religions	5,853,000		8,796,000	
Jewish	3,137,000	1.8	2,680,000	1.2
Muslim	527,000	0.3	1,349,000	0.6
Buddhist	404,000	0.2	1,189,000	0.5
New religious movements/Other	1,296,000	0.8	2,804,000	1.2
Total No Religion	14,331,000	8.2	34,169,000	15.0
Atheist	n/a	n/a	1,621,000	0.9
Agnostic	1,186,000	0.7	1,985,000	0.5
Refused	4,031,000	2.3	11,815,000	5.2

Source: American Religious Identification Survey. Reprinted with permission.

Box 14-3

America's 'Civil Religion'

If American religion is so diverse, and religion is typically seen sociologically as an integrative force, then what religion integrates American society? According to Robert Bellah, "there actually exists alongside of and rather clearly differentiated from the [Christian] churches" another religion which is equally "elaborate and well-institutionalized" (1967: 1). Overtly borrowing a term from Rousseau's *The Social Contract*, he called this second faith America's "civil religion." Central to this civil religion is the concept of "God," "a word that almost all Americans can accept but that means so many different things to so many different people that it is almost an empty sign" (3). The civil religion does not ordinarily make reference to Jesus or to specific beliefs and doctrines that might be divisive. As he admitted, the God of civil religion "is not only rather 'unitarian,' he is also on the austere side, much more related to order, law, and right than to salvation and love" (7). Neither the god nor the civil religion as a whole is "in any specific sense Christian," but the god is not a general god, and the civil religion is not a "religion in general" (8). Bellah believed America needs a civil religion because no sectarian religion, even Christianity, can or should be injected into civil affairs, yet there are occasions and circumstances in which a religious invocation seems appropriate, even essential. Bellah thus suggested that the civil religion provide a religious sanction that (most) Americans can accept. But why is a religious sanction required at all? His answer was that a society and its institutions require *legitimization* and *transcendental goals*. Religion not only explains but legitimates social arrangements; in the United States, where the people are sovereign and their will law, the civil religion assures citizens that "the ultimate sovereignty" lies with God. This both ensures the goodness and value of the laws and institutions and also provides a ground for judging and criticizing them: "The will of the people is not itself the criterion of right and wrong. There is a higher criterion in terms of which this will can be judged; it is possible that the people may be wrong" (4). Further, the sense of transcendental goals means that American decisions and actions are "going somewhere," part of a greater plan and a greater good—literally, that Americans are doing God's work on earth. This makes their history and their policies virtuous and important by definition. Even this does not exhaust the efficacy of the civil religion. It is "ceremonial" but not *merely* ceremonial; the civil religion achieves "national solidarity" (13) in a way that no other more sectarian religion can because it calls on "God" as a national symbol—one that means whatever the hearer wants it to mean. In other words, the fact that "the meaning of 'God' is by no means so clear or obvious" allows listeners and participants to hear and feel and believe whatever they are so inclined. It does not ask them to believe anything in particular but merely to believe something" (3).

conservative, to condemn adultery as immoral and wrong, and to expect God's intervention in nature. In fact, the political views of the various kinds of believers differ in a nearly straight line:

- Authoritative God believers: 10 percent liberal, 68 percent conservative

- Benevolent God believers: 21 percent liberal, 51 percent conservative

- Critical God believers: 28 percent liberal, 36 percent conservative

- Distant God believers: 45 percent liberal, 26 percent conservative.

(Comparatively, atheists in the United States are 63 percent liberal and 16 percent conservative, making Distant God believers politically more similar to atheists than to their Authoritative God coreligionists.)

Other research supports the link between religion and important social variables. The Pew Forum U.S. Religious Landscape Survey measured religion and political party affiliation (see Table 14-4). For instance, the data show that Evangelicals and Mormons identify themselves more as politically conservative than do Catholics, mainline Protestants, non-Christians, and the nonreligious.

Two final points are worth making about American religion. The first concerns the personalistic nature of religion in the United States. Many sociologists, from Robert Wuthnow to Thomas Luckmann, have commented on Americans' individualistic approach to religion, not only choosing their religion voluntarily but

Table 14-4

Religious Affiliation and Political Party Affiliation in the U.S.

Religion	% Republican or Leaning Republican	% Democratic or Leaning Democratic
Catholic	33	48
Mainline Protestant	41	43
Evangelical Protestant	50	34
Historically Black Churches	10	77
Mormon	65	22
Jewish	24	66
Muslim	11	63
Buddhist	18	66
Unaffiliated	23	55

interpreting, mixing, and even inventing the religion that is right for them. In interviews with Americans about their religion, a woman named Sheila told Robert Bellah that her religion was "Sheilaism." Others have noted that Americans often seem to be on a personal religious quest or journey, what Wuthnow called a spirituality of seeking. Extending this theme, Richard Madsen writes that for Americans, religious "membership is based on an active voluntary choice" (2009: 1269), such that "religious individualism is the American religion" (1270).

The individualist quality of American religion means that Americans choose a religion for

© George Muresan, 2012. Under license from Shutterstock, Inc.

personal reasons, in particular according to how the religion "feels" to them. Religious "satisfaction" is a critical element of the religion that one selects. This also suggests that Americans tend to "try out" a number of religions before they settle on one; this accounts for the "seeking" characteristic of American religion. But Madsen stresses that Americans tend to *find* a religion eventually; they do not seek indefinitely, so "the most typical religious act in America is not seeking but seeking/finding" (1283). Change of religious affiliation, thus, is part and parcel of the American religious experience. But Madsen adds that "When people shift affiliations, it is mostly *within*, not between these broad traditions" such as Protestant or Catholic, etc. (1293). In other words, the rate of conversion from, say, Catholic to Jewish or even from Catholic to Protestant is relatively low. Instead, people tend to convert from one mainline Protestant denomination to another, or from one variety of Judaism to another. The implication of this discovery is that American religion is a set of continents or large islands, and people are more likely to relocate within their continent or island than to hop from one continent/island to another. Madsen characterizes this arrangement as the "archipelago" of American religion, in which Americans tend to move to a "nearby" religion but seldom to a remote one. Part of the explanation of this tendency is the power or pull of one's starting religion or religious tradition. As Madsen summarizes it, American religion is *porous* but it is also viscous, and "the viscosity of ritual tradition limits the effects of this porosity" (1294).

The second point follows the first. Since Americans tend to choose their religion for individual/emotional reasons, Americans tend to choose particularly individualistic and emotional religions—but still ones within the Christian tradition. As a result, two of the fastest-growing categories of American religion are evangelicalism and Pentecostalism. Evangelicalism is a form of (mostly Protestant) Christianity that emphasizes individual experience and salvation—the "born-again" experience—and the authority of the Bible. "Evangelical" is not a religion or even a denomination but a style of Christianity, with which over one-third of Americans identify. Evangelicalism is associated with traditional or conservative social and moral attitudes, and in the late twentieth century the evangelical movement became politically active in the form of organizations like the Moral Majority, the Christian Coalition, and Focus on the Family. Pentecostalism is another style of (mostly Protestant) Christianity that stresses an even more personal encounter with "the holy spirit," resulting in "spiritual gifts" like speaking in tongues, prophesying, and the power of healing. Among its recent institutional forms is the Vineyard movement.

FURTHER TOPICS IN THE SOCIOLOGY OF RELIGION

Sociologists, from the earliest days of the field until today, have turned their attention to a number of important issues and changes in religion, including secularization, new religious movements, and fundamentalism.

Secularization

As can be easily appreciated, sociologists from Comte and Marx to Durkheim and Weber thought that they saw—and often expected and even desired—a decline in religiosity, at least in the Christian world. Comte believed that religion was an idea for an earlier and more primitive kind of society, while Marx theorized religion as a kind of false consciousness, a substitute for "real" social justice and one that would fade away when real justice was achieved. Weber was the most explicit in describing the relationship between religion and "modern" society: As sociology essentially teaches, a religion is intimately interdependent with its wider social setting. However, for Weber the social setting of "modernization" was basically inhospitable to religion. It was not that modern people hate religion but rather that the attitudes and practices of modern society were like an infertile field in which religion could not grow. Specifically, Weber regarded modernization as a process of increasing urbanization, industrialization, bureaucracy, rationalization (not necessarily increasing "rationality" but increasing efficiency, calculation, and standardization), and secularization. Weber called this the "disenchantment" of the world and was not entirely happy to see it come, since it was part of the so-called "iron cage" of modernization.

Since the founding days of sociology, "secularization theory" has become a familiar if not taken-for-granted aspect of the field. Through the 1960s, the assumption was generally that religion would not survive in the modern world, and religiosity was a doomed anachronism. Even in those days, though, secularization was understood in a variety of ways. For the functionalist Talcott Parsons, it meant differentiation. Religion, which had formerly pervaded the society and culture, was becoming a distinct and separate institution in society, a subsystem of the greater social system. This was not necessarily disastrous for religion. In a way, consolidating into a discrete institution could strengthen religion and also establish a formal, institutional link between it and the rest of society. Religion could also become *more* integrated with society by abandoning some of its more specifically "religious" facets and becoming more social and more secular.

Peter Berger also explored the question of secularization, which he defined in his famous *The*

Sacred Canopy as "the process by which sectors of society and culture are removed from the domination of religious institutions and symbols" (1967: 107). Collectively and institutionally, religion retreats to its limited domain of "church," while individually, religion becomes a less important and less motivational force. One of the main reasons for secularization, he proposed, was religious pluralism: as many religions came to coexist in a society, the society had to distance itself from religion and take a neutral stance (e.g., the well-known "separation of church and state"). "Public" religion in such a situation would be divisive and impolite. Note that this analysis is exactly the opposite of Rodney Stark's, who thought that many competing "religious firms" would instead *increase* the religiosity of society.

Whatever its particular form, secularization theory has proved to be basically wrong about the relationship between religion and modern society. Phenomena like fundamentalism and new religious movements or "cults" have demonstrated the resilience of religion (see below). Yet, there is little doubt that religion is not as unified or as pervasively powerful as it may once have been. For instance, as the American Religious Identification Survey data illustrate, the number of people who do not identify with any religion has risen dramatically in recent years. Not all—or even most—of these unaffiliated or disaffiliated people consider themselves "atheists," so sociologists have had to devise other terms and concepts for them, one of the catchiest of which is the "nones." The "nones" are the folks who, when asked about their religion, reply, "None."

Joseph Baker and Buster Smith (2009a, 2009b) have conducted a couple of research projects on the nones, finding social determinants and social characteristics of the category. Nones, as Wilson and Sherkat also mentioned, are more likely to have been raised in religiously unaffiliated families and to have participated in religion less as children. They are also more likely to be married to nones and to have a peer group of nones (whether these latter are causes or effects of nonreligiosity is an open question). Wilson and Sherkat also discovered that nones are a diverse category, consisting of atheists, agnostics, and "unchurched believers," with different characteristics. Atheists, not surprisingly, were the most completely antireligious group, with the lowest rates of religious affiliation (less than 20 percent), of religious activity like prayer, and of self-description as "spiritual." Over half of agnostics were affiliated with a religion, with just less than half avowing some sort of "spirituality" for themselves and half at least occasionally praying. The "unchurched believers" were more like regular believers than like atheists or agnostics: comprising perhaps 50 percent of all nones, most of them pray and regard themselves as "religious" and "spiritual."

A productive approach to secularization, then, is not so much to oppose "the religious" to the "nonreligious" or "antireligious" as to look for alternative ways to be religious and social determinants of those alternatives. David Ley and Bruce Martin, based on Canadian data, suggested that the new urban lifestyle sometimes dubbed "gentrification" was related to lower levels of conventional religiosity. The secularists in their study, who were also the urbanites, shared a set of traits and experiences: "the young adult stage in the life-cycle (20–29 age-group), small households, post-secondary educational attainment, and professional or managerial occupations" (1993: 223). Related to these demographic features were changes in the nature of social life in the urban neighborhood, which "does not disappear, but it is redefined around a new set of axes expressive of changing community values" (228). More amusingly, Ley and Martin described how "Sunday brunch congregations at neighborhood restaurants are four times more numerous than the congregations of local churches" (229). Most importantly, though, they also stated that these same districts "have become the core of the New Age movement" in certain cities.

What such research implies is that religion is not so much vanishing as transforming. In other words, people are not necessarily *less* religious, they are just *differently* religious. Colin Campbell revived Ernst Troeltsch's concept of "mystical religion" to suggest that urban, educated, middle- and upper-class people may be attracted to a less institutional and even more individualistic kind of religion, the kind associated with New Age religions and "spirituality." Campbell reminded us that Troeltsch himself believed spiritual/mystical religion to be uniquely compatible with modern society because it "had a basic affinity with the idealistic and aesthetic individualism that was a feature of the educated classes" (Campbell 1978: 155). Such a modern spirituality is more abstract but also more inclusive than institutional religion; it is tolerant as well as syncretistic, absorbing multiple influences from religions and nonreligions alike. It is therefore creative and personal, open to interpretation, and comparatively "indifferent" to issues of "truth"—and therefore more immune to refutation. Campbell concluded that such a mystical/individual style of religion has "adaptive superiority" (152) over other sorts of religion in a modern, scientific, pluralistic context.

Fundamentalism

The strongest evidence of the inadequacy of traditional secularization theory is the emergence of a particularly militant kind of religion generally known as fundamentalism. Fundamentalism, like evangelicalism or Pentecostalism, is not a specific religion but rather a style of religion. In fact, fundamentalism is not a uniquely religious concept, as a person or group can be "fundamentalist" about anything, so long as she/he tries to preserve or revert to the "fundamentals"—the original and/or basic ideas and practices—of that thing. Fundamentalism then, in all its forms, is not only a movement but a movement *against* something. Religious fundamentalism is religion *in opposition*, and as a thoroughly modern phenomenon, it is religion to some extent opposed to modernity.

George Marsden, for instance, has defined a fundamentalist as "an evangelical Protestant who is militantly opposed to liberal theologies and to some aspects of secularism in modern culture" (1990: 22). But that cannot do, as there could be no non-Protestant fundamentalisms, let alone any non-Christian ones. Of course, in the United States, fundamentalism as such began in the early 1900s as a Protestant resistance to the modernizing of religion and society, but that does not make fundamentalism an inherently Protestant phenomenon. Fundamentalism can and does appear as an option in any and all religions, and when it does it takes the form of, as Gabriel Almond, Scott Appleby, and Emmanuel Sivan (2002) titled their book, "strong religion."

In their review of the sociology of fundamentalism, Michael Emerson and David Hartman relate its prominence and pervasiveness to Weber's ideas about modernization and Berger's concept of the "sacred canopy." As a sacred canopy, religion was supposed to function as an embracing source of identity and integration. However, under the forces of urbanization, rationalization, and pluralism, "modernization rips the sacred canopy, and, at best, people are left with sacred umbrellas" (Emerson and Hartman 2006: 129). Fundamentalism, thus, can be seen as an attempt to secure the patch of religious coverage that still exists and to restore religion (as understood by any particular fundamentalist movement) to its former place and function. For fundamentalists, "Western versions of modernization rush over them in a tidal wave of change, ripping apart communities, values, social ties, and meaning. To these changes, some groups say, 'No'" (131). This is why, in addition to their strong religious beliefs, "fundamentalists are strong traditionalists on matters of family and gender relations" (135). They are also often strong nationalists on matters of political identity. American fundamentalists tend to glorify not only God but country, seeing America as a special

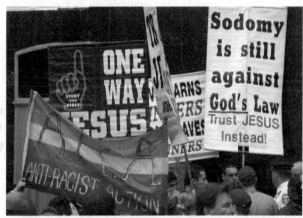

© Benjamin F. Haith, 2012. Under license from Shutterstock, Inc.

Christian society, just as Hindu fundamentalists (practitioners of *Hindutva* or "Hindu-ness") tend to glorify not only Hinduism but India, seeing India as a special Hindu society. And Hindu fundamentalism, like Islamic fundamentalism, experiences one other threat that most American fundamentalists do not: Western society, including Christianity, as a foreign, invasive, and socially disruptive force.

Finally, while fundamentalism is a style of religion very much in the name and the service of "tradition," it is also a highly modern kind of movement itself. As Lechner asserts, in modernist societies, "sociocultural order becomes revisable in principle" (1985: 245): We moderns, individualist market actors that we are, can choose and must choose, including the very social ideas, relations, and institutions that we will live by. Fundamentalism may seem, and claim, to be "a mode of revitalization aimed at (re)asserting and (re)establishing absolute values, (re)organizing different spheres of life in terms of those values, and thereby dedifferentiating aspects of (social) life" (245), but it is also a choice and an option. One can be a liberal/mainline religionist, one can be a secularist, one can join a new religious movement, or one can join a fundamentalist movement. But no matter what, one chooses, and one's choice is only one of an indefinite number of options. Fundamentalism is, therefore, a possible form or style of modern religion, but it "is inevitable in an age which has destroyed so many certainties by which faith once expressed itself and upon which it relied" (252).

Chapter 15

Top-Down Power: The State

In the early weeks of 2011, the world watched as revolutions broke out in the Arab world, first in Tunisia and then Egypt, where longtime autocracies (Zine el Abidine Ben Ali had ruled in Tunisia since 1987, and Hosni Mubarak in Egypt since 1981) were overthrown by popular mass movements. In both countries, political dissatisfaction and economic inequality had simmered for decades. Foreign countries like the United States had long advocated democracy for the region; spreading democracy was one of the explicit motivations for the invasions of Afghanistan (2001) and Iraq (2003). However, it was only when Tunisia's Ben Ali declared himself the winner of a fifth term by a vote of 89.6 percent and when a protester named Mohamed Bouazizi set himself publicly on fire in response that diverse elements of the society such as union members, human rights activists, and the unemployed took to the streets. After a month of protests and one hundred deaths, Ben Ali fled Tunisia on January 14, 2011. Inspired by this success, demonstrations against Egypt's Mubarak began on January 25, with workers joining students and other protesters with general labor strikes in early February that essentially shut down the country's economy. On February 11, 2011, Mubarak resigned.

In both cases, observers credited much of the success of the movements to new electronic media like Facebook and Twitter, and the protests in Egypt were immediately coordinated by young, media-savvy leaders. And because of the collapse of these widely unpopular governments and of the circulation of the news in the Arab world and beyond, protests also broke out in other countries, from Bahrain and Saudi Arabia to Syria and Libya—with Libya's dictator Muammar Gaddafi finally captured and killed in October 2011.

One of the first questions that socially aware thinkers asked was how people should organize and govern themselves. The ancient Greek city-states knew of each other's political systems, and Plato and Aristotle analyzed and compared those systems. Indeed, the English word "politics" derives from the Greek name for the city-state, the *polis*, and in 350 BCE Aristotle's book, *Politics*, appeared, in which he asserted that the human is a "political animal," that is, that humans always—and most happily—live in well-ordered societies. Plato went so far as to imagine an ideal society in *The Republic*, where every aspect of social life was overseen by an enlightened leader (a philosopher-king) and protected by a class of Guardians. Further and more important, every aspect of social life was carefully designed to contribute to the good of society, from education and physical exercise to arts and music.

Neither Plato nor Aristotle was a sociologist, yet both agreed and stressed that politics was about much more than "government" or even "power." Every society is what Durkheim called a "moral community," a collectivity of people who ideally share a set of values, most critically a notion of the "good society." As Aristotle wrote in the first sentence of *Politics*, "every community is established with a view to some good; for mankind always act in order to obtain that which they think good. But, if all communities aim at some good, the state or political community, which is the highest of all, and which embraces all the rest, aims at good in a greater degree than any other, and at the highest good" (Aristotle 2011).

Politics, then, is and always has been a thoroughly social matter. Politics involves networks, groups, and institutions, but also beliefs, values, interactions, and inequalities of various kinds. Accordingly, politics has preoccupied social

theorists for centuries; in fact, "political philosophy" was the precursor to much of modern sociology. Nicolo Machiavelli, for instance, in his famous *The Prince* (written in the early 1500s) offered advice to the would-be monarch on how best to govern his realm, ultimately concluding that it was better to be feared than loved. In the mid-1600s Thomas Hobbes turned to a different question, the supposed history of political institutions. In his 1651 *Leviathan* he speculated on life in the absence of a central government and concluded that once upon a time humans had lived in a "state of nature" without rules or rulers. In this state of nature and of rough individual equality, if two or more people sought the same things they would necessarily become competitors and enemies. The outcome, he believed, was a war of all against all, which produced a life that was "solitary, nasty, poor, brutish, and short." Here, we see a social theory premised on a certain view of human nature, in this case a nature defined by "three principal causes of quarrel," namely competition, diffidence, and glory. In other words, social theory and political theory were (and are) moral

Protesters in Tahrir Square in Cairo, Egypt, 2011.

theory. Hobbes' conclusion was that humans need a strong leader, a king, to curb their inherently selfish and violent nature.

A century later Jean-Jacques Rousseau asked the same question but came to the opposite conclusion. In his 1762 *The Social Contract* Rousseau (writing after the reign of a strong king, Louis XIV) suggested that in the "state of nature" humans were relatively equal and happy and, above all else, free. To secure that equality, happiness, and freedom, they voluntarily entered into a "social contract" that established certain institutions and powers—in a word, a government. However, as the U.S. Declaration of Independence—a statement of intention to create a government on the basis of the social contract—clearly contends, "whenever any form of government becomes destructive of these ends, it is the right of the people to alter or abolish it and to institute new government." Thus, Rousseau's message was that governments (as phrased once again by Thomas Jefferson) "are instituted among men, deriving their just powers from the consent of the governed" and therefore that different societies might derive different contracts and that contracts/political systems might change over time.

TOWARD A SOCIOLOGY OF POLITICS

In the nineteenth century there were various efforts to establish just political systems for the benefit of the governed. Even before 1800, the American and French revolutions, like the Tunisian and Egyptian ones mentioned earlier, had toppled governments that the revolutionaries regarded as unfair and oppressive. Early figures who would contribute to the formation of sociology such as Alexis de Tocqueville and Saint-Simon were witnesses to these events. Auguste Comte (1798–1857) and Karl Marx (1818–83) lived through the widespread European revolutions of 1848, leading Marx to compose his *The Eighteenth Brumaire of Louis Bonaparte* in 1851–52, analyzing the (unsuccessful) revolution in France. It was also this political turmoil, and the economic

Thomas Hobbes

© Georgios Kollidas, 2012. Under license from Shutterstock, Inc.

processes underlying it—urbanization, industrialization, and capitalism—that transformed Marx from a philosopher to an economic and political theorist and that produced his theory of "scientific socialism" describing the historical forms of society as results of the evolving modes of production. Again, as with Plato and Aristotle, politics—the right establishment and regulation of social order—was a central concern of nineteenth-century thinkers and early sociologists, set within the more general context of the "good society."

Politics and Power

Politics from the sociological point of view refers to the concepts and values, the practices and relationships, and the institutions organizing how people achieve and maintain social order. It involves such matters as decision making, conflict resolution, rule creation and enforcement, defense, offense, and diplomacy. We tend to identify politics with "government," but of course government is only the most formal and institutional expression of politics. In the sense of politics offered by thinkers from Plato and Aristotle to Marx, the term covers much more than government, including the most basic experiences of socialization as well as education, class structure, religion, and the "micropolitics" of everyday interpersonal interaction.

Fundamental to politics is the concept of power. In fact, one more technical definition of politics might be the processes and practices by which individuals, groups, or institutions acquire and exercise power. Max Weber defined power as "the probability that one actor in a social relationship will be in a position to carry out his will despite resistance, regardless of the basis on which this probability rests" (1997: 152). More generally, we might think of power as the capacity of an individual, group, or institution to control the course and outcome of social interactions. The upshot of these sociological definitions is that power is not a "thing" and certainly not a property of a "powerful" person or group, but rather a social relationship. Dennis Wrong (see below) has said that power is "a particular kind of social relation. . . . People exercise mutual influence and control over one another's behavior in all social interaction—in fact, that is what we *mean* by social interaction" (1968: 673). Like Weber and Wrong, political scientist Hannah Arendt has insisted that power is entirely social:

> Power corresponds to the human ability not just to act but to act in concert. Power is never the property of an individual; it belongs to a group and remains in existence only so long as the group keeps together. When we say of somebody that he is "in power" we actually refer to his being empowered by a certain number of people to act in their name. The moment the group, from which the power originated to begin with . . . disappears, "his power" also vanishes. (1969: 44)

In short, no matter how much force a leader may be able to exert, power always requires the complicity, the cooperation, or at least the submission of those who are under the power. (The Tunisian and Egyptian, and American and French, revolutions demonstrated how tenuous "power," even dictatorial power, really is.)

Sociologists also recognize that power comes in multiple forms and has multiple bases, specifically

- Authority
- Persuasion
- Coercion

Authority

Weber discussed authority extensively, defining it as legitimate power, that is, power that those under power believe that the power holder has a legitimate right to exercise. The point that Weber emphasized was that "legitimacy" is a crucial aspect of power: if followers feel that the power of a person, group, or institution is legitimate, appropriate, just, and rightful, then they are more likely to submit to it. In fact, granting legitimacy is in itself a form of submission.

Charisma is the personal charm or grace of the individual that makes others want to follow him/her.

© Sanjay Deva, 2012. Under license from Shutterstock, Inc.

For Weber, authority could come in three, sometimes overlapping, varieties. The first type is traditional authority, which usually derives from custom or habit, generally from practices of the past. For instance, much of the authority of royalty or of religious figures is traditional. This sort of power is often represented or performed in rituals and through symbols. When a king or queen is coronated or when an American president is inaugurated, there are rituals: oaths are taken, flags are displayed, music is played, and sometimes objects like crowns or scepters or books are handled. For scholars (and college graduates), robes and mortarboards or tams are worn to signify their accession to and possession of traditional authority.

Weber's second type of authority is rational-legal authority, which derives its legitimacy from formal and often written rules, from explicit offices, and from the competence one shows in navigating these systems. The terms of rational-legal authority are laws, regulations, policies, documentation and files, specialized training, degrees and appointments and ordinations, contracts, elections, and all the bureaucratic apparatus that Weber associated with modern society (although there were, to be sure, rational-legal forces operating in premodern societies).

Charismatic authority comprised Weber's third type of authority. Charisma comes from some personal quality of the power-holder, from the strength of his or her personality, or from some purported "revelations, heroism, or other leadership qualities of an individual" (Weber 1919: 2). It is an ineffable charm, a force of will, a "gift of grace." It is a characteristic of many successful prophets and politicians: Gandhi had it, as did John F. Kennedy and Ronald Reagan. Some leaders actively promote it in a "cult of personality," as with Stalin or Saddam Hussein or Kim Jong-Il. People are naturally inclined to affiliate with and follow such "powerful" personalities.

Persuasion

Leaders with authority often have and use persuasion, the ability to influence or manipulate people to do the things they want those people to do. Persuasion usually involves the capacity to control some socially valued practice or commodity. For instance, one of the most common and important sources of persuasion is speaking: being persuasive often means being able to give reasons, to present an argument, to be convincing, or specifically, to make a good speech. American formal politics is largely a matter of speechmaking and debating. Persuasion also can come from control of access to valuables like money and grades as well as more symbolic goods like prestige, respect, or reputation. Notice that a formal political agent like a police officer has simultaneously traditional authority (the power of the uniform and badge), rational-legal authority (the power of the office and the law), and ideally, persuasive power (the ability to explain the importance of proper behavior).

Coercion

Coercion is the use or threat of force. It is the power of the fist and the gun. For Arendt, coercion only appears where power fails: there is no need to use force when authority and persuasion work, and force is thusly always illegitimate (think of the coercion practiced by Gaddafi against "his people" in Libya). Coercion too is social. At the very least, it is people using force on other people. But more, coercion almost always entails some form of social organization, an institution of force like the police or the army, and it is always a social relationship. People may surrender to superior force, but at a certain point they may be willing to suffer injury and death to overthrow that force.

Sociological Advances in the Study of Power

Since Weber's time, because power is such a crucial concept in politics and society, the thinking on the nature of power has continued to mature. For instance, during his time in prison in Italy for his communist activities, Antonio Gramsci reconsidered the standard Marxist view of power, which had power situated in the "base" or material/economic aspect of society, the mode

Dennis Wrong on Defining Social Power

The fact that power is always and necessarily a social relationship means that it is never really "in" the power-holder but *between* the power-holder and those held in power. This further means, as Wrong discussed in his essay on the problems and difficulties of defining power, that power relations are never completely "asymmetrical" or one direction, that is, top-down (1968: 673). "Thus if we treat power relations as exclusively hierarchical and unilateral, we overlook an entire class of relations between persons or groups in which the control of one person or group over the other with reference to a particular scope is balanced by the control of the other in a different scope" (674). He called this "intercursive power" or the situation in which "the power of each party in a relationship is countervailed by that of the other, with procedures for bargaining or joint decision making governing their relations when matters affecting the goals and interests of both are involved" (674). The consequence of this bilateral or symmetrical nature of power is that power relations are constructed rather than "given" and that they can be negotiated, contested, and even defeated. Wrong described four ways in which "power subjects may attempt to combat or resist the power of an integral power holder" (675):

1. First, "they may strive to exercise countervailing power over him in order to transform his integral power into a system of intercursive power," which Wrong basically recognized as "democracy."

2. Second, "they may set limits to the extensiveness (the number of power subjects), *comprehensiveness* (the number of scopes), and *intensity* (the range of options within particular scopes," which Wrong equated to constitutional government.

3. Third, "they may destroy his integral power altogether, leaving the acts he formerly controlled open to free and self-determined choice," which Wrong considered anarchy.

4. Fourth, "they may seek to supplant him by acquiring and exercising his integral power themselves," in other words, revolution or some other form of power-competition within the system.

Finally, Wrong observed that "having power" and "exercising power" are not identical: individuals, groups, and institutions may possess power, or the potential for power, that they do not use or do not even realize that they possess. Therefore, *if* an actor is believed to be powerful, *if* he knows that others hold such a belief, and *if* he encourages it and resolves to make use of it by intervening in or punishing actions by others who do not comply with his wishes, *then* he truly has power and his power has indeed been conferred upon him by the attributions, perhaps initially without foundation, of others. But if he is unaware that others believe him powerful, or if he does not take their belief seriously in planning his own projects, then he has no power and the belief that he has is mistaken. (679)

of production. Gramsci instead proposed that an important kind of power, which he called hegemony, emanates from the "superstructure" or ideology of a society, taking the form of a kind of moral and intellectual leadership exerted by those in higher social positions on those in lower positions. Later interpreter Raymond Williams understood "superstructure" not only as explicit legal and political institutions but also as "forms of consciousness" (a worldview) and "political and cultural practices" in and through which people work out their social, economic, and political relations (1977: 77). For Gramsci, then, "government" (see below) referred to the actual apparatus of official political power and enforcement, while "hegemony" meant the "'spontaneous' consent given by the great masses of the population to the general direction imposed on social life by the dominant fundamental group [i.e., the dominant class]; this consent is 'historically' caused by the prestige (and consequent confidence) which the dominant group enjoys because of its position and function in the world of production" (1971: 12). In a word, hegemony is *invisible power*, taken-for-granted power, "naturalized" power. One of the most important processes for the construction and inculcation of this social consciousness, Gramsci insisted, was education, which was intended "to raise the great mass of the population to a particular cultural and moral level, a level (or type) which corresponds to the needs of the productive forces for development, and hence to the interests of the ruling class" (258).

More recently, Steven Lukes (1974) stressed the need to attend to the invisible or inaccessible aspects of power. Specifically, Lukes regarded the familiar overt kind of power, relating to conspicuous behavior, decision making, and of course actual conflict, as merely the first dimension of power. The second and more subtle dimension relates to control over the political agenda, what questions are asked and how issues are defined (what has been called "convening power"). The third and most covert dimension of power consists of influence over people's thoughts and wishes, their values and preferences, leading them to misunderstand their own interests—to want what is not in their interest and to oppose what is. In so doing, power can prevent conflict or even the expression of differences and grievances by producing thoughts and perceptions that are fundamental distortions of social reality. One example of this type of analysis is Thomas Frank's *What's the Matter with Kansas?* (2004).

Most influentially, Michel Foucault explored the kind of invisible power identified by Gramsci and Lukes in terms of language and the human body. According to Foucault, every society includes or is a "discursive regime," a certain way of talking about the world including the social relationships in the world. This social discourse establishes the limits of what is possible to think in a particular time and place and how we frame questions and seek answers. One example would be the contemporary discourse of "rights," which has definitely not been a part of all societies' talk. Perhaps more insidious is what he called "techniques of power." By studying institutions like the prison, the hospital, or the mental asylum, Foucault identified precise and often taken-for-granted techniques of control such as surveillance, record keeping, diagnostic labels, physical restraint, and of course, detention or imprisonment—often applied directly to the body and thus representing "a 'physics' or an 'anatomy' of power, a technology" (1977: 215). Most covert and pervasive of all are what he called "technologies of the self" or socially specific knowledge and habits or strategies that "permit individuals to effect, by their own means or with the help of others, a certain number of

operations on their own bodies and souls, thoughts, conduct, and way of being, so as to transform themselves in order to attain a certain state of happiness, purity, wisdom, perfection, or immortality" (1988: 18). This is the political side of socialization, in which individuals are first made into social actors and then continually called on to monitor and evaluate themselves.

The Distribution of Power: Pluralism vs. Power Elite

In the modern world and among much of the general public, power is generally equated to "government," but that perception is inadequate. Power is more dispersed and often more informal than government. This leads to a question that has preoccupied sociologists as well as political scientists: *where* exactly is power? The two main contrasting perspectives are

1. pluralism

2. power elite

The pluralist position claims that power is more or less diffused through a society, that is, there are multiple and competing social sites of power. For instance, in modern democracies (see below), there are ordinarily at least two—and often many more—political parties vying for and sharing power. There are also many interest groups in society with different amounts and kinds of power. Some of these interest groups are formally institutionalized, as in the NAACP (National Association for the Advancement of Colored People), the ASPCA (American Society for the Prevention of Cruelty to Animals), the AARP, the NRA (National Rifle Association), and many more. Some of these groups and organizations are composed of people with a certain shared physical or social characteristic, while others contain people with a single interest or agenda. Some, like the American Medical Association (AMA) or the American Sociological Association (ASA), represent a profession and serve not only to create relationships, share knowledge, and set standards within the profession, but to promote the interests of the profession to the wider society and government. Some interest groups are stable and longstanding, while others are new or ad hoc, appearing and disappearing as needs and circumstances merit.

Thus, in the pluralist view, power can never be monopolized by one group or party. Rather, power and the policies and laws that emerge from it are the product of a negotiation or struggle, often a compromise, between these various power groups and pressure groups. Temporary or lasting coalitions may develop between groups, but their interests—as well as their leaders—remain relatively distinct. However, in 1956 C. Wright Mills asserted that interests and even leaders are not as distinct as pluralism contends, and therefore, that power is not nearly as distributed as in the pluralist model. Rather, as the title of his book, *The Power Elite*, suggests, most of the crucial power is centralized in a few hands which

are, further, highly interlocked. Early in his book, Mills wrote:

> The power elite is composed of men whose positions enable them to transcend the ordinary environments of ordinary men and women; they are in positions to make decisions having major consequences. . . . For they are in command of the major hierarchies and organizations of modern society. They rule the big corporations. They run the machinery of the state and claim its prerogatives. They direct the military establishment. They occupy the strategic command posts of the social structure, in which are now centered the effective means of the power and the wealth and the celebrity which they enjoy. (1956: 3–4)

In a word, a small number of people occupy "the top command posts of society," which are concentrated in three main fields—government, military, and business. These three social areas are deeply enmeshed: business leaders become government leaders and vice versa, while

Protesters in Los Angeles exercise the pluralist "power of the people" against government and corporations.

© Gerry Boughan, 2012. Under license from Shutterstock, Inc.

Box 15-1

The Global Elite

While Mills' book was written explicitly to describe the power elite in the United States, it is applicable to most if not all modern societies, as well as most if not all complex and stratified societies throughout time. Contemporary European, Middle Eastern, and Latin American states have their power elite, as did ancient Greece, Rome, and Egypt. Nor is it unique to capitalism: present-day communist China and the former Soviet Union exhibited similar ties between political, military, and economic leaders. In fact, the power elite are not constrained by national boundaries at all. Many prominent families from other countries send future leaders to the United States or other prestigious nations for education. The last shah of Iran was educated in Switzerland, while Benazir Bhutto of Pakistan obtained a degree from Radcliffe College of Harvard University. In a 2011 article in *The Atlantic* Chrystia Freeland concluded that globalization has contributed to "the rise of a new super-elite that consists, to a notable degree, of . . . hardworking, highly educated, jet-setting meritocrats who feel that they are the deserving winners of a tough, worldwide

economic competition—and many of them, as a result, have an ambivalent attitude toward those of us who didn't succeed so spectacularly." Even more importantly and problematically, "they are becoming a transglobal community of peers who have more in common with one another than with their countrymen back home. Whether they maintain primary residences in New York or Hong Kong, Moscow or Mumbai, today's super-rich are increasingly a nation unto themselves." Most interestingly, Freeland insists that the new global elite still maintains strong interpersonal ties like past elites, but the current site of much of this mingling and networking is the international conference circuit. At meetings like the World Economic Forum, the Aspen Ideas Festival, or Google's Zeitgeist event, figures from Archbishop Desmond Tutu to former president Bill Clinton, Google CEO Eric Schmidt, and Starbucks CEO Howard Schultz talk, socialize, speculate on, and plan the future of the global society—the society that the rest of us will be living in some day.

military and business are mutually dependent (the military needs corporate contractors to provide their supplies, and corporations need military contracts), and government and military often and ideally coincide (the American president is also the military commander-in-chief).

Surrounding and intermingling with the three primary fields of leadership are a coterie of "advisers and consultants, spokesmen and opinion-makers" who are often "the captains of their higher thought and decision," not to mention "those professional celebrities who live by being continually displayed but are never, so long as they remain celebrities, displayed enough" (Mills 4). And not only do these various types share power and interests, but they also share attitudes and values. This is partly because they come from similar social backgrounds and partly because they undergo similar "apprenticeships." Thomas Dye (2002) has calculated that 54 percent of top business leaders and 42 percent of the highest government officials in the United States attended just twelve universities such as Yale, Harvard, Stanford, and Princeton. Hence, the power elite often know each other personally, adding

informal to formal connections. They literally sometimes intermarry, and they may travel or vacation together.

Of course, the pluralist and power elite models are not mutually exclusive. There may be a small clique of society with an inordinate amount of official and unofficial power, while the rest of society divides up the remaining (and perhaps substantial) power. As Wrong and others have stated, power is never one-dimensional or one-directional—and the power elite in Tunisia and Egypt, not to mention the former Soviet Union, have certainly learned that lesson.

TYPES OF STATE POLITICS OR 'GOVERNMENT'

Every piece of land on earth (with the possible exception of Antarctica) has been claimed by some state—occasionally more than one. All people are affected by state politics; therefore, state politics is the most significant kind of politics for most human beings today, although certainly not for all. It is imperative, then, to understand how states shape our individual and collective existence.

In a lecture published as *Politics as a Vocation*, Weber offered a simple definition of the state: "a human community that (successfully) claims the *monopoly of the legitimate use of physical force* within a given territory" (1919: 1). This deceptively brief definition carries a lot of social import. First there is the question of territory: a state is by nature a territorial unit, a land with (ideally) clear and recognized boundaries. The population within those boundaries is thereby subjected to the power of the state (through such mechanisms as "citizenship"). Second there is the question of "legitimate force" and what makes its coercive power legitimate. The state, within its territorial domain, grants itself sole right to arrest, to punish, and in some cases, to kill its members; it even maintains institutions of legitimate force, such as police departments, prison systems, and armies. Individuals and substate groups cannot have their own police or prisons or armies, except by permission of the state (states like the United States may and do "hire out" these functions to private prison-operating companies like Corrections Corporation of America or private "security" or mercenary contractors like the company formerly known as Blackwater—which has changed its name to Xe—or Airborne Tactical Advantage Company). Moreover, the state (perhaps hegemonically) insists that its force and its monopoly over that force *are* legitimate, that the state has a right to use force and uses that force rightly. Obviously, not everyone necessarily agrees.

This raises a critical point that is explored later, namely, the *claim* and the *success* of the claim to coercive monopoly. A state may assert a monopoly of legitimate force, but members of the society may contest that assertion. The citizens of Tunisia, Egypt, and Libya certainly contested it, as did the colonists of pre-independence America. So, individuals or groups within and under the authority of the state may not respect the state's claim to its legitimate monopoly of force, nor may other states or nonstate groups respect it. Therefore, the state's monopoly of force is always

a social accomplishment and may ultimately fail, in the form of revolution, separatism, conquest, invasion, or other such means.

Nevertheless, while in possession of the mechanisms of power, the state must organize that power in some fashion. The main varieties of official state politics, or roughly "government," have included:

Monarchy Probably the oldest and most common arrangement of state power is monarchy, literally "one-rule." A single individual—often a king or emperor—claims the right to rule, based on some combination of tradition, rational-legal authority, and military might; such power is usually hereditary, as the monarch attempts to transfer power to his/her kin. Further, the ruling family frequently uses notions of "nobility" or "royalty" to justify their rule, as well as religious legitimation such as "the divine right of kings" (Europe) or "the mandate of heaven" (China). The classic statement of monarchy came from France's King Louis XIV, who said, *"L'état c'est moi"*—I am the state.

Not all monarchies are the same. Contemporary England (formally the United Kingdom) is an example of constitutional monarchy, in which the powers of the king or queen are described and limited by a constitution. The so-called Holy Roman Empire of medieval Europe was an elective monarchy, in which a council of noblemen selected a monarch from the royal family. And of course the power of all monarchs is not equal; rather, it depends on charisma and military prowess of the ruler, as well as the circumstances of the society and the unruliness of his/her subjects (since power, again, is never completely monop-olized). In fact, monarchs like England's Charles I and France's Louis XVI not only lost their thrones but their heads.

Aristocracy Derived from the Greek for "excellent-power," aristocracy ideally refers to rule by the "best" members of a society. These rulers might be the richest or the most educated or the most sophisticated people in the state. In many cases, they have labeled themselves as "noble" or in some manner superior to the "commoners" of society. Plato's *Republic*, for instance, describes an aristocratic state in which a certain class of people, the Guardians, was trained to rule.

Oligarchy Similar to an aristocracy, an oligarchy ("few-rule") exists when a minority of people dominates the state. Ancient Sparta was an oligarchy, as the minority Spartans ruled over the majority of enslaved helots; likewise, some observers regard South Africa during its apartheid phase as an oligarchy with the minority white population dominating the nonwhite majority. In many cases, the oligarchs are the wealthy segment of society, but the term "plutocracy" has been reserved for situations in which a small number or class of rich individuals directs the state.

Dictatorship Based on the Roman office of "dictator" ("one who speaks") who exercised absolute power during emergencies, a dictatorship is characterized by power greatly or totally centralized in the hands of one person, whose power does not come through royal claims. The person may seize power (like Julius Caesar), acquire power initially through constitutional means (like Adolf Hitler), or inherit power from a kinsperson (like Kim Jong-Il). Once obtained, dictators regularly attempt to pass their power to their children or other chosen successors. A common modern variation on dictatorship is a military dictatorship, in which one or more army officers act as the head of state; in some instances this may be transitional between civilian governments (as has happened in Brazil and ideally is happening in Egypt), while in other cases the military may intend to rule indefinitely (as with Pinochet in Chile, Suharto in Indonesia, or the military junta in Myanmar/Burma).

Totalitarianism The term "totalitarianism" is usually reserved for political systems in which the state attempts to regulate every aspect of social life; in other words, its social power is "total." The word is typically attributed to Giovanni Amendola who in 1923 coined it to describe the new fascist government of Italy under Benito Mussolini. Like other totalitarians such as Hitler and Stalin, not only are the state and its

Augustus Caesar, monarch of the Roman Empire.

© adersphoto, 2012. Under license from Shutterstock, Inc.

mythical leader (its *Führer*, its *Duce*, its *Vozd*) given complete primacy—Mussolini summarized the position as "Everything within the state, nothing outside the state, nothing against the state"—but the system is highly organized by and around a political ideology such as "national socialism" (Hitler's Germany) or communism (Stalin's Soviet Union). Everything from economic production to the family and religion is brought under the control of and made to serve the interests of the state, and every aspect of society is politicized, with the charismatic authority of the leader emphasized. The main mechanism of the modern totalitarianism is the political party, with a single party exercising power—or even permitted to exist. Totalitarianism seldom allows political parties to compete, either because the leaders have no desire to lose power or because they believe they are acting on behalf of "the people." Thus, the party—the Nazi party, the Fascist party, the Communist party—typically claims to represent or *to be* the people.

Democracy Literally meaning "people-rule," democracy implies that the members of society share and exercise power, making their political decisions collectively. (Of course, communist governments have also claimed to be democracies, with the alleged "party of the people" in power.) Democracy greatly depends on how "the people" is defined. In ancient Athens, "the people" referred to citizens of the city, which was largely restricted to property-owning males. All those citizens were eligible to assemble, speak, and vote. Small societies can practice such "direct democracy," but larger ones obviously cannot, which is why large and complex societies practice "representative democracy" in which eligible citizens choose (elect) representatives to assemble, speak, and vote for them. Citizenship and voting rights still determine who may participate in this selection process (in the United States, African Americans could not vote until 1870, and women could not vote until 1920), and in "majority rule" representative democracies, a thin majority of eligible voters may have chosen the government over the objections of an almost equal number of voters.

Democracies may organize their powers in diverse ways. The United States uses a presidential system with a separate bicameral (two-chamber) legislature; the very real possibility exists that the presidency and the legislature—or even the two different "chambers" of Congress—can be controlled by different parties. This is one example of the intended "checks and balances" in the American Constitution, preventing any one person, party, or branch of government from accumulating too much power. At the same time, it leads to divided and sometimes deadlocked government, as the President and the Congress compete to advance their agendas.

Another and more common democratic structure is the parliamentary system, in which the party that wins the majority of seats in the legislature (the parliament, from the French for the "talking" institution) earns the right to "form a government" and to install its leaders as the executive branch (the "prime minister" and other ministers). The parliamentary system ideally avoids the problem of divided government and guarantees that one party can implement its policies. In reality, however, most parliamentary societies contain more than two political parties, so no party may win a clear majority of votes. In that case, competing parties may have to cooperate to form a "coalition government." Coalition governments, as often result in Israel, tend to be unstable (which is why such governments rise and fall quickly) and to empower small and often radical parties. Finally, democracy and monarchy are not entirely incompatible, as the United Kingdom (or other states like Japan or Sweden) continues to have an elected parliament with day-to-day political power and a constitutionally limited monarch who is the nominal head of state but does possess some real power, too.

Republic While monarchy and democracy are not mutually exclusive, monarchy and republic are. A republic (from the Latin *res publica* for "public affair") is a system of government without royalty or nobility, in which "the public" or "the people" are regarded as sovereign. The United States is a republic (notice that the Pledge of Allegiance characterizes the United States as a republic and not a democracy), since it officially outlaws noble titles like "Lord" or "Sir." More important, in contrast to Louis XIV who personally asserted to be the state, sovereignty is embedded in "law" rather than in a person: no person in a republic, not even the prime minister or president, is ideally above the law.

SOCIOLOGY OF VOTING

In the United States and most democracies, the quintessential political act is voting. (Other political acts, such as running for office, are considerably less common.) In the United States, voting is largely conducted through political parties: Most Americans are affiliated with a political party, and only Americans who are registered to vote may cast a ballot. For over 150 years, the two dominant political parties in the United States have been the

© Everett Collection, 2012. Under license from Shutterstock, Inc.

Republican and the Democratic parties; other parties existed earlier in history (the Republican party was only founded in 1856), and third parties have come and gone in recent years, but only those two parties have controlled the presidency and the Congress in the past century and a half.

According to a Rasmussen poll (http://www .rasmussenreports.com/public_content/politics/ mood_of_america/partisan_trends), 35.1 percent of Americans were Republicans in 2011, while 34.3 percent were Democrats. It is also possible to register as an "independent," and approximately one-third of Americans do. For most of the past century, the Republican Party has tended to be associated with "conservative" ideas and policies, with the Democratic Party more associated with "liberal" ideas and policies. Affiliation with the parties and their agendas tends then to vary along a number of social criteria. African Americans have historically been more likely to support Democratic candidates. In 1988 eighty-six percent voted for Michael Dukakis; in 1996 eighty-four percent voted for Bill Clinton, and in 2000 ninety percent voted for Al Gore. Hispanics also have generally voted more Democratic. Jews, too, have trended toward Democrats, with 78 percent voting for Clinton in 1996 and 79 percent for Gore in 2000. Whites and Christians, particularly in the southern states, are more likely to support Republican candidates.

An even more fundamental issue in the United States is voter participation. The United States does not make voting compulsory, so not all Americans vote or even register to vote. According to a Census report for the election of 2008, seventy-one percent of eligible voters were registered, and 64 percent of those potential voters actually did cast a vote; that means that less than half of the eligible voters participated in the election. By race, non-Hispanic whites (66 percent) and blacks (65 percent) were more likely to vote than Hispanics (49.9 percent) or Asians (47.6 percent). Women (65.7 percent) were slightly more like to vote than men (61.5 percent), married (69.9 percent) more than never married (53.5 percent), and homeowners (67.8 percent) more than renters (51.6 percent). Voting increases continuously with age, income, and education.

One element of the political struggle between parties within the United States involves the areas or districts for which representatives are elected. Of course, Americans elect one president for the entire country (not by direct popular vote, but through an "electoral college" that apportions "electoral votes" by state, most often on a winner-take-all basis) and two senators per state. However, Americans also elect members of the House of Representatives as determined by the population of each state. Each U.S. state is apportioned a certain number of seats and empowered to design the territories or districts that will elect and be represented by its Congressional representatives. (At the level of state government, state senators and representatives are also chosen on the basis of yet other voting districts.) Therefore, how those districts are arranged is crucial to party interests: Districts that hold a majority of Republican citizens are more likely to vote for a Republican candidate, and districts with a majority of Democrats are more likely to vote Democratic. Every decade, based on the census, states may engage in "redistricting" or redrawing their congressional and state-governmental districts, which is often an exercise in attempting to establish an electoral advantage for the party in power at the state level. These practices, including the drawing of odd or spurious district boundaries known as "gerrymandering," profoundly affect the distribution of political power for years.

Table 15-1

Party Affiliation September 2010: Percent Democratic or Leaning Democratic

Gender: Men	44	Education: High school or less	43
Gender: Women	39	Education: Some college	42
Race: Non-Hispanic White	38	Education: College graduate	45
Race: Black	81	Education: Postgraduate	52
Race: Hispanic	50	Religion: Protestant	41
Age: 18–29	51	Religion: Catholic	46
Age: 30–49	42	Religion: No religion	55
Age: 50–64	43	Income: Less than $24,000	49
Age: 65 and older	42	Income: $24,000–60,000	46
Region: East	50	Income: $60,000–90,000	45
Region: Midwest	43	Income: Over $90,000	42
Region: South	41	Marital status: Married	38
Region: West	43	Marital status: Not married	53

Source: Gallup Daily Tracking, September 1–13, 2010
http://www.gallup.com/poll/143009/Democrats-Establish-Narrow-Edge-Party-Affiliation.aspx

EMERGING TOPICS IN POLITICAL SOCIOLOGY

In addition to the conventional, historic interests of the sociology of politics, a variety of new subjects have come to capture sociological attention. Among these are war and terrorism, the rise of substate and antistate (including but not limited to right-wing) political groups, and globalization and neoliberalism.

Sociology of War

War has been a part of social experience at least since the evolution of state societies, if not before. There is, in fact, a lively debate about whether war is endemic to the human condition, but the answer depends partly on how we define war. Keith Otterbein, for instance, defines it as "armed conflict between political communities" (1968: 278), whereas Anthony Wallace extends the definition to "the sanctioned use of lethal weapons by members of one society against members of another" (1967: 179), and Bronislaw

Malinowski characterized it as "an armed contest between two independent political units, by means of organized military force, in the pursuit of a tribal or national policy" (1941: 523).

By all of these and most other definitions, war is a fundamentally political and social phenomenon. The famous scholar of war, Carl von Clausewitz, went so far as to assert that war is merely diplomacy or politics by other means. Firstly, as an act of power or "an act of force to compel our enemy to do our will" (von Clausewitz 1984: 75), it qualifies as a political undertaking by Weber's definition. Secondly, it requires some social-political identity (a political community, an independent political unit) and some social-political goals or interests. Thirdly, it involves a high degree of social-political mobilization and coordination: a government does not fight a war, a society does. Or, to be more precise, it involves a three-way synchronization between a political system (state), its war-making institution (military), and the general society.

A number of questions preoccupy sociologists, including *why* political communities engage in war, *how* they engage in war, and *what effects* war has on those communities. Meyer Kestnbaum notes the "materialist bias" in studies of war, which focuses on the practical/economic interests served by going to war, such as acquiring land or resources. While not discounting those, it is also true that war is not solely a rational decision and is never an entirely self-interested one (it would be in many soldiers' self-interest *not* to go to war, since they could die there). He thus alludes to the complex "cognitive, evaluative, and even emotional" processes—those processes themselves heavily socially constructed—by which people "make sense of themselves and of the world in which they live and the variety of ways these efforts at sense-making may shape and be shaped by warfare" (2009: 238).

Thus, sociology can investigate how a society is mobilized for war. A war-making polity (usually a state; see below) must recruit, supply, transport, and command its army, but the army is not only an institution but a subset of the society—that is, the members of the army come from the society—and a war takes the participation and support of many other institutions besides the army. In other words, the state depends on a "broad expanse of those it ruled to find persons to take up arms, to provide the resources necessary for armed conflict, to support war efforts, and ultimately to endure dislocation and devastation and to become casualties and victims" (Kestnbaum, 239). One method that a state can use is conscription or the draft, but it is even more desirable when citizens volunteer to serve in the military. The state thus employs a number of methods to induce people to serve voluntarily, many of them reminiscent of Gramsci's hegemony or Foucault's techniques of power, such as appeals to patriotism, nationalism, pride, duty, and fear.

As Kestnbaum reminds us, war itself is a very political practice, with its own norms and rules. Western societies have long pondered the "correct" or "just" way to initiate and prosecute a war. The result is a body of thought known as "just war theory," which maintains that a war is proper and good if it meets certain social conditions, such as being declared by a legitimate authority (e.g., a government), being based on a good cause (which is an entirely social question), having a

fair chance of success, and conforming to certain standards or rules of war. A "good war" in this sense does not target civilians, does not torture prisoners, and does not unleash certain weapons (say, biological and chemical weapons). Different societies, unfortunately, may follow different rules or define concepts like "combatant" or "prisoner" or "torture" differently.

Finally, Kestnbaum mentions the relationship between war and signification or meaning, or more generally how "processes of war-making leave a durable imprint on states, societies, and arms bearers of all varieties, well beyond wartime itself" (Kestnbaum, 247). One area of effect is *memory*, that is, how collective social memories are created, energized, and perpetuated; a few recurring practices are speeches, memorials and shrines, and rituals such as parades and holidays. Another area is institutional and identity effects; for instance, various commentators have noted that in times of war a society becomes more conservative, more xenophobic, and more centralized. It tends to emphasize its traditional values and its cultural (and physical) boundaries. And in a recent study, Brian Gifford (2006) confirmed one of the common assumptions about war: States with a relatively significant commitment to war-making (in the form of a large standing army and, therefore, high military spending) tend to put less attention on and money into the social welfare of their citizens—although, interestingly, states that use compulsory military service spend more on social welfare than those that use volunteer soldiers, perhaps to offset the negativity of the draft.

Terrorism

Terrorism has been defined in a number of ways, such as "the use of covert violence by a group for political ends" (Laqueur 1987: 72), "politically motivated violence perpetrated against noncombatant targets by subnational groups or clandestine agents, usually intended to influence an audience" (Ruby 2002: 10), or "the unlawful use of force or violence against persons or property to intimidate or coerce a government, the civilian population, or any segment thereof, in furtherance of political or social objectives"

(Federal Bureau of Investigation 1995). These definitions make two points. First, terrorism is *political* in some sense; it involves a political cause or goal and some relation to extant political power, usually a subordinate relation. As Laqueur stressed, the grievance of terrorism is usually "tyranny" (real or perceived), and the terrorist views himself/herself as struggling against oppression. Sometimes the terrorist believes that there is already a war underway, in which the terrorist act is merely one battle. Thus, terrorism is really a tactic of war, or to paraphrase von Clausewitz, terrorism is war by other means.

Second, as covert or illegal force, terrorism is perceived *by its victims as illegitimate*. It does not conform to the norms of war as designed and followed by the targets or the world community: it is not authorized by a valid source (a state or government) or for a valid cause, it does not exempt noncombatants, and it uses weapons and tactics that are condemned in the familiar rules of war. However, terrorism is an understandable strategy for certain perpetrators, particularly weak groups who cannot hope to prevail on a conventional field of combat. In particular, nonstate groups (ethnic, class, and religious) who do not possess armies and armaments are more likely to opt for the tactic of terrorism—and to see it as legitimate.

Terrorism itself is not new. A radical ancient Jewish group called the *sicarii* adopted the tactic of assassinating Roman officials or Jewish collaborators, with the goal of striking fear in these enemies of traditional Judaism and to foment

violence that might lead to resistance against and expulsion of the hated occupiers. "Terror" first became an explicit concept and political tool during the French Revolution (1790s), when it was considered to be a rightful strategy against counterrevolutionaries and "enemies of the people," with the goal of establishing a "republic of virtue." It became an increasingly popular and common weapon in the nineteenth century, when political extremists used violence in an attempt to undermine the social systems they so despised. Their targets were most often individual political leaders like U.S. Presidents Lincoln (1865), Garfield (1881), and McKinley (1901), Russian Emperor Alexander II (1881), French President Marie François Carnot (1894), Italian King Umberto (1897), and most fatefully Austrian Archduke Franz Ferdinand (1914).

The anarchist Nechayev expressed the anger and passion of the terrorist in his "Catechism of a Revolutionary." For the man of revolutionary violence, bent on destroying an entire social system, all ties to the social and moral order were broken, and his only knowledge and care were destruction. Everything and everyone else had no value, and all that stood in the way of the ultimate goal was criminal and immoral while he was above crime and morality. Political extremists of all sorts absorbed the lesson of Nechayev. From the Bolsheviks, Khmer Rouge, and Shining Path, to the Red Brigade; from the Japanese *kamikaze*, Tamil Tigers, Irish Republican Army, and Irgun to the Chechens, Serbs, and Croats; to the Ku Klux Klan and various "militia" organizations, terror campaigns have been inspired by what the Hindustan Socialist Republican Association in India enthusiastically called "the philosophy of the bomb." The key development of the late twentieth century was a shift in strategy from targeting individual politicians to targeting the general population and nonpolitical institutions.

Substate and Antistate Politics

Throughout the nineteenth and early twentieth centuries, the greatest nonstate and antistate violence came from the "left" in the form of socialist, communist, and antimonarchist movements—all intended to end an old social order and inaugurate a new one. Since the mid-twentieth century, the tide has shifted, and the preponderance of violence and overall political mobilization has come from the "right" in the form of fascist, nationalist, ethnic, and religious movements, often originally intended to resist the leftist ones. Much of this politics and political violence was committed by states, as in Chile and Argentina, not to mention fascist Italy and Nazi Germany. But, as the discussion of terrorism indicates, states are not the only political players in the contemporary world. This raises the issue of what Brubaker and Laitin have called the "decay of the Weberian state," that is, the decline "in states' capacity to maintain order by monopolizing the legitimate use of violence in their territories and the emergence in some regions . . . of so-called quasistates, organizations formally acknowledged and recognized as states yet lacking (of possessing only in small degree) the empirical attributes of stateness" (1998: 424).

In other words, states no longer exercise a total monopoly on military force nor on political organization and identity. Groups below the state level, *substate* groups, such as ethnic groups, race groups, class groups, and religious groups, also claim the right of legitimate force, based on their claim of a legitimate political identity—sometimes more legitimate than the state. Carole Nagengast has gone so far as to say that the classic state is in crisis because of the contradiction between the ideals of the state and the ideals of the peoples within those states. One of the central goals of the Weberian state was "assimilation, homogenization, and conformity within a fairly narrow ethnic and political range, as well as the creation of societal agreement about the kinds of people there are and the kinds there ought to be" (Nagengast 1994: 109). But substate identities and cultures have persisted, and particularly as the promises of the state for equality and prosperity have gone unrealized, the identities and cultures have become increasingly politicized and increasingly impatient. Thus, many groups have developed their own agendas, created their own political institutions and parties, adopted their own symbols, and often enough acquired their own weapons.

Box 15-2

Richard Hofstadter on the 'Paranoid Style' in American Politics

"American politics has often been an arena for angry minds," Richard Hofstadter wrote almost fifty years ago (1964: 77). Even then he could say that "in recent years we have seen angry minds at work mainly among extreme right-wingers, who have now demonstrated . . . how much political leverage can be got out of the animosities and passions of a small minority." This paranoia, he argued, manifested as "exaggeration, suspiciousness, and conspiratorial fantasy." The specific objects of the conspiracy fears and fantasies have altered over time—the Masons, the Catholics, the African Americans, the Communists, the Hispanics, the Muslims, the Liberals, and so on. In every case, Hofstadter opined, the paranoid right-wing "feels dispossessed: America has been largely taken away from them and their kind, though they are determined to try to repossess it and to prevent the final destructive act of subversion." Frequently, the government itself is believed to have been infiltrated by the Other and the Enemy, whether communist, Jew, or homosexual. This sense of existential threat naturally makes the paranoid political actor think that she/he is living on "the barricades of civilization," in a life-and-death struggle with anticivilization. "The enemy is clearly delineated: he is a perfect model of malice, a kind of amoral superman—sinister, ubiquitous, powerful, cruel, sensual, luxury-loving." Therefore, violence is more than merited: "the paranoid is a militant leader. He does not see social conflict as something to be mediated and compromised, in the manner of the working politician. Since what is at stake is always a conflict between absolute good and absolute evil, what is necessary is not compromise but the will to fight things out to a finish." And finally, as Rydgren assessed above, "The paranoid style is not confined to our own country and time; it is an international phenomenon." We see it in the twenty-first century in such groups as the English Defense League (http://www.englishdefenceleague.org), which sees itself as the barrier between true British culture and identity and the rising tide of anti-British culture, especially in the form of Islam.

In particular, the rise of the Radical Right has captured the interest of sociologists. Jens Rydgren studied it as an international phenomenon, noting certain common characteristics such as "xenophobia (and sometimes racism), ethno-nationalism, sociocultural authoritarianism, and antisystem populism" (2007: 242).

> The new radical right-wing parties share an emphasis on ethno-nationalism rooted in myths about the distant past. Their program is directed toward strengthening the nation by making it more ethnically homogeneous and by returning to traditional values. They generally view individual rights as secondary to the goals of the nation. They also tend be populists in accusing elites of putting internationalism ahead of the nation and of putting their own narrow self-interests and various special interests ahead of the interest of the people. Hence, the new radical rightwing parties share a core of ethnonationalist xenophobia and antiestablishment populism. In their political platforms this ideological core is embedded in a general sociocultural authoritarianism that stresses themes such as law and order and family values. (242-3)

In other words, a radical right-wing party or movement "gives priority to sociocultural issues, in particular to issues related to national identity, and its central political program can be understood as 'a response to the erosion of the system of ethno-national dominance'" (244). This is why the Radical Right tends to be nostalgic, looking back toward an idealized past when the group and/or state were strong, wealthy, and happy. It typically seeks to close its social (and often physical) boundaries, to reaffirm its "traditional" culture and values, and to give the group and/or state a new birth, a fresh start.

Trans-State Politics: Globalization and Neoliberalism

Finally, not only is the Weberian state under assault from "below," from the substate (and more or less "traditional") identities of tribe, race, class, and religion, but also from "above." Best known as globalization today, there is also an emerging set of superstate or trans-state forces, institutions, and identities that suggests a new stage in the evolution of political society. Some of these new forms are explicit and formal, such as the European Union, while others are more subtle and informal.

Many sociologists and other scholars see a kind of "world polity" coalescing, in which states will be one among a number of players. However, a variety of other kinds of groups and institutions already exist and are continually created in this evolving global system. One sort of institution is the intergovernmental organization (IGO), which is established and run by member-states; some examples include the International Criminal Court, the World Bank (International Bank for Reconstruction and Development), the International Monetary Fund, the World Health Organization, the World Trade Organization, and of course, the United Nations. There are also many nongovernmental organizations (NGOs) that exist to promote particular interests and agendas. Among these are the Association for Sustainable Human Development, the Earth Charter, the Global Policy Forum, the Institute of World Affairs, the League of Women Voters, Nuclear Age Peace Foundation, and hundreds if not thousands of others. In addition, multinational corporations (MNCs) participate in the world polity.

The result is what Brubaker and Laitin called "a thickening web of international and nongovernmental organizations" (1998: 425)—a kind of global social network—within which states, businesses, and race/ethnic/class/religious groups live and operate. While in a sense this has meant a weakening of classical state politics, it has hardly meant the end of the state or of politics. First, states are still crucial actors in the global polity, not only continuing to maintain the only legitimate military forces, but they also hold the seats in the various IGOs that increasingly shape global interaction. Second, the global polity has developed some of its own structures and networks and, in a profound way, *increased* the amount of regulation and law in the world. Halliday and Osinsky in particular have noted the growth of the globalization of law, meaning "the worldwide progression of transnational legal structures and discourses along the dimensions of extensity, intensity, velocity, and impact," particularly but not exclusively in four social areas: "(a) the construction and regulation of global markets, (b) crimes against humanity and genocide, (c) the diffusion of political liberalism and constitutionalism, and (d) the institutionalization of women's rights" (2006: 447). As a consequence, law—and certain cultural conventions and concepts like "rights"—may become more standardized across societies. But it also may become more omnipresent, more invisible, and therefore, more inescapable; power and politics are no longer restricted to "the government" and morph into a phenomenon that is everywhere and nowhere, with globalized techniques of influence and control that Foucault has dubbed *governmentality*.

Finally, a major component of the emerging and thickening global political system is the market, as discussed and advocated by neoliberalism. David Harvey, a leading scholar of neoliberalism, defines the term as "a theory of political economic practices that proposes that human well-being can best be advanced by liberating individual entrepreneurial freedoms and skills within an institutional framework characterized by strong private property rights, free markets, and free trade" (2005: 2). However, in regard to the embeddedness of the economy, "free markets" are not independent of states. Rather,

> The state has to guarantee, for example, the quality and integrity of money. It must also set up those military, defense, police, and legal structures and functions required to secure private property rights and to guarantee, by force if need be, the proper functioning of markets. Furthermore, if markets do not exist (in such areas as land, water, education, health care, social security, or environmental pollution) then they must be created, by state action if necessary. But beyond these tasks the state should not venture. State interventions in markets (once created) must be kept to a bare minimum because, according to the theory, the state cannot possibly possess enough information to second-guess market signals (prices) and because powerful interest groups will inevitably distort and bias state interventions (particularly in democracies) for their own benefit. (2)

To be more precise, the state and the global market-policy must promote a specific set of policies and values, including:

- deregulation—the state should put as few restrictions as possible in the way of market actors and the self-regulating "invisible hand" of the market

- privatization—more and more of the productive aspects of the economy and society should be turned over to private ownership, and more and more of its resources should enter the realm of commodities

- reduction in the state's responsibility for social services—in the interests of low taxes and maximum competitiveness, the state should and has no option but to decrease its involvement in areas of poverty alleviation, healthcare, welfare, education, retirement insurance, etc. These areas should also become sectors for market activity (in the form of private schools or school vouchers, private health insurance, private retirement savings, and so forth)

WAR AND PEACE EFFORTS

When people think about history, sometimes they use a war model to explain social events. Students may learn about the Revolutionary War, move on to the Civil War, have minor mention of the Spanish American or French and Indian wars, and then move into discussion of World War I, then World War II, followed by Korea, Vietnam, and the Middle East Wars, including the Gulf War and the current wars in Afghanistan and Iraq. While there may be some mention of peace, it is usually in the context of discussion of social movements or the Nobel Peace Prize. The United States and the world have rich histories in which peace predominated. It is curious why war, not peace, has been the organizing conceptual framework for understanding societies. In this section, a brief discussion of war, followed by peace, will occur. But first, the issue of conflict will be explored.

It is normal and natural for people living in a collectivity to disagree. It is to be expected that societies and cultures who come from different backgrounds and experiences may not view phenomena the same ways. Even within families, tension and conflict are inevitable. However, disagreeing or being different does not mean that people will choose to become violent. In order to understand war and peace, it is first necessary to understand the social functions of conflict.

According to conflict resolution theorists (Thomas & Kilmann, 2010), when tensions occur, people resort to common ways of resolving them. These include accommodation, avoidance, collaboration, compromise, and coercion. With accommodation one person or side surrenders their own needs and wishes to please the other party. Avoidance is where one avoids conflict by denying or ignoring it, changing the subject, buying time, or removing oneself from the situation. With collaboration techniques, people who disagree decide to work together to find a mutually beneficial solution in a process of mediation, where the problems are openly discussed and a third party helps resolve the disagreement. In compromise, differences are settled by mutual concessions or changes in the stances of opposing parties. Lastly, in coercion one side forces its point of view onto the other without concern for the other side's position or the relationship. Since World War II, diplomacy and arms control have increased, as have international communication and trade. A variety of international organizations have emerged to assist nations with growth and development, and to avoid conflict, violence, and war. Nonviolent methods of conflict resolution are almost always tried first, before violence and war are enacted. Sometimes peaceful solutions to emotionally charged problems are difficult to achieve. Peace takes time and committed effort by both parties.

Sociologists discuss the role of sanctions to control the behavior of others in order to achieve socially desirable goals. Sanctions, as we recall from earlier in this book, may be positive or negative, formal or informal. With respect to managing potential conflictual situations, an informal positive sanction would occur when someone provides rewards or incentives for good behavior instead of addressing the bad. A positive formal sanction occurs when awards are made on a public level, such as receipt of the Nobel Peace Prize or the key to the city for being citizen of the year. A negative informal sanction is when someone is scolded, chastised, or made to feel embarrassed or guilty. A negative formal sanction would consist of arrest, imprisonment, execution, or war. Positive sanctions are usually not expensive and are good motivators for desired behaviors, whereas negative sanctions tend to foster anger, resentment, or retaliation. They are expensive socially and financially. Therefore, from a humanist point of view, war and conflict are undesirable. But from a social point of view, they may be functional indeed.

Theoretical Views of War and Peace

It is important to remember information from Module 1 concerning culture and the creation of values and norms. Not everyone views war and peace the same way (Aron, 2003; Brown, 1998). From a functionalist perspective, the goal of society is homeostasis, balance, and equilibrium. This means smooth operations of a social system. So in an ideal sense, war is dysfunctional to those goals. However, war can be very functional from the point of view of those who stand to gain honor, wealth, land, resources, prestige, or power as a result of it. Warfare requires the use of a military industrial complex, which produces jobs and monetary rewards for both workers and business owners. From that point of view, war can be functional indeed. Therefore, both war and peace can be functional for society—depending on one's values.

Conflict theorists allege that those with powerful interests and resources may use them to overtake an enemy or territory. The powerful are able to overtake the powerless, and the goal of a warfare state is to be able to fight off future invaders or oppressors. The mere presence of weapons may deter an enemy from violence. In war,

A building burns during heavy bombardment of Baghdad, Iraq, by U.S.–led forces in 2003. Although some would argue that war is sometimes necessary, death and destruction are an intrinsic part of war.

Dept. of Defense photo by SSGT D. MYLES CULLEN, USAF.

many innocent people and soldiers may be wounded or killed, and the social and environmental areas may be destroyed in the process. Often it is those who are socially powerless or seen as unfortunately expendable, not elites, who are harmed, in a process known as collateral damage. Sometimes conflict may be necessary in order to establish a new social order that is more receptive to the needs of the people, as in the case of overthrowing Hitler in World War II.

When war occurs, it is always conveyed as something necessary with benefits for a particular group of people, but the death, disability, pain, and suffering are often downplayed—otherwise people may not be eager to support it. From the symbolic interactionist point of view, both sides in a disagreement know the norms and values that predominate in a society. Those in power know that to violate those norms and values would not be supported by the majority of people. It is therefore incumbent on each of them to find ways to portray their positions as in the best interests of the people, and in the best interests of society. This is no small task. Ultimately, this manipulation of information and justification of why one side is best is why war is so confusing for people, and why they are willing to take sides in a conflict when they actually don't know very

much about the essence of the conflict itself. One group of soldiers or individuals may be willing to take the lives of people they have never met because they believe the others are dangerous. Sometimes, people are ruthless and insensitive to the needs of others. Other times they are fighting for a cause they believe is just and in the best interests of those they love. Sometimes, people take sides in a conflict merely because they think they should. Use of the media has been important for both sides of a conflict laden situation; if they can get the television commentators, radio announcers, and writers of Internet articles to persuade listeners of their point of view, then they become those in positions to define reality. And, as Peter Berger reminded us in Module 1, reality can be arbitrary.

Is fighting a power that is exploiting the people good or bad? But who is exploiting whom, and why? Is attacking a nation that is perceived to be a danger an honorable and heroic act, or is it an aggressive and morally improper behavior? These are value-based decisions. The position that societies, and individuals, take is complicated indeed. Ultimately, individuals make a decision that they think is best—but this is usually without access to full information on what is going on behind the scenes. Individuals are generally not privileged to know details of the choices behind warfare. All they know is what they think they know, which may or may not accurately reflect reality.

When challenging an established power system, we know that those in power will not willingly abdicate their positions. How they are coerced to change their view depends largely on what they will receive in return. Stakeholders, be they individuals, governmental factions, or societies, will naturally choose a course of action that is in their own vested interests. So when might war be functional? It could be functional if people are being mistreated and the citizens support a moral imperative to do something about it. It could be functional when there are major corporations that stand to make a lot of money, such as corporations that make airplanes, weapons, or other related businesses. War could be functional when a society seeks to overtake lands or people that will yield them a strategic advantage in the future. There are many ways that war can be functional to a society, or to vested interest groups within it. War can also be devastating to a society; people may die or be injured; they may lose their housing and institutions, and services may be compromised or damaged, families may be torn apart, buildings and infrastructures may be eliminated, lifestyles may be gravely compromised, and the costs of war may skyrocket and shackle the nation with debt that will take generations to repay.

War

War is a system of premeditated, organized violence aimed at dealing with an internal or external conflict, usually with aggressive acts, social discord and disruption, and high morbidity and mortality. A military industry and set of related institutions are created for the engagement of war. Sociologist Quincy Wright (1942) studied war and found that there were five root causes. These included perceived threats (example: Iraq having weapons of mass destruction, which was later shown not to be the case but the public perceived they did as a justification for war); political objectives, in which war is a political strategy to increase wealth, prestige, and power (example: Roman Empire); wag-the-dog rationale to detract public opinion from internal problems; moral objectives, such as rallying around freedom or the immorality of another country's behavior (example: U.S. involvement in World War II); and absence of alternatives, such as when a country has no choice because they are being invaded by others. The view of war will always depend on if one is on the offense or the defense. The opposing side is referred to as the enemy, and enemies are the recipient of labeling that paint a particular picture of them, whether that picture is totally accurate or not. Weapons, armor, and modes of both aggression and protection are part of the culture of war.

A Brief Overview of War

Conflict is a normal social phenomenon and has existed between tribes and nations throughout the history of humankind. Conflict need not escalate into war, but technological inventions have made warfare more likely. Hand-to-hand combat has been replaced with computerized killing where troops never even see the faces of those who perish. Chariots have been replaced by tanks, planes, boats, and missiles. Bows and arrows have been replaced with grenades; guns of today have only a vague resemblance to guns of long ago. Cannons were first used in 14th century Europe during the Hundred Years War, and they hoisted stones, not crafted cannonballs. Technological developments trans-formed war into a more impersonal and horrific experience, with chemical warfare beginning during World War I, the atomic and nuclear bombs of World War II, and biochemical warfare during the Vietnam war. Space warfare now exists, as does cyberwarfare, making warring techniques dramatically different than those used hundreds of years ago.

There are a variety of ways to sociologically classify war, such as civil war, regional war, world war, cyberwar, or terrorism. Another classification system is attrition warfare, maneuver warfare, and revolutionary war. In this system, attrition warfare focuses on large units of military forces who will follow predetermined orders and attempt to destroy the enemy's ability to fight, such as in World War I and World War II. It can result in large numbers of dead and injured and can be measured in the numbers of enemy destroyed and in ground captured. Maneuver types of wars are designed to destroy the enemy's will to fight, such as Desert

World War I is an example of attrition warfare, in which each side attempts to wear down the enemy.

© Susan Law Cain, 2014. Used under license from Shutterstock, Inc.

Storm in Iraq, where key support structures were destroyed to break the morale of the enemy, and where soldiers are trained to take risks and take advantage of situations as they emerge. Revolutionary war, such as in the United States, Vietnam, Burma, or Ireland, tends to be bloody, expensive, and long-lasting, and it uses nontraditional methods against the enemies. This type of war is more about beliefs and emotions, where killing an enemy is a means to an end, not an end itself. As a result, innocent people may be killed, rebels may exist, and it may take a very long time to end this type of conflict. A third classification system alleges that there are three major types of war, including absolute war, agonistic fighting, and instrumental war. Absolute war is unregulated and unrestricted, and designed to annihilate those defined as evil and lawless. Agonistic fighting is regulated in accordance to norms, such as the British in the Revolutionary War with the colonies. Instrumental war requires expediency and may or may not be guided by rules (Spier, 1941). Types of war, then, may have different goals, means, and forms. Warfare of 2020 will not look like the type of warfare used in 1920.

Terrorism

Terrorism is the warfare approach of major concern during the early 2000s. It is a premeditated, politically motivated violence that is directed against a noncombatant group of people. It consists of the use of violence, or the threat of violence, by a group of individuals as a political strategy to evoke change. Terrorism can occur within small, weak organizations which seek to dismantle a stronger, more visible power. It can also occur as state terrorism, such as Iraq, where Saddam Hussein used state power to crush opponents. Terrorists tend to be people who feel excluded from access to traditional and legitimate means of power. Feeling marginalized with no ability to be a change agent as part of the system, they are forced to effect social, political, or economic change from the outside. They almost always use unconventional means, and often adhere to violent strategies to get people to comply

with their demands. Fear is a significant behavioral motivator in peoples everywhere, so by keeping people afraid, terrorists know they have a greater chance of achieving their goals. Terrorism is also used as a strategy by people who are economically frustrated and are seeking to improve their status. As an example of this, during the 1970s people in Iraq lived in a relatively stable middle-class economy, but in the 2000s over one-third live in poverty (Anderson & Taylor, 2009). Global stratification exacerbates the likelihood of terrorism, especially when a transnational capitalist class with unprecedented wealth and power exists. At this moment in time, the transnational capitalists are from the Western nations, which fuels anti-American and anti-European actions. When there is a sense of sacred purpose associated with a violent act, such as with suicide bombers, the emotional intensity around terrorism increases. Terrorists may operate outside the bounds of normative behavior and create fear through a variety of nonconventional attacks. Targets are typically civilians, as opposed to the military.

Peace

Peace is an ongoing lifestyle, not one particular action. Peace proponents allege that there is no way to peace, because peace is the way. Those who advocate for peace, such as Mahatma Gandhi, try to live in everyday ways that practice this conviction. Peace is an attitude and value that transfers into beliefs and norms. Peace can be reflected in resistance to war, pacifism, nonviolence, diplomacy, and negotiation to resolve differences, or at least come to a respectful understanding of each other's positions.

Brief Overview of Peace Efforts

Government entities have long pursued peace. They usually try diplomacy, sanctions, and nonviolent measures before war is undertaken. The pursuit of peace has been a value in every society over time. If we look back into history, we see a rich legacy built around the importance of peace. Ancient Greece and Rome were often credited for creating the Amphictyonic League, which

Alfred Nobel created the Nobel Peace Prize as part of his will because he regretted the deaths and injuries caused by his invention, dynamite.

© catwalker, 2014. Used under license from Shutterstock, Inc.

prohibited one city-state from destroying the ability of others to care for their people. During the Olympic games, a month-long truce was established so that no one could bear arms or make war. The Pax Romana, or peace truce, lasted more than 200 years, from 27 BC to 180 AD. Religions of many types advocated for the peace of God to reign. In the early 1600s Maximilien de Bethune developed a grand design for peace in Europe. Dutchman Hugo Grotius wrote the book *On the Law of War and Peace,* which formed the basis of international law. Voltaire advocated for democracy to be the main governmental vehicle for the creation of peace. The Hague in the Netherlands became a major location for governmental disputes to be resolved. Swedish chemist Alfred Nobel invented dynamite and regretted the deaths and injuries caused by his invention, and in his will he set up a fund to reward people who made the world a better place. The first Nobel Peace Prize was awarded in 1901, and has been given yearly since then to a variety of individuals. This wide range of individuals and their contributions can be found in Box 15-4. The League of Nations and the United

Box 15-3

Applying Sociology

Who Is Brave and Who Is a Coward?

It is curious that while most religions and philosophers applaud the value of peace and see the importance of peaceful pursuits, people who choose not to fight are labeled as cowards, weak, or sissies, and are often ridiculed for their lack of bravery and willingness to fight. The meaning of bravery could be used to incorporate nonviolence and pacifism; peace advocates have countered with the position that peace is patriotic.

According to Rev. J. Bryan Hehir, president of Catholic Charities USA, peace is difficult to achieve. It is not a "soft-headed idea." "Everyone recognizes that war is hard: It requires courage, bravery, risk and sacrifice. But peace is hard, also; it takes the same qualities of courage, bravery, risk and

sacrifice. . . . War has a beginning and usually a definitive end. There are victories, treaties, settlements. Peace is an ongoing effort; we achieve it, then we have to solidify it."

Martin Luther King, Jr., reminded us that peace is not merely a distant goal that we seek, but a means by which we arrive at that goal (King, 2011). It is similar to that said by A. J. Muste, who noted that there is no way to peace—peace is the way (McNair, 2002).

Mahatma Gandhi (n.d.) said, "If we are to teach real peace in this world, and if we are to carry on a real war against war, we shall have to begin with the children." This is why the socialization of children is of utmost importance. If we socialized children today with the values that were best for the world, in twenty years we would have an entire generation committed to kindness and humanity.

Source: Sanford, John. (2003, June 18). Peace requires 'bravery, risk.' Stanford Report. Stanford, CA: Stanford University. Retrieved from http://news.stanford.edu/news/2003/june18/bac-618.html

Box 15-4

Applying Sociology

Nobel Peace Prize Winners

Nobel Peace Prize winners come from all around the world, and they have contributed to the well-being of the world in a variety of ways. More about the Peace Prize and a complete list of winners can be found at the Nobel website (http://nobelprizes.com/nobel/peace/)

Examples include:

- 2010 Liu Xiaobo for his long and non-violent struggle for fundamental human rights in China
- 2008 Martti Ahtisaari for 30 years of international efforts to resolve conflicts
- 2007 Intergovernmental Panel on Climate Change and Albert Gore for efforts to disseminate knowledge about man-made climate change
- 2006 Muhammad Yunus and Grameen Bank for economic and social development efforts
- 2002 Jimmy Carter for efforts to promote world peace
- 2001 United Nations and Kofi Annan for efforts to promote world peace
- 2000 Kim Dae June for work toward peace and reconciliation in Korea
- 1998 John Hume and David Trimble for efforts to find a peaceful solution to conflict in Northern Ireland
- 1997 International Campaign to Ban Landmines and Jody Williams for work to ban and clear anti-personnel mines
- 1994 Yasser Arafat, Shimon Peres, and Yitzhak Rabin for efforts to create peace in the Middle East
- 1993 Nelson Mandela and Fredrik DeKlerk for efforts to create peace and solidarity in South Africa
- 1992 Rigoberta Menchtu Tum for support for human rights for indigenous peoples
- 1991 Aung San Suu Kyi for human rights in Burma
- 1989 Tenzin Gyatso, the 14th Dalai Lama, for support of peace and the people of Tibet
- 1983 Lech Walesa for human rights in Poland
- 1979 Mother Teresa, Order of the Missionaries of Charity in India
- 1977 Amnesty International for protecting prisoners of conscience
- 1970 Norman Borlaug, International Maize and Wheat Improvement of Mexico
- 1965 UNICEF for the protection of children worldwide
- 1964 Martin Luther King, Jr., for his work in civil rights
- 1962 Linus Pauling for efforts to ban nuclear weapons tests
- 1952 Albert Schweitzer, missionary surgeon in Gabon
- 1947 American Friends Service Committee for work toward peace
- 1933 Jane Addams, sociologist, International President of the Women's International League for Peace and Freedom
- 1919 Thomas Woodrow Wilson for the League of Nations

Nations were created to allow nations a forum to discuss problems and negotiate conflicts. Religious prophets from the Judeo-Christian-Islamic traditions advocated for peace, as did Chinese sages such as Lao-zi and Confucius, the Buddha, and the leaders of the Baha'i faith. Peace is not owned by any one religious or ideological group, but is universally appreciated as a lifestyle approach that can lead to greater social harmony and inner satisfaction. Presidents and scientists such as Albert Einstein and Albert Schweitzer incorporated peace tenets into their work, as did Martin Luther King, Jr., as he mobilized the Civil Rights movement, and as Caesar Chavez did in his farm-worker rights movement and Nelson Mandela in breaking apartheid in South Africa. These are just a few people whose everyday pursuits of peace have been recognized for making a difference in the world.

Alternatives to War

Living in a diverse, highly changing world means that people may not always see things the same way, and that they may disagree. But as the conflict theorists point out, conflict and tension are not necessarily bad—they can force debate and dialogue that can result in the creation of new norms, new social structures, and new ways of seeing and doing things. A great deal of money is spent on warfare and the institutions and infrastructures that support it. There will always be human and social debate on whether this is money well spent, in the cost-benefit analysis of all the needs of many different constituencies in the world. War is an option for dealing with conflict, but it is not the first option. Millions of people work for peace every day, and it is important to recognize that this is part of the human story too.

Chapter 16

Bottom-Up Power: Social Movements and Social Change

SOCIAL CHANGE

Throughout this book, we have used sociological theories and studies to point out that there are many aspects of society that are stable and ongoing, such as the institutions of the family, the economy, politics, religion, the quest for health, and the like. It has also been pointed out that society is in chronic flux, and that where people live, what they do, and how they act may change from time to time and place to place. Change is the name of the game. The interface between stability and change creates opportunities, tensions, and social transformation.

Sociologists point out that social change is universal, and it will occur everywhere, although it may vary in its speed and location. Some social changes are important, like the computerization of almost everything, and some will be fleeting or relatively unimportant in the big picture, such as body art. Social change may be intentional, such as the creation of automobiles and highway systems, or it can be unintentional, such as what people can wear or take onto airplanes. Social change may be controversial, because it forces people to give up some lifestyles in order to have other ones. For instance, the civil rights, women's rights, and gay rights movements have all been met with opposition from people who felt Blacks, women, and gays should stay in their place, and out of the mainstream of society. Yet all of these movements have resulted in allowing people with talents to better use them for personal satisfaction as well as the betterment of society.

Often, the world changes so fast around us that it takes awhile to mentally gear up to the changes around us. This is called cultural lag—when the physical world around us changes faster than our emotional and cognitive ability to deal with those changes (Ogburn, 1922). For instance, older people may find themselves to be technological immigrants because they are challenged to use computers, cell phones, texting, electronic chat forums such as Facebook or Twitter, or even the remote on the television with deft speed and accuracy.

Because of the increased diversification of populations, cultural diffusion has occurred as people share ideas and different ways of thinking and behaving. Increased use of media and

Tens of thousands of Egyptian protesters rallying in the streets were eventually able to oust longtime president Hosni Mubarak in 2011—a powerful example of how individuals can catalyze social change.

© Hang Dinh, 2014. Used under license from Shutterstock, Inc.

technology results in changing cultures. People in undeveloped nations may use cell phones to talk with relatives around the world, and to check their e-mail and watch the news or films or listen to music that comes from far away. Tension and conflict cause social change too; the entire world has changed its ways of thinking and acting since the 9/11 World Trade Center attacks. Tension and conflict take a society in very different directions than tolerance and negotiation. As Dr. Helen Caldicott states in the film *The Last Epidemic,* each one of us has the power to be as powerful as the most powerful person ever on earth by what we say and what we do. Societies have a reciprocal relationship with individuals—they shape opportunities and create limitations on people, but each person's actions influence others, and collectively merge together to influence how a society functions.

BACK TO THEORY AND THE IMPORTANCE OF THE SOCIOLOGICAL IMAGINATION

In this book, you have been provided with a brief overview of the field of sociology. Each topic covered here is a field of its own, with a rich body of research and literature. The American Sociological Association (http://www.asanet.org) can provide a wealth of information to people who are interested in learning more about specific topics, the field, further education, or jobs.

One of the goals of this text has been to challenge attitudes and to provide you with the knowledge that there are multiple ways of looking at any social issue. Who is right, who is wrong, and what should be done are all topics of social construction and are open to debate. It is important that you consider why you feel the way you do about social phenomena, and where those attitudes came from. As pointed out early in the text, we are all products of our environment; children are socialized in accordance to the values and norms deemed essential by their parents and social institutions. Whether we grow up in the United States, China, or Afghanistan, the same social principles are at work. Sociology provides us with a way of understanding similarities and differences within a conceptual framework.

Professor Gordon Fellman of Brandeis University asks whether we view the world from a cooperative or competitive framework. This is an important thing for us to consider. If we see the world and everyone in it as all working together, facing the same struggles and trying to help each other and make a positive difference in the world, the world looks very different than it does to the person who sees the world as a dog-eat-dog fight in which the cards are stacked against them, and the only way people get ahead is to step on the backs of others. How do you greet the world? Your views matter—to you, and to all of us.

Information creates knowledge, which creates action. Students of today will become society's leaders tomorrow. The choices will be in their hands. As Einstein said in one of his less mathematical moments, a human being is part of a whole, called the universe. Humans experience their personhood, their thoughts, and their feelings as something separated from others. However, he points out this is an optical delusion of our consciousness. The world, and everyone in it, is interrelated.

Eric Heubeck (2001), an advocate of the "New Traditionalist Movement," offers sage advice on how to build a successful modern social movement:

> [T]he truth of an idea is not the primary reason for its acceptance. Far more important is the energy and dedication of the idea's promoters—in other words, the individuals composing a social or political movement. . . . We will never succeed in taking over political structures until we can convince the American people that we can be trusted to take them over, and to do that we must win the people over culturally—by defining how man ought to act, how he ought to perceive the world around him, and what it means to live the good life. . . . [We must] develop a network of parallel cultural institutions existing side-by-side with the dominant leftist cultural institutions. . . . We will not try to reform the existing institutions. We only intend to weaken them, and eventually destroy them. . . . We will use guerrilla tactics to undermine the legitimacy of the dominant regime. We will take advantage of every available opportunity to spread the idea that there is something fundamentally wrong with the existing state of affairs. . . . We must be feared, so that [our opponents] will think twice before opening their mouths. . . . We will initially operate according to the belief that it is more important to win over the elites (or create a new, better one) than to build up a mass movement. . . . We must reframe this struggle as a moral struggle, as a transcendent struggle, as a struggle between good and evil.

Sociology was conceived at a time of, and is largely a product of tumultuous and world-historic social change. Saint-Simon (1760–1825) and his student and secretary Auguste Comte (1798–1857) lived through the French Revolution, the early phase of the industrial revolution, and, for Comte, the widespread European revolutions of 1848. Karl Marx (1818–83) was also a witness to industrialization, urbanization, the events of 1848, and the subsequent upheavals of the Paris Commune in 1871. These men and many others were conscious of living through profoundly (and often disastrously) changing times.

As a consequence of their lived experience, the founders of sociology enshrined three notions in the new discipline: (1) humans tend to act in groups and they are strongly influenced by those groups, (2) human groups develop their distinctive patterns and institutions of interaction, and (3) those patterns and institutions change over time. Thus, the two most fundamental questions for sociology were and continue to be how social order is established and maintained, and how social order is contested and changed.

THE SOCIOLOGY OF SOCIAL CHANGE

Early nineteenth-century thought was strongly influenced by the philosophy of Hegel, for whom history was the unfolding of a cosmic mind or spirit (*Geist* in German) as it came to better know itself. For Hegel, a few great men embodied and facilitated this process, like Napoleon. However, the century also produced thinkers who emphasized action over mind, groups over individuals, and the masses of humans over a few great men. And they were not always as optimistic as Hegel.

Thirty-nine years old at the outbreak of the French Revolution in 1789, Saint-Simon supported the revolution's ideals of liberty and equality, as well as lauding the development of science and industry. For him, men of accomplishment like industrialists, engineers, inventors, financiers, and intellectuals were the future of humankind, and science and industry would bring social improvement. Indeed, society should and would throw off the "unproductive" elements like the nobility and the priesthood and arrive at a new order in which industrial owners, industrial workers, and an aristocracy of scholars and artists would rule society. Saint-Simon's follower Auguste Comte, influenced by the events of the day as well as the emerging evolutionary perspective, formalized this hopeful view into a series of stages of society. In the first "theological" stage, social order was based on given social categories like kinship, as well as on tradition and religion. In the second "metaphysical" stage, society was organized in terms of philosophy, universal concepts, and rationality, although without much factual knowledge. However, the coming "positive" stage was founded on science, technical know-how, and especially the application of this knowledge to the solution of social problems. For both Saint-Simon and Comte, then, scientific knowledge and industrial production would make a better life and society for people.

Marx, as we have seen, also envisaged a final solution to the troubles of society, but he provided a more practical analysis of those troubles. First, he saw the basis of every society (of what we have called a social formation) as its economic or material practices, that is, its productive activities and relationships; this is the Marxian "mode of production." Two results followed: when a society's mode of production changed, other aspects of society consequently changed, and every society contained seeds of its own change in the form of "contradictions." Thus, when a new technology or an environmental shift or simply a growing and migrating population impacted society, the social and ideological aspects of life would be expected to alter. Further, a society like nineteenth-century urban industrial Europe created new social characteristics and categories (such as "exploited industrial worker") that would eventually cause or demand social change. Change in society, then, was normal and inevitable, and Marx felt that one great final change was coming *but* that it would have to be shepherded by specialists and an organization. He and his colleague Friedrich Engels were not just observers but participants in this process. The famous "Communist Manifesto" of 1848 was a document commissioned by the Communist League in England, and sixteen years later in 1864 Marx and Engels organized the International Workingmen's Association in London, which became known as the First Socialist International. As an outcome of their work, a Social Democratic Party was formed in Germany in 1869, followed by a Spanish Social Labor Party (1879), a Belgian Labor Party (1885), and an Austrian Social Democratic Party (1888), among many others. In 1889 the Second Socialist International was held, and Marxian social and political thought were institutionalized (six years after his death).

The other founder of sociology, Durkheim, was centrally concerned with social change, too, although some prominent twentieth-century sociologists thought that he neglected the subject. Talcott Parsons commented on "how conspicuous

by its absence from his thought is any clear-cut theory of social change" (1968: 448), and Lewis Coser concluded that "he did not duly appreciate the import of social innovation and social change" (1960: 221). However, while he may have approached social change differently than modern scholars, and while he may not have provided a complete theory, Durkheim's work certainly struggled with the problem of social change.

Probably Durkheim's best-known contribution on social change is his distinction between mechanical solidarity and organic solidarity. He described two quite different types of society, depending on the principles of integration in that society—in the one case kinship ties and shared "collective representations," in the other case economic dependence and the division of labor. According to John Harms' analysis of Durkheim's thinking on social change, the key to Durkheim's view on social change and on society in general was *morality*: "That Durkheim's sociology (and analysis of social change) was inspired by a deep concern for the 'moral crisis' of Europe and France is supported by the fact that in all his major works . . . and the majority of his published lectures . . . the issue of a 'moral crisis' is presented" (Harms 1981: 395). The nature of the crisis was an absence or breakdown of the collective representations, of the shared beliefs and values and norms, found in earlier and more integrated societies as a result of modern changes in moral density or "the amount of interaction or the rate at which particular consciousnesses come into contact with each other" (403). When people have regular and sustained contact with a few

© Rob Kints, 2012. Under license from Shutterstock, Inc.

others, the moral density is typical of mechanical societies. However, when certain changes in social existence occur—particularly increased population size, increased population concentration (as in cities), and technological advances (that allow more and faster communication and interaction)—the moral density shifts to that of organic societies, with many social consequences. People either find new ways to organize and relate, or they find themselves without ways to organize and relate, that is, in a condition of anomie.

Weber too showed a profound interest in social change. In fact, perhaps his most important contribution was the view that each society must be understood as a particular behavior-and-meaning system in a particular time and place. His study, for instance, of capitalism in early modern Europe analyzed how economic, intellectual, and religious changes interacted to produce a new social order based on capitalism. One other figure bears mentioning, who has not appeared in our discussion before. Oswald Spengler wrote an important book in 1918 titled *The Decline of the West* in which he argued that a society is like an individual or organism with its own life cycle. Over a millennium or so, a society or civilization passes from birth or emergence, through a period of growth and creativity, to a phase of formality and rigidity, and then ultimately to decline through war, overpopulation, and a general pessimism about the future. However, out of the exhaustion of a dying society, a new and vibrant one could be born.

THE SOCIOLOGY OF SOCIAL MOVEMENTS

As this book and the discipline of sociology have amply demonstrated, societies are always in motion, although that motion may be gradual, unplanned, and even invisible to members. However, individuals and groups—especially in recent history—have often set out to move their societies intentionally, that is, to effect minor or major changes in the norms, values, relationships, institutions, and power arrangements of their societies. These activities, which could be considered a

subset of collective behavior but which have characteristics different from mere crowds and fads and crazes, have been called social movements.

Lorenz von Stein has been credited with introducing the term "social movement" to social scientists in his 1850 book *History of the French Social Movement from 1789 to the Present*. However, the term was already in use by some observers as well as some activists, such as Marx, who referred in his "Communist Manifesto" of 1848 to "historical movements" and "the proletarian movement." Similarly, a German newspaper of the same year asserted that "social movements are in general nothing other than a first search for a valid historical outcome" (quoted in Tilly and Wood 2009: 6). As such, these were precisely the events that Saint-Simon, Comte, and obviously Marx were living through and writing about.

For a number of reasons, social movements have great sociological importance. For one thing, they are a particularly common kind of social behavior in the contemporary world. One might reasonably claim that modern society is a swirling field of social movements. Further, they are a particularly effective kind of social behavior: they produce change in society. Finally, far from being chaotic instances of antistructure, they represent distinct kinds of social organization, while they also shed light on general social processes, such as group formation, identity, strategy, and ideology.

The sociology of social movements concerns itself with four big questions:

1. What are the social conditions or circumstances in which social movements emerge?

2. How do social movements recruit, retain, and mobilize members? Put another way, why do some individuals join movements while others do not?

3. What are the means that social movements use to achieve their goals, that is, their tactics?

4. What are the outcomes of social movements? What kinds of changes can and do they effect on society?

Social Movements and Deprivation

One of the earliest and most obvious answers to the question "Why social movements?" was deprivation or relative deprivation. The idea is manifest in both Blumer's and Smelser's approaches to collective behavior, not to mention the Marxian analysis of history and social change. One year before Blumer's classic formulation on collective behavior and social movements, Robert Merton offered a perspective on social change that evinced characteristics of Durkheim's and George H. Mead's sociology. Merton distinguished "society" or the distribution of social statuses and roles, as well as socially approved means of acquiring those statuses/roles, from "culture" or the beliefs, values, goals, and interests of a society. Culture teaches us what to desire and strive for; society situates us in the system of goods and power. Normally (Merton assumed) cultural goals and social structures operate in equilibrium, so "a dissociation between culturally defined aspirations and socially structured means" would lead to disequilibrium and "aberrant conduct" (1938: 674). Especially in social conditions of anomie (Durkheim), individuals compared themselves to significant others (Mead) and found their circumstances dissatisfactory, that is, they experienced deprivation relative to others. The result would often be some form of deviance, including "innovation" or "rebellion."

For Marx, too, comparative disadvantages—or more strongly, active exploitation and alienation—were the source of proletarian unrest and the future communist revolution. The idea of unrest or social strain was subsequently picked up by Blumer and Smelser, leading Blumer to insist that social movements arise "in a condition of unrest, and derive their motive power on one hand from dissatisfaction with the current form of life, and on the other hand, from wishes and hopes for a new scheme or system of living" (Blumer 1939: 255). Most scholars who emphasized deprivation further tended to understand it in economic or material terms: deprivation meant deprivation of money or land or housing or jobs, etc. Thus, the prediction was

that circumstances of deprivation were the most likely to produce social movements and that the most deprived members of society were the ones most likely to participate in social movements. In short, the poorest people or the lowest class should be the most restless.

However, by the 1970s sociologists were noticing flaws in the relative deprivation thesis. John McCarthy and Mayer Zald (to whom we return below) said explicitly that recent research

> has led us to doubt the assumption of a close link between preexisting discontent and generalized beliefs in the rise of social movement phenomena. A number of studies have shown little or no support for expected relationships between objective or subjective deprivation and the outbreak of movement phenomena and willingness to participate in collective action. (1977: 1214)

Even worse, studies like Craine Brinton's comparative analysis of revolutions concluded that social dissatisfactions and deprivations probably exist in virtually all societies and that the revolutionary participants tend not to come from the very lowest classes but are often middle-class, well educated, and professional. Indeed, he quoted the Russian revolutionary Leon Trotsky, who declared: "In reality, the mere existence of privations is not enough to cause an insurrection; if it were, the masses would always be in revolt" (quoted in Brinton 1965: 33).

Social Movements and Mass Society

Similar to deprivation theory, supporters of mass society theory believed that modern twentieth-century society, with its large, urban, impersonal social systems, generated a social actor who was alienated or detached from society or who felt insignificant in his/her anonymous bureaucratic society. This was a common and influential point of view in the middle of the twentieth century, especially during the 1950s with its withering criticisms of the "lonely crowd" (Riesman, Glazer, and Denney 1950), the "organization man" (Whyte 1956), and the "one-dimensional man" (Marcuse 1964). As the subtitle of Herbert Marcuse's book (*Studies in the*

Ideology of Advanced Industrial Society) indicated, much of the angst of the mass-society school was directed at the social and psychological effects of industrialization or what Theodore Roszak called the "technocracy," the rule of the machine and those who make and manage machines. Technocracy (literally "know-how power") "is the ideal men usually have in mind when they speak of modernizing, up-dating, rationalizing, planning"; it calls "for efficiency, for social security, for large-scale coordination of men and resources" (1970: 5), reducing all social life to "purely technical scrutiny" and to "purely technical manipulation" (6).

Against such a dreary backdrop, social movements would constitute the true Marxian "sigh of the oppressed." Many critics, like Marcuse and Roszak, not only desired but foresaw a coming liberation from the impersonality of mass society. In fact, Roszak believed that he saw it in the youth "counter culture" of the 1960s, the hippie movement, "a culture so radically disaffiliated from the mainstream assumptions of our society that it scarcely looks to many as a culture at all, but takes on the alarming appearance of a barbaric intrusion" (42). But such barbarism was the last hope for humanity and community in the eyes of many contemporaries.

Social Movements and Resource Mobilization

In the 1970s, the focus of sociology shifted from *why* social movements occur (that is, the social-structural preconditions) toward *how* they occur (that is, the processes by which they coalesce and proceed). One of the key concepts in regard to movement formation and action was resource mobilization, and some of the key figures in the new approach were Mancur Olson (1965) and Anthony Oberschall (1973). Olson launched the challenge to Merton's deprivation theory and Marx's class theory by arguing that the underlying assumption of rational self-interested individuals acting in concert to achieve group goals was false. Rather, unless the group is very small or there is some form of coercion or supra-individual motivation, individuals will not

act collectively to pursue collective interests. In more modern parlance, a rational, self-interested individual would not bear the cost of social action, when other "free-riders" might not join the movement but still enjoy its accomplishments. In short, there must be something else over and above individual dissatisfaction. By drawing a critical distinction between collective behavior ("infrequent and unusual") and social movements ("large-scale, collective efforts to bring about or resist changes that bear on the lives of the many"), Oberschall (1996: 2) drew attention to the organizational factors that make and keep a social movement integrated and mobilized.

Together, these new insights led to a concentration on the resources that potential movement leaders and members can call on and precisely how they do call on and employ those resources. McCarthy and Zald, in their pivotal article, advocated "detailed attention to the selection of incentives, cost-reducing mechanisms or structures, and career benefits that lead to collective behavior" (1977: 1216). This viewpoint stressed

- the aggregation of resources (money and labor): "Because resources are necessary for engagement in social conflict, they must be aggregated for collective purposes"

- some minimal form of organization necessary to carry out the aggregation and use of available resources

- the support of individuals and organizations from outside the movement's constituency (i.e., it is not only members of the group/class who may contribute to the movement)

- the costs and rewards involved in social movement activity

While early resource mobilization theorists such as these still thought of "resources" in primarily economic/material terms, they also added other useful ideas about strategy and tactics (specific practices for "mobilizing supporters, neutralizing and/or transforming mass and elite publics into sympathizers, achieving change in targets" and such) and about the relation of the movement to the wider society (nongroup resources including "communication media and expense, levels of affluence, degree of access to institutional centers, preexisting networks, and occupational structure and growth") (McCarthy and Zald, 1217).

The Organizational Field of Social Movements

As we have come to see, the sociological perspective on collective behavior and social movements has changed over recent decades from a presumption of disorganization and individual pathology (collective behavior as lacking social characteristics) toward an appreciation of the social nature and structure of such activities. Having discovered the social structure of movements, sociology has extended its account of the social movement system.

Foundational to this approach is the work of McCarthy and Zald, who introduced the concepts of social movement organization and social movement industry. The insight here is that a social movement is not simply a mass of atomized individuals, like Blumer's acting crowd. Rather, an effective social movement must institutionalize,

with specific and formal organization and leadership. Such a formal institution they called a social movement organization (SMO), "a complex, or formal, organization which identifies its goals with the preferences of a social movement or a counter-movement and attempts to implement those goals" (McCarthy and Zald 1977: 1218). Some examples would include the National Organization of Women (NOW) in the feminist movement, the National Association for the Advancement of Colored People (NAACP) or the Southern Christian Leadership Council in the Civil Rights movement, and Focus on the Family or the Moral Majority in the Christian Right movement.

As McCarthy and Zald explained, an SMO not only has a goal or agenda, but it is also has leaders (who might be considered the "elites" or "entrepreneurs" or "avant-garde" of the movement), members, and—above all—resources. These resources include money, sometimes professional staff, physical facilities like buildings, energy (as in the paid work of its staff and the volunteer efforts of its membership), alliances or competitions with other movements or movement organizations, and cultural legitimacy. It also has

Box 16-1

Organizing the Organizational Field: The Role of Foundations

An underappreciated aspect of the organization of social movements is the role of foundations—large, powerful, and rich institutions that can influence the behavior and relationships of specific SMOs and entire SMIs. Tim Bartley (2007) discusses one such example in the area of environmentalism, specifically forest certification. There are, of course, many disparate SMOs in the environmental/forest protection industry, including the Sierra Club, EarthFirst!, the National Audubon Society, and Greenpeace. In 1993 the Forest Stewardship Council (www.fsc.org) was formed to develop global standards for forest management and to accredit businesses, organizations, and communities in the forestry industry. Obviously this introduced a new player, new power, and new forms of governmentality into the environmental SMI. The result is that the FCS was instrumental in "field-building" in the movement—bringing groups together, providing money, coordinating efforts, and professionalizing specific SMOs. This

therefore meant organizational and tactical changes in those particular organizations, not the least of which was a decline in radicalism and a shift toward more moderate and mainstream actions and goals. Beyond the level, then, of individual social movement entrepreneurs, foundations can act as "institutional entrepreneurs." Sarah Lyon (2011) found much the same process in the subject of "fair trade" coffee, where multinational corporations and nongovernmental organizations, such as the International Coffee Organization and The Fairtrade Foundation, had several profound effects on local coffee growers, coffee consumers, and the entire production chain in between. The two main insights from these investigations are that "social movement organizations are embedded in multi-organizational fields" and "that foundations are often key players in the formation and structuration of organizational fields" (Bartley 2007: 232).

relationships with different kinds of people, whom they categorized as adherents (members and beneficiaries of the movement), "conscience adherents" (people who are not members and do not stand to benefit but nevertheless support the movement, e.g., white people who supported the Civil Rights movement of the 1960s), "potential beneficiaries" (those who may gain from the movement but do not belong to the organization, like all the women who are not members of NOW), and non-adherents and even enemies.

Any important movement probably contains more than one SMO, sometimes hostile to each other. For instance, in the early twentieth century, the African American movement was divided by the integrationist NAACP and the separatist Universal Negro Improvement Association of Marcus Garvey. The latter advocated international black unity and a return to Africa—which won it an unlikely ally in the Ku Klux Klan, which endorsed that plan. McCarthy and Zald referred to all the SMOs that share the same basic social goal, that cooperate or compete in the "field" of the social movement, as a "social movement industry" (SMI). Finally, at the highest level, and on the analogy of an economy with its various "sectors" of activity like manufacturing and farming and service, they applied the term "social movement sector" to all the social movement industries in a society. Their model then, fittingly for a resource mobilization theory, described a veritable economy of social movements.

This led the authors to a number of prescient observations and predictions. For one, the more money and other resources available to an SMO, the more likely it is to use movement professionals—full-time staff, lobbyists, and such. Small SMOs are more dependent on amateurs and volunteers. For another, also on the economic model, the more an SMO depends on isolated constituents rather than a centralized membership (in other words, dispersed people who merely pay dues or make contributions), the more time and energy the organization has to devote to advertising (television, mailings, etc.) and the more its "resource flow [will] resemble the patterns of consumer expenditures for expendable and marginal goods" (1230). Finally,

the larger and more organized the social movement industry and the total social movement sector, the more likely that "social movement careers" will be possible—that is, the ability of one to find a job in social-movement work or to hop between SMOs. If a movement is sufficiently successful, it may even create new career opportunities, such as affirmative-action or sex-discrimination officers.

Finally, Nancy Whittier added yet another nuance to the organization of social movements by looking at the micro level of groups and especially at what she called "political generations." Any movement and its associated SMOs face two standard sociological problems—persistence over time and socialization of new members. By examining the women's movement in the 1970s and 1980s, she was able to analyze the relations and differences between long-time or "core" members of groups and new recruits, who comprise different political generations or "individuals (of varying ages) who join a social movement during a given wave of protest" (1997: 762). She divided these subgroups even more minutely into microcohorts, "clusters of participants who enter a social movement within a year or two of each other and are shaped by distinct transformative experiences that differ because of subtle shifts in the political context." Her interesting finding was that generations and microcohorts (the old guard and the young guns, etc.) tend to maintain their separate identities, agendas, and strategies—each

© jbor, 2012. Under license from Shutterstock, Inc.

formed by the time in which they matured as persons and became active as members—but that the SMOs and the overall social movement change over the years as new generations and cohorts replace the old. In the end, there is not a single monolithic women's movement or even SMO like NOW; rather, a movement and its constituent organizations change as a consequence of the altering external social conditions (including acceptance or rejection) and the intergenerational differences that redefine the movement and even its fundamental identity.

Tactics and Strategies: The Social Movement Repertoire

The last questions we address here are the methods and techniques of social movements: What kinds of societal-change activities do they engage in, and Which activities are effective? This is the next step in the *how* question about social movements: "How do activists choose from among the strategies, tactics, targets, organizational forms, and deliberative styles available to them?" (Polletta and Jasper 2001: 292).

A valuable way to think about this matter is in terms of a social movement repertoire (sometimes called a repertoire of collective action), which refers to all the possible tools and tactics available to a social movement sector in any particular time and place. We might also refer more specifically to the set of means and methods that any specific social movement organization has chosen to adopt. For instance, no SMO could include the Internet in its repertoire until recently, but now virtually every SMO does. Conversely, some tactics are available to or appropriate for certain SMOs or social movements while others are not. The strike is a ploy of the labor movement but not so much of the environmental movement (although the student movement might use a version of the strike or walk-out, and the women's movement could even use a "strike" against husbands). Meanwhile, some devices have fallen out of favor (like lynching or torture) or were never regarded as legitimate in the first place (such as assassination).

A short list of items in the contemporary social movement repertoire includes strikes, sit-ins,

---

Box 16-2

Durkheimian Sociology as a Social Movement

Sociology did not just happen. In a way, sociology—like any new idea or discipline—is every bit as much a social movement as Civil Rights or feminism or environmentalism. Launching and promoting sociology required some energetic leaders and entrepreneurs, some group organization, and some formal institutionalization. Some of the early heroes of sociology have already been encountered in this book (Saint-Simon, Comte, Marx), but none was more influential than Durkheim. Not only was Durkheim, according to Alexander Tristan Riley's (2010) recent book, an indefatigable advocate of sociology, but he also gathered a group around him and established various elements of a sociological institution. The key members of Durkheim's group were Marcel Mauss, Henri Hubert, and Robert Hertz. Activating pre-existing social networks, Mauss was actually Durkheim's nephew (son of his sister), while Hubert was best friends with Mauss, and Hertz was a student of the older triumvirate. Naturally, a main transmission point for early sociology—and another institutional resource exploited by

Durkheim and his circle—was the university system, in which Durkheim taught first at the University of Bordeaux (from 1887) and then in Paris at the Sorbonne. In fact, Durkheim began his academic career in the philosophy department, as there was no sociology department yet, and as part of the institutionalization of sociology he received the first full professorship in social science at Bordeaux in 1896. From these platforms he was able to secure a place for sociology in the academy (over objections from the philosophers) and to influence a great many students. Even more, he served as what Riley calls a "master of ceremonies" for the fledgling science, defining many of its terms and problems. He also obviously wrote extensively, including on the method of sociology, and even produced his own sociological journal (with his inner circle of followers), *L'Année Sociologique* or "Sociological Year," through which he and his collaborators could develop and steer sociology.

marches, debates, boycotts, lobbying, voting, petitions, lawsuits, letter-writing campaigns, newsletters and pamphlets, books, television, and radio, websites and blogs, vandalism, and violence or passive resistance (civil disobedience). Different SMOs in the same SMI may adopt a different playbook of tactics: Greenpeace is relatively peaceful (although it will sail fast boats between whales and whaling ships), while the Earth Liberation Front has used strategies that many consider terrorism, such as setting fire to buildings in the wilderness or putting metal spikes in trees to break saws (and sometimes injuring loggers). An SMO may also change its tactics over time, for example, hardly any women burn their bras any more, and the student sit-in so common in the 1960s is uncommon today.

One general activity that virtually all SMOs participate in today, especially if they know what they are doing, is called "framing." The idea of a frame can be found in the work of Erving Goffman, who stressed the construction and representation of meaning in social action. A frame is a context of interpretation, a shared meaning, a particular view of the world or some part of that world. As Robert Benford and David Snow explain, "collective action frames are action-oriented sets of beliefs and meanings that inspire and legitimate the activities and campaigns of a social movement organization (SMO)" (2000: 614). Such views of the movement and its wider society "are constructed in part as movement adherents negotiate a shared understanding of some problematic condition or situation they define as in need of change, make attributions regarding who or what is to blame, articulate an alternative set of arrangements, and urge others to act in concert to affect change" (615).

The point and importance of framing is that how an SMO sees and publicly represents its mission will deeply affect public opinion on the subject, recruitment to the movement, mobilization of members and conscience adherents, tactics, and the legitimacy of the SMO and the movement. Some frames, not surprisingly, work better than others, but frame construction always presents options and problems. Should

the movement be inclusive or exclusive, rigid or flexible, narrow or wide, idealistic or realistic, intellectualist or emotional? Is its goal, and its interpretation of the problem, credible to the society? Does it resonate with the society? Much of this process involves crafting images and telling stories—for the animal-rights movement, perhaps images of suffering animals and stories of endangered species. Frames may also advance likable spokespersons or animated characters, like Smoky the Bear. And they frequently attempt to play on the myths and history of a society, for instance by comparing the liberation of African Americans from racism to the freeing of the Hebrew slaves from Egypt.

Framing is also likely to express the goals and interests of the movement in grander and more motivational language. This language frequently includes, as just indicated, concepts like "justice" or "rights" or "freedom/liberation." When competing social movements work toward exactly opposite purposes, they may both try to claim the moral high ground in this way. Consider the "pro-life" and "pro-choice" movements, since both life and choice are American values. Movements from Civil Rights to animal rights adopt the highly evocative "rights" discourse.

Finally, framing depends to a large extent on the resources that a movement or SMO can mobilize, and one of the most valuable resources is *collective identity*. Collective identity, the "we" of the movement, can provide a natural constituency (e.g., the collective identity "woman" or "gay" suggests an automatic set of potential adherents for a movement). It also helps identify a problem and propose a solution. And most important, it can confer legitimacy like no other. As an (ostensibly) authentic group, the movement can claim a sort of entitlement to its interests, a sort of collective right.

However, contrary to early thinking, collective identities are not always ancient or "real" or prior to social mobilization. In many cases, collective identities are *constructed* by the process of social movement formation, and in all cases these identities are affected—contested, defined, and redefined—by that process. The movement helps determine who "we" are and what "our" interests are. The use of identity is always strategic; it really is a social resource. As Francesca Polletta and James Jasper remind us, "Activists may define their identities in different ways depending on the strategic situation. If they are representing their group to a public audience, they may cast themselves as more unified and more homogeneous than they would in a setting of fellow activists" (2001: 294). And ultimately, the social movement may be the collective identity of the group. In her study of political interest groups, Elisabeth Clemens concluded that "Organizational forms may be a source of shared identity. The answer to 'who are we?' need not be a quality or noun; 'we are people who do these sorts of things in this particular way' can be equally compelling" (1997: 50).

COLLECTIVE BEHAVIOR AND SOCIAL MOVEMENTS IN THE TWENTY-FIRST CENTURY

As society changes, so do the collective behaviors, social movements, and identity groups that form it and are formed by it. In recent years, then, the attention of sociologists has turned to new and emerging questions of social change and the ongoing contestation and construction of society.

New Social Movement Theory

One of the most interesting and important developments in contemporary social movements has been the appearance of movements that seem to have little to do with deprivation and not much to do with economic or material conditions ("class")—or even with individual rationality—as such. These new social movements have called forth a new social movement theory that emphasizes "post-materialist" interests and identities.

Central to such new movements is what we just called "collective identity," or better yet,

culture. As understood by Stephen Buechler, new social movement theory accordingly makes a number of claims about these identity- and culture-based movements:

- They tend to "underscore symbolic action in civil society or the cultural sphere as a major arena for collective action alongside instrumental action in the state or political sphere."

- They stress "the importance of processes that promote autonomy and self-determination instead of strategies for maximizing influence and power."

- They emphasize "the role of postmaterialist values in much contemporary collective action, as opposed to conflicts over material resources."

- They generally "problematize the often fragile process of constructing collective identities and identifying group interests, instead of assuming that conflict groups and their interests are structurally determined."

- They note "the socially constructed nature of grievances and ideology, rather than assuming that they can be deduced from a group's structural location."

- They recognize "a variety of submerged, latent, and temporary networks that often undergird collective action, rather than assuming that centralized organizational forms are prerequisites f or successful mobilization" (1995: 442).

Examples of such movements abound, including many religious movements, ethnic/nationalist movements, sex/gender-based movements, the so-called "culture wars," and a vast array of others.

Right-Wing and Nationalist Movements

Prominent among the new social movements are nationalist and religious movements, often designated as "right-wing." In the early era of social movements (from the French Revolution through the Russian/Communist Revolution), social movements were seen as largely phenomena of the "left," that is, of the "workers" or the "peasants" as opposed to the "elites." Only the lower classes were considered "revolutionary" (they were sometimes called "the dangerous classes"), because supposedly only they were deprived. However, since the middle of the twentieth century, leftist movements have dramatically receded or been beaten back, to be replaced by rightist movements that celebrate the state and the "traditional culture."

The most obvious of these right-wing movements was fascism, known in Germany as "national socialism" or Nazism. In its German, Italian, and Japanese versions, all interests were subservient to the state, which allegedly represented "the society," which itself was premised on a shared cultural *and racial* identity. While fascism as such was defeated in World War II, many right-wing movements—often fomented by governments as a sort of "revolution from above"—appeared in subsequent decades, frequently claiming to protect the society from leftist/communist threats. One familiar example was the "dirty war" in Argentina from 1976 until 1983, during which suspected subversives and dissidents were arrested, tortured, executed, or simply "disappeared."

Not all right-wing movements have been so deadly, although others like the Ku Klux Klan in the United States have committed their share of

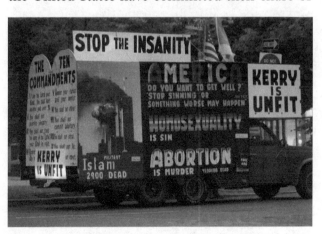

© Mark Yarchoan, 2012. Under license from Shutterstock, Inc.

violence, too. Kathleen Blee and Kimberly Creasap, therefore, distinguish between "conservative" movements, which they define as ones "that support patriotism, free enterprise capitalism, and/or a traditional moral order and for which violence is not a frequent tactic or goal," and "right-wing" movements, or ones that "focus directly on race/ethnicity and/or promote violence as a primary tactic or goal" (2010: 270). Both represent new social movements since they are not primarily about class or deprivation (although the groups certainly often present a "frame" of threat). As Blee and Creasap state, American conservative movements—of which the Tea Party is a clear example—tend to form around "anticollectivist economic policies, fervent patriotism, and/or traditionalism and conventional morality," with specific agenda items such as tax revolts, campaigns against social welfare, anti-environmental movements (global warming), opposition to supranational entities like the United Nations or World Court (the presumed "world government"), and traditionalist morality, the Bible, evolution, antipornography, and anti-abortion and antigay rights (271).

Conservative and right-wing movements have existed for a long time in the United States (consider the KKK and the John Birch Society), but a pivotal change occurred in the 1970s with the rise of the "New Right." Two contributors to the empowered New Right were "the alliance of freemarket advocates and social conservatives, traditionally separate wings of U.S. conservatism," and "the entry of large numbers of conservative Protestant evangelicals into secular political life" (Blee and Creasap, 273). The institutions of the new "Christian Right" included the Moral Majority, Focus on the Family, the Promise Keepers, the Christian Coalition, and Concerned Women for America.

As various observers have noted, these cultural traditionalists have not been shy about using a modern social movement repertoire. Among their tactics have been political pressure, boycotts, publishing, and the use of the media and new technology. From theme parks like The Holy Land Experience (www.holylandexperience.

com) to websites like the KKK/Knights Party (www.kkk.com) to popular music like the little Aryan girls who made up "Prussian Blue," conservative/right-wing movements have proven to be savvy organizers and entrepreneurs. Michael Lindsay (2008), in fact, has investigated how these movements have been successful at creating alliances with elites in business, government, and the military (Mills' "power elite") through foundations, prayer breakfasts, major social events, training programs, and of course, a network of personal and professional ties. Such connections give the movement what Lindsay calls "convening power," that is, "the ability to bring disparate groups together, for example, by introducing a congressional staffer to a senior media executive. It is the ability to set agendas and to coordinate activity, but it is more than simply establishing a legislative agenda. It entails interaction and coordinated effort where elites are able to bridge network disjunctures for mutual advantage" (75).

Islamic Movements

Everyone is familiar with Islamic movements in the contemporary world—or at least thinks they are. What most people recognize as Islamic movements is limited to "Islamic fundamentalism" or "Islamic terrorism," which is often further seen as the same thing. However, in reality Islam is a complex and dynamic religion with many contrasting and even conflicting movements and social aspirations. Mazen Hashem has produced one of the few

© arindambanerjee, 2012. Under license from Shutterstock, Inc.

sociologically useful examinations of Islamic activism, which grows from different roots and faces different challenges than social activism in the Western or Christian world. Hashem insists that Islamic activism—which is *not* identical to "popular Islam" or "Islamic fundamentalism"— is an intersection of two variables. The first is some orientation to the *sharia* or Islamic "law" or "socio-religious teachings" (2006: 23), of which there are many. The other is some particular scope of social aim and ambition, whether local, global, or individualistic. Local Islamic movements set their sights on provincial issues like restoring mosques (e.g., the mosque in Ayodhya, India, that was torn down by Hindu activists in 1992) or supporting Islamic social institutions like the *madrasa* (Islamic school) or *waqf* (Islamic endowment of land or buildings). Global movements strive to strengthen or spread Islam across national boundaries, often in opposition to "modernity" or "the West." Individualist movements stress personal piety, moral behavior, and "the legitimacy of Islam-as-culture" (35).

Some examples will illustrate the point. Muslims outside Islamic-majority societies face special challenges, particularly in a country like France. There, Islam contradicts the official secularism of society as well as its unofficial "Frenchness." Thus, as John Bowen recounts, Muslims in France have explored several approaches to being "French Muslims" or "Islamic Frenchmen." The trick in France (as elsewhere and for all religions) is "how to adapt Islamic texts and traditions to local, contemporary ways of life" (2010: 8). Among the choices made and institutions established are diverse (and often opposing) interpretations of Muslim belief and behavior. Some argue that "Islamic norms should be inflected across differing social settings, such that Muslims living in one place would be exempted from rules that otherwise would apply" (13), while others insist that the wider society should be seen—and even reformed—through Muslim revelations. As a result, new public thinkers and activists have appeared, offering different messages. Mosques have been opened, some of which engage the general French society and some of which attempt to maintain Islamic subcultures within France. Schools and other educational centers have been set up, providing diverse services from prayers and lectures to book sales and certification of *halal* (Islamic-acceptable) food. One specific case is the Center of Studies and Research on Islam outside Paris, where locals can find "two large classrooms; a library with books on immigration, French law, and Islam, in both French and Arabic languages; a lunchroom; and several offices" (66). One surprising controversy among French Muslims is whether they should use the French banking system to borrow money for mortgages and such, since the religion forbids high interest rates and perhaps the very notion of interest rates.

In Turkey the issues are different. Turkey is a majority-Muslim society with a secular state, and many officials of the state view Islam with some suspicion. A number of movements have formed there, including the so-called Gülen movement, named after its founder, Fethullah Gülen. He took his direction from an earlier movement begun by Said Nursi and often dubbed the Nur movement, which was a type of modernist Islam. Among its goals was an effort "to prove that science and rationalism are compatible with religious belief. He wanted to contemporize Islam by Islamicizing contemporary institutions, practices, and discourse. He wanted to 'protect' the people 'from unbelief, and those in the *madrasas* from fanaticism'" (Yavuz 2003: 5). Focusing on personal faith and everyday transformation (an instance of Hashem's "individualist"-type movement), Nursi stressed education and founded *dershanes* or reading circles. When Nursi died in 1960, the movement fragmented, including a splinter-group led by Gülen that developed into a distinctly nationalistic kind of Islam, a "Turkish Islam." Most interestingly, the Gülen movement subsequently went international, opening more than three hundred schools and centers around the world, particularly in Central Asia, where large numbers of Turkish people live. For them, the movement represents a kind of global Turkish

cultural and religious revival. (There are, incidentally, a number of Gülen schools in the United States.)

Speaking of revival, and expanding on the Muslim norms of money mentioned above, an almost unknown initiative within Islam known as the Murabitun movement pursues an Islamic renaissance by promoting the idea of a new gold currency that would replace the world's paper money. For proponents, the "introduction of the gold dinar is the first and necessary step toward an Islamic form of emancipation, a revolution that will set the oppressed free from nationalism, secularism, and capitalism" (Bubandt 2010: 112); through this single symbol, "social revolution and religious renewal fuse into a moral utopia" (114).

SOCIAL MOVEMENTS CHANGE THE WORLD

Sociologists have long studied movements (Smelser, 1963). Some movements are short lived and may be considered to be fads, while others result in sweeping social change. Social movements are important ways for collectivities of people concerned about a particular issue to bring it to the public's attention and evoke new behaviors and structures as a result. Social movements are organized activities that encourage or oppose some aspect of social action. They are a part of collective behavior, or actions of large numbers of people that may be perceived to be outside mainstream ways of doing things. Collective behavior represents the views of a group of people, not individuals, and tends to be planned. Movements are not irrational and quickly created but designed with goals and objectives in mind, even when in response to unexpected circumstances, like Hurricane Katrina. The members often act quickly to respond to new and changing circumstances and develop new strategies and tactics to produce desired results. Most social movements make a concerted effort to make their views public and to gain support for them. Supporters will organize meetings, rallies, and demonstrations, and work for increased education about the issues and policy support for them. In order for social movements to be seen as legitimate, they must be supported by large numbers of individuals who share a collective vision of what they believe should be accomplished, and a will or commitment to the accomplishments. The public must see the issues as important and worthy of attention (Tilly, 1978).

Types of Social Movements

Social movements can be classified into distinct types (Jenkins & Klandermans, 1995; Larana, Johnson, & Gusfield, 1994). One type is personal transformation movements, which aim to change individuals and the way they think and act. The evangelical and New Age religious movements both try to help people achieve a sense of personal meaning in life, but they do so using quite different approaches. Yet they can both be seen as personal transformative movements, both are highly organized, both have financial as well as ideological gain from the conversion of members, and both network like-minded individuals with others who share their beliefs, giving them a sense of community and purpose.

A more extreme variation of the personal transformation movements are the redemptive movements, which target individuals in an attempt to dramatically change their lives, such as religious organizations that encourage their members to be born again. Alternative social movements propose limited change in certain groups of individuals, encouraging them to give up one set of behavior for another. Examples of this may be seen by Planned Parenthood encouraging the use of birth control, or by the AIDS prevention community for the use of condoms.

Another category of social movements are political or social change movements, which aim to change some part of society. Political movements may include the Tea Party or Moral Majority movements, which seek to gain members who share a conservative agenda of how governmental and individual behavior should be regulated. Some of the movements that fall into this category straddle the political and social arenas, such as the Civil Rights movement

of the 1960s or the gay rights movement of the 2000s. Reform movements seek change through and within mainstream institutions and use traditional means. The charter school movement in the United States is attempting to change the form and quality of education from within the public school sector. Trade unions may be created to make the workplace safer for employees. Radical social movements may seek more fundamental change within existing institutions, or challenging them altogether. They often work outside of the major institutions to achieve their goals. As examples of movements working to achieve environmental change, the Sierra Club works within mainstream institutions while Greenpeace tends to use more dramatic actions to protest the killing of whales, seals, and other creatures.

Revolutionary social movements are designed to create widespread social transformation and may call for extreme measures in order to do so. An example would be the Russian Revolution in the early 1900s. Reactionary movements are designed to resist change that members believe would be better, such as the one Hitler organized in order to promote the Aryan nation or white Anglo-Saxon Protestant supremacy. Revolutionary movements operate in opposition to social values and changes and often want to move back to some idealized version of the past. It is important to note that there are a variety of movements and they share the commonalities of mobilization and strategy (Gamson, 1990; Goodwin & Jasper, 2004; Tucker, 1991).

Stages of Social Movements

Social movements tend to evolve in stages—they are not expected to last long-term. The first stage, emergence, is when widespread social change is deemed desirable by an identifiable group of people. It is often mobilized by a charismatic leader or set of individuals committed to a cause. The second stage is coalescence, when the movement defines itself, recruits members, and devises goals and actions. The third stage is bureaucratization, in which the movement becomes better organized, with specific roles and

Youth march in the Annual Lesbian, Gay, Bisexual, and Transgender Pride parade on Fifth Avenue in New York. Is there a social movement that resonates strongly with you?

© gary718, 2014. Used under license from Shutterstock, Inc.

responsibilities of its members. This stage is critical because it helps a social movement have a better chance of long-term survival. The last stage is when the movement declines, either because it has been incorporated into mainstream institutions, or because it loses resources or members or has been unable to mobilize on its goals. Thus, the life cycle of a social movement indicates that it will grow and change, and over time will no longer exist (McCarthy & Zald, 1977; Blumer, 1969; Tilly, 1978).

Social movements are important vehicles to helping a society grow and change. Let us now explore some major social movements in more detail.

Anti-Poverty Movement

Every society has had a segment of the population that has been poorer than other groups. During the Great Depression of the 1930s in the United States, a large segment of the population was poor. Poverty was often thought to be a result of personal problems or imperfections, but during the 1960s, when the relationship between poverty, racism, sexism, and ageism became apparent, social movements occurred to do something about economic inequality. President Johnson waged a war on poverty that resulted in the creation of programs that constituted a social safety net that were designed to keep people out of

poverty. However, more recent political administrations have not advocated as much for the poor. The number of homeless people has increased, and social movements have also emerged to assist them (Cress & Snow, 1996; Vissing, 1996; Harrington, 1961).

Civil Rights Movement

The Civil Rights movement in the United States began in the 1960s and fought to create racial equality. Before that time, segregation of Whites and Blacks was commonplace and often reinforced by the laws of the nation. Martin Luther King, Jr. is usually recognized as the movement's charismatic leader. Other Black leaders included Rosa Parks, Malcolm X, and Medgar Evers. They drew on the inspiration of people like Sojourner Truth, Harriet Tubman, and the nonviolence of Mahatma Gandhi. The civil rights movement was regarded as a success, resulting in the Civil Rights Act of 1964, which outlawed discrimination against Blacks and women. The movement that began with Black Americans has since morphed into civil rights movements of other racial, ethnic, and religious groups (Cone, 1992; Rosales, 1997).

Women's Movement

The women's rights movement has a long history, commonly attributed in the United States to the formation of the National Women Suffrage Association in 1869 by Elizabeth Cady Stanton and Susan B. Anthony to achieve voting rights for women by means of a congressional amendment. Debate over women's rights has occurred around the world since ancient times, with some cultures more or less supportive of gender equality. Even today in many parts of the world, women have few rights. While women have achieved greater protection and more rights, it is important to note that the Equal Rights Amendment to the U. S. Constitution has not been ratified (McMillen, 1992).

Elderly Rights Movement

Elderly individuals today have access to a variety of legal protections, but this was not always the case in the United States. Many found themselves sick, poor, and unable to care for themselves. As a result, programs such as Social Security were created. But that program did not provide all the help elders needed. During the 1960s, the American Association for Retired Persons (AARP) worked with government agencies to improve the lives of elders, and groups like the Grey Panthers sought an activist approach to aging. Their efforts were successful; the 1961 White House Conference on Aging highlighted the problems of inadequate health care, social services, and nursing home care facing the elderly; the Older Americans Act of 1965 established the federal Administration on Aging and a nationwide network of Area Agencies on Aging and nutrition amendments of 1972 added programs to feed older people. Civil rights of older people were also written into legislation; the Age Discrimination in Employment Act of 1967 protects applicants and employees older than age 40 from discrimination, and the Age Discrimination Act of 1975 prohibits discrimination on the basis of age in programs receiving federal financial assistance. The age for mandatory retirement was raised to 70 in 1978 and eliminated for most workers in 1986 (Powell, Branco, & Williamson, 1996).

Children's Rights Movement

The children's rights movement has increased protection of young people around the world from issues such as abuse and sexual exploitation, employment, involvement in war, and access to education, health care, and a quality life. The main organization advocating for child rights and protections is the United Nations. It created a Convention on the Rights of the Child that all UN nations in the world have signed, except for Somalia and the United States. Children are one of the poorest and most exploited groups on the planet, so it is fair to say that while the children's rights movement has created some significant improvements for children, there is still much to do to protect them (Children's Defense Fund, 2011).

Gay Rights Movement

A homosexual rights movement was first thought to be mobilized in the 1920s in Germany. It was not until post-World War II when the gay movement became active in the United States, as returning gay soldiers and sailors began living in large cities like San Francisco and New York. The civil rights movement encouraged other social movements, such as the women's movement, elderly movement, and the movement for gay rights. As with many social events, a triggering incident may occur to push people into action. This was the case when the 1969 Stonewall riot in Greenwich Village of New York occurred. An active gay liberation front began, followed by the election of Harvey Milk in San Francisco as the nation's first gay official. The movement has since morphed into supporting gay, lesbian, bisexual, transsexual, and transgendered individuals. While AIDS is not a disease exclusive to the gay community, it has been a cause around which the community could unify (Marcus, 2002).

Disabilities Rights Movement

There are many reasons why an individual may be disabled, such as mental illness, physical impairment, cognitive issues, deafness, or blindness, to name but a few. When people focused on their disability as an individual problem, little was done about it since it was perceived to be a personal trouble. But as it became identified as a public problem shared by many different types of individuals, a movement began to advocate for the rights of all disabled persons. People who were wheelchair-bound led the charge, but it was quickly picked up by others whose disabilities had kept them silent. The civil rights revolution for the disabled began with the 1973 amendments to the Vocational Rehabilitation Act and later the Americans with Disabilities Act. Although similar language was included in the 1964 Civil Rights Act and the 1972 Education Amendments Act, the new wave of disability activism began with efforts to implement amendments which banned discrimination against any qualified handicapped individual in any program receiving federal financial assistance. The American Coalition of Citizens with Disabilities movement pushed for a strong compliance and enforcement program,

On July 26, 1990, President George H. W. Bush signed the Americans with Disabilities Act, which seeks to provide equal access for those with disabilities to employment, services, transportation, and more.

© spirit of america, 2014. Used under license from Shutterstock, Inc.

which has encouraged social institutions to be more sensitive and attentive to the needs of those with disabilities (Shapiro, 1994).

Environmental Movement

Writings by Henry David Thoreau at Walden Pond in Massachusetts during the 1800s are often attributed to the creation of the environmental protection movement. The Audubon Society and scouting programs also brought attention to the preservation of nature. So did Teddy Roosevelt and John Muir, who popularized conservation. Rachel Carson's book *Silent Spring* (1962/2002) popularized the idea that nature has a delicate balance and humans are disrupting it to their own detriment. In 1963 the United States first created environmental protection laws, first for clean air, then to enforce water quality standards and protect wilderness areas. The fight against pollution became more rampant and covered not

just air and water, but foods, pesticides, housing contaminants, and the proper disposal of both industrial and nuclear waste. Animal protection and habitat areas became part of the environmental movement as well, although they have splintered into social movements in their own right. The environmental movement and governmental legislation like the Environmental Protection Act (EPA) and organizations like the Food and Drug Administration (FDA) have helped create healthier communities for citizens. Environmentalists have made convincing arguments to the public for the need for social change and protection of nature as a limited resource. The environmental movement continues to be actively engaged because there remains significant tension between corporate interests, individual needs, animal rights, and the effects on nature, locally, nationally, and globally (Kline, 2007).

Green Movement

The green movement has been led by scientists and food production specialists, in conjunction with major food-producing organizations, to encourage the use of technology and techniques to increase food production worldwide. This includes developing high-yielding varieties of grains, new irrigation systems, and new distribution systems for seeds, fertilizers, and pesticides. The notion underlying this movement is that healthy foods could be made available to everyone, thereby reducing hunger and environmental toxification. The Green Revolution has helped nations like Israel produce foods from previously barren land, but has not been fully developed in Africa, where famine continues, as does increased need for foreign aid. The green movement also has encouraged people to purchase organic and local foods instead of those that were grown far away and shipped in. Over the last 20 years, Community Supported Agriculture (CSA) has become a popular way for consumers to buy local, seasonal food directly from a farmer. The term *environmental sustainability* has emerged to reinforce the notion that any environmental practice must be used to sustain, not destroy, the ecosystem. The movement also encourages recycling; there are over 413 million tons of garbage produced annually, which is an increase of 25 million tons from 2006. When the recycling movement began, it focused on paper (litter) and slowly added items. People interested in recycling would have to transport their own items to paper drives for items to be recycled. Today many cities either have curb-side recycling or they have town recycle centers, where glass, plastics, wood, metal, and other items are recycled and where trash can be disposed of in a non-hazardous manner. Recycling has been successful because advocates worked with community leaders and devised plans for removing the items that were cost-effective and manageable (Sale, 1993).

Animal Rights Movement

This social movement advocates for the humane care of animals. There is wide disagreement about whether animals are sentient beings, which contributes to how people feel they should be treated. Animals are regularly used as sources of food, both directly for their flesh and indirectly for by-products such as milk or oil. If animals are to be killed, many cultures have their own standards about what, how, and when. For instance, both Jewish and Muslim faiths have humane food slaughter procedures dictated by their faiths. This is different from slaughtering that may occur in meat processing plants or factories. The animal rights movement has included saving the whales, protesting the killing of Canadian harp seal pups, and killing that can lead to the extinction of many species, including many of the big game in Africa. The Humane Society and the American Society for the Prevention of Cruelty to Animals (ASPCA) have long sought to protect animals from pain and suffering. More recently, organizations such as People for the Ethical Treatment of Animals (PETA) have emerged to bring animal rights to the forefront. Some animal rights advocates oppose eating or wearing animal products. Appropriate use of animals for product and medical testing is also a concern for animal rights advocates. In many Scandinavian nations the courts have strong anti-abuse laws and have ruled on a variety of legal rights for animals. They include food, water,

housing, and care, as well as keeping animals in isolation and away from members of their own species. Many zoos and aquariums have established standards that will lead to more natural lifestyles for their captive animals, birds, and marine lives. Research indicates that many primates and sea mammals have intelligence and emotions that rival those of humans. Animal rights advocates have made some inroads with how animals are treated and cared for, but they have not achieved their goals yet (Singer, 2009).

Human Rights Movement

This social movement advocates for the fair and just treatment of all human beings, anywhere. It is based on liberties assured in the U.S. Bill of Rights. Human rights are also a part of many religious ideologies. It also builds on the human rights laws and standards of many other nations, over the history of humankind. The United Nations is a premiere agency to advocate for assuring equal rights throughout the world. International treaty mechanisms are usually cumbersome and can be subject to political obstruction, which has resulted in human rights violations. The movement continues to fight for the fair and just treatment of all (Stammers, 2009).

Moral Majority Movement

The Moral Majority was a social movement that focused on incorporating evangelical Christian views into political lobbying. It was founded in 1979 and lasted for about a decade. Reverend Jerry Falwell used a television show to communicate views of the movement to a national audience. The leaders of the Moral Majority worked with a network of conservative clergymen to advocate for issues deemed important to the movement, such as a traditional vision of family life and opposition to the Equal Rights Amendment, abortion, and homosexuality. It also sought to convert non-Christians to the faith. Members of the movement felt their views represented the majority of citizens who were believers in moral values (Snowball, 1991).

The Tea Party

The Tea Party is a recent grassroots political movement in the United States that endorses particular candidates for public office and sponsors local and national protests. The Tea Party movement has no central leadership (although Sarah Palin of Alaska is sometimes regarded as its spokesperson) but is composed of a loose affiliation of national and local groups that determine their own platforms and agendas. Its members tend to be Republican, conservative or libertarian, and they call for reduced government spending, lower taxes, reduction of the national debt and budget deficit, strict interpretation of the Constitution, support of family values, and endorsement of a new contract with America (Rasmussen & Schoen, 2010).

Progressive Movement

The progressive movement began in the 1800s with demands for social reforms designed to help the average American citizen, and has continued since in one form or another. The progressive movement has advocated for health care for all; worker safety; government reform; improvements in education, medicine, finance, insurance, industry, railroads, and churches; and it has led anti-corruption efforts. The New Deal of President Franklin Roosevelt and President Lyndon Johnson's War on Poverty and Great Society programs are examples of how the

Tea Party supporters protest at the Oregon state capitol in 2009.

© Cheryl Casey, 2014. Used under license from Shutterstock, Inc.

progressive movement has affected society. It advocates for having more people involved in the political process and has a conviction that government has a responsibility to treat all citizens in a fair manner in all aspects of economic and social life, and that government must play a role in solving social problems (McNeese, 2007).

There are certainly more social movements that have existed, and exist now. The ones listed here provide merely a smattering of possibilities to provide the reader with an idea of the wide range under the conceptual umbrella of collective behavior and social movements.

What Could the Future Look Like?

No one knows for sure what tomorrow will bring. Social scientists look at the data and try to make predictions. There are some facts that seem likely. One is that there will be an ever-growing population on the planet, and the bulk of the growth will occur in Asia, Africa, and Latin America. This will inevitably change the balance of power as it is known today. It will also affect the resources needed to provide for them. This will inevitably impose new stressors and challenges on the population. Two, there will be increased diversification of the population in virtually every way—in race, religion, ability, and views. This will require that the leaders of tomorrow have good interpersonal and communication skills to treat others respectfully, and negotiate successfully when there are differences. Three, technology will continue to increase and create new inventions, opportunities, and challenges. Four, the world itself will be called on to meet the impact of so many new people and ways of doing things. How well it will be able to do so remains a question.

For instance, pollution has increased all across the globe. Concern over the environment has increased dramatically in the last 50 years, as increased pollution and climate changes have occurred. Few individuals (2%) report being very concerned about the environment as a major social problem; most people focus on problems like crime, war, and economic well-being. However, on average, every American has at least 116 toxic chemicals in his or her body that did not exist 75 years ago, produces five pounds of garbage a day (much of which is plastic and will not biodegrade), and consumes more water and natural resources than four dozen people in less developed nations (Benokratis, 2009; Biello, 2008). So much plastic is discarded that huge gyres have been found in isolated areas of the ocean, with expansive beaches that consist of granulated plastic pieces. There are five major gyres, one in each of the oceans, that have become the garbage dumps of the world. Many of these plastic and trash dumps are estimated to be as large as North America. The long-term impact of this type of pollution remains to be seen, but is projected to have catastrophic effects (Greenpeace, 2011).

Clean water is a necessity of life, and its quality is essential for good health. Water pollution has been the focus to date, but other water issues are looming. As population increases, so will the need for fresh water, and it is likely that the amount of available water will not be able to keep up. While water is renewable from rains, with rainforests being depleted, the environmental set of checks and balances may be at a tipping point. Water is already being sold when once it was free, and debates on the ownership of water have ensued. For instance, to whom does the water in the Great Lakes belong? Michigan? Wisconsin? Minnesota? Or are people in the desert Southwest entitled to a water pipeline, just as mainland residents felt entitled to oil in Alaska that was piped down for use in the lower 48 states? Is Canada, which bounds the Great Lakes to the north, equally entitled to the water? Or do governments not own the water, but do corporations, such as Nestlé, which own

many of the water sales companies? One can anticipate that such arguments will be waged in the years to come. In the future, water will be an increasingly important issue as a source of acquisition conflict, as a political force, a military tool, and a target, as well as a target for terrorists (World Water Council, 2011; Kirby, 2000; Evans-Pritchard, 2008).

Air quality becomes an issue as technological advances are made and wastes are not managed. Smokestacks and tailpipes emit toxins into the atmosphere, which are picked up and deposited many miles away, resulting in high air pollution even in rural areas. Companies may balk at the cost of strict air control mechanisms, which pit business and individual needs against each other. As the population increases, so does the amount of feet walking on the ground, which disrupts dirt and creates dust clouds that produce air pollution of a human-made force (National Geographic, 2011).

There is an energy crisis in many parts of the world, as people struggle to find ways to heat their homes, cook, and acquire electricity. Businesses struggle with this as well, since they are dependent on energy to run their operations. Wood, coal, and petrochemical products have predominated until this point. Electric cars, solar energy, and wind and water power are all used somewhat, but massive financial investment in those technologies has not yet occurred. Nuclear energy remains a controversial choice of energy. Only 15% of the energy consumed in the United States comes from renewable sources. Americans make up 5% of the world's population but consume over a quarter of energy and emit five times the world average of carbon dioxide pollution (Kimmel & Aronson, 2009).

Energy. Food. Water. Breathable air. Global warming. Housing. Jobs. Money. Happiness. There are many fundamental issues necessary for a society to address.

Index